In Defense of Farmers

Our Sustainable Future

SERIES EDITORS

Ryan E. Galt
University of California, Davis

Hannah Wittman
University of British Columbia

FOUNDING EDITORS

Charles A. Francis
University of Nebraska–Lincoln

Cornelia Flora
Iowa State University

In Defense of Farmers

The Future *of* Agriculture *in the*
Shadow *of* Corporate Power

Edited by JANE W. GIBSON and SARA E. ALEXANDER
Foreword by JOHN K. HANSEN

University of Nebraska Press
LINCOLN

The University of Nebraska Press is part of a land-grant
institution with campuses and programs on the past,
present, and future homelands of the Pawnee, Ponca,
Otoe-Missouria, Omaha, Dakota, Lakota, Kaw, Cheyenne,
and Arapaho Peoples, as well as those of the relocated
Ho-Chunk, Sac and Fox, and Iowa Peoples.

Publication of this volume was assisted by the Virginia
Faulkner Fund, established in memory of Virginia Faulkner,
editor in chief of the University of Nebraska Press.

Library of Congress Cataloging-in-Publication Data

Names: Gibson, Jane W. (Jane Winslow), editor. |
Alexander, Sara E., editor.
Title: In defense of farmers: the future of agriculture in the
shadow of corporate power / edited by Jane W. Gibson and
Sara E. Alexander; foreword by John K. Hansen.
Other titles: Our sustainable future.
Description: Lincoln: University of Nebraska Press, [2019] |
Series: Our sustainable future | Includes bibliographical
references and index.
Identifiers: LCCN 2018047752
ISBN 9781496206732 (cloth: alk. paper)
ISBN 9781496230546 (paperback)
ISBN 9781496215895 (epub)
ISBN 9781496215901 (mobi)
ISBN 9781496215918 (pdf)
Subjects: LCSH: Agricultural industries. | Farmers.
Classification: LCC HD9000.5 .I48 2019 | DDC 338.1—dc23
LC record available at https://lccn.loc.gov/2018047752

Set in New Baskerville ITC Pro by Mikala R. Kolander.

To all the world's farmers
and
To the futures of our children and grandchildren

THE MAN BORN TO FARMING

The grower of trees, the gardener, the man born to farming,
whose hands reach into the ground and sprout,
to him the soil is a divine drug. He enters into death
yearly, and comes back rejoicing. He has seen the light lie
down
in the dung heap, and rise again in the corn.
His thought passes along the row ends like a mole.
What miraculous seed has he swallowed
that the unending sentence of his love flows out of his mouth
like a vine clinging in the sunlight, and like water
descending in the dark?

—Wendell Berry, *Farming: A Handbook* (1979)

CONTENTS

ILLUSTRATIONS

Figures

Tables

FOREWORD

JOHN K. HANSEN

From Mother Earth's geological perspective, one hundred years is less than the blink of an eye. Yet in that short span of time, farming and food production has changed more in the last one hundred years than it has from the beginning of civilization and the cultivation of crops to 1900. This thoughtful and straightforward book helps us better understand the history, current status, and likely direction of farming and the forces that shape and control it.

The contributing authors take turns peeling away the countless layers of the onion of conventional wisdom and the assumptions that surround farming and food issues. In its own way, this book provides a badly needed "fact check" of the widely held theories and assumptions that drive the public explanation of how our food system works.

My lifetime of working on farm, food, renewable energy, climate, market concentration, and trade issues has repeatedly taught me to think structurally in order to best understand the drivers, players, policies, and patterns. I view this book as a helpful structural roadmap of farm and food policy history and direction. Given the worldwide level of vertical integration and market concentration, thinking structurally and globally is essential.

One hundred years ago, modern day agriculture looked much the same as it had looked for centuries, except for the development of steam engines and railroads. In 1918, my great-grandfather Julius and great-grandmother Christina were raising their six children in the farmhouse they had built in 1905–1906 that we still use, and they were farming the 320 acres in western Madison County, Nebraska, with teams of horses, a few mules, and a lot of hard manual labor provided by the industrious Hansen boys and their occasional hired man. Great-grandfather Julius was threshing oats for his family and their neighbors with their new steam-powered tractor with the steel wheels that he owned together with our neighbor.

Great-grandmother Christina had a very large garden and no electricity. To keep food cool, she used the hand-dug cistern with the cool water that came from the windmill along with block ice stored in the cellar with straw and tarps under the basement. She hired young girls to help her with the cooking, butchering, cleaning, canning, and gardening, all done by hand from before the crack of dawn until dark.

Rural electrification was still two decades away, but for entertainment, after supper and before darkness set in, they listened to the Atwater-Kent radio whose batteries were recharged by the windmill-powered battery charger. The neighbors would come to listen to this amazing new technology, eat cake and sandwiches made for the occasion, and drive their horses home in the dark without lights. I still have that radio.

One summer afternoon, my grandfather, Carl, born in 1890 and approaching his ninetieth birthday on August 10th, provided a clear-eyed summary of the changes he had seen in his lifetime. Grandpa told me that he remembered what the prairies looked like when his family first plowed them with a horse-drawn plow. He still remembered the wagon trails that snaked around the hills that went to the various towns before county roads were built. He said that as a small boy he helped plant the trees for the tree claim land next door.

As a farmer who toughed out the Great Depression, Grandpa described in detail how day turned into night from the dust storms from Oklahoma, and the damage the drought and wind caused the family and the livestock, including the respiratory problems of livestock and humans. He smiled as he remembered the welcome Roosevelt-sponsored shelterbelts he helped plant, and how he helped build the first terraces in Madison County on our farm. When he described his feelings about living long enough to see a man walk on the moon, his eyes began to water.

Always the keeper of history, Grandfather Carl reminded me that the Midwest was settled by serfs like our family who came from Europe in hopes that with a lot of hard work and a little luck, the serfs in the new country could one day own and control their own land. He reminded me that in 1892 his great-grandparents, Ole and Anne Hoeffen, had homesteaded a few miles from our farm for just that reason. His great disappointment was that many farmers, whose ancestors fled the old country to escape the cruelty of the feudal system of land ownership, were so quick to volunteer for the new corporate version of the old feudal system. "They learned nothing from their own histories," he lamented.

As a farm leader, I know all too well that our nation's traditional system of independently owned and operated family farms raised and sold our products into functioning markets that were accessible, competitive, transparent, and fair. This kind of marketplace is being replaced by the vertically integrated, capital and energy intensive, industrialized, corporate-owned version of the feudal system our ancestors fled. In order to avoid the financial risks of the marketplace, independent owner-operators surrender their independence and control of their own operations for the security and limited rewards of "take it or leave it," non-negotiated, one-sided contracts with vertical integrators. One of my friends lamented that he had become a poorly paid operator of a bed and breakfast for corporate-owned hogs. "I do all the work and own all the regulatory responsibility and the buildings, and the company owns the hogs and the profits. My banker thought it was a good idea."

The history of farming is one of very few short-lived economic booms and lots of long and deep economic busts that used to be called panics. According to the USDA data, farmers now receive a smaller share of the consumer food dollar than at any time in history. While the titles of the economic structure have changed over the years, the European feudal system, the southern plantation system, and now the vertically integrated, industrialized, corporate-owned production system, all include top-down control and decision-making, while the folks who do the work, assume most of the risk, and provide the labor become marginalized and exploited. For instance, poultry processors continue to report record profits while their poultry contract producers have not seen a raise in their compensation for fifteen years.

The majority of net farm family income continues to come from the off-farm jobs necessary to subsidize the lack of profitability of farm operations that gross hundreds of thousands of dollars but lack the margin needed to feed and clothe the owners and operators who take the risk and do the work. Rural America continues to lose farmers and ranchers; small towns continue to dry up; and rural youth continue to migrate to population centers that provide economic, social, and cultural opportunities. The concentration of land grows, as does the average age of farmers. Not all change represents progress.

Who is making the money? The corporate economic interests that farm the farmers continue to increase their profit margins at the expense of both food producers and food consumers. Former U.S. senator Fred Harris aptly summarized the farm situation when he said, "The number one problem in America today is that corporations have no soul to save nor butt to kick." Amen.

Our nation's farm, food, trade, and antitrust policies continue to be driven by mega-agribusiness players who continue to "invest" in candidates with their campaign contributions that see things their way, and at the expense of the families that produce and eat our food. No matter how much money, power, market share, and control today's international food and agricultural supply corporations have, they want more.

Our Congress is supposed to protect the public interest but, from a regulatory standpoint, has become the corporate fox's best friend. Congress not only allows the corporate fox to eat our public interest chickens but all too often actively helps the corporate fox raid the henhouse. For example, it is clearly not in our nation's national food security interests to allow the Chinese government to take worldwide control of hog production and hog processing, yet the Chinese government was allowed to buy Smithfield Foods, by far the largest U.S. hog producer and processor.

Farmers and food producers have not been getting the national farm and food policy they support for a very long time. For years, polls and surveys show that consumers want to buy their food from families that farm. Yet mega-agribusiness has used their campaign contributions to hijack national farm and food policy. In our democracy, there are two primary forms of power: money and people. For too long, big money has had its way with food and farm policy. Farmers and food consumers have a common set of interests. They need to work together to harness the power of organized effort.

Food production is about so much more than just food. Food security is national security. We must produce our food that protects our nation's precious soil and water resources for future generations. How do we put a price tag on the importance of the social and cultural link between human beings and the earth from which they come and to which they will one day return?

Given the climate change crisis that is overtaking our world, shouldn't we be talking about what kind of food production system emits the least carbon, uses the least energy, and sequesters the most carbon? If we are serious about fighting for the future viability of our planet, we must move food production back toward more diversification, and more and better resource managers who have a stewardship ethic. Family farm and ranch agriculture is that system.

When farming is profitable, agriculture is a primary economic driver of new tax revenues and economic activity because, like manufacturing, it produces new wealth. When farmers make money, they buy new machinery, improve their homes and farm buildings, make improvements to their operations, hire more help, and spend their money locally. After all, what is more basic to the overall health and welfare of our nation than the production of food that our very lives depend on?

As sure as the spring comes, the sun shines, and plants come to life, there are signs of hope. Food consumers increasingly care about who grows their food and how they do it. I find hope in the local food movement, direct marketing efforts that connect food producers with food consumers, urban agriculture, community gardens, and conventional farmers' growing interest in soil-building strategies and the use of cover crops. All provide rays of hope for a better future.

Thanks to the authors of this extraordinary book it is possible for us to understand our increasingly complicated and industrialized food production system and its many facets as we work together to shape the future of farming for the benefit of farmers, food consumers, rural communities, our national security interests, future generations, and Mother Earth.

ACKNOWLEDGMENTS

The Society for Applied Anthropology provided the venue for presentation of the ideas that became the chapters of *In Defense of Farmers*. We especially appreciate the support and editorial advice generously given by Don Stull throughout the production of this volume, and the diligence of its contributors as they developed their work for publication. External reviewers David Griffith and Michael Broadway carefully read all the chapters and provided thoughtful and insightful comments and suggestions. We also wish to thank our very helpful and patient editors at the University of Nebraska Press, Bridget Barry and Emily Wendell, and Baylor University's Department of Anthropology and the University of Kansas for financial support. Not least on the list of those to whom we are indebted and grateful are the farmers who invited us into their lives and shared their experiences.

In Defense of Farmers

Introduction

A Food System Imperiled

JANE W. GIBSON

We humans have tested many ways to feed ourselves. Some livelihood patterns—hunting and gathering, nomadic pastoralism, and swidden horticulture—have proved successful for millennia and still support small populations in marginal areas of our planet. The origins of our latest experiment with food production can be traced to the horticulturists who, simply at first, applied new energy to ecosystems. They burned competing vegetation and planted in the nutrient-rich ash, used hand-hewn tools such as digging sticks, domesticated plants by selecting the most desirable specimens, applied manure, and defended gardens against predators. The result was more energy available in the form of food for human consumption, making larger human populations possible, and driving food producers to increase productivity further. The use of domesticated draft animals, plows, and irrigation increased the land area under cultivation, required more human labor, and fortified private property institutions. Growing demand by nonfood producers further stimulated the production of food surpluses. The industrial revolution brought more technological innovations based on steam, electricity, and fossil fuels, first to farms in the western world where railroads, highways, and the shipping industry delivered commodities to growing towns and cities. Populations continued to

1

grow and people in industrial societies began to live much longer lives than their ancestors. Indeed, so successful has been this experiment in industrial food production that, as we are frequently reminded, the world's population will reach ten billion by 2050, necessitating a 50 percent increase over 2013 food supplies (FAO 2017, x). Thus, it is greatly disconcerting that producers of most of the world's plant and animal foods today operate at such a disadvantage, under conditions over which they have less and less control, that their livelihoods are in jeopardy.

In our global food system, farmers respond to declining profit margins related to rising costs and falling commodity prices with an urgent pursuit of increased yields and production efficiencies that, according to the president of the Nebraska Farmers Union, has been insufficient to cover farmers' costs of production in the United States for the last several years (John Hansen, pers. communication, October 11, 2017). Indeed, increased yields explain the precipitous decrease in crop prices, and, according to the *Wall Street Journal*, U.S. farm income has fallen for four years in a row, reducing farmer income by half since 2013. These alarming findings led the National Farmers Union to set up a farm crisis web page with information about debt, mediation, disaster relief, and suicide prevention (Newman 2017).

Effects of the most recent cost-price squeeze mirrors the historic pattern seen in the United States, evident in the latest U.S. Census of Agriculture (USDA–NASS 2017). The total number of farms continues to decline, despite growth in the smallest farms since 2000. Farm structure reflects continued development of a bimodal distribution in which mid-sized farms are gradually disappearing. The majority of small farms (80.2 percent with < 309 acres) control a disproportionately small share of total land in farms (30.6 percent), and a few enormous farms (4 percent with > 2656 acres) control a large and disproportionate share of land (24 percent). And while each region of the world is unique in its farming traditions, aspirations, growing conditions, and investment capabilities, the adoption of industrial production technologies and practices proceeds apace, including digital technologies (Deichman et al. 2016). Technological diffusion is impelled by trade negotiators, especially from the United States, and agribusiness corporations working to remove all trade barriers to the globalization of industrial agriculture (Ikerd n.d.).

Despite technological innovations, new technologies that have boosted productivity have not been able to overcome a slowing down of yield increases. Degraded natural resources, biodiversity losses, and the transboundary spread of pests and diseases undermine efforts to increase productivity (FAO 2017, x). Technologies that have driven yield increases and falling food prices also contribute to loss of soil fertility, deforestation, and climate change. These concerns add to problems of food waste in a world with 800 million chronically hungry people and two billion who experience nutritional deficits (FAO 2017, xi). Given population projections and these discouraging facts, not only are many farmers at risk of losing their livelihoods, but the majority of the world's non-food producers, including those of us who are currently well-fed, are at increased risk of food shortages. Compounding this bleak prospect, increased income inequality in the world means a rising threat to access for those unable to pay for sufficient quantities of food.

The old saying that we do not know where our food comes from is indeed true, particularly if what we mean is that we know little about farmers and the system in which they labor. Instead, the popular imagination is fueled with images that fall into one of two camps. At one extreme, as purveyors of agricultural inputs and equipment would have it, farmers are hard-working heroes, expected to shoulder the responsibility of feeding the growing, hungry global population with the help of the latest in science and technology research. A counternarrative, produced by some environmentalists, depicts farmers who rely on industrial production practices as socially and environmentally destructive.

The elements of truth in these caricatures of industrial farming do little to help us understand either food system vulnerabilities or opportunities to prepare for a challenging future. And while only a few countries dominate the world market for agricultural exports, this system of production is a global affair. Whether depicted as heroes or villains, producers on every continent face enormous challenges, not least their dependence on nonrenewable and declining resources; shrinking profit margins and volatile, uncompetitive markets; land management problems related to tillage, monoculture production, and grazing; new threats to production caused by climate change; and loss of social, material, and moral support as rural communities decline. These issues speak to the need to understand the constituents and dynamics of the global food system, and to enlist the help of farmers to gain that understanding.

In this volume, we offer case material from four countries—the United States, Canada, Brazil, and Bolivia— all of which embrace industrial agriculture's commodities, technologies, and practices to varying degrees. By concentrating on countries with the most sophisticated production technologies to produce the largest quantities of grains, soybeans, and animal proteins in the world, we mean to focus attention on the farmers whose labors, decision-making, and risk-taking can teach us about the implications and limitations of our global industrial food system for the future. And because farmers, their families, and their communities sit on the front lines of that future, the quality of rural life, the health of ecosystems, the biodiversity they support, and the success of the global food system rest on the hard decisions farmers must make in the context of powerful forces beyond their control. Yet with few exceptions, farmers and the experiences and views that inform their decisions remain inaudible in the din of policy and agribusiness discourses. In this volume, we bring farmers' expertise to bear on discussions of what kind of future their work will underwrite.

What's in a Name?

Names matter. They can embody strength, beauty, heroism, danger, and beliefs and assumptions that demonize or canonize. The most technologically complex farming practiced in the world today, and the focus of this volume, goes by many names: conventional, chemical, intensive, industrial, modern, factory, mechanized, corporate, productivist, large-scale, and capitalized agriculture. We use the terms "industrial farmers" and "industrial agriculture" to highlight particular production practices that illustrate how farms tend to emulate modern factories: industrial farmers specialize in the commodities they sell; they operate in a highly competitive, global market; they rely on sophisticated machine, chemical, and genetic technologies; and they pursue efficiency and profit, necessitated by a global capitalist system. Thus, we group together farmers who practice their art in particular ways without reference to farm size or sales class. Whereas industrial farmers do not feed a majority of the world, nor yet make up a majority of the world's farms, in technologically complex countries such as the United States and Canada, they do constitute nearly all farms, from very small operations with sales under $10,000 a year to the largest farms with sales over a million dollars. What this suggests is that wherever industrial agriculture is adopted, because of its tendency to concentrate land and sales, it may well become the dominant system of food production. Further, joining this system defined by particular and evolving production practices and technologies will also mean becoming part of the transformation of that food system.

Changing institutional arrangements and technologies have imposed a new agricultural order on the global food system that will be expected to deliver up mass-produced wheat, rice, corn, sorghum, soybeans, poultry, beef, pork, and dairy products, not to mention fuel and fiber. This new order is distinguished in important ways. As the first chapters of this volume unequivocally demonstrate, the food system is undergoing a significant restructuring through both horizontal and vertical integration (Mooney 2017).

We begin with the deeply troubling pattern of horizontal integration as the processes of mergers and acquisitions create bigger and fewer players in the agrichemical, fertilizer, genetics, farm machinery, processing, and retail sectors. In chapter 1, Mary Hendrickson, Philip Howard, and Douglas Constance demonstrate the consolidation of corporate power whose effects will be further explored in subsequent chapters. These authors demonstrate the concentration and domination of agribusiness firms resulting in inequitable social and economic organization of the system, and the near absence of market competition. They argue that these conditions severely constrain and disadvantage farmers, workers, consumers, and communities. They also consider the growth of resistance against what they see as an inequitable and unsustainable global food system.

The next two chapters take up the problem of vertical integration in the United States and Bolivia. In chapter 2, Don Stull draws from twenty years of fieldwork in western Kentucky to examine the widespread adoption of vertically integrated and concentrated supply chains in poultry production. He shows the significance and consequences of this production and distribution model for contract growers, local communities, and the environment, and he extends the analysis to "chickenization" of the beef, pork, tobacco, and grain industries.

Chapter 3 looks at the spread of the chickenization model

in Bolivia where Sarah Kollnig links industrial poultry production to social, environmental, and political realms. Kollnig provides an intimate portrait of a concentrated poultry operation and shows how the arrival of vertically integrated chicken-meat production is displacing small- and medium-scale producers as well as backyard chicken tenders. Kollnig foregrounds the role of the Bolivian state in supporting the industrialization of chicken in partial fulfillment of its promise of *Vivir Bien*, living well. Yet the promise remains a distant hope as we see how the model exacts ecological costs and exacerbates social inequality. Bolivian families, however, have found ways to domesticate industrial chicken-meat production by incorporating its products into long-held traditions.

Among other features that distinguish the new agricultural order is its detachment or alienation of food producers from the land, despite the fact that production of plant and animal proteins cannot be accomplished without soil. In chapter 4, Jane Gibson considers the implications of the fourth industrial revolution in which farmers adopt digital technologies whose corporate developers envision automated farming systems controlled by an Internet of things. She argues that automation using precision and robotic technologies distances farmers from ecosystems, and that associated "best practices" engender a wholly new kind of knowledge about farming and nature. Deskilled producers must rely increasingly on off-farm experts as production moves toward "smart farms" without farmers.

The emergence of new relationships between farmers and ecosystems raises questions about stewardship of the natural world in the interest of future generations' needs. In chapter 5, Casey Walsh presents a case study of groundwater depletion by California vineyards during the recent, prolonged drought. He examines implementation of the Sustainable Groundwater Management Act and contestation over water among agribusinesses, municipalities, and residents of the Central Coast. Walsh focuses on how each group of actors in this conflict maximized power and minimized costs to property and participation, science and expertise, and notions of sustainability.

Groundwater depletion is caused by over-pumping, but the need is exacerbated by climate change, a problem expected to worsen and require innovative adaptations. The 2014 report of the Intergovernmental Panel on Climate Change estimated the impact of climate change on undernutrition and "concluded with high confidence that climate change will have a 'substantial negative impact' on per capita calorie availability, childhood undernutrition, and child deaths related to undernutrition in low- and middle-income countries" (Porter et al., 2014, cited in FAO 2017, 43). In chapter 6, Sara Alexander describes the threat of climate change faced by Texas wheat farmers. In response to the urgent need to understand the complex relationships between climate change and production decisions, she shows how farmers' perceptions and responses to risk grow out of more than economic principles and productivity standards. They are also shaped by intuitive reasoning and socialization that derive from shared worldviews, social complexities, values, and cultural norms.

The next chapter addresses farmer innovation in production practices at the institutional level where agribusiness money and power limit what farmers can know and learn. In chapter 7, Katherine Strand examines changes in Canadian agricultural research funding and in the practice of farmers' "witnessing" research results. Strand analyzes the consequences of the change from an earlier model of state-funded research collaboration involving both extension and farmers to replacement of the state's role with corporate funders who control the research agenda and the demonstration of results.

Chapter 8 also considers transmission of production practices, this time shining a light on farmer agency in Brazil.
The Cerrados region, once believed to be agriculturally
worthless, is now abuzz with intensive soybean cultivation.
Andrew Ofstehage compares migrant Mennonite and midwestern U.S. farmers' different modifications of the "Brazil
model" of production. He underscores not only farmers'
ability to diverge from standards and expectations, but
also the variability and flexibility of production methods
as farmers bring to bear their own experiences and values,
and adjust to new social and ecological conditions.

In chapter 9, Jane Gibson and Benjamin Gray situate
farmers in their social worlds and introduce the problem
of depopulation of rural counties in western Kansas. In this
chapter, grain farmers talk about their experiences of loss
as their social worlds collapse with outmigration of kin and
friends, and the shuttering of local businesses, social ven-
ues, schools, and public service facilities. Gibson and Gray
reframe the problem of community decline as community
transformation and ask how farmers now meet their material and social needs. The answer illuminates the emergence of digitally reconstituted communities that protect
the agribusiness market for farm inputs while affording rural
families a way to preserve elements of the moral economy
through virtual networks. But the loss of face-to-face relationships also inspires concerns about rural residents' abilities to interpret and respond effectively to the structural
causes of demographic decline.

In the concluding chapter of the volume, John Ikerd
proposes a way forward. He reflects on his own story as a
conventional agricultural economist who saw how the production models he advocated failed to feed the hungry or
support farmers and their communities. Thus began his
long career focused on development of sustainable agriculture, the subject he addresses in chapter 10 as a "wicked

problem" that arises within a complex, interconnected, dynamic system. Using a metaphor of the small movements of a rudder that cause a whole ship to turn, he argues for local commitments to community food security, rooted in a declaration of enough good food as a human right. Food must nourish bodies, but it must also nourish local economies and communities.

Sustainable agriculture is one name that defines production practices and philosophies in opposition to industrial agriculture. Among others, alternative, organic, ecological, permaculture, and small-scale agriculture represent the growing number of farmers in the developed world and perhaps the majority in the world that agribusinesses have begun to colonize. In truth, both industrial and alternative "types" of farmers hide the significant variation within each group from local ecological adaptations and from decisions and adjustments farmers make based on experience, knowledge, and the shifting sands of farm policies, climate change, production costs, and commodity prices. The typology thus obscures the fact that farmers, in whatever groups others may lump them, have much in common. Family farms dominate both groups. For example, the last U.S. Census of Agriculture shows that 97 percent of America's 2.1 million farms are family-owned (USDA 2012) and all are subject to political, economic, and ecological forces beyond their control. Such observations suggest that the rhetoric that divides industrial from alternative farmers may at times separate them to everyone's detriment. While we maintain the language of industrial farming in this volume, the movement of industrial practices and technologies into the developing world make our authors' investigations and revelations based on farmers' own insights and experiences valuable tools for those wishing to understand what industrial farming means to farmers, and what the challenges they face portend for us all.

References

Deichman, Uwe, Aparajita Goyal, and Deepak Mishra. 2016. "Will Digital Technologies Transform Agriculture in Developing Countries?" Policy Research Working Paper 7669. May 2016. 2016 World Development Report Team & Development Research Group. Environment and Energy Team. https://openknowledge.worldbank.org/bitstream/handle/10986/24507/Will0digital0t0veloping0countries00.pdf?sequence=1.

FAO. 2017. *The Future of Food and Agriculture: Trends and Challenges.* United Nations. Rome. https://www.scribd.com/document/345628822/FAO-2017-The-future-of-food-and-agriculture-trends-and-challenges.

Ikerd, John. n.d. "The Globalization of Agriculture: Implication for Sustainability of Small Horticultural Farms." Accessed October 1, 2017. http://web.missouri.edu/ikerdj/papers/TorontoGlobalization.html.

Mooney, Pat. 2017. "Too Big to Feed: Exploring the Impacts of Mega-Mergers, Consolidation, Concentration of Power in the Agri-food Sector." *IPES-Food.* October. http://www.ipes-food.org/images/Reports/Concentration_FullReport.pdf.

Newman, Jesse. 2017. "U.S. Farm Income Seen Falling for Fourth Straight Year." *The Wall Street Journal.* Updated February 7; https://www.wsj.com/articles/u-s-farm-income-seen-falling-for-fourth-straight-year-1486486691.

Porter, J. R., et al. 2014. "Food Security and Food Production Systems." In *Climate Change 2014: Impacts, Adaptation, and Vulnerability. Part A: Global and Sectoral Aspects.* Contribution of Working Group 2 to the Fifth Assessment Report of the Intergovernmental Panel on Climate Change. Cambridge: Cambridge University Press.

U.S. Department of Agriculture. 2012. *Census of Agriculture: Highlights.* National Agricultural Statistics Service. https://www.agcensus.usda.gov/Publications/2012/Online_Resources/Highlights/NASS%20Family%20Farmer/Family_Farms_Highlights.pdf.

———. 2017. *Farms and Land in Farms: 2016 Summary.* February. https://www.nass.usda.gov/Publications/Todays_Reports/reports/fnlo0217.pdf.

1

Power, Food, and Agriculture

Implications for Farmers, Consumers, and Communities

MARY K. HENDRICKSON, PHILIP H. HOWARD, AND DOUGLAS H. CONSTANCE

The system by which most relatively affluent global consumers obtain their food is globalized and industrialized in the same fashion as the rest of the global capitalist system.[1] An increasingly smaller number of actors within global supply chains make many of the decisions about the food we eat, from where and how it is grown, to how we will obtain it. While this system has produced and marketed a great many tasty and diverse calories for those who can afford to participate, the costs of this system have been borne by farmers, food workers, rural communities, and the ecology in which we are all embedded. In the way it is shaped and organized, the food system is very much like other industries, but food (and water) is unlike other consumer goods. Everyone on the planet needs to eat nutritious foods every day to live a healthy and productive life. Thus, we believe food should not be treated like other commodities, and the people who produce food, along with a stable agroecosystem, should be protected as critical to society.

The purpose of this chapter is to show how a minority of global actors make many of the decisions about what food is produced—where, how, by whom, and for whom—and highlight the implications of these decisions for farmers, consumers, communities, and their environment. The structuring of the relationship along the supply chain from farm to plate, and the globalizing of these relationships, has harmed our ecology, rural communities, and the livelihoods of farmers and food workers. We explain how farmers and consumers—who have myriad concerns about the implications of the agrifood system—are mostly excluded from decision-making through the continued consolidation of critical points of the supply chain. Decisions are increasingly made by CEOs to meet the narrow demands of shareholders of global agrifood firms, whose main concern is to increase their power more than similar firms. Still, farmers and consumers are not passive bystanders to these trends and have organized in multiple ways to stop, shape, or opt out of them.

Impacts of Social and Economic Organization in Agrifood

The organization of the agrifood system has important consequences for the life chances of farmers, farm and food workers, communities, and the environment. In the last fifty years, food and farming in the United States and across the world has been reorganized toward an industrialized system that reduces food—a physiological necessity that has important cultural and social meanings—to a commodity to be produced as cheaply as possible and sold to the highest bidder. Even the comparatively wealthy farmers in the United States, Canada, and Europe end up as relatively powerless participants in food chains over which they have little or no control. Farmers face limited choices in which inputs to use, which crops or livestock to produce, and which markets to sell their goods. Meanwhile, food and farm workers in the United States are some of the most food insecure people in a country where one in eight households may not know where their next meal is coming from (Coleman-Jensen et al. 2016). That a highly industrialized and capitalized agrifood system can produce abundant calories and still leave hungry people, many of them involved in the production of food, shows that the tradeoffs

Hendrickson, Howard, Constance

Table 1. Principal farm operator household finances, by USDA farm typology, 2015

Item	Residence Farms	Intermediate Farms	Commercial Farms	All Farms
Number of farms	1,215,011	631,942	185,346	2,032,300
Income, median dollars per household				
Farm income	-2,100	788	146,466	-765
Off-farm income	82,987	55,750	40,250	67,500
Earned income	62,500	31,789	22,500	38,270
Unearned income	24,000	25,013	9,000	25,013
Total household income	82,925	59,102	197,980	76,735

Source: Data from USDA Economic Research Service, https://www.ers.usda.gov /webdocs/DataFiles/48870/table02.xls?v=42704.

farmers, workers, and the environment are making are not worth the cost to people, communities, and the ecosystem in which we are embedded.

Let's start with the fact that fewer farmers are able to make a full-time living from farming. Just 40 percent of the two million farms in the United States list farming as the primary occupation of the farm operator. Less than 200,000 American farms are classified as "commercial" by USDA, meaning that they have gross farm sales exceeding $350,000. At first glance, this "upper 10 percent" of farm households appear to be doing well, having a median net farm income of over $146,000 in 2015 and median household income nearing $200,000—triple the median U.S. household income (Posey 2016; USDA 2015b). Yet nearly a third of farm households listing farming as a principal occupation reported a median of *just $788 in farm income* in 2015, even though they had higher median household income due to off-farm income (USDA 2015b).

These changes exact real tolls on farmers. In the early 2000s, when Midwestern commodity agriculture was reeling from low prices, a Missouri farmer told Hendrickson that he used to look around to see if any farmers were getting out of farming so he could get their land to farm. Now he looks around and sees that he has no neighbors. As one can see in table 1, three-fifths of U.S. farms are residential where the operator does not consider farming as their primary occupation, while about a tenth gain significant income from farming, leaving a floundering "intermediate" set of farms. Some of these farms may be considered part of the declining "Agriculture of the Middle" (Lyson, Stevenson, and Welsh 2008), defined as the decrease in the number of farms in midsized categories (USDA uses $350,000 to $999,999 in annual agricultural sales, USDA 2015a). While fewer than 6 percent of all U.S. farms, midsized farms accounted for about one-fifth of all agricultural sales and farmland, and over one quarter of net farm income. Farmers of the middle are often left out by the large commodity chains we describe in this chapter, but also find fewer other midrange businesses to cooperate with (such as processing plants, distributors, or grocers) or to supply them with inputs and right-sized equipment for planting, harvesting, storing, processing, or distributing their products (Legun and Bell 2016).

Given difficult economics, these "intermediate" sized farms may feel particular pressures to farm in ways incongruent with their values or beliefs. For instance, James and Hendrickson (2008) found evidence from Missouri farmers to suggest that financial pressures can increase a farmer's willingness to tolerate unethical conduct. Concentrated markets may cause farmers to feel financially pressured, especially as they become relatively dependent within production networks organized by transnational agrifood firms (Hendrickson, James, and Heffernan 2013). Concentrated markets for inputs or agricultural products narrow the range of choices that farmers *can* make about how they treat their land, animals, and workers, and even what kind of farming they decide to enter (Hendrickson and James 2005). For instance, a farmer may want to enhance soil quality by practicing multiyear rotations with three to five different crops but is prevented because he cannot find regional markets for sunflowers or wheat rather than just soybeans and corn (Roesch-McNally et al. 2017). Farmers may also want to practice diversified crop and livestock farming but cannot find available markets for smaller livestock numbers (for a summary of these agricultural practices of the middle farmers who are too large to direct market and too small to compete in global commodity chains see: Lyson, Stevenson, and Welsh 2008). For example, it is essentially impossible for Midwestern farmers who want to use non-genetically modified soybeans to access seeds that do not contain GM traits, as nearly 100 percent of soybeans now contain at least one herbicide tolerant trait.[2] Stuart and Schewe (2016) document how seed corn contracts in Michigan constrain the choices of farmers, causing them to over-apply fertilizer to maximize yield, resulting in greenhouse gas emissions and water pollution, while Stuart (2009) found that farmers in California felt pressured by their buyers to use practices they felt were ecologically destructive and unethical. In short, constrained choices can force farmers into the "kinds of decisions that they otherwise would not have chosen for ethical or other reasons" (Hendrickson and James 2005, 283)

The decisions these farmers must make also impact their communities and their ecology. For example, in their meta-analysis of the relationship between agricultural structure and community well-being, Lobao and Stofferahn (2007) found detrimental effects of industrialized farming on communities, such as increased income inequality or poverty and population decline; these negative effects were reported in 82 percent of 51 studies. A more detailed exploration of community impacts can be found in Gibson and Gray, (chapter 9 of this volume). Many U.S. farmers feel forced into specialized monocultures that separate livestock from crop production both at the farm level and at larger regional geographies (Lyson 2004), with widely documented negative ecological impacts such as soil loss and degradation, changes in water quality, and the rise of herbicide resistant weeds (Eller 2014; Hendrickson 2015). Ecological and community impacts are often interdependent. For example, Monsanto's introduction of dicamba-tolerant soybeans and cotton as the latest measure to fight herbicide resistant weeds created new problems as dicamba drifts when applied in anything less than perfect application conditions, causing damage to a wide range of crops, including neighboring non-dicamba tolerant soybeans.[3] In 2016 and 2017 this damage caused considerable tension in rural communities, pitting neighbor against neighbor; conflict over dicamba damage was cited in the murder of an Arkansas farmer by a neighboring Missouri farmhand.[4] In addition, these agricultural systems both contribute to climate change and must adapt to it (explored further by Alexander in chapter 6 of this volume). The industrial agrifood system's lengthening supply chain lacks tight ecological and social feedback loops, compromising adaptive responses that promote resilience (Lamine 2015; Hendrickson 2015).

Analyzing the Structure of Food and Farming

The current structure of the agrifood system can best be thought of as a series of competing global production networks in which dependence and power are highly correlated (Carstensen, Lianos, Lombardi, and MacDonald, 2016; James, Hendrickson, and Howard, 2013; Wilkinson, 2006; Hendrickson et al. 2008). A key concept is defining power in the food system, specifically who has it, how we can document and measure it, and how it is articulated in the structure that we document. Power is a crucial element of who can make decisions in the food system, decisions that shape the life chances of farmers and workers who produce our food, the vibrancy of the communities in which they live, and the ecology on which future food production depends. Those of us involved in the Missouri School of Agrifood Studies (Bonanno 2009) have documented increasing concentration in different sectors of the U.S. agrifood industry through a series of concentration tables, reports, and articles (Constance et al. 2014a). We hoped that by documenting the market relationships in the agrifood system, we would help farmers, consumers, and communities understand the system they were part of in order to transform it.

Our approach is different from other scholarship in economics and law that has primarily addressed concerns about agricultural consolidation by studying one aspect—horizontal integration, that occurs when firms in one sector (for example, pork processing) consolidate into fewer firms—at one scale, national markets (Crespi, Saitone, and Sexton 2012; Fuglie et al. 2011; MacDonald 2016). These scholars often express little concern about increasing market consolidation, adopting the mainstream economics position that increased efficiency produced economic gains, and maintaining that firms did not use their market power to increase prices or to discriminate against producers.

We admit there are weaknesses in looking only at concentration in certain commodities, or employing monopoly-only models of the agrifood system. For instance, while firms may organize themselves into global production networks, those networks may still compete with each other while disadvantaging farmers and ecosystems (Hendrickson et al. 2008; Heffernan, Hendrickson, and Gronski 1999). Current concentration and monopoly models also do not address the issue of vertical integration and other structural issues in the agrifood value chain. To remedy these problems, some scholars have worked to differentiate between buyer and seller power, or to examine the differing levels of concentration that can harm producers, consumers, or the public good in different situations (Foer 2016; Carstensen 2008; Carstensen et al. 2016).

Following Nitzan and Bichler (2009), Howard (2016a, 11) proposed a more encompassing look at capital as power— "that corporations quantify their perceived influence through 'capitalization'"—which can be viewed as a measure of their expected future earnings, discounted for perceived risks. This means that "capitalism as a system is therefore better understood as a mode of power rather than a mode of production." Mode of production refers to the way we collectively produce what we need to survive as a society and the social relationships that form around it. Mode of power, in contrast, does not assume that capitalists are driven to increase production (nor consumption), but only their own power relative to everyone else, even if it reduces well-being. This approach highlights the need to understand the social, political, and economic relationships that structure the agrifood system. At the core of all these works is the desire to describe and understand the power relationships that arise in an industrialized, highly capitalized agrifood system in order to address their negative impacts.

Methods

The Missouri School method documents economic concentration in an accessible format that illustrates the breadth and depth of concentration in major agricultural commodities and in different sectors of the agrifood system (see figure 1). We report the market shares in major agricultural commodities, agricultural inputs, and food retailing in CR4 tables (CR4 is the concentration ratio [CR] of the combined market share of the top four [4] firms in each market). We glean the data from trade journals, company annual reports, government reports, academic journals, and financial newspapers. Sources used in this chapter include: trade journals and newspapers such as *Successful Farming, Farm Futures, European Seed, Reuters,* and *Fortune;* government reports from USDA's Economic Research Service and Grain Inspection Packers and Stockyards Administration (GIPSA), as well as United Nations agencies such as the Food and Agriculture Organization (UNFAO) and the Committee on Trade and Development (UNCTAD); nonprofit research briefs where we agree with the methods used including from ETC Group, Food and Water Watch, and Oxfam; and academic journals in law, economics, policy, and sociology.

We are particularly interested in the top four firms in a specific market for two reasons. First, when four firms control more than 40 percent of a market the oligopolistic/oligopsonistic structure can confer market power to those firms (Breimyer 1965; Connor et al. 1984; Heffernan 2000; Hendrickson and James 2005). Second, the theory of small group behavior indicates that actors in small groups generally inform their own actions through *observation* of other actors, rather than through *discussion* (Olson 1965). As noted above, CR4 is a rather simplistic monopoly model that provides an imperfect assessment of power relationships within a particular commodity (James, Hendrickson, and Howard 2013). The utility of the CR4 tables is the snapshot of the dominant players in and across particular commodities, which helps farmers and community members understand the wide reach of corporate actors. Because we are interested in concentration issues across the agrifood system, one of our major contributions is the identification of the top firms by name to document the progress of cross-commodity integration. Reading company reports, trade journals, and financial newspapers allows us to glean information about potential strategies that different actors pursue, as well as industry insights into the implications of those strategies.

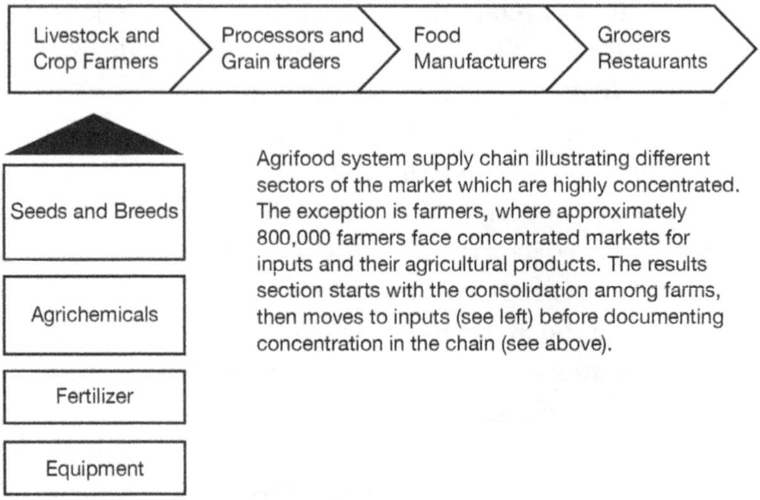

| Livestock and Crop Farmers | Processors and Grain traders | Food Manufacturers | Grocers Restaurants |

Seeds and Breeds

Agrichemicals

Fertilizer

Equipment

Agrifood system supply chain illustrating different sectors of the market which are highly concentrated. The exception is farmers, where approximately 800,000 farmers face concentrated markets for inputs and their agricultural products. The results section starts with the consolidation among farms, then moves to inputs (see left) before documenting concentration in the chain (see above).

FIG. 1. Agrifood system supply chain. Created by authors.

The Structure of the Agrifood System

In the following pages, we provide a snapshot of different markets across the agrifood chain (see figure 1), which starts with the inputs farmers use to produce agricultural commodities, the commodity markets into which they sell, and the food processing and food retailing sectors that have driven a large number of changes in the marketplace in the last twenty-five years. We describe each link of the chain, the way markets have changed, and the implications of those changes. But first, we provide a look at what has happened to farmers in the last fifty years.

We have lost one-third of the U.S. farms that existed in 1964, and half of the remaining two million farms produce less than $10,000 in annual sales (USDA 2012). Using the median size of crop acres or number of animals, MacDonald (2016) shows increasing consolidation at the farm level in the United States, where median farm size in cropland more than doubled between 1982 and 2012, and increased even more rapidly in livestock (see table 2). Illustrating that the "Agriculture of the Middle" is declining and perhaps facing extinction, he documents that "the number of farms with milk cows or hogs fell by about 70 percent, while those with fed cattle [steers/heifers for market] or contracts for broiler production fell by 30 percent" (MacDonald 2016, 5).

The trends toward large-scale farms in the United States (mirrored in Canada) have been on the leading edge of global shifts, suggesting what may happen elsewhere as agrifood industrialization diffuses globally. Lowder, Skoet, and Raney (2016, 27) document how farms in low- and middle-income countries decreased in size after 1960 but began increasing during the last decade of the twentieth century, while "average farm size increased from 1960 to 2000 in some upper-middle-income countries and in nearly all high-income countries." Oya (2013) reminds us that farm

Table 2. Structural change in U.S. livestock production

Item	1987	2012
Midpoint farm sizes		
Broilers (annual sales/ removals)	300,000	680,000
Cattle feeding (annual sales/removals)	17,532	38,369
Hogs (annual sales/ removals)	1,200	40,000
Milk cows (herd size)	80	900
Number of farms with		
Contract broiler production	22,000	15,830
Cattle feeding	112,109	77,120
Hogs	243,398	63,246
Milk cows	202,068	64,098

Source: Data from James M. MacDonald, "Concentration, Contracting, and Competition Policy in U.S. Agribusiness," *Concurrences Competition Law Review* 1 (2016): 5.

scale does not neatly describe the relations of production; rather, we need to understand global agrifood commodity relationships, or as we conceive of it, the *mode of power* that is shaping how people can participate in the food system.

Concentration in Input Markets

Fewer and larger farms signifies that farmers are replacing management and inputs produced on the farm with capital-intensive inputs purchased off the farm, especially in the production of pork, poultry, dairy, and row crops and within large vegetable, fruit, and nursery operations. Consolidation in the input markets then becomes a serious concern for farmers who remain. In the past two decades, mergers of enormous firms have occurred in the farm machinery, fertilizer, seeds, and agrichemical sectors. Of increasing concern is ownership of data, codes, and programming upon which commercial

Hendrickson, Howard, Constance

farmers have come to rely; even smaller scale row-crop farms use GPS systems to manage soil fertility, irrigation, and especially yield data, while farmers with recently purchased tractors or combines cannot legally fix the machines themselves (Carolan 2017; Gibson, chapter 4 of this volume).

We begin with seeds. The introduction of Round-up Ready seeds in the mid-1990s spurred rapid consolidation among seed companies (see figure 2) and convergence between seed and chemical companies (Howard 2009b). Monsanto became the dominant seed firm with the acquisition of more than fifty formerly independent firms (see table 3). Fuglie et al. (2011) estimated a CR4 of 54 percent in the global commercial seed market, with certain segments even more concentrated (for example, the global vegetable seed market at CR4 of 70 percent and the U.S. cottonseed, corn seed, and soybean seed markets at CR4 over 50 percent; see figure 2). In the last two years, major mergers between the largest seed and chemical companies have taken place. Bayer merged with Monsanto, and Dow with DuPont to make Corteva. Depending on requested divestures, the new firms could control half of the global commercial seeds market (see table 3). This "merger activity in [the seed sector] illustrates rapid transformation from an already concentrated industry to a tight oligopoly on a global scale" (Lianos, Katalevsky, and Ivanov 2016, 1).

Much of this concentration has been spurred by proprietary agricultural biotechnology that makes it illegal for farmers to save seed and promotes tight coordination between seed and chemical companies. Agrochemical firms like Syngenta, Monsanto, and DuPont entered the seed industry in the past two decades (UNCTAD 2006), with six global firms (Monsanto, DuPont, Syngenta, Bayer, Dow, and BASF) estimated to control three-quarters of all private sector plant breeding research, nearly three-fifths of the commercial seed market, and over three-quarters of

Concentration in the seed industry increased for corn and soybeans in 2015

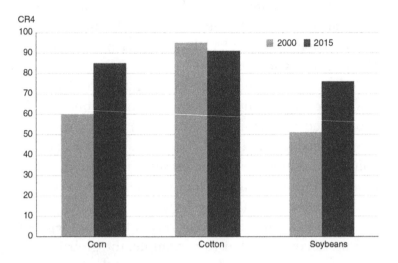

Note: CR4 is the share of sales held by the four largest sellers in the industry.
Sources: USDA, Economic Research Service using data from the USDA Agricultural Marketing Service (cotton) and the Farm Journal (corn and soybeans).

FIG. 2. USDA seed market data prior to 2016 merger announcements. Source: https://www.ers.usda.gov/webdocs/charts/83018/april17 _feature_macdonald_fig01.png?v=42825.

Table 3. Global seed and agrichemical companies

Seed Company and Global Rank on Global Seed Sales	Concentration Ratio of Global Proprietary Seed Market (Current)	Merger Partner	Percent of Global Proprietary Seed Market of Combined Firm (Estimated)
Monsanto (1)		Bayer (7)	29%
DuPont (2)		Dow (8)	18%
Syngenta (3)			9%
Vilmorin (4)	4–54%		5%
WinField (5)			
KWS (6)			
Bayer Crop-Science (7)		Monsanto (1)	
Dow Agrosciences (8)	8–63%	DuPont (8)	

Agrichemical Company and Global Rank	Concentration Ratio of Global Agrichemical Market (Current)	Merger Partner	Percent of Global Agrichemical Market of Combined Firm (Estimated)
Syngenta (1)		ChemChina (7)	29%
Bayer Crop-Science (2)		Monsanto (5)	25%
BASF (3)			12%
Dow Agrosciences (4)	4–62%	DuPont (6)	16%
Monsanto (5)			
DuPont (6)		Dow (4)	
ChemChina (7)		Syngenta (1)	
Nufarm (8)	8–87%		

Source: Data from information in ETC Group (2013) and Keith O. Fuglie, et al. (2011), "Research Investments and Market Structure in the Food Processing, Agricultural Input, and Biofuel Industries Worldwide" (Washington DC: USDA Economic Research Service).

global agrochemical sales (ETC Group 2013).[5] ChemChina acquired Syngenta, which was the third-largest global seed company and largest agrochemical company with over one-fifth of the global market in 2011. If all these mergers proceed without required divestures, three firms would sell 70 percent of agrichemicals globally (see table 3).

No one can explain better than farmers what is happening. In 2010, a number of farmers testified at workshops on agricultural competition organized by the U.S. Departments of Justice and Agriculture. In Iowa, Todd Leak from North Dakota gave a farmer's view of the changes we documented:

> I farm 2,000 acres with my brother in central Grand Forks County, North Dakota. . . . I'm a soybean farmer for thirty years, and maybe about a decade ago [in 2000], I was free to choose from about a hundred different varieties of non-GMO soybeans. . . . Today there's about 123 varieties of GMO soybeans that I have to choose from and about twelve non-GMO. Of those twelve non-GMO varieties, six of those are for the specialty food grade . . . market . . . [six] that remained to me were developed in the 1980s and 1990s and their disease packages, their host resistance are far less than the GMO varieties, and their yield is only about 70 percent of the GMO varieties, and that is not because of the GMOs. GMOs do not increase yield. There is no yield gene trait. The issue is that all of the research, all of the breeding, is going into proprietary genetically modified varieties. . . . I am therefore forced as a farmer to have to go to the seed companies, these few seed companies that are left, to purchase my seed. (U.S. Departments of Justice and Agriculture 2010, 126–27)

Many—but not all—farmers at the Iowa hearing agreed. Fred Bower, a Minnesota farmer and seed dealer, lamented the decrease in the number of seed companies from fifty

Hendrickson, Howard, Constance

when he started farming in the 1970s to four in 2010. He complained that farmers were "not being treated properly as far as price. When the amount of seed dealers goes down, the competition decreases, and they kind of run the show of what they want to say is the price. It was way better to have more seed companies involved than to have fewer seed companies at the present time and pay through the nose" (U.S. Departments of Justice and Agriculture 2010, 132). An Indiana farmer pleaded, "I need a choice of seed. I'm down to planting three varieties of public soybeans" (U.S. Departments of Justice and Agriculture 2010, 139).

As farmer Leak's testimony indicated, it is difficult to disentangle seeds, chemicals, and agriculture biotechnology. Moss (2016, 11) reported that in 2009, prior to mergers, the Big 6 firms "held greater than 95% of trait acres for corn, soybeans, and cotton in the U.S." A recent article in *Successful Farming* highlights new linkages that will arise with the proposed merger between Bayer-Monsanto:

> Monsanto is largely in the seeds and traits business, while Bayer concentrates on chemicals. . . . 74% of Monsanto's 2016 sales came from seeds and traits, with the remaining 26% coming from crop protection chemicals. Bayer's flipped the other way. It derived 85% of its 2016 sales from crop protection chemicals, with just 15% coming from seeds and traits. Little overlap exists between the companies in the global seed and traits space for corn and soybeans. Monsanto's 36% market share in corn would not change if the firms combined. In soybeans, Monsanto's current 27% market share would rise to just 28% if the Bayer Monsanto merger went through. (Gullickson 2017, n.p.)

Because access to genetically modified traits is so important in the current seed market, the Big 6 firms have engaged in a number of cross licensing agreements, which increases sector consolidation and already high barriers to entry (Howard 2015; for a history of how these agreements have developed, see Howard 2016a). There is also the much-despised patent enforcement at the farm level controversy, such as Monsanto's tactics aimed at enforcing patents that included videotaping and photographing farmers, and infiltrating community meetings to the point where their investigators were termed the "seed police" (Bartlett and Steele 2008, n.p.).

Livestock genetics are also highly concentrated, especially for poultry and swine production (see table 4). Research on nearly all of global poultry genetics and close to two-thirds of cattle and swine genetics is controlled by four firms (ETC Group 2013; see also Gura 2007). Concentration in both seed and livestock genetics raises a number of important issues, including that farmers must now use more capital to access genetics while also having fewer choices about what kinds of seeds or breeds to use. Genetic concentration is a growing concern, especially in terms of disappearing livestock breeds (FAO 2015), which means that animals may be more susceptible to evolving pathogens or could be less resilient in the face of climate change (Howard 2016a; Hendrickson 2015).

While improved seeds and breeds increased agricultural productivity (yield), about half the gains made in the twentieth century are the result of inorganic fertilizers, particularly for crop nutrients such as nitrogen (N), phosphorous (P), and potassium (K) (Aziz et al. 2015). Maintaining and enhancing soil fertility has been one of the key struggles of human civilization; Montgomery (2012) argues that many great civilizations have collapsed due to the exhaustion of soils. Europe's imperialistic search for external sources of nitrogen was resolved through the development of synthetic nitrogen (Foster and Magdoff 2000), while industrial mining techniques facilitated trade in phosphorous and potassium.

Table 4. Concentration in livestock genetics

Turkeys	Laying hens	Broilers	Swine
EW Group	EW Group	EW Group	Genus
Hendrix Genetics	Hendrix Genetics	Tyson	Hendrix Genetics
		Groupe Grimaud	Groupe Grimaud
			Smithfield/WH Group
CR2 99%	CR2 94%	CR3 95%	Four firms control 2/3 of research & development

Source: Data from Philip H. Howard, *Concentration and Power in the Food System: Who Controls What We Eat?* (New York: Bloomsbury Academic, 2016), based on data from ETC Group (2013).

These developments created a capital-intensive fertilizer industry controlled by transnational firms with substantial support from national governments. Global fertilizer companies such as Yara, Potash Corp, Agrium, Mosaic, OCP (Morocco), and a Russia-based potash cabal dominate the market (Taylor and Moss 2013). In 2018, Potash Corp and Agrium completed their merger, which created the largest fertilizer company in the world, Nutrien. Global fertilizer producers have been able to act "in a coordinated fashion" on price, but buyer power in the India and China markets has curtailed those actions (Taylor and Moss 2013, 9). The United States and Canada have legally sanctioned export cartels in fertilizers, primarily in the phosphorus industry where a duopoly between Potash Corp and Mosaic, called PhosChem, controls 52 percent of the world's phosphorus trade. PotashCorp, Agrium, and Mosaic also cooperated in a legally sanctioned export cartel, *Canpotex*, which accounted for 61 percent of the world potash trade (Taylor and Moss 2013).

The global farm machinery sector has also consolidated

rapidly in the past three decades. John Deere is the largest domestic and global agricultural machinery firm, followed by CNH Industrial (a merger of Fiat and CNH Global) and AGCO, which includes many iconic brands such as Massey-Ferguson, Gleaner, and White. In 2011, ten global firms had sales greater than $1 billion, accounting for over one-third of the global market. In just fifteen years between 1994 and 2009, the four largest machinery manufacturers increased their market share from 28 to 50 percent of global sales (Fuglie et al. 2011).

Concerns about consolidation in the agricultural machinery market arise in two different arenas. One regards digital information in terms of who captures it, who uses it, and who owns it. Precision agriculture utilizing GPS is an important tool to monitor soil fertility, crop yields, and input use. Nearly three-quarters of U.S. corn acres employ precision agriculture practices (Carolan 2017). Precision agriculture has significant ecological benefits, particularly in the reduction of fertilizer and pesticide use (Burger 2016). Input reductions jeopardize the sales of the Big 6 seed/chemical firms, hence their interest in acquiring farm management software and digital companies. Precision agriculture relies on the transmission of large amounts of data from tractors, harvesters, sprayers in crop production, and from electronic tags, feeding equipment, and milking equipment in livestock production. Farmers have concerns about the ownership of this data, as well as the value of such big data to powerful market actors. Brian Marshall, a member of the American Farm Bureau Federation, testified before the U.S. Congress that "virtually every company says it will never share, sell or use the data in a market-distorting way, but we would rather verify than trust" (Plume 2014). Plume also writes that large companies are trying to figure out how to position themselves for the future, when more farmers will participate in data sharing. Monsanto's ownership of Climate Corporation, which specializes in collecting and analyzing soil and weather data to allow farmers to make "data-driven" decisions, was considered a key enticement for Bayer's offer to buy Monsanto, as Bayer has lagged behind in developing data platforms.[6] As Monsanto's CEO, Hugh Grant, says, "The company of the future won't just be selling seeds and chemicals, but seeds and chemicals and data as a service" (Murray 2016, n.p.; for a detailed discussion see Gibson, chapter 4 of this volume).

A second concern regards innovation, which has long been a source of pride for farmers who adapted their machinery to improve its fit with their needs. Magazines like *Farm Show* and *Successful Farming* provide multiple examples of farmers "hacking" machinery and sharing their insights with other farmers. In a rare case, the U.S. Department of Justice blocked a proposed merger of Deere and Precision Planting (Monsanto) because the merger would hamper farmer innovation in retrofitting their planting toolbars. Still, the top two precision planter manufacturers control over 80 percent of the high-speed precision planting equipment market (U.S. Department of Justice 2016). Some analysts predict greater levels of bundling of input packages, comparable to when chemical firms took over the seed industry. As longtime agricultural concentration observer Pat Mooney writes, "The dominant farm machinery companies have invested heavily in satellite and sensor information and Big Data management. With this data, the machinery companies stand to know more about the inputs and outcomes of every field than any other company and even the farmer. Machinery companies have the 'box' in which the other input companies have to put their seeds, pesticides and fertilizers" (2017, 4).

Beyond the Farm Gate

While farmers face decreased choice regarding input markets, they also must market their agricultural products to just a few processors or grain traders. Globally, Archer Daniels Midland (ADM), Bunge, Cargill, and Louis Dreyfus move the vast majority of grain trading between nations (Murphy, Burch, and Clapp 2012; Howard 2016a). In the U.S. grain sector, four or fewer firms control nearly all of cane sugar processing and over four-fifths of the wet corn milling, beet sugar processing, and soybean crushing markets (Adjemian et al. 2016). For flour milling, just one joint venture, Ardent Mills (co-owned by Cargill, ConAgra, and CHS), controls approximately one-third of the market, leaving farmers in some parts of the country with few options to sell their wheat (Howard 2016b).

The same situation exists in the livestock sector (see table 5). Farmers rely on the same dominant firms across the entire protein (chicken, pork, and beef) sector, including Tyson Foods, JBS, and Smithfield (held by WH Group from China). While we report primarily U.S. data, the rise of just a few firms dominating the protein sector is a global phenomenon.

Take the case of Tyson Foods, a firm explored in more detail by Stull in chapter 2 of this volume. After rising to dominance as the largest poultry company in the United States, Tyson began to diffuse its "Southern Model" (Constance 2008) of poultry production into Mexico in 1988 through a joint venture with Mexican and Japanese companies. By 2003 it was the second-largest poultry firm in Mexico. During this same time, Tyson acquired or developed joint ventures with numerous companies around the world. In 2001, it bought Iowa Beef Packers (IBP) and became the largest meat packer in the world with major holdings in beef and pork added to its poultry (broilers and turkey) portfolio. Tyson perfected its global expansion model in Mexico and then moved aggressively into the emerging markets in Brazil, India, China, and other countries (Constance et al. 2010).

Table 5: Concentration in the U.S. protein sector

Commodity and CR4	Firm Rankings
Broilers (51% CR4)*	1. Tyson Foods**
	2. Pilgrim's (owned by JBS)
	3. Sanderson Farms Inc.
	4. Perdue
• Note that JBS and Tyson each have more than double the market share of either Sanderson Farms or Perdue.	
Turkeys (57% CR4)*	1. Butterball**
	2. Jennie-O
	3. Cargill
	4. Farbest Foods
Steer and Heifer Slaughter (85% CR4)*	1. Tyson**
	2. JBS
	3. Cargill
	4. National Beef
• Note that the top three firms have three-fourths of the market.	
Pork Slaughter (66% CR4)*	1.Smithfield/WH Group***
	2. JBS
	3. Tyson
	4. Hormel

CR4 refers to the percent of the market controlled by the top four firms.

* *Source*: Data from GIPSA, "Packers and Stockyards Program Annual Report" (Washington DC: USDA, 2016), https://www.gipsa.usda.gov/psp/publication/ar/2016_psp_annual_report.pdf.

** *Source*: Data from Watts Poultry USA, "Watts Poultry USA's 2017 Broiler Companies," March 2017, 17–18, http://www.wattpoultryusa-digital.com/201703/index.php#/18; Tyson Factbook.

*** *Source*: Data from *National Hog Farmer*.

Brazil's JBS followed Tyson's model with several acquisitions starting in the early 2000s to surpass Tyson and become the largest meat company and beef packer in the world. These purchases included the assets of Swift Foods (beef) in the United States, Australia, and Latin America; Cargill's pork operations in the United States; and Pilgrim's Pride (poultry) in the United States and Mexico. JBS benefitted from substantial investments from Brazilian government-owned banks, but it was forced to sell some operations in 2017 after admitting to corruption in Brazil (Howard 2017). Interestingly, government support gave JBS an advantage over Tyson in Latin America, and as a result, Tyson sold its Mexico and Brazil divisions to JBS in 2014.

Smithfield, facing credit issues after the financial crisis in 2007–2008, was acquired by WH Group, a Chinese firm that has significant ties to the Chinese government (Howard 2017). WH/Smithfield is the world's largest pork producer, with 1.1 million sows in production worldwide, including holdings in the United States, Mexico, Poland, and Romania, and it is rapidly expanding its poultry operations in China.[7] WH Group has announced its intention to be the world's largest packaged-meats firm (Sito 2016). At the time of this writing, WH Group is seeking to acquire beef and poultry assets in Europe and North America, aiming to access cheap grain for feedstuffs and strong demand for meat products (Polansek and Zhu 2017). These global meatpackers have increased significantly in size over the last decade, partly due to government subsidies (Howard 2017). Their global scope also allows these firms to circumvent national regulations, such as import bans or higher tax rates, via the use of subsidiaries in other countries (Degen and Wong 2012).

Consolidation in the livestock sector has been accompanied by increased use of contracts and forward contracting, with a transparently negotiated cash market all but disappearing.[8] According to USDA's GIPSA (2016), nearly three-fifths of steer and heifer slaughter is procured using a formula pricing system that references an exogenous price (either based on a dwindling cash market or cattle futures), with

Hendrickson, Howard, Constance

only 30 percent procured through the cash market, which is half what it was in 2007. In the past, cash markets have been valued by farmers as they were established in places where several buyers might bid on a single group of cattle or hogs and the farmer had the choice of whether or not to accept that price. Today, cash markets are residual markets where farmers have limited time and options in which to make a sale. An Iowa farmer, Eric Nelson, illustrated this in the 2010 workshops: "The fewer competitors, particularly in my cattle operation, it's not unusual in a week's time that we're down to fifteen and twenty minutes cash market per week compared to a grain producer who maybe has 1,500 minutes a week in order to make grain sales, and it's because there are only a handful of end users in the cattle market" (U.S. Departments of Justice and Agriculture 2010, 62).

The situation is worse in pork production where only 2 percent of hogs are marketed through negotiated cash markets, with the remainder procured through formula pricing and marketing agreements (GIPSA 2016). The latter two forms often relied on the cash market as the basis for their own formulas for paying producers. The disappearance of the cash market indicates that the hog sector has moved into very similar marketing arrangements as have existed in broilers, eggs, and turkeys for several decades (Breimyer 1965). These arrangements do not use a transparent marketplace to negotiate the actual price per pound or animal; instead, broiler integrators use a complicated and purposefully opaque formula to pay their growers. Thirty-five large hog producers now own two-thirds of U.S. sows, with the top four firms owning 1.74 million sows or about 30 percent of the total.[9] Economists sometimes refer to these as "thin" markets, or markets where there are "few purchasers, low trading volume and low liquidity" (Adjemian et al. 2016, 2). Small producers are often left out in thinning markets because of the costs of using contracts as well as the economies of scale that favor larger producers. The structure of these end markets is reflected in what's happened on farms (see table 2), where less than 10 percent of farms with hogs and pigs produced 50 percent of all hogs and pig sales, with similar numbers for dairy and poultry (Adjemian et al. 2016). While farmers may not have the data that scholars do, they know the problems. During hearings on competition in agriculture, farmers "charged that the thinning of spot markets reduces market transparency, denies producers opportunities, reduces their bargaining power, and yields prices not accurately reflecting underlying supply and demand" (U.S. Department of Justice 2012, 12).

Retailers Drive Changes

The consolidation described above is matched by that in food retailing, where retailers have been accused by farmers and workers of exerting market power to force lower prices back upstream through the system to the farm gate (U.S. Department of Justice 2012). The top four food retailers (Walmart, Kroger, Albertson's, and Ahold Delhaize) sell over 60 percent of U.S. groceries—the result of Walmart's entry into food retailing in the late 1980s, a move that prompted national and international mergers (Howard 2016a).[10] Walmart also brought a different business model to groceries, focusing on supply chain efficiencies and negotiating with suppliers for the lowest price, which in turn motivated mergers among suppliers. For example, Tyson acquired IBP to supply the whole protein case (everything from chicken legs to pork chops to hamburger) to Walmart (Hendrickson et al. 2001). Many food manufacturers, especially in the packaged food space, might derive at least 20 percent of their net sales from Walmart stores.[11] Food and Water Watch (2013, 2) summed up the grocery landscape this way: "The top companies controlled an average of 63.3 percent of the sales of 100 types of groceries. . . . In 32 of the

Hendrickson, Howard, Constance

grocery categories, four or fewer companies controlled at least 75 percent of the sales. In six categories, the top companies had more than 90 percent of the sales, including baby formula and microwave dinners. . . . Retailers exert leverage by picking and choosing their suppliers, but suppliers rely on a few retailers for the bulk of their sales."

In the summer of 2017, a new disruption in food retail emerged with Amazon's acquisition of Whole Foods. Kowitt (2017) suggests that the $800 billion grocery business and its suppliers may be in for a new round of cost-cutting reminiscent of what happened to publishers and bookstores as Amazon built its book business. For example, the new parent firm immediately dropped Whole Foods' prices on organic rotisserie chicken, bananas, apples, and avocados by approximately 30 percent. Cost cutting in the food industry is often (if not exclusively) borne by farmers, workers, and small businesses.

Finally, we should mention that concentration in the restaurant and food service market can also be a concern for farmers and other suppliers. Four firms have over 40 percent of the fast food market (McDonald's, Yum! Brands, Doctor's Associates, Inc. [Subway], and Wendy's) (Howard 2016a). Two distributors, Sysco and U.S. Foods, dominate food distribution to food services such as restaurants, hospitals, and hotels/hospitality concerns.[12] One firm, 7-Eleven, has nearly one-quarter of the U.S. convenience store market (Howard 2016a). Consolidation in this sector means that the very firms who have power over farmers find themselves in a less powerful position vis-à-vis food distributors or grocers. Market power exercised at the retail level extracts concessions from the food processor, which in turn extracts concessions from the farmer who has no one (outside of the farm ecology or farmworkers) to extract concessions from. More practically, farmers providing alternative produce, meat, or dairy items can find themselves in a "catch-22" situation: too small to supply a distributor, yet too large to direct market.

In summary, the industrialization and consolidation of agriculture means that farmers specialize in certain crops or in a single animal sector; specialization requires significant capitalization. Markets for seeds, fertilizers, pesticides, and farm machinery have consolidated in the last two decades, constraining the choices farmers have regarding seed varieties, animal genetics, soil fertility practices, and pest/weed management strategies. Knowledge and information in managing farms (i.e., precision agriculture or genetically modified seeds) have also commodified during this time, becoming a significant source of power for transnational firms. Farmers face limited choice of where to sell their products as major grain and livestock markets are consolidated. Finally, large grocers exert power over suppliers in consolidated food retail markets.

Discussion: Resisting and Reshaping the Agrifood System

While it may seem that the structural conditions in the agrifood industry are insurmountable, in reality they are created and shaped by human actors. The "Emancipatory Question," as Constance puts it, then becomes "what kind of agrifood system might decrease injustice and inequality" and how do we achieve it (Constance 2009, 9)? Along with Ikerd (chapter 10 of this volume), we showcase how farmers in North America and across the globe, along with workers and consumers, have fought back against the changes we described above, to stop them, to shape them, or to go around them.

First, the bad news: resistance to this highly coordinated, capitalized, and industrialized agrifood system has been fragmented and less than successful at stopping the larger trends (Constance et al. 2014a). After four decades of anti-trust reinterpretation to a singular focus on efficiency and price (Howard 2016a), farmers joined with allies in pressing the Obama administration for movement on antitrust issues, resulting in a series of workshops in 2010 exploring competition in agriculture and food markets.[13] Yet what began as a bang ended with a whimper when the final report issued by the U.S. Departments of Justice and Agriculture claimed that "anticompetitive mergers and discussions represented only a portion of the concerns voiced at the workshops," and that claims about "fairness, safety, promotion of foreign trade, and environmental welfare" were outside the purview of antitrust law (U.S. Department of Justice 2012, 3). In another form of grassroots resistance, organic production and distribution systems grew out of environmental concerns about overuse of synthetic chemicals, health concerns about what those chemicals did to human bodies, and social concerns about small-scale farmers. Today, however, the organic challenge has become "standardized resistance" (Howard 2009a, 2016a) with coopted certification schemes that have shoehorned a broad movement into a narrow set of production practices (Jaffee and Howard 2010; Guthman 2008). Other farmers and consumers have turned to local food systems as a way to subvert the consolidated food system. But these projects, founded on authentic relationships and democratic participation, are often being stripped of their potential for radical transformation as they scale up to find efficiencies and lose sight of original goals (Mount 2012; DeLind 2011). Indeed, this is exactly what scholars would expect in a system embedded in the "mode of power" we described.

Still, there have been some small successes, particularly in the areas of removing objectionable ingredients (e.g., "pink slime" or rBGH in milk), improving animal welfare practices through both market (e.g., cage-free poultry in the U.S.) and government regulation (e.g., banning sow gestation crates in the European Union), and marginally improving wages through consumer campaigns (e.g., Coalition of Immokalee Workers) (Howard 2016a).

It would be tempting to stop here, acknowledging that the existing mode of power is very difficult to transform. However, our commitment to the possibilities of transformation requires us to examine patient, long-term struggles. In fact, following Bichler and Nitzan (2012), it may be that the all-encompassing mode of power described in this chapter is approaching the limits of what society will accept (e.g., the seed industry is having difficulty increasing prices to farmers, and declining beer sales are forcing the two global brewers to look to non-alcoholic beverages for growth). While Bichler and Nitzan are optimistic that at some point resistance will overcome agrifood capitals' ability to continue to concentrate and its power will disintegrate, this hope remains an unanswered empirical question.

Restoring Fairness and Competition in Agrifood

Against all odds, farmers continue authentic calls for justice through democratic institutions such as the courts and government policy. In 1996, a group of cattlemen filed suit against what was then called IBP (later Tyson) alleging that the firm was large enough to control prices. The lawsuit claimed that the firm artificially depressed prices by around 5 percent, thereby giving the company one free cattle out of every twenty cattle purchased (Harris 2004). The suit, filed under the Packers and Stockyards Act of 1921, was given class status in 2001 and proceeded to trial in 2004 (Taylor 2007). The jury awarded a $1.3 billion verdict for the plaintiffs, but the judge almost immediately overturned the ruling and the U.S. Supreme Court refused to hear the appeal. At the 2009 Organization for Competitive Markets annual meeting, the lead plaintiffs' attorney, David Domina, urged the audience to stay engaged and to fight for new competition policies at the Congressional level because the judicial system had been unsympathetic to these claims.[14] While this is a depressing story that starkly underscores the weak position of producers under the current mode of power, it is significant that a jury—which had access to the financial details presented at trial—found for the plaintiffs, legitimizing their complaint. Moreover, antitrust scholars have expressed some concern that the judge muddled the statutes and thus the legal proceedings when overturning the verdict (Taylor 2007). The case did contribute to provisions in the 2008 Farm Bill to amend the ninety-year-old Packers and Stockyards Act (PSA). After a long fight, a new rule went into effect in 2012 (Greene 2016). Despite having won in both Congress (new interpretations of PSA) and the Obama administration (new rules), activist farm organizations lost the battle because Congress refused to appropriate money for USDA's GIPSA to enforce the PSA.

These so-called GIPSA rules were also influenced by the work of farmers and their allies in the early 2000s, when sixteen state attorneys-general drafted a model "Producer Protection Act," some of which was adopted in individual states (Peck 2006; Wu and MacDonald 2015). Along with the beef producers mentioned above, contract poultry growers have fought long and hard to get new rules for contract growers into federal policy. In December 2016, USDA announced a set of "Farmer Fair Practices Rules" to target the most harmful practices aimed at poultry growers and to restore fairness within the PSA by defining unfair practices and undue preferences.[15] While broadly supported by organizations such as the National Farmers Union, the Organization for Competitive Markets, contract poultry growers associations, and even the American Farm Bureau, the rules are unpopular with organizations that have mixed memberships of industry and farmers and ranchers, such as the National Pork Producers Association and the National Cattlemen's

Beef Association (*Farm Futures* 2017). The Rules were withdrawn by the Trump administration in 2017.

Although unsuccessful, these fights demonstrate that resistance is important in shaping the playing field, building new alliances with consumers, and planting seeds for the future. In recent years, media attention has illuminated the plight of contract growers through sharp comedy on John Oliver's *Last Week Tonight* in 2016 and in Chris Leonard's 2014 exposé of the poultry industry, *The Meat Racket*. On another front, economists like Wu and MacDonald (2015, 5) acknowledge that tradeoffs between *efficiency*, the need to reduce unnecessary costs to increase economic gains, and *distribution*, which is dividing the gains fairly, may need to be addressed. By separating regulations derived from antitrust law from those derived from tort law, concerns around competition could "facilitate regulatory oversight of policies that enhance transparency, protect property rights, and prohibit misinformation and fraud." Contrary to the economics view that protections for producers, workers, consumers, or the environment decreases efficiency and thus creates a smaller economic pie to divide up, Wu and MacDonald (2015) suggest that government enforcement of property rights or protections against fraud or misinformation actually facilitates efficiency, thereby implying that protections for farmers from exploitation of market power could offer wide benefits.

Building New Linkages in the Food System

Many of those fighting for contract growers and antitrust reform are simultaneously working to create new linkages in the agrifood system. In North Carolina, the Rural Advancement Fund International (RAFI-USA) helped farmers fight discriminatory lending practices, predatory contracts, and financial distress, while also providing support for alternative markets and production practices. In the

Hendrickson, Howard, Constance

1980s, for example, Tom Trantham was resigned to selling his high-producing dairy cows before working with RAFI to implement a sustainable grazing plan that reduced costs and allowed access to new markets for on-farm bottled milk.[16] The Missouri Rural Crisis Center waged battles against farm foreclosures caused by the 1980s Farm Crisis, fought the "chickenization" of the hog industry through a pork check-off vote, and founded a producer cooperative, Patchwork Pork, to market naturally raised pork from members' farms. In Kansas, Organization for Competitive Markets cofounder Mike Callicrate, an original member of the Pickett vs. Tyson lawsuit, developed Ranch Foods Direct, a company that includes cattle finishing, a mobile meat processing unit, a Colorado Springs retail outlet, and a processing/slaughter facility.[17] Elizabeth Henderson of Peaceworks Organic Farm in New York raises and distributes organic foods through a community-supported agriculture farm; she also cofounded the Domestic Fair Trade Association and advocates for fair markets. In Wisconsin, the Farmers Union created a food hub cooperative to market members' products to local stores, restaurants, and schools.[18] To push back against the centralization and commodification of knowledge in farm machinery, farmers organized themselves into Farm Hack, a global community of innovative farmers building and modifying farm implements—and then sharing their "hacks" with others (Carolan 2017). These examples show how farmers embedded within the highly industrialized, capital-intensive system struggle to reshape commodity markets while also seeking to create alternatives that can transform agrifood system relationships.

Ongoing Farmer-Peasant Struggles

Agrifood industrialization and concentration is not restricted to North America. Smallholders around the world face many of the same constrained choices with far fewer resources

(Hendrickson et al. 2008). Olivier de Schutter, former United Nations rapporteur on the right to food, called for agroecological farming practices that reduce the dependence of small-scale farmers on capital-intensive inputs and create local and regional food markets (de Schutter 2010a). De Schutter founded the International Panel of Experts on Sustainable Food Systems (IPES) that uses evidence-based research to inform policy debates on food systems around the world. In 2016 and 2017 IPES released three reports dealing with concentrated agrifood systems and impacts on health and ecology.[19] However, the most widespread and potentially transformative movement is that oriented to food sovereignty which seeks to move decisions over food—from production to consumption, from seeds to land, and from market access to food safety—from the corporate realm into the hands of farmers and eaters around the world (see Ikerd, chapter 10 of this volume).

"Food sovereignty is best understood as a radical democratic project that, on the one hand, exposes the power dynamics within the current global food system, and on the other hand, cultivates new spaces (at all levels) for inclusive debate on a whole set of different issues related to food, agriculture and provisioning" (Desmarais 2017, 3). Originating in the myriad peasant and farmer groups that together make up La Via Campesina, the movement rejected the dominant food security discourse that sought to maximize food production and enhance food access through a corporate neoliberal regime that focused on markets as a solution (Wittmann, Desmarais, and Wiebe 2010).[20] The definition of food sovereignty remains fluid, despite the best efforts of academics. A Zimbabwean farmer, Elizabeth Mpofu, chastises those who don't understand that the movement is simultaneously within, against, and beyond our current mode of power (neoliberal capitalism):

Hendrickson, Howard, Constance

We are not trying to create the perfect definition, for a dictionary or for a history book. We are trying to build a movement to change the food system and the world. To build a powerful movement, you need to add more allies. And as you add more allies, you have more voices. More contributions. More issues to take into account. So your concept grows, it evolves, it broadens. To understand what Food Sovereignty is for La Via Campesina, yes, it is a vision of the food system we are fighting for, but, above all, it is a banner of struggle, an [*sic*] ever evolving banner of struggle.[21]

The food sovereignty perspective forces us "to rethink our relationships with food, agriculture and the environment. But, perhaps the most revolutionary aspect . . . is that it forces us to rethink our relationships with one another" (Wittmann, Desmarais, and Wiebe 2010, 4). What this means is that a farmer on an industrialized wheat farm in Saskatchewan can find purpose and solidarity with a peasant farmer from Zimbabwe, or an American corn producer, on issues of agriculture, food trade, and agroecological production. The meeting and sharing of these disparate interests provide an alternative view of the potential for transformation of the food system. As Desmarais (2017) says, food sovereignty is ultimately about the return to creating community, prioritizing relationships as best we can above the market.

Conclusion: Contested Agrifood Transitions

In this chapter we have sought to describe the current mode of power—the drive of agrifood firms to increase their own power relative to everyone else, even if it reduces well-being—that is at work in the global food system. We have detailed the consolidated and concentrated markets that farmers face from buying inputs to selling their products—situations that exist across the globe from the United States to China. Farmers face constrained choices for everything from seeds and livestock genetics, to fertilizers and chemicals, to commodity processing. Global behemoths, many with assistance from national governments, dominate markets for seeds, pesticides, fertilizers, genetics, livestock and grain processing, food manufacturing, and food retail. Globalized markets centralized in the hands of a few decision-makers decide what food to produce, where and how to produce it, who will produce it, and who will eat the resulting products. Such constrained choices make it difficult for farmers to use practices that protect their ecosystems, that treat workers well, that strengthen their communities, and that provide for economic development in their regions. They also make it difficult for everyone else as consumers and activists to support these farmers in making their preferred choices, and steer us toward locking in existing power relations.

However, as the number of agrifood firms decreases, and the negative impacts of capitalists' power become more visible, new *linkages* are emerging between farmers and eaters, farmers of the North and the South, environmental groups, labor activists, small food businesses, animal welfare advocates, and others. Perhaps the best way to encapsulate the ongoing resistance to a globalized, industrialized agriculture is to examine the proposed solutions to the looming problem of making sure that the nine billion people expected to be on earth by the mid-twenty-first century will have enough food to eat, especially as we scrape the bottom of the barrel of "*stored, concentrated energy*—fossil fuels, rock phosphate, potash, fossil water" and face higher energy and input costs, less freshwater and good soil, and increased adverse weather events (Kirschemann 2015, 51, emphasis in original). Two competing visions of agriculture have emerged as the path forward toward addressing this challenge: (1) food security through sustainable intensification, and (2) food sovereignty through agroecology (Constance et al. 2014b; Levidow 2015).

The food security discourse began in the 1940s when the United Nations' FAO was created to establish global food security. Although the FAO embraced the scientific extensification and intensification of world agriculture to boost production, it also included the Universal Declaration of Human Rights which maintained that food was an essential right of life rather than a commodity. The Cold War subverted FAO multilateralism as the United States employed bilateral food aid to counter the spread of communism. The FAO food as a right vision was replaced in 1986 when the World Bank redefined food security as the ability to buy food. In 1994 the World Trade Organization (WTO) institutionalized this market vision of food security whereby countries grow and trade agrifood products based on comparative advantage, and people buy these foods instead of grow them. The WTO's Agreement on Agriculture in 2008 furthered this vision by defining the new agriculture as a system of global entrepreneurial farmers employing sustainable intensification practices linked to agrifood transnational corporations in flexible arrangements governed by sustainability standards (Ingram et al. 2010; McMichael 2009).

As noted in the above section, the food sovereignty movement posits a counter frame to food security approaches. Represented by La Via Campesina, this view challenges the WTO-sanctioned food security framework based on free trade and corporate rights. Instead, La Via Campesina builds coalitions to create agrifood self-sufficiency through land reform, indigenous knowledge, and the regionalization of agrifood systems based on agroecological principles (Desmarais et al. 2014; Fairbairn 2012; Rosset and Martinez-Torrez 2014; Wittman, Desmarais, and Wiebe 2010). Moderate and smaller-scale agroecological farming, situated and adapted in a particular place, is more resilient to climate shocks than industrial agriculture. Domestic agrifood production is a better path to agrifood sustainability than global commodity chains (de Schutter 2010b).

At their heart, these two contrasting perspectives represent alternative conceptions of modernity (Desmarias 2007; McMichael 2014). The food security discourse separates the social and physical sciences and casts traditional agriculturalists as primitive laggards. The food sovereignty frame values interdisciplinary approaches, honors indigenous knowledge, and pursues social justice, which is the crucial fault line in agrifood studies (Allen 2008; Rivera-Ferre 2012). Food security embraces a land commodification perspective, which assumes the food supply problem is solvable through a high-tech repackaging of the adoption and diffusion approaches of the productivist paradigm that has underlined the global consolidation of the agrifood system we described in our results. In contrast, food sovereignty views land through a multifunctional lens, employing a full-cost accounting approach that internalizes the unsustainable externalities. It embraces a rights-based rather than a market-centered framework where rights are defined in collective rather than individual terms (McMichael 2014). The food sovereignty perspective proposes a repossession of the land in the face of the continuing enclosures based on accumulation through dispossession. The intellectual property rights and copyright framework advanced by the WTO is countered by a copy-left and open-source framework advanced by La Via Campesina. The battle over seed sovereignty fought between La Via Campesina and the GMO seed transnational corporations is a crucial example of the conflicting paradigms (Kloppenburg 2010).

The tension between the food security and the food sovereignty visions aligns directly with the two proposed transition paths to a sustainable global agrifood system. The food security path is based on neo-productivist solutions that have resulted in the concentrated agrifood system we described, diffused globally from Europe and North America around the world, as the new paradigm to meet the challenge of feeding the world with sustainable intensification (Almas and Campbell 2012; Levidow 2015; Marsden 2012). The food security path is patterned on utilitarian assumptions about agrifood science and rurality. The greater good for the most people outweighs the negative impacts on the few.

In contrast, the food sovereignty path, based on agroecology and social justice, employs a rights-based rhetoric grounded in a social justice agenda (Thompson 2010). The food security path includes incremental, green reforms to the existing system, while the food sovereignty path pushes for transformative change to the system (Constance et al. 2014b; Holt-Gimenez and Shattuck 2011). With little evidence, the neo-productivists promise that their high-tech green solution can feed the world, while the low-tech agroecology approach cannot. The agroecologists warn that sustainable intensification is an oxymoron at least, and more probably a "wolf in sheep's clothing."

In the end, it is likely that the industrialized agrifood system —even dressed up through sustainable intensification—will have to change if we want to continue to feed human society in ways that acknowledge our indisputable connection with, and impact on, the earth's ecosystem. The question is: can those visionary farmers and allies work fast enough for us all? Will the capitalist mode of power have sabotaged more democratic, socially just, and ecologically sustainable alternatives to the extent that we will lack the resilience needed to build a better food system?

Notes

1. This material is based upon work that is supported by the National Institute of Food and Agriculture, U.S. Department of Agriculture, Hatch under 1002034.

2. Row-crop farmers buy seeds through seed dealers who service particular regions because of the immense amounts needed. Planting one thousand acres of corn requires roughly seven tons of seed, and five tons are required for one thousand acres of cotton. Sourcing non-GM seed and their chemical inputs is laborious and offers little reward, especially if selling into commodity rather than specialty markets.

3. See blog posts from the University of Missouri Integrated Pest Management Program at https://ipm.missouri.edu/IPCM/2017/7/Ag_Industry_Do _we_have_a_problem_yet/.

4. See http://www.npr.org/2017/06/14/532879755/a-pesticide-a-pigweed -and-a-farmers-murder.

5. ETC Group (2013) notes that BASF is not a strong contender in the seed market itself, but maintains a great deal of seed research and is in partnership with the other five firms in new ventures.

6. https://agfundernews.com/big-ag-turns-digital-ag-growth-ex-senior -dupont-exec-joins-farmers-edge-board.html.

7. See *Successful Farming's Pork Powerhouses*. Accessed on July 31, 2017 at http://www.agriculture.com/pdf/pork-powerhouses-2016.

8. "A production contract usually specifies in detail the production inputs to be supplied by the contractor, the quality and quantity of the particular commodity involved, the production practices to be used, and the manner in which compensation is to be paid to the producer" (Kunkel and Peterson 2015). Forward contracting is an agreement to purchase livestock in advance of slaughter, where the base price is established by reference to prices on the Chicago Mercantile Exchange. See https://www.ams.usda.gov/market-news /livestock-poultry- and-grain-cattle-terms.

9. Annual report on the pork industry by *Successful Farming*. Available at: http://www.agriculture.com/livestock/pork-powerhouses/pork-powerhouses -2016-glut-of-pigs.

10. Statement by Wenonah Hauter, Executive Director of Food and Water Watch on June 26, 2017 regarding Amazon's acquisition of Whole Foods. https://www.foodandwaterwatch.org/news/amazon%E2%80%99s-acquisition -whole-foods-higher-prices-fewer-choices-consumers-and-more-profits.

11. CNBC: https://www.cnbc.com/2017/06/16/amazon-whole-foods-pair -up-signals-power-shift-for-the-food-industry.html.

12. Bloomberg Government Disclosure, "US Foods Holding Corp at Deutsche Bank Global Consumer Conference—Final." June 14, 2017.

13. More information on these workshops, including full transcripts of each workshop, can be found at: https://www.justice.gov/atr/events/public -workshops-agriculture-and-antitrust-enforcement-issues-our-21st-century -economy-10.

14. See http://www.dominalaw.com/documents/Domina-Speech-Annual -OCM-Meeting-8-09.pdf.

15. USDA announces Farmer Fair Practices Rule: https://www.usda.gov/media/press-releases/2016/12/14/usda-announces-farmer-fair-practices-rules-clarifications-industry.

16. See more about Tom Trantham's farm at http://www.sare.org/Learning-Center/Multimedia/Videos-from-the-Field/Sustainable-12-Aprils-Dairy-Grazing.

17. See more at http://ranchfoodsdirect.com/.

18. See more at http://www.wifoodhub.com/about-wfhc/.

19. See http://www.ipes-food.org/ for more information. In 2016, the group released "Unravelling the Food-Health Nexus" and "From Uniformity to Diversity," and in 2017 "Too Big to Feed." One author, Howard, is a member of this group.

20. La Via Campesina is an international peasants' movement representing over 200 million peasant farmers in 79 countries belonging to 164 different organizations. Their 2017 declaration says, "We, the peasants, rural workers, landless, indigenous peoples, pastoralists, artisanal fisherfolk, rural women and other peoples who work in the countryside around the world, declare that we feed our people and build the movement to change the world (emphasis in original)." https://viacampesina.org/en/.

21. https://www.iss.nl/fileadmin/ASSETS/iss/Documents/Conference_presentations/ElizabethMpofu-ISS-25_January_2014.pdf.

References

Adjemian, Michael K., B. Wade Brorsen, Tina L Saitone, and Richard J Sexton. 2016. "Thinning Markets in U.S. Agriculture: What Are the Implications for Producers and Processors?" Washington DC: USDA Economic Research Service.

Allen, Patricia. 2008. "Mining for Justice in the Food System: Perceptions, Practices, and Possibilities." *Agriculture and Human Values* 25: 157–61.

Almås, Reidar, and Hugh Campbell. 2012. "Reframing Policy Regimes and the Future Resilience of Global Agriculture." In *Rethinking Agricultural Policy Regimes: Food Security, Climate Change and the Future Resilience of Global Agriculture*, edited by Hugh Campbell and Reidar Almas, 285–300. DOI: 10.1108/S1057-1922(2012)0000018015.

Aziz, Tariq, M., Aamer Maqsood, Shamsa Kanwal, Shahid Hussain, H. R. Ahmad, and M. Sabir. 2015. "Fertilizers and Environment: Issues and Challenges." In *Crop Production and Global Environmental Issues*, edited by Khalid Ehman Hakeem, 575–98. Cham: Springer. DOI: 10.1007/978-3-319-23162-4_21.

Bartlett, Donald, and James Steele. 2008. "Monsanto's Harvest of Fear." *Vanity Fair*, April.

Bichler, Shimshon, and Jonathan Nitzan. 2012. "The Asymptotes of Power." *Real-World Economics Review* 60, no. 2: 18–53.

Bonanno, Alessandro. 2009. "Sociology of Agriculture and Food Beginning and Maturity: The Contribution of the Missouri School (1976–1994)." *Southern Rural Sociology* 24, no. 2: 29–47.

Breimyer, Harold F. 1965. *Individual Freedom and the Economic Organization of Agriculture*. Urbana IL: University of Illinois Press.

Burger, Ludwig. 2016. "Digital Farming Could Spell Shake-up for Crop Chemicals Sector." *Reuters*, May 4, 2016. http://www.reuters.com/article/us-farming-digital-idUSKCN0XV0KP.

Carolan, Michael. 2017. "Publicising Food: Big Data, Precision Agriculture, and Co-Experimental Techniques of Addition." *Sociologia Ruralis* 57, no. 2: 135–54. DOI: 10.1111/soru.12120.

Carstensen, Peter C. 2008. "Buyer Power, Competition Policy, and Antitrust: The Competitive Effects of Discrimination among Suppliers." *Antitrust Bulletin* 53, no. 20: 271–331.

Carstensen, Peter C., Ioannis Lianos, Claudio Lombardi, and James M. MacDonald. 2016. "Competition Law and Policy and the Food Value Chain." *Concurrences Competition Law Review* 1: 1–35. http://www.concurrences.com/en/review/issues/no-1-2016/on-topic/competition-law-and-policy-and-the-food-value-chain.

Coleman-Jensen, Alisha, Matthew P. Rabbitt, Christian A. Gregory, and Anita Singh. 2016. "Household Food Security in the United States in 2015." Washington DC: USDA Economic Research Service.

Connor, John, Richard Rogers, Bruce Marion, and Willard Mueller. 1984. *The Food Manufacturing Industries: Structure, Strategies, Performance and Policies*. Lanham MD: Lexington.

Constance, Douglas H. 2008. "The Southern Model of Broiler Production and Its Global Implications." *Culture and Agriculture* 30, no. 1: 17–31.

———. 2009. "AFHVS Presidential Address-The Four Questions in Agrifood Studies: A View from the Bus." *Agriculture and Human Values* 26, no. 1: 3–14. DOI: 10.1007/s10460-008-9187-0.

Constance, Douglas H., Francisco Martinez, and Gilberto Aboites. 2010. "The Globalization of the Poultry Industry: Tyson Foods and Pilgrim's Pride in Mexico." In *From Community to Consumption: New and Classical Themes in Rural Sociological Research*, edited by Alessandro Bonanno, Hans Bakker, Raymond Jussaume, Yoshio Kawamura, and Mark Shucksmith, 59–75. Bingley, UK: Emerald.

Constance, Douglas H., Mary Hendrickson, Phillip H. Howard, and William D. Heffernan. 2014a. "Economic Concentration in the Agrifood System: Impacts on Rural Communities and Emerging Responses." In *Rural America in a Globalizing World: Problems and Prospects for the 2010s*, edited by Connor Bailey, Leif Jensen, and Elizabeth Ransom, 16–35. Morgantown WV: West Virginia University Press.

Constance, Douglas H., William H. Friedland, Marie-Christine Renard, and Marta Rivera-Ferre. 2014b. "The Discourse on Alternative Agrifood Movements." In *Alternative Agrifood Movements: Patterns of Convergence and Divergence*, edited by Douglas H. Constance, Marie-Christine Renard, and Marta Rivera-Ferre, 3–46. Bingley, UK: Emerald.

Crespi, John M., Tina L. Saitone, and Richard J. Sexton. 2012. "Competition in U.S. Farm Product Markets: Do Long-Run Incentives Trump Short-Run Market Power?" *Applied Economic Perspectives and Policy* 34, no. 4: 669–95. DOI: 10.1093/aepp/ppso45.

Degen, Ronald Jean, and K. Matthew Wong. 2012. "An Examination of the Resource-Based Horizontal Acquisition Strategy of JBS—The Biggest Meat Packer in the World." *Proceedings of the New York State Economics Association* 5: 37–46.

DeLind, Laura B. 2011. "Are Local Food and the Local Food Movement Taking Us Where We Want to Go? Or Are We Hitching Our Wagons to the Wrong Stars?" *Agriculture and Human Values* 28, no. 2: 273–83. DOI: 10.1007/s10460-010-9263-0.

De Schutter, O. 2010a. "Addressing Concentration in Food Supply Chains: The Role of Competition Law in Tackling the Abuse of Buyer Power." Report of the United Nations Special Rapporteur on the Right to Food. http://www.srfood.org/images/stories/pdf/otherdocuments/20101201_briefing-note-03_en.pdf.

———. 2010b. Agribusiness and the right to food." Report to the United Nations Special Rapporteur on the Right to Food to the Human Rights Council. http://www.srfood.org/images/stories/pdf/officialreports/20100305_a-hrc-13-33_agribusiness_en.pdf.

Desmarias, Annette. 2007. *La Via Campesina: Globalization and the Power of Peasants*. Chicago: University of Chicago Press.

———. 2017. "The Power and Potential of Food Sovereignty: An Agenda for Social Transformation." Keynote Address to Twenty-Seventh Congress of the European Society for Rural Sociology, Krakow, Poland. July.

Desmarias, Annette A., Marta G. Rivera-Ferre, and Beatriz Gasco. 2014. "Building Alliances for Food Sovereignty: La Vía Campesina, NGOs, and Social Movements." In *Alternative Agrifood Movements: Patterns of Convergence and Divergence, Research in Rural Sociology and Development*, vol. 21, edited by Douglas H. Constance, Marie-Christine Renard, and Marta G. Rivera-Ferre, 89–110. Bingley, UK: Emerald.

Eller, Donnelle. 2014. "Erosion Estimated to Cost Iowa $1 Billion in Yield." *Des Moines Register*, May 3, 2014. http://www.desmoinesregister.com/story/money/agriculture/2014/05/03/erosion-estimated-cost-iowa-billion-yield/8682651/.

ETC Group. 2013. "Putting the Cartel before the Horse . . . and Farm, Seeds, Soil, Peasants, Etc." *Communiqué*, no. 111: 40.

———. 2015. "Status and Trends of Animal Genetic Resources." In *The Second Report on the State of the World's Animal Genetic Resources for Food and Agriculture*, 25–42. Rome: FAO. http://www.fao.org/3/a-i4787e.pdf.

Fairbairn, Madeleine. 2012. "Framing Transformation: The Counter-Hegemonic Potential of Food Sovereignty in the US Context." *Agriculture and Human Values* 29, no. 2: 217–30.

FAO. 2015. "The Second Report on the State of the World's Animal Genetic Resources for Food and Agriculture," edited by B. D. Scherf & D. Pilling. FAO Commission on Genetic Resources for Food and Agriculture Assessments. Rome. http://www.fao.org/3/a-i4787e/index.html.

Farm Futures. 2017. "GIPSA Rule Implementation Delayed, Comment Period Extended." February 8. http://www.farmfutures.com/farm-policy/gipsa-rule-implementation-delayed-comment-period-extended.

Foer, Albert A. 2016. "Abuse of Superior Bargaining Position (ASBP): What Can We Learn from Our Trading Partners?" Washington DC: American Antitrust Institute.

Food and Water Watch. 2013. "Grocery Goliaths: How Food Monopolies Impact Consumers." Washington DC. December. https://www.foodandwaterwatch.org/sites/default/files/Grocery%20Goliaths%20Report%20Dec%202013.pdf.

Foster, John Bellamy, and Fred Magdoff. 2000. "Liebig, Marx and the Depletion of Soil Fertility: Relevance for Today's Agriculture." In *Hungry for Profit: The Agribusiness Threat to Farmers, Food and Environment*, edited by John Bellamy Foster, Fred Magdoff, and Frederick H. Buttel, 43–60. New York: Monthly Review.

Fuglie, Keith O., Paul W. Heisey, John L. King, Carl E. Pray, Kelly Day-Rubenstein, David Schimmelpfennig, Sun Ling Wang, and Rupa Karmarkar-Deshmukh. 2011. "Research Investments and Market Structure in the Food Processing, Agricultural Input, and Biofuel Industries Worldwide." Washington DC: USDA Economic Research Service.

GIPSA. 2016. "Packers and Stockyards Program Annual Report." Washington DC: USDA. https://www.gipsa.usda.gov/psp/publication/ar/2016_psp_annual_report.pdf.

Greene, Joel L. 2016. "USDA's 'GIPSA Rule' on Livestock and Poultry Marketing Practices." R41673. Washington DC: Congressional Research Service.

Gullickson, Gil. 2017. "Why Bayer's Buyout of Monsanto Will Likely Proceed." *Successful Farming*. March 17. http://www.agriculture.com/news/crops/why-bayer-s-buyout-of-monsanto-will-likely-proceed.

Gura, Susanne. 2007. "Livestock Genetics Companies Concentration and Proprietary Strategies of an Emerging Power in the Global Food Economy." Ober-Ramstadt, Germany. http://www.mdpi.com/2071-1050/1/4/1266/.

Guthman, Julie. 2008. "Neoliberalism and the Making of Food Politics in California." *Geoforum* 39: 1171–83.

Harris, Wylie. 2004. "The Power of Concentration: Local Ruminations on Global Ruination." *The Touchstone.* https://www.iatp.org/files/Power_of _Concentration_Local_Ruminations_on_Gl.htm.

Heffernan, William D. 2000. "Concentration of Ownership in Agriculture." In *Hungry for Profit: The Agribusiness Threat to Farmers, Food, and the Environment,* edited by F. Magdoff, J. B. Foster, and F. H. Buttel, 61–76. New York: Monthly Review.

Heffernan, William D., Mary Hendrickson, and Robert Gronski. 1999. "Consolidation in the Food and Agriculture System." Report to the National Farmers Union, Washington DC.

Hendrickson, Mary, William D. Heffernan, Philip H. Howard, and Judith B. Heffernan. 2001. "Consolidation in Food Retailing and Dairy." *British Food Journal* 103, no. 10: 715–28.

Hendrickson, Mary K., and Harvey S. James. 2005. "The Ethics of Constrained Choice: How the Industrialization of Agriculture Impacts Farming and Farmer Behavior." *Journal of Agricultural and Environmental Ethics* 18, no. 3: 269–91.

Hendrickson, Mary, John Wilkinson, William D. Heffernan, and Robert Gronski. 2008. "The Global Food System and Nodes of Power." *SSRN Electronic Journal.* DOI: 10.2139/ssrn.1337273.

Hendrickson, Mary K., Harvey James, and William D. Heffernan. 2013. "Vertical Integration and Concentration in US Agriculture." In *Encyclopedia of Food and Agricultural Ethics,* edited by Paul B. Thompson and David M. Kaplan, 1–10. Dordrecht: Springer Netherlands. DOI: 10.1007/978-94-007-6167-4_216-1.

Hendrickson, Mary K. 2015. "Resilience in a Concentrated and Consolidated Food System." *Journal of Environmental Studies and Sciences* 5, no. 3: 418–31. DOI: 10.1007/s13412-015-0292-2.

Holt-Gimenez, Eric, and Anne Shattuck. 2011. "Food Crises, Food Regimes and Food Movements: Rumblings of Reform or Tides of Transformation?" *Journal of Peasant Studies* 38, no. 1:109–44. DOI: 10.1080/03066150.2010.538578.

Howard, Philip H. 2009a. "Visualizing Food System Concentration and Consolidation." *Southern Rural Sociology* 24, no. 2: 87–110.

———. 2009b. "Visualizing Consolidation in the Global Seed Industry: 1996–2008." *Sustainability* 1 no. 4: 1266–87. DOI: 10.3390/su1041266.

———. 2015. "Intellectual Property and Consolidation in the Seed Industry." *Crop Science* 55, no. 6: 2489. DOI: 10.2135/cropsci2014.09.0669.

———. 2016a. *Concentration and Power in the Food System: Who Controls What We Eat?* New York: Bloomsbury Academic.

———. 2016b. "Decoding Diversity in the Food System: Wheat and Bread in North America." *Agriculture and Human Values* 33, no. 4: 953–60.

————. 2017. "Consolidation in Global Meat Processing." *Philhoward.net.* June 21. https://philhoward.net/2017/06/21/consolidation-in-global -meat-processing/.

Ingram, Paul, Lori Qingyuan Yue, and Hayagreeva Rao. 2010. "Trouble in Store: Probes, Protests, and Store Openings by Wal-Mart, 1998–2007." *American Journal of Sociology* 116, no. 1: 53–92.

Jaffee, Daniel, and Philip H. Howard. 2010. "Corporate Cooptation of Organic and Fair Trade Standards." *Agriculture and Human Values* 27, no. 4: 387–99.

James, Harvey S., Jr., and Mary K. Hendrickson. 2008. "Perceived Economic Pressures and Farmer Ethics." *Agricultural Economics* 38, no. 3: 349–61.

James, Harvey S., Jr., Mary K. Hendrickson, and Philip H. Howard. 2013. "Networks, Power and Dependency in the Agrifood Industry." In *The Ethics and Economics of Agrifood Competition,* edited by Harvey S. James, 20: 99–126. The International Library of Environmental, Agricultural and Food Ethics. Dordrecht: Springer Netherlands. DOI: 10.1007/978-94-007-6274-9.

Kirschenmann, Frederick L. 2015. "From Soil to Sustainability." *Rootstalk: A Prairie Journal of Culture, Science and the Arts* 2, no. 1: 49–55.

Kloppenburg, Jack. 2010. "Impeding Dispossession, Enabling Repossession: Biological Open Source and the Recovery of Seed Sovereignty." *Journal of Agrarian Change* 10, no. 3: 367–88. DOI: 10.1111/j.1471-0366.2010.00275.x.

Kowitt, B. Y. Beth. 2017. "The Deal that Made an Industry Shudder." *Fortune,* June 22.

Kunkel, Philip L., and Jeffrey A. Peterson. 2015. "Agricultural Production Contracts." University of Minnesota Extension. https://www.extension .umn.edu/agriculture/business/taxation/farm-legal-series/agricultural -production-contracts/docs/agricultural-production-contracts.pdf.

Lamine, Claire. 2015. "Sustainability and Resilience in Agrifood Systems: Reconnecting Agriculture, Food and the Environment." *Sociologia Ruralis* 55, no. 1: 41–61. DOI: 10.1111/soru.12061.

Legun, Katharine, and Michael M. Bell. 2016. "The Second Middle: Conducers and the Agrifood Economy." *Journal of Rural Studies* 48: 104–14. DOI: 10.1016/j.jrurstud.2016.10.004.

Leonard, Christopher. 2014. *The Meat Racket.* New York: Simon and Schuster.

Levidow, Les. 2015. "European Transitions Towards a Corporate-Environmental Food Regime: Agroecological Incorporation or Contestation?" *Journal of Rural Studies* 40: 76–89.

Lianos, Ioannis, Dmitry Katalevsky, and Alexey Ivanov. 2016. "The Global Seed Market, Competition Law and Intellectual Property Rights: Untying the Gordian Knot." *Concurrences Competition Law Review* 2.

Lobao, Linda, and Curtis W Stofferahn. 2007. "The Community Effects of Industrialized Farming: Social Science Research and Challenges to Corporate Farming Laws." *Agriculture and Human Values* 25, no. 2: 219–40. DOI: 10.1007/s10460-007-9107-8.

Lowder, Sarah K., Jakob Skoet, and Terri Raney. 2016. "The Number, Size, and Distribution of Farms, Smallholder Farms, and Family Farms Worldwide." *World Development* 87: 16–29. http://dx.doi.org/10.1016/j.worlddev.2015.10.041.

Lyson, Thomas A. 2004. *Civic Agriculture*. Lebanon NH: Tufts University Press.

Lyson, Thomas A., George W. Stevenson, and Rick Welsh. 2008. *Food and the Mid-Level Farm*. Cambridge MA: MIT Press.

MacDonald, James M. 2016. "Concentration, Contracting, and Competition Policy in U.S. Agribusiness." *Concurrences Competition Law Review* 11: 3–9.

Marsden, Terry. 2012. "Towards a Real Sustainable Agri-Food Security and Food Policy: Beyond the Ecological Fallacies?" *Political Quarterly* 83, no. 1: 139–45.

McMichael, Philip. 2009. "A Food Regime Genealogy." *Journal of Peasant Studies* 36: 139–69.

———. 2014. "Historicizing Food Sovereignty." *Journal of Peasant Studies* 41, no. 6: 933.

Montgomery, David R. 2012. *Dirt: The Erosion of Civilization*. Berkeley CA: University of California Press.

Mooney, Pat. 2017. "Agricultural Mega-Mergers—History Lessons." *European Seed* 4, no. 2. http://european-seed.com/agricultural-mega-mergers-history-lessons/.

Moss, Diana. 2016. "Consolidation in Agriculture and Food: Challenges for Competition Enforcement." *Concurrences Competition Law Review* 2, no. 1: 10–14.

Mount, Phil. 2012. "Growing Local Food: Scale and Local Food Systems Governance." *Agriculture and Human Values* 29, no. 1: 107–21. DOI: 10.1007/s10460-011-9331-0.

Murphy, Sophia, David Burch, and Jennifer Clapp. 2012. "Cereal Secrets: The World's Largest Grain Traders and Global Agriculture." Oxfam International. August. https://www.oxfam.org/sites/www.oxfam.org/files/rr-cereal-secrets-grain-traders-agriculture-30082012-en.pdf.

Murray, Alan. 2016. "Why Bayer Wants Monsanto." *Fortune*, May 19. http://fortune.com/2016/05/19/bayer-monsanto-merger-approach-brainstorm/.

Nitzan, Jonathan, and Shimshon Bichler. 2009. *Capital as Power: A Study of Order and Creorder*. New York: Routledge.

Olson, Mancur. 1965. *The Logic of Collective Action: Public Goods and the Theory of Groups*. Cambridge MA: Harvard University Press.

Oya, Carlos. 2013. "The Land Rush and Classic Agrarian Questions of Capital and Labour: A Systematic Scoping Review of the Socioeconomic Impact of Land Grabs in Africa." *Third World Quarterly* 34, no. 9: 1532–57. DOI: 10.1080/01436597.2013.843855.

Peck, Alison. 2006. "State Regulation of Production Contracts." Available from the National Law Center, University of Arkansas. http://

nationalaglawcenter.org/wp-content/uploads/assets/articles/peck
_contractregulation.pdf.

Plume, Kari. 2014. "High-Tech U.S. Farm Machines Harvest Big Data, Reap
Privacy Worries." *Reuters*, April 9. http://www.reuters.com/article/usa
-farming-data-idUSL2N0N11U720140409.

Polansek, Tom, and Julie Zhu. 2017. "China's WH Group Targets Beef and
Poultry Assets in U.S. and Europe." *Reuters*, June 6. http://www.reuters
.com/article/us-smithfield-m-a-idUSKBN18Z29Y.

Posey, Kirby G. 2016. "Household Income 2015: American Community Survey Briefs." https://www.census.gov/content/dam/Census/library
/publications/2016/demo/acsbr15-02.pdf.

Rivera-Ferre, Marta G. 2012. "Framing of Agri-food Research Affects of the
Analysis of Food Security: The Critical Role of the Social Sciences." *International Journal of Sociology of Agriculture and Food* 19, no. 2: 162–75.

Roesch-McNally, Gabrielle E., Andrea D. Basche, J. G. Arbuckle, John C. Tyn-
dall, Fernando E. Miguez, Troy Bowman, and Rebecca Clay. 2017. "The
Trouble with Cover Crops: Farmers' Experiences with Overcoming Barriers to Adoption." *Renewable Agriculture and Food Systems* (March): 1–12.
DOI: 10.1017/S1742170517000096.

Rosset, Peter M., and María Elena Martínez-Torres. 2014. "Food Sovereignty
and Agroecology in the Convergence of Rural Social Movements." In
Alternative Agrifood Movements: Patterns of Convergence and Divergence,
edited by Douglas H. Constance, Marie-Christine Renard, and Marta G.
Rivera-Ferre, 137–57. Bingley, UK: Emerald.

Sito, Peggy. 2016. "Chinese Pork Giant WH Group May Eye Major Acquisitions by End of 2017." *South China Morning Post*, November 20. http://
www.scmp.com/business/companies/article/2047719/chinese-pork-giant
-wh-group-will-eye-major-acquisitions-end-2017.

Stuart, Diana. 2009. "Constrained Choice and Ethical Dilemmas in Land
Management: Environmental Quality and Food Safety in California Agri-
culture." *Journal of Agricultural and Environmental Ethics* 22, no. 1: 53–71.
DOI: 10.1007/s10806-008-9129-2.

Stuart, Diana, and Rebecca L. Schewe. 2016. "Constrained Choice and Climate Change Mitigation in US Agriculture: Structural Barriers to a Climate Change Ethic." *Journal of Agricultural and Environmental Ethics* 29,
no. 3: 369–85. DOI: 10.1007/s10806-016-9605-z.

Taylor, C. Robert. 2007. "Legal and Economic Issues with the Courts' Rulings
in Pickett v. Tyson Fresh Meats, Inc., a Buyer Power Case." Washington
DC: American Antitrust Institute.

Taylor, C. Robert, and Diana Moss. 2013. "The Fertilizer Oligopoly: The Case
for Global Antitrust Enforcement." Washington DC: American Antitrust Institute. http://www.antitrustinstitute.org/sites/default/files
/FertilizerMonograph.pdf.

Thompson, Paul. 2010. *The Ethics of Intensification: Agricultural Development and Social Change.* New York: Springer.

UNCTAD. 2006. "Tracking the Trend towards Market Concentration: The Case of the Agricultural Input Industry." Geneva, Switzerland. http://unctad.org/en/Docs/ditccom200516_en.pdf.

USDA. 2015a. "Census of Agriculture Highlights: Family Farms." https://www.agcensus.usda.gov/Publications/2012/Online_Resources/Highlights/NASS Family Farmer/Family_Farms_Highlights.pdf.

———. 2015b. "Principal Farm Operator Household Finances, by ERS Farm Typology." https://www.ers.usda.gov/webdocs/DataFiles/48870/table02.xls?v=42704.

U.S. Departments of Justice and Agriculture. 2010. Public Workshops Exploring Competition Issues in Agriculture. Ankeny IA. March 12. https://www.justice.gov/sites/default/files/atr/legacy/2010/12/20/iowa-agworkshop-transcript.pdf.

U.S. Department of Justice. 2012. "Competition and Agriculture: Voices from the Workshops on Agriculture and Antitrust Enforcement in Our 21st Century Economy and Thoughts on the Way Forward." May: 1–24. https://www.justice.gov/sites/default/files/atr/legacy/2012/05/16/283291.pdf.

U.S. Department of Justice. 2016. "Justice Department Sues to Block Deere's Acquisition of Precision Planting." Media release. August 31. https://www.justice.gov/opa/pr/justice-department-sues-block-deere-s-acquisition-precision-planting.

Watts Poultry USA. 2017. "Watts Poultry USA's 2017 Broiler Companies." March. 17–18. http://www.wattpoultryusa-digital.com/201703/index.php#/18.

Wilkinson, John. 2006. "Network Theories and Political Economy: From Attrition to Convergence?" *Research in Rural Sociology and Development* 12: 27.

Wittmann, Hannah, Annette Aurélie Desmarais, and Nettie Wiebe. 2010. "The Origins & Potential of Food Sovereignty." In *Food Sovereignty-Reconnecting Food, Nature & Community,* edited by Annette Desmarais, Nettie Wiebe, and Hannah Wittman. Oxford, UK. https://foodfirst.org/wp-content/uploads/2014/01/Food-Sovereignty_Intro_Origins-Potential-of-Food-Sov.pdf.

Wu, S. Y., and J. MacDonald. 2015. "Economics of Agricultural Contract Grower Protection Legislation." *Choices Magazine.*

2

Chickenizing American Farmers

DONALD D. STULL

To understand industrial agriculture, we must understand the chicken industry. In his 2005 book, *Chicken: The Dangerous Transformation of America's Favorite Food*, Steve Striffler argued that what he calls industrial chicken epitomizes both the triumph and tragedy of America's industrial food system. It transformed what we eat: since 1960, when the U.S. Department of Agriculture began keeping records, chicken production in the United States has risen almost 900 percent—it is up by 113 percent since 1990 (Meat+Poultry 2016). It has also reshaped American agriculture, leading agribusiness steadily toward vertical integration, concentration, contract growing, product branding, and further processing. In so doing, industrial chicken has exploited farmers, processing workers, and the communities that host its plants, all the while abusing animals and polluting air and water.

The poultry industry as we know it was born in the 1920s on the Delmarva Peninsula, which encompasses portions of Delaware, Maryland, and Virginia. Commercial production of broilers—eating chickens—expanded rapidly after World War II, and the "broiler belt" eventually stretched from Delmarva to North Carolina, Georgia, Alabama, Mississippi, Arkansas, and East Texas. As the broiler belt wrapped itself around much of the South, the industry was also creating what some hail as "the most advanced form of food production in the entire world" (Williams 1998, ix) and others lament as "industrial agriculture" (Heffernan 1984).

By the late 1950s a contract system was emerging that promised to reduce risk for growers and maximize profits for companies. The poultry company provided farmers with day-old chicks from the hatchery, feed, medications, and technical assistance. Farmers provided fully equipped chicken houses, utilities, and labor. They also had to dispose of dead birds and manure. In return, they received a guaranteed payment tied to the feed-conversion ratio—the less feed it takes to grow the bird to market weight—and the faster—the better (Morrison 1998, 146; Williams 1998, 50–1). By the early 1960s, independent chicken farmers, who raised their own birds and made their own decisions about how best to do it, had been transformed into chicken growers bound by a contract to raise a company's birds according to its specifications.

Today, broilers are hatched, raised, slaughtered, and processed in tightly integrated production complexes within limited geographic catchment areas by firms referred to as integrators—a reference to their business model. By combining production, processing, and distribution in the same firms, poultry companies developed the model of vertical integration that has become the exemplar for American agribusiness. The poultry industry is also tightly concentrated: twenty integrators accounted for 96 percent of all broilers produced in the United States in 2012. The top four firms—Tyson Foods, Pilgrim's Corporation, Purdue Farms, and Sanderson Farms—control 54 percent of all production (MacDonald 2014, 4; Schneider 2017).

Public demand for chicken meat began its steady—and dramatic—rise around 1960. From 1960 to 1995, U.S. broiler production grew on average 4.6 percent annually, from 1.5 to 7.4 million birds, and slaughter weight rose on average from 3.35 pounds to 4.66 pounds. By 1990 per capita chicken consumption had more than doubled, reaching 61 pounds per person in that year (MacDonald 2014, 6). Poultry integrators expanded their production facilities, encouraged existing growers to add new houses, and recruited new growers. But by the beginning of the 1990s the broiler belt was becoming saturated with chicken houses. Concerns were mounting about the industry's treatment of its growers and processing workers, as well as environmental problems related to disposal of manure and dead birds (Hall 1989). And so poultry companies began moving into new territories. One of those was Kentucky.

Big Chicken Lands in Kentucky

The expansion of the broiler belt to new territories like Kentucky was part of a broad restructuring and relocation of the meat and poultry industry. Small towns in the Midwest and South became home to beef, pork, and poultry plants in the 1970s, 1980s, and 1990s, as packers shuttered their urban plants and moved to the country to be near their supplies of animals and to cut transportation and labor costs. But these new packinghouse towns could not supply enough workers for plants reliant on large workforces and prone to high employee turnover. Quickly exhausting local labor supplies, companies recruited from farther and farther afield. This strategy translated into dramatic population increases, the rapid influx of immigrants and refugees who were heavily recruited by the companies, and continuous population mobility wherever large packinghouses were built.

For more than thirty years, I have studied the meat and poultry industry's effects on American farmers, processing workers, and host communities (Stull 2017). Elsewhere, I have discussed community impacts, working conditions in packing plants, and environmental consequences (Stull and Broadway 2013); here I will focus on poultry growers. I will also discuss the chickenization of other farmers—those who produce beef, pork, dairy, and especially tobacco—and what this may mean for American agriculture.

Absent before 1990, Kentucky now boasts four large chicken processing plants, two primary breeder hatcheries, six feed mills, three layer complexes, and 3,000 chicken houses on 850 farms in 45 of the Commonwealth's 120 counties. In less than two decades, chickens flapped past Kentucky's traditional agricultural powerhouses of tobacco, horses, and cattle to become the state's leading agricultural and food commodity. Soaring from 1.5 million broilers in 1990 to 308 million in 2014, Kentucky now ranks seventh among the states in chicken production (Keeton 2010, 6; Kentucky Poultry Federation n.d.).

Crisscrossed by interstate highways, Kentucky is within a day's drive of more than two out of three Americans (Ulack, Raitz, and Pauer 1998, 3). Plenty of corn and water, along with a dearth of environmental regulations and rural zoning, appealed to the industry. The Commonwealth's low levels of education and income, combined with declining fortunes in two of its major industries—coal and agriculture—offered a readily available supply of workers for poultry-processing plants and growers to supply them. Eager to attract outside industry, state and local governments anted up $165 million in tax credits and incentives (Associated Press 2000).

Tobacco—historically the state's primary cash crop—was under attack, and farmers were being encouraged to find alternative crops (Stull 2000). Chickens appealed to some Kentucky farmers, especially those with limited acreage, because they are raised inside massive houses, reducing weather as a factor in production. And growers are guaranteed a minimum price per pound for each bird they raise. Poultry companies also promised easy financing for minimal investment and attractive incomes in exchange for a modest amount of labor—"full-time money for part-time work," as company hawkers liked to say.

Tyson's processing plant in Robards, Kentucky, originally built by Hudson Foods, opened on July 9, 1996. The first chicken houses to serve this plant were built in September 1995. By the summer of 1999, Tyson's plant was receiving chickens from 667 chicken houses, operated by 124 growers in 10 counties. Of the 667 houses, 572 were in three counties immediately south of the processing plant. The highest number of houses, 227, were in Webster County (Tyson Foods n.d., 6).

Today this plant employs about 1,200 workers to slaughter and process 1.5 million chickens a week. At this rate, 60 broiler houses, each home to about 25,000 birds, are emptied every week.

Methods

In 1998, I began studying poultry and tobacco growers in and around Webster County, Kentucky, where I was born and am half owner of a family grain farm. For six months (July-January) I gathered data by participant observation, informal interviews, mapping, and collection of pertinent documents. I conducted thirty-three formal interviews with a purposive sample of poultry growers, tobacco growers, and growers of both. Included in those I interviewed formally or informally were grain farmers, hourly poultry workers, residents and attorneys involved in complaints against the poultry industry, city and county officials, county extension agents and specialists, bankers, service providers, clergy, business owners, and town residents. Several of those I interviewed were relatives or long-time friends or acquaintances.

I returned in July 2005 to explore the effects of the tobacco buyout and the end of the federal tobacco program, and to update my research with poultry growers. For the next six months, I carried out ethnographic research in a six-county area of western Kentucky, extending from the banks of the Ohio River to the Tennessee state line (see

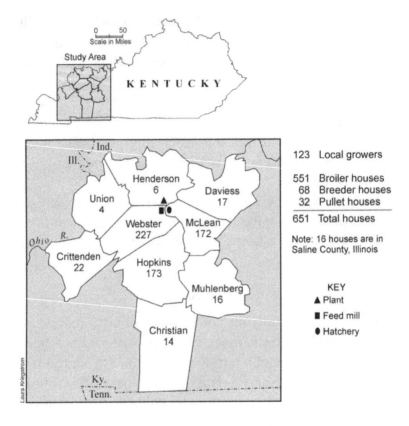

FIG. 3. Tyson chicken houses in western Kentucky, 1999. Tyson Foods. n.d. "Tyson's Live Production Teams Span Nine Counties." In "Growing the Future," 12-page advertising insert in several Western Kentucky newspapers, July 1999, 6. Originally appeared in Donald Stull, "Tobacco Barns and Chicken Houses: Agricultural Transformation in Western Kentucky" *Human Organization* 59, No. 2 (Summer 2000): 151–61. Created by Laura Kriegstrom Stull. Reprinted with permission by Laura Kriegstrom Stull and the Society for Applied Anthropology.

figure 4). I recorded two dozen formal interviews with a purposive sample of current tobacco growers; former growers; and farmers who had diversified into so-called alternative crops, including poultry, freshwater shrimp, fruits, and sod. Among these interviews were poultry growers, several of whom I interviewed in 1998. I also interviewed two county agents, a state government official, and a grower co-op official. These formal interviews were augmented with numerous informal interviews, both in person and over the telephone.

Between these two extended field seasons, and since, I regularly returned to Webster County for at least one month each year to visit relatives and friends and to keep abreast of agricultural developments. Since retiring from the University of Kansas in 2015, I have divided my time between Kansas and Kentucky.[1]

Chickenizing Western Kentucky

As I began my research on the impact of poultry production on agriculture in western Kentucky in the summer of 1998, Tyson's Robards plant was barely two years old, and its growers were still enjoying the honeymoon. That fall, a grower who had been raising broilers for about a year told me, "I kind of like fooling with 'em. It's kind of relaxing in there. You don't have to deal with people and stuff. You can just go in there and work with 'em. And they're not fussing about nothing. They don't say much (he laughs). As long as they got food and water, they're tickled. The main thing I like is the money."

He owned ten broiler houses with his father, which he figured yielded "somewhere around $8,000" a house. But poultry growers, like other farmers, do not factor the cost of their own labor into calculations of profit. This grower estimated that the ten houses required on average about five hours of labor a day, which he and his father provided

FIG. 4. The author stands inside a broiler house in 1998. Photo by
Laura Kriegstrom Stull.

with the help of a "girl." As the grower explained, "She fixes up all his chickens and stuff. Now he does the managing as far as the water lines, raising feed lines, chicken feed and stuff like that. She picks up the dead chickens for him. And, you know, does some other stuff. There are days when things happen and it takes you all day maybe. You know, water line break or something or motor go bad or something." How much the girl was paid he did not say.

In 1998, Webster County's economic development director told me the benefits from the Tyson poultry complex included 227 poultry houses and the income they generated for their owners, as well as the feed mill, which was valued at $18 million.[2] The mill employed thirty-two people and bought twelve million bushels of grain a year from local farmers at a premium of seven to ten cents per bushel. Tyson's processing plant, located just over the line in Henderson County, employed more than 1,500 people, of whom 15–17 percent lived in Webster County. It had an annual payroll of $41 million, paid $12 million in payroll taxes, and purchased $6 million in local goods and services.

A pullet grower I interviewed that November shared the economic development director's positive assessment:

> I think it has been great. It's contributed to the decline of the unemployment rate. It's brought a lot of dollars in here . . . for every direct dollar there's a whole bunch of spinoff dollars. I know that they buy a lot of things here locally. . . . Our grain farmers are getting prime money for their grain. They buy a lot of repair parts out of local firms and other stuff. . . . The wages paid out and the spinoff dollars . . . have tremendous effect on the country around here. It's upgraded water systems; it's upgraded sewage systems. It's a heck of an improvement.

"A heck of an improvement"? By 2005, a decade after the first chicken houses were built, many growers did not think so. Tyson let growers keep all the money from the first flock, so, as one tobacco farmer quipped, "they get dollar signs in their eyes." But beginning with the second flock, loan payments kicked in, and realities of income, expenses, and cash flow became apparent.

"Shawn" made $36,000 on his first flock in the summer of 1998—more than most people in the county made in a year. Energy prices soared in 2001. He spent $2,800 on electricity per flock for his six houses that summer and $25,000 to heat his birds that winter. Many of the chicks Shawn received in his next flock were blind. He and other growers complained that Tyson was extending the time between flocks to twenty days, the maximum allowed under their contract before the company had to pay a penalty. A flock takes about seven weeks to mature, and several such delays could cost the farmer a whole flock per year—the difference between profit and loss.

In the summer of 2002, Tyson's field representative told Shawn to make $10,000 in improvements to his houses. When he said he could not afford the expense, he was told to borrow the money. When Shawn said he was too far in debt to qualify for another loan, the company refused to send him more birds and terminated his contract. After deducting its expenses from the payment for his last flock, Shawn said that Tyson wrote him a check for $33.22.

Shawn's six chicken houses stood empty until 2005, when Tyson paid more than $50,000 in back taxes he owed on his farm and bought his chicken houses and the thirty-one acres they sit upon for forty cents on the dollar. He was able to retain ownership of the farm's remaining 130 acres, however. A month later a Mennonite farmer new to the area bought the houses from Tyson (for a 2.3 percent profit) and the remainder of the farm from Shawn. Five and half years later the Mennonite sold these houses to another grower

Fig. 5. Chicken catchers load some of Shawn's broilers on a live-haul truck, which will take them to the slaughterhouse. Photo by author.

for almost double what he paid for them—but still 25 percent less than Shawn's original purchase price.

Shawn's story is far from unique. Other growers I first interviewed in 1998 also suffered setbacks. Financial difficulties, dissatisfaction, and turnover are common to chicken growers. Some called it quits. Some sold out. Others declared bankruptcy, and lenders foreclosed on their houses, or Tyson repossessed them and then ran them with hired labor. Tyson's advertisement in a local newspaper for a farm manager for one of these complexes required that applicants

—Must be capable of bending, squatting, pulling, lifting, and prolonged walking and standing

—Must be able to work in dusty environment and inclement weather conditions

—High school diploma or equivalent preferred

—Couples Preferred.

The ad also warned, "Absences from the farm cannot be for more than two hours at a time."

Such working conditions keep chicken growers "in a state of indebted servitude, living like modern-day sharecroppers on the ragged edge of bankruptcy" (Christopher Leonard, as quoted in Charles 2014). It is no wonder that some growers sold out, left their houses empty, or abandoned them altogether. As a grower who quit after four years told me: "They was just saying whatever they could to get you to grow chickens. . . . It was all misleading. Money, payback, like the time you had, and the time that you had to put into it. It wasn't right. . . . It just got to where I didn't like it any more. Putting up with Tyson and being there 24/7 and I couldn't go anywhere, and picking up dead chickens . . ."

In 2005, when Tyson took over Shawn's chicken houses, it had more growers than it needed, but by 2008 the company wanted sixty new houses. By then, new broiler houses cost around $200,000 to build, $50,000 more than a decade earlier. In the meantime, Tyson was compressing the period between flocks, leaving its growers barely enough time to clean out their houses before another flock arrived. "Frank" probably spoke for many Tyson growers one Saturday morning, over coffee, eggs, and toast at a local café, after a crew finished catching his birds:

> "I feel like I just got out of jail. I've never been in jail, but getting rid of those chickens feels like it must feel to get out of jail."
>
> "Yeah," a café regular replied, "but you'll be back in jail next week."
>
> "Yes, I get birds again on Friday," he said with a sigh, as he pondered all that he had to do to get his houses ready for the next flock.

Tyson could not stay in business if all its growers were unhappy. And Frank, one of Tyson's top growers, told me, "I've made more money than I was led to believe that I would make, and most of the bad press that the poultry industry got when they arrived in Kentucky, as far as I'm concerned, almost none of it has proved to be true." He liked growing chickens, but he admitted "it probably takes more work than I thought it would. Sometimes I feel like a galley slave, but I can get up when I want to, go to bed when I want to, and I can say the hell with it for a day or so, if I want to. It beats working for a living." I could not help but see the irony in that last sentence, one I often used to describe my own work as a college professor. But all things are relative, and Frank did employ one full-time worker to help with his chickens.

The summer of 2011 was hot and dry. It was hard on chickens and hard on chicken growers. Frank lost 5,000 six-week-old broilers to the heat in early August, just one week before they were to go to slaughter. Another grower lost 50,000. Altogether, Tyson growers lost 200,000 birds in western Kentucky during that heat spell. Growers are not paid for birds that die before the company picks them up, and they must dispose of their dead birds.

Frank sold his six broiler houses in 2013. He was seventy years old, had been growing chickens for Tyson for fifteen years, and came out ahead on the sale of his houses. He didn't know whether to blame the company or the local plant manager, but his relationship with the company had soured. "Over the last six months, Tyson has proved you and your coauthor right," he admitted, referring to what Michael Broadway and I had written about the poultry industry in *Slaughterhouse Blues*. "The problem with Tyson," he concluded, "is that they think growers don't know anything and don't need to know anything, except the delivery date and the pickup date for their chickens." A county extension agent put it this way: "Tyson thinks chickens grow themselves." As a result, company representatives do not treat growers well. They understate the amount of work that goes into raising chickens and overstate the income from them. Nor do they tell potential growers that they can't really leave their birds alone for any length of time—they save that admonishment until they are under contract.

In September 2017—twenty-two years after the first chicken houses were built—forty grower complexes holding 215 chicken houses were still in production in Webster County. Another eight complexes held twenty chicken houses that were idle and seventeen houses that had been torn down or destroyed by high winds. Of the forty-eight original complexes, two-thirds (thirty-two) had been sold at least once. Some chicken houses have been sold as many as seven times, and on average they have been sold 2.8 times since construction. These complexes contain 174 houses—81 percent of the active houses. Of twenty-one grower complexes where I could determine purchase prices over time, thirteen sales were for a loss, while eight were for a gain.[3]

Companies like to say that they and their growers are financial partners in the poultry industry. And each side does put up about half the capital necessary to support the industry. But the relationship is far from equal. The integrator owns not only the birds, but the genetic patent on them. It owns the feed, medicine, trucks used to bring feed to the grower and haul his birds to its slaughter facility, and the brand under which they are marketed. The grower owns the farm, the houses where the chickens are raised, and the considerable debt incurred to finance, maintain, and upgrade them. The grower must provide the labor necessary to raise the birds, pay for water and utilities to heat and cool the chicken houses, and dispose of their manure and any birds that die before they go to slaughter.

Growers are compensated according to what economists call a "tournament pay system" (Taylor and Domina 2010, 3). The National Chicken Council (2012), which represents the industry, prefers the term "performance-based incentive structure." Whatever you call it, grower compensation is tied to performance, as measured by feed efficiency and flock mortality. Grower performance is ranked against all others whose birds are slaughtered at the same plant in the same week, and payment is then adjusted on an ordinal scale from a base price per pound live weight. In 2012, Tyson's base pay for its Kentucky growers was 5.43 cents per pound, up from its base of 4 cents in 1998. It had also implemented a new performance-based incentive structure that annualizes the pay comparisons between growers. In this rolling tournament, the economic impact of one poorly performing flock is reduced, since it will be figured along with all the other flocks the farmer grew out that year. Of course, the economic benefit of a high-performing flock is also reduced. Thus, the system levels out individual grower scores on a rolling per annum basis. In this zero-sum game, the higher payments to top-performing growers come from the lower payments to the growers at the bottom of the tournament ranking (Leonard 2014, 121–2).

By 2012, Tyson had also increased the size of its broilers from 5.5 to 6.5 pounds. Grow-out for each flock averaged forty-eight to fifty-one days but could go as high as fifty-three days before "live-haul" trucks took the birds to the processing plant. Tyson was averaging only fourteen days between flocks, which was as short as Frank would like. But, as he told me, Tyson can send you the next flock whenever it wants. When I asked what the shortest time he needed to get ready for the next flock, he replied, "Whenever Tyson says the next flock is coming."

The integrator provides teams to catch the chickens and trucks to transport them. Growers are paid only for those birds that reach the processing plant alive. But growers are not present when the birds are weighed and cannot challenge head counts, weights, death loss, or the peer rankings that determine the amount of payment per pound in the grower tournament. Growers have little recourse in disputes with integrators, and there are many stories of intimidation and abuse. The integrator can send you sick birds or "short" flocks; it can "short" you on feed or "short weigh" your birds when they are delivered for slaughter; it can keep your birds waiting at the processing plant scales so they lose weight and you lose money; it can require you to make costly upgrades to your houses; it can mandate resolution of disputes through arbitration and require you to sign away your rights to sue. And if you challenge the company, it can cancel your contract.[4]

Big Chicken on the Move Again

Poultry production expanded steadily in the 1980s and 1990s as population, per capita consumption, and exports all rose (MacDonald 2014, 6–8). Annual poultry slaughter slowed early in the twenty-first century, however, and few new poultry processing complexes were built. But that is starting to change. Sanderson Farms brought a new broiler complex online in Palestine, Texas, in 2015, another in St. Pauls, North Carolina, in 2017, and plans to open yet another Texas complex in 2019 (Thornton 2016; Fielding 2017). Holly Poultry opened a new plant in west Baltimore, Maryland, in 2017, quadrupling the company's production (Meatingplace 2017). Tyson will open the first new chicken plant it has built from the ground up since 1996 in Humboldt County, Tennessee, in 2019 (McGee 2018).

In 1968, Perdue became the first poultry company to brand its product. Fifty years later, Costco is poised to become the first retailer to fully integrate its poultry line by contracting with Lincoln Premium Poultry LLC to produce rotisserie chickens exclusively for its stores. Lincoln Premium will run the production side of the operation, but Costco will own the processing plant, and all its product will go to Costco stores. When fully operational, the plant, to be built in Fremont, Nebraska, is supposed to employ 1,000 workers to process 2 million birds a week (Clayton 2016; Gerlock 2017). The company broke ground in June 2017 on the $300 million project, which is projected to open in May 2019 (Scott 2017).

According to company statements, the Fremont plant will require roughly 404 chicken houses—332 broiler houses, 24 pullet houses, and 48 breeder houses. Lincoln Premium says each broiler house will hold 43,000 birds per flock, and each house will produce 6 flocks a year (44 days per flock, 14 days between flocks), for a total of 258,000 broilers per year per house (Clayton 2016). At this rate, 332 broiler houses would grow out 85,656,000 birds a year—considerably less than the 104 million birds that a plant slaughtering 2 million birds a week would need.

For every pound of gain, a chicken produces half a pound of dry waste. This waste, combined with the rice hulls or wood chips used to line the floors of chicken houses, is called litter. If the Costco broilers are grown to a weight of six pounds, then the 258,000 broilers each house produces annually will generate 774,000 pounds, or 387 tons, of litter a year. Its 332 broiler houses will thus produce 128,484 tons of litter a year. Spread on fields at the recommended rate of four tons per acre, this litter will fertilize 32,121 acres, or 50 square miles of Nebraska every year (640 acres = 1 square mile). If the plant reaches its slaughter capacity of 2 million birds a week, 104 million a year, then the associated litter will fertilize 39,000 acres, or 61 square miles. Either way, these are ponderous numbers.

Early on, rural western Kentuckians welcomed the poultry industry because it promised new jobs and the salaries and tax revenue they brought, new markets and premium prices for the corn and soybeans they grew, and cheap fertilizer for their fields in the form of abundant amounts of chicken litter. But they had yet to smell chickens or their litter. Tyson employees and growers like to call it the smell of money. But for those who live near chicken houses, which were built in complexes of two to twenty-four houses, there is nothing likeable about the stench of houses when flocks near maturity and the litter when it is spread on fields. By the time Tyson's Robards, Kentucky, plant opened, poultry-house neighbors were complaining of odor, flies and other vermin, groundwater pollution, and damage to roads caused by increased and overweight truck traffic. County and municipal governments tried to enact zoning ordinances to ensure adequate setbacks of poultry houses from neighbors' properties and nearby towns, but it was too late.

In 2002, the Sierra Club sued Tyson and several of its largest Kentucky growers for excessive emissions of ammonia and dust under the Clean Air Act and other federal laws. The

FIG. 6. Looking down on a complex of broiler houses, each home to more than twenty-five thousand birds, in McLean County, Kentucky. The building in the foreground with the open door stores chicken litter after it is removed from the broiler houses until it is spread on fields as fertilizer. Photo by author.

suit was settled in 2005, when Tyson agreed to plant trees around these growers' chicken houses to shield neighbors from air pollution, pay all legal fees, and compensate the neighbors who filed the suit. Tyson also agreed to continuously monitor poultry complexes for ammonia emissions for one year and report results to the Sierra Club. But two years later, an Iowa State University study found that two western Kentucky chicken houses emitted over ten tons of ammonia in one year—levels sufficient to cause respiratory harm (Stull and Broadway 2013, 173). Big Chicken is now firmly entrenched in Kentucky, and with it, the attendant harmful environmental and health consequences.

Lincoln Premium hopes to recruit 120 area farmers as contract poultry growers for the Fremont plant. In its initial publicity the company said the standard broiler complex will consist of four houses and cost about $1.5 million to construct, or $375,000 per house. According to Harvest Public Media, Tim Mueller, who raises corn and soybeans on 530 acres near Columbus, Nebraska, plans to borrow $2 million to build four broiler houses and eventually twelve more houses, which would require $6 million more in loans (Gerlock 2017). Using these figures, Mr. Mueller's houses would cost $500,000 each—considerably more than Lincoln Premium's projection. Like Kentucky tobacco farmers who took up poultry growing two decades ago, Mueller sees chickens as a way to diversify his farm operation and bring in a steady income at a time when Nebraska farmers are getting the same price for their corn they got in the early 1970s (John Hansen, pers. communication, June 20, 2017).

In the fall of 2016, Lincoln Premium's draft broiler production contract said base pay would be 6.48 cents per pound of gain. Taking into account an average inflation rate of 1.42 percent per year between 2011 and 2017, this figure is worth virtually the same as the national average of 5.77 cents per pound paid to chicken growers in 2011 (MacDonald 2012, 26). But by the summer of 2017, the company was having trouble getting enough growers interested, and it spoke of adding another cent to the base pay (Mike Weaver, pers. communication, June 19, 2017).

In 2001, a study by the National Contract Poultry Growers Association and the United States Department of Agriculture found that 71 percent of all growers whose income came solely from chicken production lived below the federal poverty line (PEW Charitable Trusts 2013). In 2011, nearly a fifth of large grower operations (five or more houses) and nearly a third of smaller ones (one or two houses) had negative net farm income—more than 20 percent of the smallest poultry farms and almost 10 percent of larger farms failed to cover cash expenses (MacDonald 2014, 37–8).

Costco and Lincoln Premium say their production contract will be different than those that bind other broiler growers to their integrators. Its growers will receive fifteen-year contracts, the length of time it will take them to pay off the bank loans needed to finance their chicken houses. It will also pay a bonus for the best performing flocks, but it will not cut growers' pay for below-average performance, a common practice in the industry (Gerlock 2017). That is good news.

Nevertheless, the contract puts virtually all the eggs in the company's basket. Although the production contract is for fifteen years, it can be terminated by the company for any number of reasons, including company economic hardship. The company has the right to make changes in housing specifications "to comply with industry standards, customer requirements, good production practices, and changes in applicable law," and it can require the grower to make capital investments during the contract period. Shawn is an example of the financial hardship—even ruin—that such requirements have meant for poultry growers elsewhere. According to a 2017 class action lawsuit filed against the five largest poultry companies in U.S. District Court in the Eastern District of Oklahoma, "Integrators often monitor Growers' debt burdens, requiring them to undertake unnecessary and expensive upgrades if they ever do near financial independence—with the intent of keeping Growers debt-laden and subservient to a specific integrator" (Fassler 2017). And at the end of that fifteen years, the company can terminate its relationship with the grower or renew the production contract only on a flock-to-flock basis. The company determines the number, frequency of placement, size, and breed of the birds placed with the grower. The contract says it will place approximately six flocks with its broiler growers each year. But the company retains the right to increase or decrease the number of flocks or the number of chicks delivered in each flock, or both, as dictated by market conditions, consumer demand, or other factors. And the company is in complete control of the health of the birds it places with each grower, the quality of the feed, and the timing of any veterinary services it may provide. To its credit, Lincoln Premium does promise to provide a certified scale to weigh broilers and feed. It says it will allow growers to observe weighing of feed delivered to their houses as well as that of live broilers picked up from their operations—provided observations "do not interrupt normal production flow of Company operations."

Concentrated animal feeding operations (CAFOs) have received widespread condemnation for air and water pollution, and the risks they pose to the health of their workers and those who live nearby. Lincoln Premium's broiler contract holds the company harmless from any and all losses, claims, damages, assessments, or legal actions arising from broiler production, and it assigns growers responsibility and liability for all noxious emissions, dead-bird disposal, and related pollution.

Lincoln Premium says it will not use a tournament system to determine grower compensation, a system presently used in 93 percent of broiler contracts (MacDonald 2012, 27). But the manner in which it calculates grower payment will be a tournament in all but name. All growers will receive the same base pay. Those growers whose efficiency is above the average of all others whose flocks were picked up in the same week can earn up to one-half cent per pound above base pay. But those growers whose rolling three-flock average is above peer average cost may be placed on a grower-improvement program. If their performance does not improve, their contracts may be terminated. Growers' attention to their flocks is a significant factor in their performance, of course. So too is the quality of the chicks, feed, and veterinary services provided by the company— and these are beyond growers' control.

The contract requires growers to waive their right to a jury trial in any disputes with the company. Growers must submit written complaints to the broiler manager, who can decide against the grower merely by choosing not to respond. The grower can then appeal to the production director, who likewise can decline to respond and thereby find against the grower. Finally, the grower can appeal to a five-member alternative dispute-resolution committee made up of two people appointed by the company, along with one company broiler grower, one company breeder grower, and one pullet grower randomly selected from among those who agree to serve. Decisions require a vote of four of the five committee members to pass—and they are not binding. Such a dispute-resolution system is fraught with possibilities for company pressure and abuse.

The company says the complex's demand for local corn and soybeans will give a major economic boost to local farmers: 300,000 bushels of corn and 3,000 tons of soybeans a week (Clayton 2016). When Hudson first came to western Kentucky in 1996, it said it would buy twelve million bushels of grain a year from local farmers—at a premium of seven to ten cents a bushel. But not long after Tyson bought the Hudson chicken complex in 1998, it stopped paying a premium, and soon thereafter the company began requiring local farmers to negotiate sales and delivery with Tyson's headquarters in Arkansas. Now grain for Tyson's Kentucky plant is just as likely to come by rail from who knows where as it is from farmers down the road.

Communities are often seduced by meat and poultry companies who describe their jobs as "good-paying." Some are. But 90 percent of workers in meat and poultry plants are hourly line workers, whose wages are below or barely above the poverty line. In the summer of 2017, line workers at Tyson's Robards, Kentucky, plant started at $12 an hour. In 2016, Lincoln Premium said line workers at its Fremont, Nebraska, plant will *average* $13 an hour. At $13 an hour, working 40 hours a week, 52 weeks a year, a worker would gross before taxes and withholding $520 a week, $27,040 a year. This is only $2,440 above the 2017 federal poverty level for a family of four ($24,600), and well below income eligibility for children to receive free meals in public schools ($31,960).

If the partnership between Lincoln Premium and Costco proves successful by industry standards, it will likely become a model for other large retailers, such as Walmart, which recently opened its own milk plant in Fort Wayne, Indiana (Hook 2018). Tyson and other meat and poultry companies have long maintained that they are in many ways controlled by the retailers who buy their products. Costco is now taking vertical integration that one final step—it will control its rotisserie chickens all the way from the genetics, through the hatchery, through the chicken house, through the processing plant, to the retail meat counter, and into the customers' shopping carts. If this venture succeeds it may well be emulated throughout the poultry industry. And if it does, can pork be far behind?

Chickenizing Other American Farmers

The pork industry has followed closely on the heels of poultry. In the early 1980s, less than 5 percent of hogs raised by American farmers went to the packinghouse under a marketing contract. By 2009, nine out of ten were owned directly by meatpackers or under contract to them. And in those three decades, 91 percent of hog farmers went out of business (Stull and Broadway 2013, 15–16).

Traditionally, meatpacking company buyers bid on pens of live cattle and paid their owners in cash. But the packers are changing how they pay for the cattle they slaughter, extending their control of the market through what is known as captive supply. For example, by 2010 more than half of cattle slaughtered in Kansas were bought on a pricing formula based on the weight and quality of meat and the byproducts each carcass yields, adjusted according to formulas or grids specified by the company. Packers also procure cattle through forward contracts, which require delivery at a future date for a predetermined price, or they may own the cattle they slaughter, finishing them at their own feedyards. JBS, the world's largest beefpacker, owned Five Rivers Cattle Company, the world's largest cattle feeding company, with a capacity of almost a million head, until it was forced to divest amid a bribery scandal in 2017 (Rochas 2017). And because beef plants secure cattle from feedyards within 150 miles or so, even cattle feeders who sell on the cash market often have only one bidder on their animals. More than half of the cattle slaughtered in the United States, and by some estimates up to 80 percent, are now secured through some form of captive supply—either forward contracts, formula pricing, packer ownership, or feeders who have only one viable buyer (Stull and Broadway 2013, 37; Domina and Taylor 2010, 3). Is it any wonder then that from 1980 to 2009, 41 percent of beef cattle producers went out of business (Stull and Broadway 2013, 16)?

Dairy has followed a similar trajectory. Between 1970 and 2011, the number of dairy farms in the United States dropped 88 percent, from 648,000 to less than 52,000 (Valenze 2015, 338). Most of the farms that went out of business were in traditional dairy states like Wisconsin, Vermont, and New York, and were small, milking fewer than 200 cows (Kardashian 2012, 9). Replacing these small farms are megadairies in places like southwest Kansas, northeast New Mexico, and North Texas. Between 2000 and 2006, dairies milking more than 2,000 cows doubled. Following the chicken model, megadairies confine their animals—a 2007 USDA survey of animal management on over 2,000 dairy farms found that about half their cows are on concrete flooring, while pasture was the predominant flooring for only 5 percent of dairy cows (Kardashian 2012, 9, 174).

Retailers are rapidly moving toward complete vertical integration in dairy. Texas-based grocer H-E-B has long operated its own dairy processing facilities, and Kroger now supplies 100 percent of its own fluid milk to all its stores. Its plant in Denver, Colorado, which opened in 2014, is fully automated and runs 24 hours a day. Albertson's opened its own milk-bottling facility in Pennsylvania in 2017, and now that Walmart has opened its own milk plant in Indiana, the die is clearly cast. Independent milk providers, such as Dean Foods, have been forced to cancel contracts with dairy farmers (Hook 2018; Hamstra 2017).

It is not an exaggeration to say that modern agriculture has been "chickenized." Wherever we look—pork, beef, dairy—we see the imprint of Big Chicken: concentrated animal feeding operations (CAFOs), vertical integration, growers forced into one-sided contracts with multinational monopsonies, the disappearance of viable markets. And it is not just meat and dairy that have been chickenized—so too have other agricultural commodities. Tobacco is especially instructive.

Tobacco was long a cornerstone of family farm agriculture in Kentucky and several other southern and border states. The federal tobacco program, established in the 1930s, limited production by establishing quotas on the amount and type of tobacco that could be grown on individual farms. Farmers sold their leaf at auction to company buyers, and the program guaranteed purchase of their leaf at a minimum price, if not by a company (for at least a penny above the federal price-support level), then by a grower cooperative, financed at no net cost to taxpayers by the Commodity Credit Corporation. By stabilizing the price farmers received for their leaf, the federal tobacco program helped many small family farms survive, even prosper. But in 2004, the program was terminated.

Tobacco farmers are now free from government regulations on how much and what kind of tobacco they can grow, but they no longer enjoy the price guarantees that previously protected them.[5] Nor can they sell their leaf to the highest bidder. Like chicken growers, they are bound to precarious contracts with a shrinking number of multinational corporations—contracts that specify how much and what kind of tobacco they can grow, at what price, and with what inputs. The tobacco company can reject all or part of their crop, leaving the grower with few, if any, marketing options. And tobacco companies annually renew farmers' contracts—or don't.

To stay in business in tobacco's new free market, Kentucky's farmers have been forced to "get big or get out." Double-digit annual increases in input costs (fuel, fertilizer, hired labor) since the end of the tobacco program have forced them, as one tobacco farmer remarked, to "go the same way as grain farmers. Fifteen or twenty years ago, a man could farm 1,000 acres and make a pretty good living as a grain farmer. Now he needs 2,000 acres to take home the same money." The same is true of tobacco farmers—this farmer has increased his tobacco acreage nine-fold in the past two decades.

Whether they raise tobacco or corn, hogs or cattle, farmers are being transformed into growers, laboring under contract to multinational agribusiness corporations rather than selling their crops or livestock on fair and open markets. Speaking of the changes facing tobacco farmers, a county extension agent, who also raises chickens for a multinational corporation, remarked on the similarities: "As contract poultry growers, you learn to exist on what you can get. There's still a lot of management decisions that we don't make, somebody else makes, and our tobacco producers are finding that out too, as the company comes out and hands them a manual and says, 'This is what we kind of want you to go by.' The companies are having a lot more to say about how [tobacco is grown]."

He is not the only one who bemoans the chickenization of tobacco. According to a farmer who was growing ten to twelve acres of tobacco, "Now, then, they're saying that Philip Morris is talking like Perdue here in the chicken business. They're talking about going into a county that tobacco has never been raised in and furnishing the money and putting up barns and start raising it."

Tobacco auctions are no more. Neither are the competitive markets and farmer autonomy that went with them. The contract-grower model, pioneered by poultry, now dominates pork, beef, dairy, and tobacco. It is increasingly prevalent in grains as well.

American agriculture is dominated by vertically integrated and highly concentrated multinational agribusinesses. According to figures compiled by the National Farmers Union, just four companies slaughter 85 percent of cattle, 74 percent of hogs, and 54 percent of chickens.

Of those companies, one—Smithfield—is Chinese-owned, and two—JBS and Marfrig—are Brazilian.

In a span of four decades, more than thirty agricultural companies have consolidated into six giants through mergers and buyouts. These six companies now control 63 percent of the seed market and 75 percent of the agricultural chemical market. And it is getting worse. The Chinese National Chemical Corporation's purchase of the Swiss seeds and pesticide company Syngenta made ChemChina the world's largest supplier of pesticides and agrochemicals. Dow and DuPont recently merged, and Bayer and Monsanto are in the final stages of merger. When these mergers are completed, ChemChina-Syngenta, Dow-DuPont, and Bayer-Monsanto will control 80 percent of U.S. corn seed and 70 percent of global pesticide sales (Unglesbee 2016).

Multinational oligopolies gobble up more and more of the agricultural and food sectors, while farmers see their share of the food dollar steadily shrink. U.S. corn and soybean growers presently receive only 29 percent of parity; dairy, pork, and beef producers receive 33, 40, and 26 percent respectively (National Farmers Union News 2016, 2). (Parity is the price farmers would receive if farm prices had increased at the same rate as expenses, using 1910–1914 as the base period). In 2016, the farmer's share of the American food dollar hit a fifteen-year low, bottoming out at 14.8 cents (National Farmers Union News 2018). The U.S. government has turned a blind eye to the rise of the new agricultural trusts and the monopolistic practices they use to control our food and the farmers and ranchers who produce it.

Competitive markets are fast disappearing and with them the welfare of farmers and rural communities. Small diversified farms are threatened with extinction in the United States unless the families that still cling to the way of life they symbolize are able to make a decent living. What Grey (2000) calls our industrial food stream has brought us cheap and abundant food, but it has also depopulated our countryside as agricultural labor has been largely replaced by mechanical, chemical, biological, and information technologies (Adams 2003, 1). An alternative food stream has emerged (reemerged, actually) as farmers seek viable ways to earn a living and consumers seek more wholesome foods. "Natural" and organic foods, farmers' markets, community-supported agriculture, food co-ops, and direct marketing to consumers are rapidly gaining in popularity. But the overall market share "captured" by this alternative food stream remains modest and in danger of co-optation by the same multinational corporations that dominate agricultural production and the industrial food stream.

The meat and poultry industry has responded to pressure from restaurant chains, public interest groups, and the general public by altering some of its production practices, such as improving animal welfare and reducing or eliminating antibiotic use (Johnston 2017). It has been much less responsive to public concern over the air and water pollution generated by its concentrated animal feeding operations and slaughterhouses (Von Reusner 2017). Nor has the industry done much to improve the wages and working conditions of its producers and processing workers. Why should it? The general public has shown little interest in worker welfare. In a 2010 national marketing survey, seven of ten respondents said they would willingly pay more for "ethically produced" food. When asked what constituted "ethical food," more than 90 percent identified three qualities: "protects the environment, meets high quality and safety standards, and treats animals humanely" (Context Marketing 2010). Working conditions and wages for farmers and other food-chain workers did not qualify as considerations for "ethical" food.

Critics of industrial agriculture, and the factory farms upon which it is built, are fond of saying that this production model is not sustainable. But that depends on what we mean by sustainable. The industrial model has dominated American agriculture at least since the end of World War II, and it is spreading, as witnessed by the geographical expansion of Big Chicken and the chickenization of American farmers. And this model is being replicated throughout much of the rest of the world: per capita meat consumption is steadily rising and with it alarming increases in obesity in many developing countries (Stull and Broadway 2013, 191–2; Jacobs and Richtel 2017).

Maybe industrial agriculture is sustainable, maybe not. That will depend on what eaters want—and buy. Right now, price and convenience are the primary considerations when Americans fill up their shopping carts or go out to eat.

There is an alternative to the industrial food stream. And, yes, its share of America's food dollar is growing. But will it prove to be sustainable? Not unless the number of independent family farmers rebounds from its steady decline over the last century and more. That will depend on whether the American family farm is able to survive, let alone prosper. Only then will an alternative model of American agriculture, one that respects land, animals, producers, harvesters, processing workers—and eaters—have a chance to become mainstream once again.

Industrial agriculture is powerful and deeply entrenched in the halls of government and, as importantly, in the habits of American eaters. The last few decades have seen victories for the alternative food stream in the "food wars" (Lang and Heasman 2004), and industrial agriculture has responded when pressure to change is significant and sustained. American farmers are resilient, and some will survive despite the many challenges that face them now and into the future. But whether they survive as diversified and independent family farmers, or as chickenized growers bound by contract to a handful of multinational food corporations, remains to be seen. Ultimately, it is American eaters who hold the answers to the future of American farmers.

Notes

1. I am a charter member and president of the Organization for Competitive Markets (OCM), a nonprofit research and advocacy organization working for open and competitive markets and fair trade in America's food and agricultural sectors. I also serve on the board of directors of the Socially Responsible Agriculture Project (SRAP), a national organization that provides support for communities affected by concentrated animal feeding operations (CAFOs). This chapter represents my own research and analysis, and not necessarily the positions of either of these organizations.

2. Poultry processing complexes consist of a hatchery, feed mill, processing plant, and the poultry houses where the birds are raised. Tyson's hatchery is located in McLean County, its feed mill in Webster County, and the processing plant in Henderson County. The hatchery, feed mill, and processing plant are only a few miles from each other but are located in different counties to maximize local tax incentives. There are three types of chicken houses. Pullet houses raise breeding stock to twenty weeks of age, when the birds are taken to breeder houses, roughly ten hens to each rooster. For about forty-five weeks breeding hens produce eggs for the hatchery, which produces chicks for the broiler houses. The vast majority of chicken houses are broiler houses, which raise eating chickens from day-old chicks until they are ready for slaughter, usually in about seven weeks.

3. I am grateful to Jeffrey Kelley, the Webster County, Kentucky, Property Valuation Administrator, and his staff for their valuable assistance in my research.

4. A more detailed description of Tyson's western Kentucky poultry complex, its growers, and its workers, can be found in Stull 2000 and Stull and Broadway 2013. This chapter draws upon and updates those works. In May 2018, Tyson Foods announced a Contract Poultry Growers Bill of Rights that guarantees: 1) The right to a written copy of their contract; 2) The right to information detailing how much they are paid; 3) The right to discuss their contract with outside parties; 4) The right to a fixed-length contract that can only be terminated for cause; 5) The right to terminate the contract with Tyson Foods for any reason or no reason at all by giving ninety-day prior written notice for broilers and turkeys and sixty-day written notice for hens and pullets; 6) The right to join an association of contract poultry farmers; 7) The right to poultry welfare standards and training on poultry welfare standards; and 8) The right of contract poultry producers to *Tell Tyson First* by contacting the company via the internet at www.telltysonfirst.com, ethics@tyson.com, or by calling 1-888-301-7304 (See Kelly 2018 and company website).

5. For a detailed review of the federal tobacco program, its termination, and the consequences for Kentucky tobacco farmers see Stull 2009.

References

Adams, Jane, ed. 2003. *Fighting for the Farm: Rural America Transformed.* Philadelphia: University of Pennsylvania Press.

Associated Press. 2000. "Kentucky Poultry Production Up 13,000 Percent." *The Gleaner* (Henderson KY), June 25, 2000.

Charles, Dan. 2014. "Is Tyson Foods' Chicken Empire a 'Meat Racket'?" *The Salt, National Public Radio.* February 19. http://www.npr.org/sections/thesalt/2014/02/19/276981085.

Clayton, Chris. 2016. "High Hopes for Costco Poultry—Experts Warn Devil Is in the Details When It Comes to Poultry Contracts." *DTN/The Progressive Farmer,* June 27. https://www.dtnpf.com/agriculture/web/ag/news/farm-life/article/2016/06/27/experts-warn-devil-details-comes.

Context Marketing. 2010. "Ethical Food." http://contextmarketing.com/sources/feb28-2010/ethicalfoodreport.pdf.

Domina, David A., and C. Robert Taylor. 2010. "Restoring Economic Health to Beef Markets." August 25. Lincoln NE: Organization for Competitive Markets.

Fassler, Joe. 2017. "Playing Chicken: A New Class-Action Lawsuit Claims that Poultry Processors Conspire to Keep Farmers Trapped and Dependent." *The New Food Economy.* February 17. http://newfoodeconomy.com/chicken-farmer-collusion-suit.

Fielding, Michael. 2017. "Sanderson Farms Announces Site for New Poultry Complex in Texas." *Meatingplace.* March 16. http://www.meatingplace.com/Industry/News/Details/72167.

Gerlock, Grant. 2017. "The Gamble of the Farmers that Raise our Chicken." *Harvest Public Media.* June 7. http://hppr.org/post/gamble-farmers-raise-our-chicken.

Grey, Mark A. 2000. "The Industrial Food Stream and Its Alternatives in the United States. An Introduction." *Human Organization* 59: 143–50.

Hall, Bob. 1989. "Chicken Empires." *Southern Exposure* 17, no. 2: 12–17.

Hamstra, Mark. 2017. "Retailers Pressure Dairy Industry with New Plants." *Supermarket News,* November 17. http://www.supermarketnews.com/dairy/retailers-pressure-dairy-industry-new-plants.

Heffernan, William D. 1984. "Constraints in the U.S. Poultry Industry." *Research in Rural Sociology and Development* 1: 237–60.

Hook, Jim. 2018. "Milk Processor Cancels Farm Contracts as Walmart Makes Own Milk." *Public Opinion,* March 12. https://www.publicopiniononline.com/story/news/2018/03/12/milk-processor-cancels-farm-contracts-walmart-makes-own-milk/417995002/.

Jacobs, Andrew, and Matt Richtel. 2017. "How Big Business Got Brazil Hooked on Junk Food." *New York Times*, September 17: 1, 12–14.

Johnston, Tom. 2017. "Uncommon Ground." *Meatingplace*, September: 27–39.

Kardashian, Kirk. 2012. *Milk Money: Cash, Cows, and the Death of the American Dairy Farm*. Durham: University of Vermont Press.

Keeton, Kara. 2010. "Something to Crow About: Kentucky Chicken Producers Challenge Equine as Top Earning Agribusiness Sector." *The Lane Report*. Lexington KY: Lane Communications.

Kelly, Susan. 2018. "Tyson Creates Bill of Rights for Its Poultry Growers." *Meatingplace*, May 3. http://www.meatingplace.com/Industry/News/Details/79452.

Kentucky Poultry Federation. n.d. "Kentucky's #1 Ag Commodity." Kentucky Poultry Federation. Accessed June 6, 2017. http://kypoultry.org/pfacts.

Lang, Tim, and Michael Heasman. 2004. *Food Wars: The Global Battle for Mouths, Minds, and Markets*. London: Earthscan.

Leonard, Christopher. 2014. *The Meat Racket: The Secret Takeover of America's Food Business*. New York: Simon and Schuster.

MacDonald, James M. 2012. "The Economic Organization of U.S. Broiler Production." U.S. Department of Agriculture, Economic Research Service. *Economic Information Bulletin No. 38*. June.

———. 2014. "Technology, Organization, and Financial Performance in U.S. Broiler Production." U.S. Department of Agriculture, Economic Research Service. *Economic Information Bulletin 126*. June.

McGee, Jamie. 2018. "Tyson Chicken Plant: Rejected in One Town, Welcomed in Another." *USA Today Network*, March 24. https://www.usatoday.com/story/money/business/2018/03/24/tyson-chicken-plant-rejected-one-town-welcomed-another/455340002/.

Meatingplace. 2017. "Holly Poultry Eyes Expansion with Opening of New Plant." *Meatingplace*, June 7. http://www.meatingplac.com/Industry/News/Details/73698.

Meat+Poultry. 2016. "USDA: Poultry Production Nearly Doubles Since 1990." *Meat+Poultry*, November 1.

Morrison, John M. 1998. "The Poultry Industry: A View of the Swine Industry's Future." In *Pigs, Profits, and Rural Communities*, edited by Kendall M. Thu and E. Paul Durrenberger, 145–54. Albany: State University of New York Press.

National Chicken Council. 2012. "March Madness: Why Contract Growing in the Chicken Industry Is Not a 'Tournament,'" March 15. http://www.nationalchickencouncil.org.

National Farmers Union News. 2016. "Farm Price Barometer, January 2016." *National Farmers Union News* 64, no. 1: 2.

National Farmers Union News. 2018. "Farmer's Share Falls to 15-Year Low." *NFU E-News* 369, May 3. http://news@nfudc.org.

PEW Charitable Trusts. 2013. "The Business of Broilers: Hidden Costs of Putting Chicken on Every Grill." December 20. http://www.pewtrusts.org /en/research-and-analysis/reports/2013/12/20.

Rochas, Anna Flavia. 2017. "Brazil's JBS Plans to Sell Moy Park, Five Rivers & Stake in Vigor Alimentos." *Meatingplace,* June 20. http:www.meatingplace .com/Industry/News/Details/73926.

Schneider, Skylar. 2017. "Stand Up for Family Farmers—Pass the Farmer Fair Practices Act." National Farmers Union, June 1. https://nfu.org/2017 /06/01/stand-up-for-family-farmers-pass-the-farmer-fair-practices-rules/.

Scott, Chris. 2017. "Costco Breaks Ground for Nebraska Chicken Plant." *Meatingplace,* June 20. http://www.meatingplace.com/Industry/News/Details/73916.

Striffler, Steve. 2005. *Chicken: The Dangerous Transformation of America's Favorite Food.* New Haven CT: Yale University Press.

Stull, Donald D. 2000. "Tobacco Barns and Chicken Houses: Agricultural Transformation in Western Kentucky." *Human Organization* 59: 151–61.

———. 2009. "Tobacco is Going, Going . . . But Where?" *Culture & Agriculture* 31: 54–72.

———. 2017. "Cows, Pigs, Corporations, and Anthropologists." *Journal of Business Anthropology* 6, no. 1: 23–40.

Stull, Donald D., and Michael J. Broadway. 2013. *Slaughterhouse Blues: The Meat and Poultry Industry in North America.* 2nd ed. Belmont CA: Wadsworth.

Taylor, C. Robert, and David A. Domina. 2010. "Restoring Economic Health to Contract Poultry Growing." Report for the Joint U.S. Department of Justice and U.S. Department of Agriculture/GIPSA Public Workshop on Competition in the Poultry Industry. May 21. Normal AL. Lincoln NE: Organization for Competitive Markets.

Thornton, Gary. 2016. "Top 10 US Chicken Producers Grow in New Directions," March 7. http://www.wattagnet.com/articles/25893.

Tyson Foods. n.d. "Tyson's Live Production Teams Span Nine Counties." In "Growing the Future," Twelve-page advertising insert in several Western Kentucky newspapers, July 1999.

Ulack, Richard, Karl Raitz, and Gyula Pauer. 1998. *Atlas of Kentucky.* Lexington KY: University of Kentucky Press.

Unglesbee, Emily. 2016. "And Then There Were Four?" *DTN/Progressive Farmer,* September 23. https://www.dtnpf.com/agriculture/web/ag/news/article /2016/09/23.

Valenze, Deborah. 2015. "Dairy Industry." In *The Sage Encyclopedia of Food Issues,* vol. 1, edited by Ken Albala, 335–40. Thousand Oaks CA: Sage.

Von Reusner, Lucia. 2017. "Mystery Meat II: The Industry Behind the Quiet Destruction of the American Heartland." http://www.mightyearth.org /heartlanddestruction/.

Williams, William H. 1998. *Delmarva's Chicken Industry: Seventy-Five Years of Progress.* Georgetown: Delmarva Poultry Industry.

3

Industrial Chicken Meat and the Good Life in Bolivia

SARAH KOLLNIG

Walking the streets of Cochabamba city, particularly at night, one finds uncountable food stands and little restaurants offering a snack. Many of the small restaurants are equipped with red plastic chairs sponsored by Coca Cola, and on the counter in the back of the room, the food is prepared for the guests. Very often, the food offered is fried chicken, kept warm under a regular light bulb, or roasted chicken turning above a furnace. Chicken is cheap, easy to prepare, and tasty. Chicken is for everyone, it seems. My Bolivian friends told me that about thirty to forty years ago, their parents and grandparents reared chickens in their urban backyards. Nowadays, urban areas in Bolivia are consumers of industrially produced chicken. Backyard chicken rearing is limited to rural areas and peripheral urban neighborhoods.

The production and consumption of industrial chicken meat have soared in Bolivia—since 2006 the production of chicken meat, measured in tons of meat produced, has surpassed the production of beef (Ormachea Saavedra 2009). The number of broilers reared in Bolivia grew by 1,500 percent between 1984 and 2015 to reach about 240 million chickens in 2015 (Ministry of Rural Development and Land 2015). The agricultural census of 2011 showed that 89 percent of the livestock population in Bolivia were broilers (Albarracín Deker 2015, 243). In comparison, in 1950, sheep

99

were the largest group of animals reared in Bolivian agriculture (Albarracín Deker 2015, 241). Since then, the share of chickens reared intensively has increased rapidly and has left the breeding of sheep, alpacas, and llamas far behind (Albarracín Deker 2015). In comparison to the number of chickens reared industrially (about 240 million chickens in 2015), the number of chickens held in traditional ways in the backyard is minimal (about six million chickens according to the Ministry of Rural Development and Land in 2015).

In 2014, the average Bolivian consumed about 77 pounds of chicken meat per year (ADA Cochabamba March 2015), which is higher than the per capita consumption in the United Kingdom or Spain (53 and 55 pounds respectively), but still below the U.S. per capita consumption (which amounts to 97 pounds–International Poultry Council n.d.). In the highland cities of El Alto and La Paz, chicken consumption is even more prominent, with per capita consumption standing at 143 pounds per year (ADA Cochabamba March 2015, 5).

This chapter analyzes the socio-ecological effects of this development and contrasts them to the discourse of *Vivir Bien* put forward by the current Morales government, which has become well known for its apparently socialist and pro-indigenous agenda. The increasing production and consumption of chicken meat has been an important political goal in Bolivia. As Albarracín Deker states, "The success and development of the poultry and beef sectors are a response to the implementation of politics, programs, and projects developed and supported by the [Bolivian] state, directed specifically at large and medium-scale enterprises" (2015, 242). Only recently, the current Bolivian government, led by the *Movimiento al Socialismo* (Movement Towards Socialism), or MAS, and president Evo Morales, has declared that the consumption of chicken meat should be further increased (*Desde 2006* January 29, 2014). In this chapter, I also scrutinize how the Morales government has been involved in the

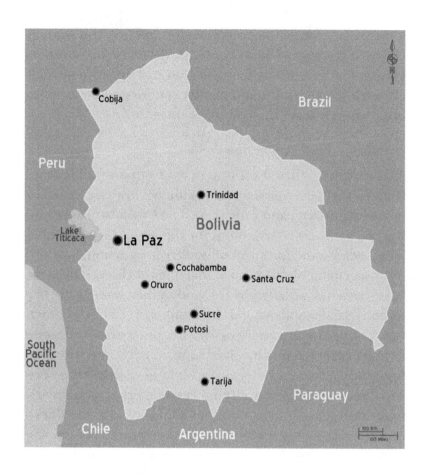

FIG. 7. Map of Bolivia. Wikimedia Commons.

industrialization of the poultry sector and how this strategy stands in contrast to the government discourse of *Vivir Bien*. I argue that this industrialization has had negative impacts on small-scale farmers and market vendors, while supporting the interests of the country's elites.

Methods

This chapter is based on one year of ethnographic fieldwork in the *departamento* ("department") of Cochabamba between July 2015 and June 2016. The Cochabamba region was chosen as a starting point for this research since it has long been on the forefront of poultry production. I carried out participant observation at meetings of chicken farmers, at markets in Cochabamba city, and in the everyday life of a middle-class neighborhood. In addition, I conducted interviews, sampling interviewees with the purpose of reflecting the diversity of actors involved in producing and distributing poultry, from small-scale farmers to civil servants. Personal contacts were important in some cases, particularly in accessing poultry farms. All in all, I spoke to two official representatives of the industrial chicken producers' associations (the ADAS—*Asociación de Avicultores*), one professor at *Universidad Mayor de San Simón* in Cochabamba specializing in poultry production, the two representatives of the association of small chicken producers (ASPYMAD—*Asociación de Pequeños y Medianos Avicultores Departamentales*), and ten associated small- and medium-scale chicken producers (in two cases, I was allowed to visit their farm as well). I also spoke to the national representative of poultry vendors and fifteen poultry vendors who either own market stalls or work at company-owned sales outlets. I received further information from civil servants at SENASAG (*Servicio Nacional de Sanidad Agropecuaria e Inocuidad Alimentaria*), EMAPA (*Empresa de Apoyo a la Producción de Alimentos*), the Ministry of Rural Development and Agriculture, and the Ministry of Economic Development. I also interviewed employees of the state-owned Development Bank, *Banco de Desarrollo Productivo*. All interviews were semi-structured, giving room for detailed elaborations from the interviewees. I spoke to some interviewees several times.

Vivir Bien as a Government Discourse

The idea of *Buen Vivir* or *Vivir Bien* gained attention internationally when it was included in the constitutions of Ecuador (in 2008) and Bolivia (in 2009) (Gudynas 2011). Ideas of *Vivir Bien* have existed in many indigenous communities, but the political momentum these ideas gained owes much to the theorization of *Vivir Bien* by intellectuals. As Burman (2017) notes, in Bolivia, *Vivir Bien* started to receive more attention from intellectuals and NGOs in the late 1980s and 1990s.

Current president Morales and his *Movimiento Al Socialismo* (MAS) passed a new constitution in 2009, which includes *Vivir Bien* as a central principle: "The State is based on the values of unity, equality, inclusion, dignity, liberty, solidarity, reciprocity, respect, synergy, harmony, transparency, balance, socially equitable participation, the common good, responsibility, social justice, and distribution and redistribution of social goods in order to reach *Vivir Bien*" (Constitución Política del Estado 2009, art. 8, II). In relation to agriculture, the new Law 144, the law of the "Communitarian Productive Agricultural Revolution" (*Ley de la Revolución Productiva Comunitaria Agropecuaria*) defines that the state will particularly support "traditional, organic, ecological" family and community agriculture to achieve food sovereignty (Ley No. 144, art. 16).

The Morales government has received international attention for its emphasis on *Vivir Bien*. However, the translation of *Vivir Bien* from a political discourse to concrete policies and changes in the everyday lives of Bolivians is a difficult task. In this chapter, I focus on the discourse of *Vivir Bien* as a social practice, particularly as part of policy-making in Bolivia. In the area of agriculture, recent policies have continued the emphasis of previous governments on industrial agriculture. The Morales government has argued that the industrialization of the national agricultural sector is an important part of its political project (Vice presidencia del Estado Plurinacional de Bolivia 2015). Industrialization has been portrayed as important in order to regain national sovereignty (Ormachea Saavedra 2009), and the supply of easily accessible food items such as chicken is an important outcome of this process. This strategy results in apparent contradictions with the government discourse of *Vivir Bien*. In what follows, I take the poultry sector as a case in point to demonstrate the socio-ecological problems that surge with the continued focus on industrialization and extractivism (the profit-oriented extraction of natural resources) implemented by the Morales government.

The Industrialization of Chicken Rearing

It is hard to get access to chicken farms in Bolivia. As we drive on bumpy roads through the countryside, we pass the chicken farms, mostly rudimentary buildings with a low wall from which a metal construction emerges to form the stables' side walls and roof. It is the yellow plastic sheets with which the sides of the stable are covered that give away the fact that this construction is a chicken farm. We see many of these farms as we drive along, but all of them have big signs in the driveway saying, "Private property, keep out."

This sign does not necessarily represent an innate hostility toward visitors, but it is a sanitary precaution: the chicken flocks are plagued by many easily transmissible diseases such as *Escherichia coli, Salmonella gallinarum,* and Newcastle's disease. The chickens are kept in a high density of ten to twelve chickens per square meter, and this intensive chicken rearing has led to the outbreak of many illnesses. In Bolivia, the individual farms are supposed to be at least one kilometer from each other to prevent the transmission of diseases, but this regulation is unenforced, and there may be farms a few hundred meters from each other.

After months of trying to get access to a chicken farm, I finally met Miguel, a friend of a friend, who rears chickens in the rural hinterland of the city of Cochabamba. Miguel is actually a musician from a well-off family, but he is currently reviving his family's farm to supplement his income. After a drive of one hour out of the city, we arrive at a dirt road. The houses along the road are small and made of clay. After taking many turns, we reach the gate of the chicken farm. Miguel asks us, suddenly switching to a serious tone, if we have been to other chicken farms recently. He disinfects the soles of our shoes and the tires of his pick-up truck, "for safety's sake," he says. On his land, he has three chicken stables, one of them functioning at the moment, and one fodder mill where he creates the right mixture of feed for the chickens. On a hill behind a tree, there is a small cottage for the caretaker, the *galponero,* and his family. A few meters to the right, Miguel's family has built a big country house. I can imagine Miguel spending a weekend of drinking and music with his friends here. I cannot imagine the caretaker doing the same. "It is difficult with these people," Miguel says, signaling to the caretaker's hut. "They don't know how to keep the place clean. They have to be instructed about everything." Although the farm needs the owner, the veterinarian, and the caretaker as central persons to manage the chicken rearing, the caretaker is the one who earns the least. He and his family are cheap manual labor.

Miguel leads us to one of the stables. As he opens the metal gates, he says, "Right now, I only have 10,000 chicks." And there they are, running around on the floor, which is a concrete floor covered with sawdust. "They are very energetic because of what we feed them," he explains. The chicks are a few days old—they have arrived from the Santa Cruz lowlands a maximum of forty-eight hours after hatching in a breeding plant. The chicks cannot hatch in the high altitude of Cochabamba. The fluffy, yellow beings are actually genetically engineered. They are offspring of the genetic lines "Ross" or "Cobb," the two types of chicken used in industrial chicken rearing in Bolivia. Many of the chicks will not survive. They will develop an infectious disease or their hearts will not be able to bear their fast growth. Miguel has a background in veterinary medicine. He just administered the first batch of vaccines to the chicks—many times, these vaccines are administered manually. It was the vaccine against Newcastle's disease, a respiratory disease in chickens that is widespread in Bolivia. They will receive several booster vaccines. All in all, the chickens will grow up to be around forty-nine days old. Then they will be slaughtered. In order to grow fast, they receive a high-energy diet consisting of soy, corn, and additives such as salts, calcium, vitamins, and amino acids. Miguel receives the ingredients from a cooperative of which he is a member.

When the chickens have reached the right age for slaughtering, Miguel calls a distributor. The distributor arrives with a truck and loads the chickens which have been placed in plastic crates. Miguel receives a price below the market price for the chickens because, the distributor argues, she has to be competitive against the big producers who control the market price. As we leave Miguel's farm, I wonder how the smaller producers can survive in the fight with the large-scale poultry producers.

Large- versus Small-Scale Producers

Being organized is paramount in Bolivia. Whether one is a worker, a small merchant, or a big entrepreneur, one has to be part of a professional association that represents the group's interests. I soon find out that the chicken farmers of Cochabamba are organized in the ADA, or *Asociación de Avicultores* (Poultry Producers' Association). Since its establishment in 1970, ADA Cochabamba has been led by Felipe Suarez, an elderly patriarch. On a warm January afternoon, he welcomes me into his office which is located in the outskirts of Cochabamba city. The office is situated in a big bungalow with several conference rooms and a separate laboratory for avian pathology. While we speak, government representatives are in a meeting with ADA staff to discuss improvements in the strategy for food safety in the chicken meat sector.

Don Felipe is proud of what he has accomplished. When ADA was founded, it consisted of five men meeting together in a rudimentary office. They had a vision: to start producing chicken meat and eggs on a large scale in Bolivia. In the beginning, the politicians did not believe that this would be either possible or useful. But the men worked hard, Don Felipe tells me, to convince the Bolivian people and politicians of the advantages of industrially produced chicken meat. As I read the booklet produced by ADA for its fortieth anniversary, I realized that the founders of poultry production in Cochabamba are part of the Bolivian elite, having grown up in the westernized, urban environment that is the breeding ground for those who have always been in power in Bolivia. They have the financial means to invest in a large-scale enterprise such as poultry production. This fact is, of course, linked to their socially privileged position. The big poultry producing companies (the biggest players are IMBA and Sofia) in Bolivia have grown in this elitist environment, as the stories told in the ADA pamphlet reveal (ADA Cochabamba 2014).

ADA represents primarily the big chicken producers. While producers like Miguel breed a few thousand chickens, the bigger producers raise over one million chickens per production cycle. In Cochabamba, as Don Felipe proudly tells me, about 80 percent of the chicken meat is produced by only six enterprises, and the remainder by hundreds (about 300 to 400) of medium- and small-scale producers. The big producers have followed an aggressive strategy of vertically integrating the chicken supply chain (see also chapter 1 of this volume by Hendrickson, Howard and Constance, and chapter 2 by Stull). The ADA pamphlet proudly tells the stories of the bigger chicken producers expanding their business into these sectors.

In my quest for more information about the chicken sector, I visit a feed mill, also located in the periphery of the city. The owner of the feed mill has been in the poultry business for decades. Don José tells me the stories that ADA did not present to me. "In order for a big poultry producer to be big, thousands of small ones have to go bankrupt. This is the logic," he tells me. So, what happened? In the beginnings of the chicken meat sector, the companies with more capital used to buy the produce from smaller producers. Nowadays, the large producers have bought these small chicken farms. Only a few large-scale producers are still buying from external farms.

Among the smaller producers, there is the widespread perception that the current government does not take them seriously. Since they did not feel well-represented by ADA, they have founded ASPYMAD, the Association of Small and Medium-Scale Poultry Producers. ASPYMAD meets in a repurposed garage with white plastic chairs. A sheet on the wall lists those who have failed to pay the membership dues.

The members of ASPYMAD are angry at the government. They had high hopes in Morales and his promise to support the smaller producers. The chairman of ASPYMAD tells me, "We are tired of the story that the government supports the small producers. It has to be said clearly: There is no support." The smaller producers have been particularly concerned about the low market price of chicken meat, which does not allow them to survive. The government, however, has not intervened directly so far.

ASPYMAD has been positioning itself against the government discourse. The association argues that the government's commitment to smaller producers does not correspond to action. The representatives of smaller chicken farmers have been contesting the government discourse. In the fight for its members' interests, ASPYMAD has also organized road blocks and other protests. ADA, on the other hand, supports the government discursively and in practice, proclaiming that, thanks to ADA, Bolivians can eat cheap protein. While ASPYMAD is concerned about a lack of support from the government, ADA president Don Felipe told me how well they worked together with the current government, particularly in crisis situations. If the government discourse of *Vivir Bien* was a valid representation of the situation on the ground, the power relations would be reversed. If there was actual support for smaller farmers, then ASPYMAD would have to be in a better situation than ADA. One issue influencing this situation is that the Morales government has been forced to make alliances with the country's elites in order to stay in power. In the agricultural sector, there has been, according to critical observers, more support for industrial agriculture than for small-scale family agriculture (Orchmachea Saavedra 2007). The MAS government regards large-scale, industrial agriculture as an important part of Bolivia's development (Ormachea Saavedra 2007). It is this continued support for the industrial sector that led Bolivian sociologist, Silvia Rivera Cusicanqui, to remark that *Vivir Bien* is a "hollow phrase" (*palabra hueca*) (*Silvia Rivera: El "Vivir Bien"* September 29, 2015). Cusicanqui reminds the reader that the Bolivian constitution recognizes three types of economic activities: private, communitarian, and state-led. According to her, the MAS government has not taken any actions to support communitarian forms of production (*Silvia Rivera: El "Vivir Bien"* September 29, 2015). At first sight, this situation seems like a discrepancy between government rhetoric and practice, but when one examines the government discourse more closely, there are, at times, situations when the dialogue itself becomes contradictory. This is particularly the case in public statements of politicians that are not worded as carefully as the written accounts of *Vivir Bien*. In a speech concluding the national agricultural summit "*Sembrando Bolivia,*" Bolivian Vice President Álvaro García Linera proclaimed that the "expansion of the agricultural frontier, industrialization and aggregated value for agricultural products" and "increasing exports and increasing markets" were central pillars of the agricultural sector (Vice presidencia del Estado Plurinacional de Bolivia 2015). This statement counts industrial, export-oriented agriculture as a central actor, and it also reflects how the government envisions the concrete pathway to the Good Life for Bolivians: through economic growth.

The Decline of Backyard Chicken Rearing

My Bolivian friends remember that their parents and grandparents used their backyards to rear chickens and turkeys, among other small animals, and for other agricultural activities. The animals were bought as chicklings from the market and fed with grains until they were ready to be eaten on a special day such as Christmas or a birthday. These memories date back thirty or forty years. In 1986, the municipality of Cochabamba banned the rudimentary, uncontrolled backyard rearing of farm animals because it was "against the hygiene and health of the population, due to the proliferation of parasites and disease vectors, and the disturbing noises caused by the animals" (Honorable Concejo Municipal 1986). It is, however, technically still permissible to keep small farm animals in controlled conditions after inspection by the municipality. This statute mirrors the development that backyard chicken rearing has been considered increasingly socially unacceptable by the more powerful parts of urban society. In the neighborhood I have studied, nobody keeps chickens anymore. Still, in poorer and peripheral neighborhoods people rear chickens for home consumption.

Chickens reared in a more traditional way, nowadays called *gallina criolla* by the people, have different properties than industrial chickens. The *gallina criolla* is not a standardized breed, so it does not produce muscle mass as quickly as factory chicken. Since the backyard chicken is bred for a longer time than the industrialized chicken, the meat is harder and has a more intense taste, and the bones are also harder to break. These properties make it more difficult to prepare a traditionally reared chicken—it is harder to divide the entire broiler into parts by breaking the bones, and the tougher meat has to be cooked for longer. As an interviewee told me, "At the beginning, the industrial chicken tasted like medicine." But nowadays, many people have gotten used to this taste and won't accept the taste of *gallina criolla*.

On one of my excursions to the smaller populations surrounding Cochabamba, I saw something interesting. Chickens, directly from an industrial chicken farm, were sold on the central square. Even the rural populations have been taken over by the poultry industry. On the one hand, the vendors have expanded the market for their industrial chicken into the countryside, and on the other hand, the local farmers have begun to regard industrial chicken farming as a source of income and have switched from traditional rearing to more industrial forms of chicken rearing. In many rural populations, the bright yellow plastic sheets covering the chicken farms have become part of the landscape.

In 2016, the Bill and Melinda Gates Foundation offered to donate chickens to Bolivian small-scale farmers, but the government was offended. The Minister of Agriculture said, "He [Bill Gates] does not know anything about Bolivia, he probably thinks we [. . .] live in the middle of the jungle without knowing how to produce" (*Gobierno califica de grosero* June 15, 2016). The current Bolivian government proudly fosters industrial chicken meat production, revealing a mainstream, Western vision of development, where development equals industrialization. This viewpoint has watered down the discourse of *Vivir Bien*.

For my Bolivian friends and family, eating *gallina criolla* has become a luxury. Self-proclaimed members of an alternative food movement are willing to pay more for a traditionally reared chicken than for factory-farmed chicken. This preference can be observed all over the world; eating healthy, organic food has become a privilege (Alkon and Agyeman 2011). It is, however, still hard to find *gallina criolla* these days. One has to navigate the hidden corners of the city's central market in order to find somebody selling one or two chickens reared in their backyard—alive. This secretive transaction presupposes that the buyer has the skills to slaughter, pluck, and gut the chicken.

Animal Health and Environment

In industrial farms all over the world, chickens are kept more intensively, in a higher population density, than other farm animals (Duncan 2011). They are also kept in an environment that doesn't allow for behavior that is natural for chickens, such as nesting and resting on perches (European Commission 2000).

Chickens for meat production are selected for their high growth rate, which causes health problems (Duncan 2011). A common health problem is Ascites in which the bird has insufficient heart-lung capacity to supply the soft tissues with oxygenated blood. This causes suffering, liver problems, and heart failure. Another common problem is skeletal deformities, particularly leg problems, which cause pain and impaired movement.

In Bolivia, drugs, particularly antibiotics, are used for the treatment of diseases and as growth promoters. The use of antibiotics as growth promoters was banned in the European Union in 2006 (European Commission 2005). The US Food and Drug Administration (FDA) recommends a "judicious use" of antibiotics in food-producing animals (Food and Drug Administration 2012). The concern leading to these measures is the issue of antimicrobial resistance; some bacteria develop resistance against the antibiotics used against them, and these resistant bacteria could attack humans as well (Food and Drug Administration 2012).

Looking for more information about the use of antibiotics in chickens, I visit the offices at SENASAG in the periphery of Cochabamba city. It is very hard to find a person who is willing to talk to me about this issue. Finally, I get an appointment for an interview with the veterinarians at the animal health lab at SENASAG. The veterinarians explain to me that there is an overuse of antibiotics in Bolivian poultry farming. As a consequence, resistant bacterial strains have developed. In some cases, none of the common antibiotics are effective anymore, which leads to the use of stronger antibiotics or to the application of combinations of antibiotics. According to the veterinarians, they have no information about whether a veterinary drug is allowed for use or banned. In fact, there are no official communications from the corresponding authority, SENASAG. As I read up on the norms for the registration of veterinary medicine in Bolivia, I realize that the regulations do not take into account concerns with animal and human health. According to United States and EU legislation (Goetting et al. 2011), almost all of the antibiotics used in Bolivia are banned from the use in laying hens. For broilers, regulations are slightly less restrictive, but some antibiotics used in Bolivia are restricted in the United States and the EU.

It is standard practice in western countries that for drugs that are allowed, a Maximum Residue Limit (MRL) is set by governmental agencies, which is not the case in Bolivia. In order to avoid residues in products consumed by humans, SENASAG recommends a "withdrawal time" for veterinary drugs. At least for laying hens, the withdrawal times recommended are, without exception, too short (Goetting et al. 2011). Also, as one of the veterinarians explains to me, Bolivia does not have the laboratory equipment to detect residues of veterinary drugs in chicken meat or eggs. This lack of diagnostic possibilities makes any regulation of residue limits futile.

Still, SENASAG controls chicken farms, and Don Felipe from ADA tells me that there already exists a certain routine between the chicken farmers and the government technicians. "A friend of mine had to travel," Don Felipe tells me, "so when the SENASAG technician visited, my friend told him, 'I won't be here next week, so I will just pay you double for now.'" This arrangement is a hint at the widespread corruption among government technicians. Apparently, the SENASAG staff charged standard fees at every visit for any kind of superficial irregularities found, which is a means for raising money rather than an actual form of control. As Ranta mentions in her work on *Vivir Bien*, it is very common in Bolivia that technicians change with every political change (Ranta 2014, 175), so public servants are oftentimes chosen for their political loyalty and not their expertise.

Returning to Miguel's chicken farm, he tells me that he only uses antibiotics when absolutely necessary. The consumer, however, has no way of telling how a chicken was reared. There is no procedure for certifying a chicken as bred with or without medication in Bolivia. The distribution system, as I describe below, does not distinguish between different types of chickens. And setting up a direct sales outlet is difficult for smaller farmers due to competition from the established vendors.

Poultry farming has become more of an industry than an agricultural activity (Gerber et al. 2007). The production sites are located strategically, depending on the proximity to markets and to the rest of the production chain, from feed supply to slaughtering. In Cochabamba, the bulk of poultry production is located close to the urban area of Cochabamba city, in the surrounding towns of Sipe, Quillacollo, Tiquipaya, and Vinto. These locations are strategically sound because the market of Cochabamba city is close, and the chicken meat can be transported easily to the even larger market of the highland cities of El Alto and La Paz (to which 67 percent of Cochabamba's poultry production is sold) (ADA Cochabamba 2015, 9). The slaughterhouses are situated in the same areas, some even in the urban area of Cochabamba city. This structural determination of the location of chicken farms is being reinforced by the lending policy of the Bolivian Development Bank—my analysis of their loans shows that the money goes principally to bigger chicken farms with promising strategic locations.

In the search for more information on the environmental impacts of poultry farming, I contact an environmental engineer. Eva visits me on a Saturday afternoon and tells me about her experiences from working with chicken farms. The chicken farmers usually do not have agricultural fields, which means that the chicken litter is sold to other farmers as fertilizer and could end up practically anywhere in the Cochabamba region. This is a sanitary problem. SENASAG regulates a minimum distance between chicken farms so that pathogens will not spread easily. If the chicken litter, which still might contain pathogens, is brought to a location near another chicken farm, there is a risk of pathogens spreading.

Eva tells me that dead chickens are usually burned or buried on site. The burning of the animals causes disturbing odors for neighboring communities, and so does the burying since the holes, initially dug deep into the ground, are filled with several layers of dead birds. The owners of smaller farms sometimes dispose of the animals' bodies in the open, which attracts stray dogs.

The slaughterhouses are usually situated near rivers for the disposal of wastewater. Eva has inspected several slaughterhouses and stresses that, due to increased controls over slaughterhouses by the authorities, some of them have installed wastewater treatment units. Nowadays, the blood resulting from the slaughtering process is separated, coagulated, and used as swine feed. The intestines are used as swine feed as well, sometimes with previous heat treatment, and sometimes in the raw state. Using the residues from the slaughtering process as feed is welcomed by pig farmers since they receive the residues for free. The downside is the associated odors, the presence of flies, and the fact that the pigs develop less rapidly than with processed feed.

The Bolivian environmental law, "Ley 1333," does not specify the environmental precautions to be taken in animal farming and slaughtering. There is a law for *Vivir Bien*, the Law 300 (2012), which to date only remains a general framework that has not been put into practice. I remember my visit at SENASAG. In the labyrinth of offices, after being sent from one person to another, seemingly without anyone feeling responsible for giving me accurate information, I get to talk to a woman who sits in a small, windowless office. She is a veterinarian. When asked about the sanitary standards for poultry production, she says, "If we closed down slaughterhouses there would be road blocks and protests." Keeping the people well-fed, it seems, comes before concerns about animal health and the environment.

Current Bolivian legislation makes many allusions to

Mother Earth and *Pachamama*, the mythical Mother of Cosmos. The preamble of the Bolivian Constitution states that Bolivia is being reconstituted "with the force of Pachamama" (Constitucion Politica del Estado 2009, preambulo). The Ley 300, in which *Vivir Bien* is defined, establishes in its first paragraph the objective to reach an "integral development in harmony and balance with Mother Earth for *Vivir Bien*" (Ley 300, art. 1). The information about the situation of animals and the biophysical environment in Bolivian poultry production suggests that these high aims are not being reached.

Connections to Soy and Corn Production

The industrialization of the poultry sector has also affected the production of the feed ingredients soy and corn. Corn is an ancestral crop for Bolivians that has been grown since precolonial times (Coe 1994). The use of corn as feed and not as food is a new development for the country and breaks with the traditional importance of the crop (Ortiz 2012). Since the 1990s, corn has been increasingly produced at a larger scale, with the production of traditional corn varieties decreasing and one hybrid corn variety increasing. Nowadays, more than 70 percent of the corn produced in Bolivia is used as animal feed, with the poultry sector demanding about 50 percent of the corn harvest (Ortiz 2012, 16). The surface of corn cultivated in Bolivia amounts to about 350,000 hectares. Medium- and large-scale producers account for 60 percent of the corn production (Ortiz 2012, 42).

Bolivia is the fourth-largest producer of soy in South America, after Brazil, Argentina, and Paraguay (Perez Luna 2007). Soy production is concentrated in the Santa Cruz lowlands. Soy has been an important cash crop in Bolivia, particularly since the beginning of the period of neoliberal governments that fostered exports in the 1980s and 1990s.

Since then, poultry producers have used soy as a main feed ingredient. Before this, the poultry sector imported fodder ingredients from the United States or neighboring countries. The large-scale production is dominated by foreign producers, mostly from Brazil and Argentina, which control about 40 percent of soy production (Perez Luna 2007, 90). Soy production follows an extractivist logic: it uses up the productive capacity of the land and then moves on to new land or to land formerly used for other products. This logic does not provide any benefits for the local population (Perez Luna 2007). Soy was the first crop in Bolivia for which genetically modified seeds (resistant to Glyphosate and patented by Monsanto) were legally allowed (Fundacion Tierra 2015a). The Morales government has implemented state control in the corn and soy sectors, emphasizing its vision of a state-led development of industrial agriculture.

I realize how important soy and corn are for the poultry sector when I visit La Paz, the city where the Bolivian government is located, and start asking in the ministries about poultry production. Particularly at the Ministry of Production and Economy, instead of talking about chicken meat, the civil servants tell me about the regulation of the soy and corn markets, which the Morales government has implemented. The regulation of these markets began in 2011, after a particularly steep increase in feed prices.

The president of ADA Cochabamba is happy about this form of government intervention because the supply of feed has always been difficult for the poultry sector. "It was the law of the jungle," Don Felipe says. According to him, soy used to be sold at a higher price for the internal market than for export, despite the fact that only a by-product of soy oil production, soy meal, is used as feed. The Morales government introduced a price range for the national market of soy beans, soy meal, and soy husk, the products used by the beef, pork, and poultry sectors. It was also regulated that the soy producers had to satisfy the demand of the internal market before exporting their produce. The smaller producers organized in ASPYMAD have been complaining that the soy assigned by the government is more expensive than the feed on the market. For the biggest producers, this entire discussion is irrelevant, since they have entered into feed production themselves and also sell feed to smaller producers.

In the corn sector, the Morales government has chosen to intervene more directly by entering into the production of corn. In 2007, the government founded EMAPA, a national agency supporting agricultural production and food security. Besides rice and wheat, corn is one of the three strategic grains in which EMAPA invests. In La Paz, I meet a proud representative of EMAPA, which is responsible for the commercialization of grains. "We support everyone," he says. "Even the big producers need support. They produce the bulk of chicken meat, which is important, and so we support them" (pers. communication, January 12, 2016). EMAPA provides seeds, fertilizers, and pesticides to producers of corn and then buys the produce in bulk. This corn goes as feed supply to the production of meat. The enthusiastic civil servant tells me that EMAPA supplies about 20–30 percent of the corn used by poultry producers.

As with soy, the process of getting access to corn is highly bureaucratic. The EMAPA representative tells me that farms that want to receive corn from the government are regularly inspected by technicians to establish the quantity of corn they need and to ensure that these farms are run according to guidelines of SENASAG. In this context, I think of ASPYMAD, which has many members who do not even have a sanitary register with SENASAG.

EMAPA is presented as a government agency that works toward *Vivir Bien*. The enthusiastic civil servant I talked to in La Paz emphasized that EMAPA particularly supports smaller producers. But only a few minutes later, he talked about the necessity also to support large-scale producers, since they contribute to food security in Bolivia with large quantities of produce. In the name of food security and opening new markets, the Morales government has been making concessions to agribusiness. Critical observers of the agricultural summit "Sembrando Bolivia" in April 2015 have voiced their concerns about the government's strong support for large-scale agriculture. At the summit, the president and the vice president of Bolivia suggested an expansion of the agricultural frontier, and agribusinesses proposed an increase in the use of genetically modified crops (Fundacion Tierra 2015b).

The inequitable distribution of feed supplies among the farmers shows that Bolivian bureaucracy privileges large-scale producers. The conditions set by the government agencies EMAPA and SENASAG can only be met with difficulty by smaller producers. Furthermore, the plan of a state-managed basic food supply has not worked out well, with EMAPA recently being involved in a corruption scandal (*En caso "granjas fantasmas"* October 29, 2017). Other government agencies supposedly founded to support small-scale farming have been involved in similar scandals, such as the *Fondo Indígena* (*Bolivia: el millonario caso* December 6, 2015).

Changes in the Chicken Meat Market

The emergence of the industrial poultry sector has also brought about changes in the distribution of chicken meat. The market system in place, based on a relationship of mutual trust between vendor and customer, now has an emerging competitor: a more formal system of distribution that provides the comfort of modern shopping and is organized and owned by the large poultry producers.

One Saturday—market day—my husband and I take the battered minibus number six that stops just outside our door.

We find a place to sit on greasy, stained seats and hear the latest news from Cochabamba shouted into our ears from the driver's sound system. As we start our journey in the rich north of the city, we pass big houses hidden behind high walls, then travel through the city center with the shops that are just opening their doors. Here the scenes get livelier: people squat on the floor to eat breakfast and vendors display their merchandise on cloths spread over the pavement. Slowly, the landscape changes with more shops in more rudimentary market stalls and more vendors on the pavement. We have reached the central market of the city, *La Cancha*. The city council estimates that this market comprises about 15,000 market stalls plus the same number of ambulant vendors. Most of the vendors are women, and most of these women have worked their way out of extreme poverty. We make our way through the dark maze of aisles between the market stalls. The smells and visual impressions are overwhelming. An elderly woman sells herbs, and next to her, a woman sells plastic toys imported from China. Finally, in the heart of the *Cancha*, a sweet smell, mixed with a slight hint of decay, tells us that we have reached the meat section. Next to beef cuts, cows' hearts, and tongues placed on rudimentary tables, the market women are selling chicken. The rosy meat, mostly entire chickens, is stacked on metal tables, and on the roof and the sides of the market stalls, the brand names and logos of the big chicken meat producers are intended to attract customers.

Neither the provenience nor the quality of the meat can be determined with certainty at these market stalls. The distribution system of chicken is as complex as the maze of the *Cancha*, but in general terms, the meat comes either from a smaller producer who sold to a distributor or from the direct distribution set up by the bigger chicken meat producers. My husband, who is from Cochabamba and thus moves expertly in the *Cancha*, says, "We won't buy our chicken here." We walk on through the labyrinth, passing the vegetable section where the smell of spicy *locoto* and *kirkiña* herbs is in the air, and arrive at the section *friales*. The *friales* look more properly like butchers' shops, usually garage-like places refined with white tiles, where the meat is offered still in the open, but at least protected with a mosquito net from flies. We buy our chicken here. We know the *caserita*, as the market women are affectionately called, and she always sells us good quality meat at a good price.

When people go to the market, they know where to buy their products—they look for their *caserita*. The *caserita* is the market woman who is trusted by the client (the vast majority of market vendors are women). Through the experience of going weekly to the market, the client knows who will sell a good quality product, have a fair price, and sell a well-measured quantity of the product. The *caserita* often offers a taste of the products she is selling, such as a piece of fruit, and she always concedes a *yapa*, a small addition to the amount sold, such as one or two additional potatoes. Failure to offer a *yapa* can lead the client not to return to the *caserita*. The *caserita* relationship sometimes goes further than that: the client and the *caserita* (who will call the client also *caserito* or *caserita*) become people who get a glimpse into each other's worlds. (Indeed, one historian told me that originally *caserito/a* was the way the *client* was addressed, with *caserito/a* being derived from *casa* [house] and therefore denominating the "house-owner." The "-*ito*" is a typically South American suffix used to express affection, such as when people would call me "Sarita" instead of "Sarah." It is assumed that, since the market relation is supposedly one of reciprocity, with time both client and vendor started to be called *caserito/a*.) I have heard clients advise their *caseritas* on how to cure illnesses (and vice versa), ask about their respective children, or kindly tell the *caserita* that she has gotten the math for the final price wrong. This

FIG. 8. Market stalls at the Cancha. Photo by Sarah Kollnig.

FIG. 9. A newly opened shop selling chicken meat provided by the
brand "Pio Rico." Photo by Sarah Kollnig.

caserita relationship provides a social bridge between people from distinctly different social strata. Apparently, this is a relationship of reciprocity, but if one looks more closely, one realizes that it is the client who has more power in this relationship. The client has the purchasing power to take advantage of the vendor's underpaid labor, and particularly the client who has a more westernized identity has the cultural superiority in the conversations with the *caserita*, where the client often ends up giving their *caserita* advice. Still, this relationship creates trust: if one is new in town and doesn't have a *caserita*, the market vendors might sell meat at any price, of bad quality, and in an ill-measured quantity. In a survey about the price for raw chicken meat, I found the highest price at a market stand whose vendor was not my *caserita*.

In the chicken meat sector, an alternative distribution system has been established over the last few years: shops directly operated by the big producers. These shops are not run by a *caserita*, but by an employee of the brand owner, with the brand advertised in bright colors and supported by TV, radio, and print marketing campaigns. In these shops, the price is publicly visible at the entrance; the customer receives a bill; and the meat is refrigerated. People trust that these brands deliver superior quality as well as a fair price and weight. The majority of people I talked with in a middle-class neighborhood prefer to buy chicken of a particular brand rather than no-name chicken meat. Advice given to me as a foreigner is to buy the local chicken brand. At the market, the *caseritas* sell chicken meat of certain brands as well as no-name chicken meat, but their market stalls are painted with ads of the larger chicken meat producers to attract clients.

This tendency has also changed the social relationship between wholesale suppliers and vendors. The brands' stores employ vendors, while the market vendors are economically independent from their suppliers. The market vendors are involved in socially embedded economic relationships, referred to as *compadrazgo*. This relationship is forged by naming a fellow vendor or supplier as the godfather of one of their children and also sponsoring each other's celebrations, such as paying for the band in a wedding (for a classical analysis of these relationships see Mintz and Wolf 1950). In the weeks before the carnival celebrations, there is the big fiesta sponsored by *compadres* and *comadres*, which traditionally started in the markets as a celebration for all market vendors and suppliers.

The downside of these close-knit social ties at the market is that it has made it difficult for new vendors to enter the market. The members of ASPYMAD, the small chicken producers' association, mention at their meetings that they would like to become more independent from intermediaries and sell their produce directly to customers. But they are afraid of the intermediaries who protect their *compadres* and *comadres* by destroying any competition. As a member of ASPYMAD put it, "The intermediaries own the *Cancha*" (pers. communication, October 6, 2015).

The *caseritas* selling in the markets are iconic figures in Bolivia and in all Andean countries (Weismantel 2001). Indeed, the image of the market woman in her traditional clothes, particularly the many-layered felted *pollera* skirt and the high hat, sitting behind a mountain of fresh fruit, has become a mythical and touristic image. For tourists and national elites alike, the market woman represents the essence of an indigenous culture and links to the image of indigeneity presented in the government discourse of *Vivir Bien*. In leaflets and on webpages, there are many images of people in colorful traditional clothes, working the land or selling at the market. In Bolivia and many other places, indigeneity has always been linked to uncleanliness. Talking to civil servants about the condition of *La Cancha* and other markets, I hear that the market vendors are inherently incapable of keeping the markets clean. As Mary Weismantel notes, the unhygienic circumstances of the market are normalized by the authorities. The markets, so many civil servants argue, are in bad shape because of the nature of the market women and not because of political neglect (Weismantel 2001). With this reasoning, the authorities create arguments for consumers to prefer supermarkets or, in the case of chicken, modern *agencias*, to markets, and indirectly support the agenda of the big players in the food sector to push the small vendors out of business.

But meeting this goal is easier said than done. Markets such as *La Cancha* are controlled by powerful intermediaries, called *comerciantes*, who have worked hard to make their way to the top. The *comerciantes* have emerged from the popular strata and often have indigenous roots; they are newcomers to the cities and are starting to claim their part of the urban territory and commerce (Tassi et al., 2013). An account of this merchant society goes beyond the scope of this chapter, but what is important at this point is that the Morales government has discursively supported yet, in practice, hindered the development of this sector. Discursively, the government supports alternative, communitarian economic activities. In practice, the *comerciantes* are marginalized for not conforming to the rules of mainstream economic activities.

Toward the Good Life?

Traveling from the city of Oruro toward the city of La Paz, a huge billboard greets the traveler, announcing that several hundred million dollars have been invested by the government in a four-lane highway between the two cities. The billboard shows Evo Morales, wearing a white hardhat, decisively pointing with his hand over the land, as if he were building the road himself in that moment. Below the picture there are a few words: *Obras para Vivir Bien* (Construction projects for *Vivir Bien*). To me, this billboard sums up the tensions inherent in the government discourse of *Vivir Bien*. In words, Evo Morales preaches respect for Mother Earth. Yet in deeds, he implements highway projects, supports hydroelectric dams, and promotes industrialization of food production that disadvantages small-scale producers and market vendors of chicken meat.

The "cracks" within the official discourse of *Vivir Bien* make it clear that the Morales government is aiming at a further industrialization of the agricultural sector, supporting the agenda of the nation's elites. As my analysis of data and interviews provided by the diversity of actors in the poultry sector shows, long-standing political support has paved the way for the centralization of this sector.

Official acts—from municipal policies against backyard chicken rearing to government lending strategies—have successfully undermined the small-scale, subsistence rearing of chickens. In today's Bolivia, small-scale farmers are at risk of food insecurity (Castañón Ballivián 2014), and city dwellers have lost their ability to provide for themselves. Small market vendors are facing strong competition from modern sales outlets, driven by the centralized system of poultry production as well as racist prejudices against market women. The chicken farms that have survived centralization base their profitability on the exploitation of workers. It was not possible for me to access the facilities for slaughtering and processing chicken meat, but international evidence (Striffler 2005; OXFAM 2016) shows that working conditions are dire throughout the poultry processing chain. The industrial production and processing of chicken meat also come with severe negative impacts on animal health and the environment.

To the outside observer, the industrialization of the agricultural sector and the ideal of *Vivir Bien* might contradict each other. But to the Morales government, this is apparently not a contradictory situation, but in line with its interpretation of development. Bolivia's political economy has been dependent on the extraction of natural resources since colonial times. The model of development that continues to reign in Bolivia is *extractivist,* entailing a profit-oriented extraction of natural resources. Eduardo Gudynas calls the leftist governments of Bolivia, Ecuador, and Venezuela the "Brown Left" (Gudynas 2017). These governments have been doing away with environmental restrictions on the exploitation of natural resources and are increasingly enmeshing themselves in contradictions with their discourse of *Vivir Bien.* As Gudynas formulates it, "In the Andes, on some days plans for *Buen Vivir* are made, while on other days corporations, lately Chinese ones, are welcomed in order to deepen extractivism" (Gudynas 2017).

In political acts and discursively, extractivist development has been portrayed as the golden path to prosperity for Bolivia (Kaijser 2014). The Morales government sees state-led resource extraction and industrialization as the road to national sovereignty (Ormachea Saavedra 2009). In the agricultural sector, gaining sovereignty for the Morales government has meant further industrialization as well as state control in the supply of basic cereals (which functions alongside a vast black market).

The Morales administration argues that extractivist development will benefit the population through the redistribution of the revenues from nationalized industries (Ranta 2016). Lalander (2017) claims that the current Bolivian government had to make a trade-off between environmental protection and social redistribution, and that it chose the latter over the former. Government representatives interviewed by Lalander emphasize that *Vivir Bien* cannot mean environmental protection alone and that socio-economic development also has to be achieved. As Alexandra Moreira,

Minister of the Environment, said, "Defending *Vivir Bien* does not mean that we will remain backwards, neither technologically, nor in terms of development, nor as humans" (quoted in Lalander 2017, 76). Very similar ideas were articulated in the interviews with Bolivian government officials conducted by Ranta in 2014. This approach to social redistribution portrays particularly the indigenous population as passive recipients of state benefits rather than as revolutionary subjects (Ranta 2016). In material terms, economic redistribution has not taken place, and the lion's share of profits still goes to international actors or national elites (Arze Vargas 2016).

Within this developmentalist paradigm of the Bolivian government, *Vivir Bien* has become a smokescreen for the continuation of extractivism and industrialization. Following Burman (2017), this interpretation of *Vivir Bien* is possible based on differences that run as deep as ontology: in the process of translating *Vivir Bien* from indigenous practices to a mainstream discourse, it has become westernized, reinterpreted under a modern ontology that separates the social and the natural. Only through such an interpretation, the destruction of the natural environment as well as the continuation of social injustices have become possible under the guise of *Vivir Bien*. The positioning of the Bolivian government as defending the rights of indigenous peoples and Mother Nature has become oriented toward the international realm, such as climate change negotiations (Kaijser 2014), while at home, business as usual continues.

The contradictions emerging between the discourse of *Vivir Bien* and state practice have been criticized by Bolivian scholars and nongovernmental organizations (*Silvia Rivera: el "Vivir Bien"* September 29, 2015; Arze Vargas 2016; Fundación Tierra 2015; for international critique see Gudynas 2017). Inconsistencies between discourse and practice, as well as corruption scandals, have split the indigenous and workers' social movements—the stronghold of the Morales government—into a fraction supporting the government and a more critical group. The government has declared that it still has the broad support of the people and is preparing for a fourth run of Morales for presidency. Before the next presidential elections in Bolivia in 2019, the situation may become turbulent. And in times of turbulence, the resilience of a food system is tested. Already now, the Morales government is unable to keep up the promised state support for small-scale agriculture and basic food supply. Subsistence activities such as raising backyard chickens have been undermined by state policies and replaced by supply from a handful of corporations. The case of chicken meat shows that the industrialization of Bolivian agriculture has created dependencies that are compromising the ability of the Bolivian people to support themselves in times of crisis.

References

ADA Cochabamba. 2014. *40 Años Asociación de Avicultores de Cochabamba. Memoria Institucional.* Cochabamba: ADA Cochabamba.

———. 2015. *Boletín Estadístico Anual. Gestion 2014.* Cochabamba: ADA Cochabamba. March.

Albarracín Deker, Jorge. 2015. *Estrategias y Planes de Desarrollo Agropecuario en Bolivia. La Construcción de la Ruta del Desarrollo Sectorial (1942–2013).* La Paz: CIDES-UMSA / Plural.

Alkon, Alison Hope, and Julian Agyeman. 2011. *Cultivating Food Justice. Race, Class, and Sustainability.* Cambridge MA: MIT Press.

Arze Vargas, Carlos. 2016. *Una década de gobierno. Construyendo el Vivir Bien o capialismo salvaje?* La Paz: CEDLA, February 2016. http://cedla.org/blog/grupopoliticafiscal/wp-content/uploads/2016/04/revista_gpfd_17_una_decada_de_gobierno.pdf.

BBC Mundo. 2015. "Bolivia: el Millonario Caso de Corrupción que Involucra a Exministros, Parlamentarios y Dirigentes del Partido de Evo Morales." December 6. http://www.bbc.com/mundo/noticias/2015/12/151205_millonario_escandalo_corrupcion_partido_evo_morales_bm.

Burman, Anders. 2017. "La Ontología Política del Vivir Bien." In *Vivir bien: Reciprocidad y Ecología en los Andes,* edited by K. D. Munter, J. Micheaux, and G. Powels, 155–73. La Paz: Plural.

Castañon Ballivián, Enrique. 2014. *Two Sides of the Same Coin: Agriculture and Food Security in Bolivia*. La Paz: Fundación Tierra.

CEPLAG (Centro de Planificación y Gestión). 2013. *Desarrollo Local: Cochabamba y sus Unidades Territoriales de Planificación*. Cochabamba: CEPLAG.

Coe, Sophie D. 1994. *America's First Cuisines*. Austin: University of Texas Press.

Constitución Política del Estado. 2009. http://bolivia.infoleyes.com/shownorm .php?id=469.

"Desde 2006, El Consumo de Cinco Alimentos Creció en Promedio 46%." 2014. *La Razón*, October 29. http://www.la-razon.com/economia/consumo -alimentos-crecio-promedio_0_1988801115.html.

Duncan, I. 2011. "Animal Welfare Issues in the Poultry Industry: Is There a Lesson to Be Learned?" *Journal of Applied Animal Welfare Science* 4, no. 3: 207–21.

"En Caso 'Granjas Fantasmas,' Juez Encarcela a Extecnico de Emapa por Corrupción." 2017. *Pagina Siete*, October 29. http://www.paginasiete.bo /seguridad/2017/10/29/caso-granjas-fantamas-juez-encarcela-extecnico -emapa-corrupcion-157557.html.

European Commission. 2000. *The Welfare of Chickens Kept for Meat Production (Broilers). Report of the Scientific Committee on Animal Health and Animal Welfare*. http://ec.europa.eu/food/animals/docs/aw_arch_2005_broilers _scientific_opinion_en.pdf.

———. 2005. *Ban on Antibiotics as Growth Promoters in Animal Feed Enters into effect*. http://europa.eu/rapid/press-release_IP-05-1687_en.htm.

Food and Drug Administration. 2012. *Guidance for Industry. The Judicious Use of Medically Important Antimicrobial Drugs in Food-Producing Animals*. http://www .fda.gov/downloads/AnimalVeterinary/GuidanceComplianceEnforcement /GuidanceforIndustry/UCM216936.pdf.

Fundación Tierra. 2015a. *Apuntes Críticos para la Agenda Agropecuaria. Una Breve Evaluación de sus Implicaciones Elaborada por la Fundación Tierra*. La Paz: Fundación Tierra. http://www.ftierra.org/index.php?option=com _mtree&task=att_download&link_id=133&cf_id=52.

———. 2015b. *Los Acuerdos de la Cumbre Agropecuaria se Convierten en Tres Decretos y Seis Proyectos de Ley*. La Paz: Fundación Tierra. http://www.ftierra.org /index.php/transformaciones-agrarias-y-rurales/558-los-acuerdos-de-la -cumbre-agropecuaria-se-convierten-en-tres-decretos-y-seis-proyectos-de-ley.

Gerber, P., C. Opio, and H. Steinfeld. 2007. *Poultry Production and the Environment: A Review*. http://www.fao.org/ag/againfo/home/events /bangkok2007/docs/part2/2_2.pdf.

"Gobierno Califica de 'grosero' Ofrecimiento de Bill Gates de Regalar Gallinas a Bolivia." 2016. *Los Tiempos*, June 15. http://www.lostiempos.com /actualidad/economia/20160615/gobierno-califica-grosero-ofrecimiento -bill-gates-regalar-gallinas.

Goetting, V., K. A. Lee, and L. A. Tell. 2011. "Pharmacokinetics of Veterinary Drugs in Laying Hens and Residues in Eggs: a Review of the Literature." *Journal of Veterinary Pharmacology and Therapeutics* 34, no. 6: 521–26.

Gudynas, Eduardo. 2011. "Buen Vivir: Today's Tomorrow." *Development* 54, no. 4: 441–47.

———. 2017. "La Izquierda Marrón." *America Latina en Movimiento*, March 2. http://www.alainet.org/es/active/53106.

Honorable Concejo Municipal. 1986. *Ordenanza Municipal No. 88/86.* Cochabamba: Honorable Concejo Municipal.

International Poultry Council. n.d. "Chicken Meat Per Capita Consumption for Top Chicken Meat Producing Countries." http://www.internationalpoultrycouncil.org/industry/industry.cfm.

Kaijser, Anna. 2014. *Who is Marching for Pachamama? An Intersectional Analysis of Environmental Struggles in Bolivia under the Government of Evo Morales.* Lund: Lund University Publications.

Lalander, Rickard. 2017. "Indigeneidad, Descolonización y la Paradoja del Desarrollo Extractivista en el Estado Plurinacional de Bolivia." *Revista Chilena de Derecho y Ciencia Política* 8, no. 1: 49–83.

Ley No. 144. 2011. *Ley de la Revolución Productiva Comunitaria Agropecuaria.* http://www.ftierra.org/index.php/recursos-naturales/111-ley-n-144-de-la-revolucion-productiva-comunitaria-agropecuaria.

Ley No. 300. 2012. *Ley Marco de la Madre Tierra y Desarrollo Integral para Vivir Bien.* http://www.ftierra.org/index.php/recursos-naturales/110-ley-n-300-marco-de-la-madre-tierra-y-desarrollo-integral-para-vivir-bien.

"Maíz Transgénico Afectaría Soberanía Alimentaria." 2015. *La Patria*, April 25. http://www.lapatriaenlinea.com/?t=maiz-transgenico-afectaria-soberania-alimentaria&nota=218259.

Ministry of Rural Development and Land. 2015. *Existencia Total de Aves Parrilleros Según Departamentos.* La Paz: Instituto Nacional de Estadística.

Mintz, S. W. and E. R. Wolf. 1950. "An Analysis of Ritual Co-Parenthood (compadrazgo)." *Southwestern Journal of Anthropology* 6, no. 4: 341–68.

Ormachea Saavedra, Enrique. 2007. *Revolución Agraria o Consolidación de la Via Terrateniente? El Gobierno del Mas y las Políticas de Tierras.* La Paz: CEDLA.

———. 2009. *Soberanía y Seguridad Alimentaria en Bolivia: Politicas y Estado de la Situación.* La Paz: CEDLA. http://www.cedla.org/content/1350.

Ortiz, A. I. 2012. *Los Maices en la Seguridad Alimentaria en Bolivia.* Santa Cruz: CIPCA. http://www.cipca.org.bo/images/cuadernos/documentos/los-maices_cipca.pdf.

OXFAM America. 2016. *No relief. Denial of Bathroom Breaks in the Poultry Industry.* Boston MA: OXFAM.

Pérez Luna, Mamerto. 2007. *No todo Grano Que Brilla es Oro. Un Análisis de la Soya en Bolivia.* La Paz: CEDLA.

Ranta, Eija M. 2014. *In the Name of Vivir Bien. Indigeneity, State Formation, and Politics in Evo Morales' Bolivia.* Helsinki: Unigrafia.

———. 2016. "Toward a Decolonial Alternative to Development? The Emergence and Shortcomings of *Vivir Bien* as State Policy in Bolivia in the Era of Globalization." *Globalizations* 13, no. 4: 425–39.

"Silvia Rivera: el "Vivir bien," Palabra Hueca que no se Cumple para Nada." 2015. *Pagina Siete,* September 29, 2015. http://www.paginasiete.bo/2015/9/29/silvia-rivera-vivir-bien-palabra-hueca-cumple-para-nada-71718.html.

Striffler, Stephen. 2005. *Chicken: The Dangerous Transformation of America's Favorite Food.* New Haven CT: Yale University Press.

Tassi, Nico, Carmen Medeiros, Antonio Rodríguez-Carmona, and Giovana Ferrufino. 2013. *"Hacer Plata sin Plata," El Desborde de los Comerciantes Populares en Bolivia.* La Paz: PIEB.

Vice presidencia del Estado Plurinacional de Bolivia. 2015. *El Vicepresidente Aaseguró que los Acuerdos de la Cumbre Agropecuaria son Mandatos para el Gobierno.* April 22. http://www.vicepresidencia.gob.bo/El-vicepresidente-aseguro-que-los.

Weismantel, Mary. 2001. *Cholas and Pishtacos, Stories of Race and Sex in the Andes.* Chicago: University of Chicago Press.

4

Automating Agriculture

Precision Technologies, Agbots, and the Fourth Industrial Revolution

JANE W. GIBSON

Food production, one of the world's oldest and most important economic activities, has evolved from small bands of
foragers seeking stands of wild grains, to mass production
of genetically modified monocultures destined for global
markets and produced with chemicals, computers, and
satellite-guided, auto-steered machines. Many farmers call
this progress. Yet farmers simultaneously acknowledge that
the benefits of this dramatic intensification of production
and expansion of scale made possible by modern industrial
farming methods and machines have come with costs to ecosystems and biodiversity, farmers' and consumers' health,
and rural communities. The search for mitigation of such
technologically induced problems focuses, both predict-
ably and ironically, on more new technologies.

The application of digital technologies to agriculture
is the latest innovation in the long history of agricultural
automation. These technologies have the potential to fin-
ish what the agricultural and industrial revolutions began:
the substitution of machines for human labor and the production of food, fiber, and fuel on "smart farms." Such possibilities suggest the importance of societal discussion and
thoughtful debate that considers not only what is to be
gained but what could be lost.

In this chapter, I explore the social implications of the

automation of agriculture with a focus on digital technologies as illustrated by two related and sometimes overlapping cases: precision agriculture and robots, or "agbots." I begin with a brief history of agricultural automation to introduce what has been labeled the Fourth Industrial Revolution (Schwab 2015). Next, I define, offer examples, and present the case for digital agriculture advanced by technology producers and industry analysts. Farmers, who are the market and potential users of precision and robotic technologies, then speak to their own interests and concerns about these technological innovations. Drawing from these data and the work of various social scientists, I offer a discussion of the implications for farmers' skills and knowledge, relationships with agroecosystems, best practices, farmer identities, and society. I conclude with speculation about the future of industrial agriculture, taking into account farmers' sense of the inevitability of technological change as well as resistance to it. I consider the tradeoffs between farmers who know land and soil, and machines that may lead us to an industrial farm sector staffed by IT experts instead of farmers.

Methods

This project grows out of research funded by the National Science Foundation's Experimental Program to Stimulate Competitive Research (EPSCOR) carried out from 2011–2014 in the state of Kansas. To consider the implications of the digital revolution on America's farms, I have drawn from interviews in the EPSCOR project conducted with 151 Kansas farmers of whom we asked their views of "proper" farming and the roles of technology and technological innovations. These interviews were transcribed and queried using NVivo software. Extending that work into the present, I interviewed equipment dealer representatives; read technology websites, newsletters, and other publications; watched YouTube videos; joined online robotic research groups and farmer organizations; attended webinars; and read farmer and techie blogs. Though contributors to online sites may publish their own names, names are withheld in this chapter following the conventions of confidentiality and informed consent. Some of what farmers have to say reports their direct experience with sophisticated technologies, and some is speculative as farmers find themselves swept along in a fast-moving, competitive, and increasingly sophisticated technological environment.

From Automation to the Fourth Industrial Revolution

Automation is the method, technology, or system of controlling a process that, whether or not by design, minimizes human intervention. Our ancestors imagined automation at least three millennia ago and began to employ it in both playful and serious ways. As early as 2200 BP, the Chinese invented a multitube seed drill, a tool that allowed planting in evenly spaced rows (Temple 1991). The most significant on-farm inventions in the West began to appear in the eighteenth century. Among others, in 1767, Richard Arkwright invented the first fully automated, water-powered spinning mill (Liu 1994); James Watt patented the first steam engine in 1769 (Liu 1994); and, in 1785, Oliver Evans developed the first completely automated process with an automatic flour mill (Jacobson and Roueek 1959, 8).

These and other technologies, growing out of the long history of automation and mechanization, mark the beginning of the Industrial Revolution and the second historical discontinuity after the Neolithic gave rise to agriculture itself. The Industrial Revolution restructured society by both contributing and responding to labor shortages in rural areas while stimulating increased production by a growing urban work force. It enabled economic specialization, increased consumption of mass-produced and more affordable products, and deepened class distinctions (Wyatt

2003, 1–2). On the farm, mechanization and automation also improved production efficiencies, transformed farming practices, and changed farmer skills and identity. As metabolic energy was replaced by coal, steam, gas, and electricity, new machines and the benefits of economies of scale drove land consolidation and the restructuring of agriculture, processes that continue today.

Despite the long history of automation, farm mechanization is a relatively recent phenomenon because farmers have had to be conservative when it comes to changing what they do and how they do it. Farmers have little control over the conditions of production—they cannot control the weather, input costs, lending rates, or the price they can expect for their products. Much of farmers' time, energy, and money, unsurprisingly, goes into exercising control where they can to minimize risk. Indeed, farmers are so committed to "what works" that plow technology changed very little in the two thousand years from the time of the Roman Empire to about the middle of the nineteenth century. In 1859, when steam energy was first harnessed to the plow and threatened to replace draft animals, Abraham Lincoln gave a speech to the Wisconsin State Agricultural Society that reflected his own skepticism about its potential for success: "It is not enough that a machine operated by steam will really plow. To be successful, it must, all things considered, plow better than can be done by animal power. It must do all the work as well, and cheaper, or more rapidly, so as to get through more perfectly in season; or in some way afford an advantage over plowing with animals, else it is no success" (Basler 1953).

Lincoln never farmed, yet he understood that farmers' desires for such machines grew out of their wish to produce more per acre. Good harvests defined success and could translate into higher incomes. No less important was the drive to develop new machinery by manufacturers whose potential market in the nineteenth century constituted the country's largest occupational group. No machine has made a greater difference on the world's farms and for equipment developers than the tractor. The first tractor powered by an internal combustion engine appeared in 1903, and Henry Ford's assembly line began mass production in 1917. Still, adoption proceeded slowly; it wasn't until the middle of the twentieth century that even half of U.S. farmers owned a tractor.

Tractors made other machines possible, impelling development in the twentieth century of a wide range of implements that mechanized every step of production, from tillage to planting and harvesting. Second only to tractors were harvesters that Massey Harris, in 1938, made self-propelled and capable of combining both cutting and threshing in a single operation, resulting in their common name, combines. Such mechanical advances laid a strong foundation for further automation that increased "efficiency, reliability, and precision, reducing the need of human intervention" (Edan et al. 2009, 1096).

Industrial farmers use many kinds of automated machines: tractors, trucks, plows, drills, sprayers, combines, pumps, and more. In general, automation relies on control systems of various types. Modern control of farm machines incorporates binary code and uses electronics for monitoring and control, both features of the first automatic digital computer invented in 1939 at Iowa State College (Campbell-Kelly and Aspray 1996, 84). Conversion to digital control systems spread rapidly in the 1970s as hardware costs began to fall (Rifkin 1995), giving rise to what some have labeled, controversially, the Fourth Industrial Revolution.

Precision Agriculture and Agbots

The historic synergy between agricultural and industrial revolutions has brought the Fourth Industrial Revolution to

American farms. This technological, economic, and social shift began in the middle of the twentieth century, arising from a widespread "digital revolution" that transformed industries ranging from the print media to medicine. Fusing technologies "that blur the lines between the physical, digital, and biological spheres," the Fourth Industrial Revolution is distinguished by "its velocity, scope, and systems impact." Klaus Schwab, founder and executive chairman of the World Economic Forum writes, "The speed of current breakthroughs has no historical precedent. When compared with previous industrial revolutions, the Fourth is evolving at an exponential rather than a linear pace [and] is disrupting almost every industry in every country. And the breadth and depth of these changes herald the transformation of entire systems of production, management, and governance" (Schwab 2015).

Significant technological developments have occurred in artificial intelligence, the Internet of Things, nanotechnology, 3-D printing, autonomous vehicles, energy storage, and quantum computing. Industrial agriculture is one sector targeted by industry for this revolution, bringing together several of these breakthroughs in a technology-driven production method called "precision agriculture," and also in the form of agricultural robots, sometimes called "agbots." Digital technologies applied to automation in agriculture create the possibility of a future of "smart farms" made up of multiple technologies, integrated into a system operated by a central digital controller: a computerized command center. Such agricultural ambitions present unique challenges, some of which already have been solved while others are on developers' drawing boards.

The Case for Precision Agriculture

Marketers of precision agriculture technologies say these systems make farmers smarter. Put simply, "precision ag"

FIG. 10. AGCO's vision of a smart farm, displayed at the 2016 Agbot
Challenge. Photo by Jane Gibson.

is field micromanagement, sometimes called satellite farming or site-specific agriculture (Dejoia and Duncan 2015). These two concepts are not in conflict, though one suggests farming from outer space and the other farming the soil beneath one's feet. The basic principle is that gathering different kinds of data to identify the variability of field conditions allows growers to respond appropriately to that variation when planting, fertilizing, watering, applying chemicals, and harvesting crops. On the large industrial farms that practice precision ag in the United States, both satellites and soil are part of the same integrated production process, as information is captured on the ground, or from above it, and transmitted as digital data via satellite to another ground-based, digital technology. At the high-tech end of the spectrum, this blurb from an IBM website shows how precision ag is technologically defined:

> With precision agriculture, control centers collect and process data in real time to help farmers make the best decisions with regard to planting, fertilizing and harvesting crops. Sensors placed throughout the fields are used to measure temperature and humidity of the soil and surrounding air. In addition, pictures of fields are taken using satellite imagery and robotic drones. The images over time show crop maturity and when coupled with predictive weather modeling showing pinpoint conditions 48 hours in advance, IBM Research is able to build models and simulations that can predict future conditions and help farmers make proactive decisions. (IBM n.d.)

According to the USDA, "access to detailed, within-field information can decrease input costs and increase yields" (Schimmelpfennig 2016). Both costs and yields depend on particular circumstances, however, because in the redistribution of inputs over variable soil conditions, averages may stay the same. And because productivity depends on multiple factors, precise applications of fertilizers, for example, may not be enough to increase yields even though costs may be reduced (Phillips 2016). From 2006 to 2014, the cost of corn seed per acre increased by 164 percent (Schnitkey 2015). Fertilizer costs were even higher. The total costs of seed, fertilizer, and chemicals as a portion of farm revenue increased from 32 percent between 1990 and 2006 to 48 percent in 2016 (Schnitkey and Sellars 2016). To continue farming, growers have no choice but to minimize costs everywhere they can because costs rise, prices vary with the volatile global market, and profits tend to fall.

One area in which farmers can be assured of cost savings is in the use of GPS guidance systems. Sam Allen, CEO of Deere & Co., claims that using his company's GPS system with autosteer, a farmer using a 60-foot boom can reduce the overlap in planting seed and applying fertilizer and chemical applications from six feet to two inches (CNN Money 2013). These guidance systems also allow farmers to work after dark or in a fog. Not surprisingly, GPS guidance, introduced in the 1980s, is the fastest growing innovation in the agricultural equipment industry (Edan et al. 2009, 1096), but soil mapping and variable-rate technologies all show increased adoption for nearly all the major grain crops. The International Plant Nutrition Institute (Phillips 2016) documented a significant jump in adoption of some precision ag technologies in only a decade. From 4 percent in 2005, 52 percent of U.S. farmers were using GPS guidance systems by 2015. From 14 percent in 2005, 43 percent used GPS-derived yield monitors ten years later. IPNI projects significant increases by 2018 in these technologies as well as in GPS-enabled sprayers and planters. With marketing focused on productivity and efficiency, the precision farming market is expected to grow from $3.2 billion in 2015 to $7.87 billion by 2022, more than double in six years with a compounded annual growth rate of 13.47 percent (marketsandmarkets

.com 2018). AgGateway, AgEagle, Aglytix, Agribotix, and other companies with longer histories and better name recognition—IBM, Monsanto, John Deere, and DuPont, for example—are dedicating money and time to development of precision agricultural technologies.

GPS guidance, mapping, variable-rate application technologies, sensors, and other precision technologies generate efficiencies that make them very attractive to farmers. To this list, developers of predictive analytic programs claim to add highly accurate weather forecasts that make it possible to avoid heavy rain that would otherwise wash pesticide and nutrient contaminants off the farm and into waterways. In this way, conservation of farmers' resources can be seen to benefit both the farm business and the environment.

In general, efficiencies can arise from the better fit between the variable and specific needs of a crop and the inputs the farmer applies, and from greater accuracy in applying those inputs. To get this better fit, precision technologies can generate data on topography, soil nutrients, moisture, pH, tilth, root-zone capacity, soil compaction, yield variability, and other characteristics that can be mapped, measured, and analyzed for optimal input prescriptions to improve yields for particular areas of a farm and reduce input costs by minimizing waste. As each innovation enters the market, it is announced with claims about efficiencies, profits, productivity, the environment, and the need to feed the world's growing population.

The Case for Agbots

Precision agriculture systems have begun to incorporate robots that are designed for precision work. A number of robotic technologies are already available commercially while others are in various stages of development. Robotics is a branch of industrial automation that emerged shortly after World War II in response to the perceived need for a quicker way to produce more industrial and consumer goods (Kurfess 2005). Since this beginning, engineers have incorporated digital logic, servos, and solid-state electronics into faster robots now integrated into many industries, including agriculture. As reported by CBS News on July 14, 2013:

> Researchers are now designing robots for these most delicate crops by integrating advanced sensors, powerful computing, electronics, computer vision, robotic hardware and algorithms, as well as networking and high precision GPS localization technologies. . . . Though they cost millions of dollars, farmers say, the robots are worth the investment: they could provide relief from recent labor shortages, lessen the unknowns of immigration reform, even reduce costs, increase quality, and yield a more consistent product. "There aren't enough workers to take the available jobs, so the robots can come and alleviate some of that problem," said Ron Yokota, a farming operations manager at Tanimura & Antle, the fresh produce company that hired the Lettuce Bot.

Taylor Farms of Salinas, California, has addressed its labor shortages with adoption of an automated romaine harvester that cuts five lettuce heads at once using a water knife. The harvester brings in more lettuce faster and with a dramatically reduced human crew whose job is to ride on the harvester, inspect lettuces, and prepare them for shipping (Taylor Farms n.d.).

In the past, fruits and vegetables destined for the fresh food market have resisted mechanical harvest technologies partly because growers could hire the readily available army of low-wage migrant workers to do the job, farmworker unions and advocates lobbied against the job displacement such technologies would mean, and because of the crops' sensitivity to bruising and other damage that machine technologies had yet to master. In the region of

California known as "America's Salad Bowl," large-scale producers, who must find ways to deal with the consequences of Washington's anti-immigration policies and still join the global competition, are looking to the robotics industry for help (Martin 2017, 21).

As noted above, tractors and combines with "autosteer," a self-driving system that relies on GPS and satellites for guidance, are robotic systems that have become standard equipment for most American farmers. Robotic milking machines have been available commercially since the early 1990s. Worldwide, farmers are the largest market for unmanned aerial vehicles (UAVs) though, in the United States, regulation of UAVs, or drones, for commercial use may have slowed their adoption in agriculture. With changes to FAA regulations, especially regarding altitude limits and line-of-sight requirements, U.S. farmers will be able to use UAVs as they do in countries such as Japan and South Korea: to identify weed, disease, and pest infestations; to deliver chemicals and seed to fields; and for precision ag field mapping. Prices of drones vary but range from $1,500 to over $25,000 (Patel 2016).

Among other interesting agbots on the market is Bosch's "Bonirob," a robot advertised in 2015 for its ability to eliminate weeds without pesticides, relying instead on the precision application of microwaves. In 2017, the robotic platform, operated remotely or independently, promised more than weed control: with "four independently steerable drive wheels and the ability to adjust track width," it can transport various application modules to the field and perform multiple functions including field testing for things like soil compaction (Bosch n.d.).

In addition to what private companies already sell and have in the development pipeline, the USDA has funded a three-year study at the University of California to develop "Robot-Assisted Precision Irrigation and Diagnostics," a system to deliver the right amount of water plant by plant (Anderson 2016). Farmers are already using infrared sensing and drones to determine which plants have received too much or too little water. In a world where it is estimated that 85 percent of fresh water is used for irrigation, and groundwater supplies are in trouble, one might argue that such conservation innovations cannot come too soon.

Perhaps in grim anticipation of a time when biological pollinator populations will be insufficient for commercial crops such as almonds and blueberries, the Wyss Institute of the Harvard School of Engineering and Applied Sciences has been developing insect-scaled microrobots called RoboBees. The goal of the team is to create a swarm of tiny robots that will be able to cooperate and perform the agricultural service that biological bees do (Ma et al. 2013).

Others engaged in agbot research and development have responded to the "AgBot Challenge," a competition held on Gerrish Farms in Rockville, Indiana, in May 2016, 2017, and again in 2018. Steve Gerrish is a farmer and entrepreneur who has been working with investors to help develop and commercialize new technologies, most recently focused on agriculture. Gerrish and his team developed a key element for the success of robotics and, in the future, smart farms. This is BATS or Broadband Antenna Tracking System. "BATS allows all high bandwidth, high-speed links on a private network. It's completely local to you. We're now applying that innovation to agricultural problems" (Bedord 2016). BATS will assure observation and intervention in the operation of autonomous machines, something operators cannot do with small signals such as those that stream data on cell phones. Yielding some insight into the complexity of robotic technologies and their integration with other complex systems, the AgBot challenge allowed Gerrish to field-test the complicated BATS system on experimental robotic equipment while moving both toward commercial applications in agriculture.

Fig. 11. 2016 Agbot Challenge contender designed to plant two seed varieties in response to variable soil conditions. Photo by Jane Gibson.

The first AgBot Challenge elicited proposals from over six hundred land grant colleges and universities and from eighty robotics groups. Judges selected eleven teams of engineers from universities, private company developers, high schools, and other institutions to compete for $100,000 in prize money. In May 2016, four winning teams shared the money for inventions that could "autonomously load seed, then plant and fertilize a two-acre parcel." The first-place winners of the competition, members of an engineering team from the University of Regina, designed software to control a robotic planter that looks like an unmanned tractor with dual seed hoppers.

The 2017 AgBot Challenge invited competitors to focus on seeding again, as well as weed-and-feed technologies. Seeding entrants were to develop a robot that would "autonomously plant two or four 1,000-ft rows of corn at a time and autonomously turn at each end"; be able to change seed variety and seed population; "stream real-time video from both the front and rear" of the agbot; and "have the ability to autonomously dock and load two varieties of seed and starter fertilizer, while weighing the seed and fertilizer and communicating in stream" (AgBot Challenge 2017a). Weed & Feed competitors were challenged to produce a robot that could autonomously maneuver and turn at the end of 1,000-ft. rows, autonomously observe and identify three common weeds within and between crop rows, "arrange for weed to die either chemically or mechanically" as the AgBot moved through the field, and provide real-time visualization of fertilizing and treating plants to a base station (AgBot Challenge 2017b).

Sponsorship of the two AgBot Challenges reveals the strong corporate interest in agricultural applications of robotics. On the list are Yamaha, Monsanto, John Deere, Precision Planting, Blue River Technology, Sumitomo Chemical, Co-Alliance, Barnes & Thornburg LLP, AGCO, The Climate Corporation, Family Farms Group, Purdue Foundry, Purdue Agriculture, and Tom Farms. These complex and expensive technologies promise to increase efficiencies and yields for the world's growing populations, address labor shortages, and reduce production costs. To meet these high expectations, they will also have to be able to deal with the realities of crop production.

Unlike other industry applications, agricultural technologies have to be able to respond to highly variable seasonal and environmental conditions between farms and within fields. Furthermore, technologies have to solve particularly challenging problems such as continuously changing weather and soil conditions; variability in produce size, shape, delicacy, and location; and the presence of dust, dirt, and humidity (Edan et al. 2009, 1095-6). This means that either the precision requirements in automated agricultural systems will have to be lower than in controlled industrial settings, or the level of machine sophistication will have to be much higher. Artificial intelligence (AI) and "deep learning" may offer solutions.

Deep learning leads machine-learning research and product development that steers artificial intelligence (AI) and biomimicry of human intelligence toward autonomous, self-teaching systems that use neural networks to solve problems (Marr 2016). Deep learning systems, like humans, produce conclusions from analysis of any kind of data: sound, images, speech, and writing. The computing construct is "based loosely on the architecture of the human brain . . . When exposed to vast amounts of data, deep learning systems develop basic pattern recognition, enabling algorithms to train themselves to perform tasks and adapt to new data" (Tractica 2017). Blue River Technology, for example, is building "See & Spray" machines they claim will reduce the use of herbicides for weed control and keep chemicals off crops and soil. "Machine learning decides how to treat each individual plant. And robotics technology enables the smart machine to take precise action in the field" (Blue River Technology n.d.). Industry analysts believe such capabilities can answer the unique challenges capricious nature presents for new developments and applications of precision and robotic technologies.

With its global reach, the robotics industry is rapidly growing. Tractica, a self-described "market intelligence firm," reported "an increase in the number of large, midsized, and startup companies showing deep interest in the development and deployment of [agricultural robotic technologies]" (Sahi and Wheelock 2016). Tractica anticipated that the overall agricultural robot market would reach $73.9 billion by 2024. Driving industry growth are labor shortages, labor costs, and challenges and complexities of farmworker labor; population growth and strain on the food supply; global warming; increases in indoor farming; and general automation of agriculture (Tobe 2015). Tractica also identifies obstacles to the adoption of robotics:

> Market challenges remain for development of the sector, however, such as unclear value propositions, limited awareness of robotic systems among growers, insufficient robotic solutions, the difficulty of matching human-like dexterity with machines, fragmented technology development, weak administrative support, and infrastructure issues. Against the backdrop of these market drivers and barriers, Tractica forecasts that shipments of agricultural robots will increase significantly in the years ahead, rising from 32,000 units in 2016 to 594,000 units annually in 2024. (Tractica 2016)

Research and development are being conducted by both public and private organizations in the United States, Europe, Asia, and Australia, where industrial agriculture is already heavily reliant on digital technologies. The participants are unsurprising and expand the list of AgBot Challenge sponsors to include, among many others, the U.S. Department of Agriculture and analogues in other countries; public and private research universities and institutes; and multinational agribusiness corporations. This assemblage of policy makers, innovators, and investors has for a century shaped and reshaped farming practices with the introduction of various technologies—new seed stock, increasingly sophisticated and powerful machines, and chemical applications—aimed at the market of large-scale, industrial producers, the group whose views in the present discussion have yet to be heard.

Views from the Farm

A recent study found that European farmers believe that precision and automation represent the future of industrial agriculture and that these changes will require farmer "professionalization" (Corsini et al. 2015). Thus Fourth Industrial Revolution technologies challenge farmers in new ways that create ambivalence about their adoption. Discomfort with new kinds of hardware and software and their practical requirements is apparent in how farmers talk about them.

To begin, farmers may have difficulty selecting which company's products to buy, as this farmer, contributing to an online discussion, explains: "Well, I've already written some messages about different modern technologies. I see them as vary [*sic*] useful and innovative. They make our life easier. But when there is a wide range of such programs and equipment it is hard to choose which is priority for your farm. And there is [the] eternal dilemma [of] what provider [or] company to choose: already famous in agriculture or brand new, which offer innovative products."

Further, while most farmers are good, even expert, at repairing and maintaining analog equipment, few are digital technology innovators like Steve Gerrish. The rate of

FIG. 12. GPS-operated tractor. Photo by Larry Schwarm.

innovation causes concern about the reliability of unfamiliar equipment that requires continually changing software and remote specialists to keep it operational. From another online discussion, a farmer told this story:

> I spent most of a Monday sitting on a tractor, reading a book on my phone, while the tractor downloaded updates that make it function as it was supposed to. . . . In the end a service man had to replace a doodad. But I got a glimpse of the struggle to maintain control of the technology we use and how close we are to owning equipment that does not function without the purchase and/or approval of whoever owns the technology that makes it function.

Companies such as John Deere use copyright-protected software and may require farmers to use company-approved technicians. When repair is not illegal, companies make it difficult for independent repair shops and farmers to purchase the tools they need to do the work themselves. In response, farmers have organized a movement under the banner "Right to Repair" to push for legislation, currently in twelve states, that "would require equipment manufacturers to offer the diagnostic tools, manuals and other supplies that farmers need to fix their own machines" (Fitzpatrick 2017). Fitzpatrick writes, "The battle over Right to Repair is about more than malfunctioning tractors. . . . It's about a spirit of self-sufficiency that's baked into the DNA of blue collar America" (Fitzpatrick 2017). Added to the challenges of rapidly changing software and the right to be able to maintain and repair the new equipment, one farmer noted wryly, "The Amish with their teams of plow horses don't have to plug their animals into a USB port and download anything."

Related to this farmer's experience is the problem of proprietary software and short-lived companies. One wrote on a social media site, "If the expensive tool you bought requires software to perform that is not purchased with the tool, . . . [and] subsequently requires periodic updates from the company that owns the software—and may or may not be the company that sold the tool (in fact may be a company with a shorter life than yours)—What on earth did you purchase???"

In this scenario, such large investments appear highly risky. Another farmer wrote, "How soon will we be using a tractor with thousands of hours on it that won't function because the technology is no longer supported? Or the replacement technology is not affordable? or available? Will we see a time when we rent the use of equipment by the season as we do seed technology? Doesn't that extraordinary cost look even more expensive with those thoughts in mind?"

Some worry, too, that the massive amounts of data that digital systems can generate may create new areas of vulnerability. Two farmers posting to a social media site help us understand this view. The first worries about ways his data might be used: "Microsoft is leading the trend to charging a subscription on an annual or other basis for using software, and you may not even be able to put it on your machine but have to use it from the cloud (if you can reach the cloud). As you generate more and more information, there is more and more incentive for others to want to have access to it for regulatory or business reasons."

The second sees the appropriation of data about his farm as a way for others to take control of the operation, rendering his own expertise superfluous: "When there is enough information so that the woman at a desk in Chicago knows as much about your side hill seep, clay knob, glacial till and wetland as you do, it may be only money and technology that keep her from watching her robot machinery plant, fertilize and harvest, all the while respecting your gravestone on the peak of that nice ridge you enjoy resting on."

And then there are the complexity and messiness of real world conditions that seldom if ever match the glossy color brochures meted out by dealers. A farmer participating in an online discussion asked for help with a problem he was having with the AgLeader autosteer installed on his John Deere tractor. He wrote: "[It was] new[ly] installed last fall for ammonia work and now for planting. . . . Sometimes it will wander maybe eight–twelve inches to the right and then same back to the left and [I] cannot get [the] steering response to slow down. [I] talked to [the] rep and he told me some adjustments but no changes. . . . In corn it seemed to leave a perfect mark when I used the markers but the rows would not be straight like the neighbors."

He got an answer that reveals the need to understand the language that relates old to new technology, and how complicated it can be to match his neighbors' pretty rows, if not the brochure: "Try adjusting your cross track setting. If that doesn't help, go in to the guidance and steering tab, then the wrench next to the Ontrac 3, then adjust steering button, then look for heading gain. Adjust your heading gain (most likely up) and see if that will help any. Ontrac 3 is great and very accurate, however I will say, if your tractor has much play in the gearbox (as 4650s can sometimes have) it takes a lot of adjusting to get it right. If all else fails, try [the] Ag Leader tech support line."

The "if all else fails" conclusion expresses what is probably the most common concern about the new digital technologies: farmers don't understand them and must rely on experts. Three farmers illustrate this issue. The first, a Kansas farmer, said in an interview, "I'm using some technology through John Deere company, which has probes in the soil, and that's beamed to a satellite, which I don't *sabe* all this stuff. They download it into a computer, and I'm computer illiterate, but my office manager isn't." Another Kansas farmer commented, "I'm not opposed to technology,

156   Gibson

I'm just not technologically savvy. . . . I use experts, I hire experts to take care of those things." The third farmer from an online site is talking about installing a program on his tractor: "I recently downloaded the latest software for 500. What happens now? Do I just stick it in the back and it will take me through it or should I get a degree first? Thoughts?"

Other issues have also arisen about which farmers express concern. Intellectual property rights and the loss of control over investments begin with the problem of price—houses can be less expensive than some of the newest equipment. A farmer on a community agriculture blog wrote, "Somehow I think it will be cheaper to hire labor in [another] country than pay the bill to have the robots do the work. . . . I just can't imagine getting all warm and fuzzy about watching a robotic tractor work. But someone else will . . . ? I just hope somebody doesn't invent a robotic accountant."

Discussion

Farmers' reservations about the new precision and robotic technologies can be summarized as follows:

The technological options on the market are too numerous and too complicated.

Farmers can neither maintain nor repair the new digital equipment and software because of intellectual property laws, inability to purchase the necessary tools, and unfamiliarity.

Farmers' need for new hardware can render useless what they have purchased without additional purchases.

Software becomes quickly obsolete.

Farmers must rely on off-farm IT specialists and pay the additional cost of hiring them.

Short-lived companies could leave farmers without support.

New farm technologies are very expensive.

Farm-generated data may be appropriated by government agencies for regulatory purposes or to render farmers themselves obsolete.

Real-world conditions can complicate and limit the capacity of digital equipment to do what it is designed to do in the lab.

Equipment upgrades and software are too complicated for farmers to install and use.

However, unlike the nineteenth century Luddites who destroyed machinery in open rebellion against machine displacement of worker livelihoods, farmers interviewed for this project see technological change as inevitable and tantamount to progress.

Yet some actively resist the technological treadmill, a practice not unknown in rural areas (see Wyatt 2003, for example), through preferential purchases of used equipment without digital advantages or its complications. Nevertheless, successful farmers, they say, are those who stay current in education about best practices that entail the incorporation of the latest technologies.

In the twentieth century, people began to refer to the concept of technology in the singular and as an independent abstraction that stands as a powerful symbol of modernity (Schot and Bruheze 2003, 229). With fast-paced, never-ceasing innovation by manufacturers in search of new profit frontiers, however, what it means to be modern is destined to remain a moving target. Yet most Kansas farmers interviewed, like American consumers in general, tend to equate nonadoption of current technology with deprivation and inequality, believing that adoption confers advantages on the haves over the have-nots. This attitude underpins farmers' views of progress; federal funding of research and devel-

Fig. 13. TechTracking movement of farming equipment south of
Colby, Kansas. Photo by Larry Schwarm.

opment through subsidies, grants, and tax deductions; and the public policy focus on removing obstacles to technology adoption (Wyatt 2003, 68).

Some farmer concerns do date to the nineteenth century when newly introduced wide frames threatened the status and livelihoods of skilled knitters and stockingers, and resulted in the production of cheap, poorer quality goods (Luddites n.d). Farmers of the past and those today who operate on a smaller scale can be seen as artisans, skilled in the management of agricultural production, sensitive to variation and change in the landscape and environment, and knowledgeable about their own agro-ecosystems. Yet especially since World War II, farming has become increasingly industrial, coming to emulate the factory model of mass production. Modern, large-scale producers' relationships with their agro-ecosystems is increasingly mediated by crop consultants, soil reports from the lab, and digital readouts. This new way of knowing is a new way to connect to the land. The practices of an artisan-farmer, paced by the inevitable but irregular beat of nature, are set aside to respond to the metronomic rhythm demanded by techno-scientific management. The producer is distanced from the ecological process, the final product, and from the consumer, sometimes by great distances. Mechanization and automation have enabled both intensification and extensification of monoculture grains and soybeans, much of it grown for export, domestic livestock and poultry feed, and the ethanol market. In this model of production, where the grain goes when it leaves the co-op and how it is processed and used are of little concern to industrial producers.

"Labor-saving" machinery has also displaced farmworkers where labor is in abundance as much as it has helped to solve the problem of labor shortages in rapidly urbanizing areas. Today, reduction in the number of available farmworkers because of recent immigration policies in the United

States is expected to increase the demand for precision-based efficiencies and robotics, especially from farms in the largest sales classes, for all production tasks from planting to harvesting. But this technological solution to labor shortages and declining profit margins means that farmers must face the sometimes daunting task of learning very different skills to operate and maintain computer-driven farm equipment. While mechanization has always simultaneously produced and responded to labor shortages in rural areas, the demands of new digital technologies create a shortage of farmers with the necessary skills.

In the digital farm world, growers who survive the paradigm shift of the Fourth Industrial Revolution must either become or hire IT specialists whose primary responsibilities, especially with the introduction of robotics, may relocate management from field to office. Aging farmers may be especially challenged by this redefinition of what it means to farm. In 2012, census data on farmer age distribution showed that the largest group of farmers was over 65, representing a third of all farmers. Those under 45 constituted only 16 percent (Widmar 2015). While the number of new farmers each year is falling, beginning farmers are more likely to have at least a four-year college degree (United States Department of Agriculture 2017). The shortage of tech-savvy farmers may be filled by this group, so the continued consolidation of land into even fewer, bigger industrial farms can be operated by future farmer and IT specialists, or by robots.

The Slavic root of the word "robot" is *rabu*, meaning "slave," a term akin to *orbh*, a root of the term "orphan," or parentless child (Harper n.d.). As programmable machines, robots are designed to replace human labor when workers are in short supply or are too expensive, or when work poses serious risks. Such linguistic roots, however, suggest other important distinctions between human workers and mechanical ones, differences that point to robots' advantages over people. First among these, robotic "slaves" must always do what they're programmed to do and, to date, can do nothing else. Second, as "orphans," robots are undefended by a social network of kin, friends, and coworkers. They cannot organize for better working conditions or higher wages. Robots can carry out complex actions simultaneously, automatically, unaffected by immigration policy, and uninterrupted by the setting sun or fatigue. In these ways, and from the point of view of their owners, robots may be seen as perfect farmworkers.

Whether generated by robots or precision technologies, owner-operators have to be able to interpret and appropriately apply new kinds of information to their production systems. The effect is to deskill the grower, and devalue the knowledge and work he performed, or continues to perform, in the absence of labor-displacing automation. Digital technologies thus induce a seismic shift that takes mechanization farther than ever before in not only reducing the need for workers but in fundamentally transforming the nature of labor and undermining the power of workers worldwide. In the application of advanced forms of digital automation, the effect of capitalism in reducing the meaning and value of work to motion and performance is complete, and in that world, human workers cannot compete with machines.

Farmers may feel incompetent in the strange, new production milieu. And because the technologies and information generated are unfamiliar to them, and companies have found ways to restrict farmers' abilities and rights to repair, a new class of experts has emerged. These specialists represent a growing industry whose product is expertise in digital agricultural technologies. Keeping in mind farmers' concerns about short-lived firms, over 90 percent of all U.S. equipment dealers provide customer support services (Phillips 2016), and new software is on the market to assist independent consultants with ways to manage their clients' data while expanding their consulting firms.

Tom Goddard, a senior policy advisor with Alberta Agriculture and Forestry, began writing about precision agriculture as early as 1997. He points to another role played by experts: "An observation I make is that [precision farming] is championed, promoted by the private sector machinery technology companies, helped along by consultants that are looking for a nice discrete saleable package" (pers. communication, March 8, 2017).

Now, not just machines, but new kinds of experts stand between farmer and land, and these experts help drive the evolution of "best practices" that force traditional methods and their practitioners to make way for those who grew up with computers and studied data management and analysis at universities. Farmers may perceive no real choice in the matter, even those determined to keep debt and fear of obsolescence at bay by buying used equipment without the advantages of precision features. They agree that investment in new technologies will be necessary if they are to remain competitive and survive in their high-risk business.

A farmer has little control over the costs of doing business, the conditions under which he will carry out the operations of his business, and the price of the products he produces for market. This level of uncertainty in the face of the unknown makes every technology that promises control and efficiency almost irresistible—but not without reservation, as we have seen. What Shoshana Zuboff reported about other workers' views of factory modernization describes farmers' views of the latest in agricultural modernization equally well. She wrote, "The discussion . . . betrayed a grudging admiration for the new technology—its power, its intelligence, and the aura of progress surrounding it. That admiration, however, bore a sense of grief. Each expression of gee-whiz-

Buck-Rogers breathless wonder brought with it an aching dread conveyed in images of a future that rendered their authors obsolete" (Zuboff 2006, 305).

As one farmer asked, "Is technology taking over farming? Is technology going to take over farming so much one day that farmers will be out of jobs?" Zuboff adds, "As long as the technology is treated narrowly in its automating function, it perpetuates the logic of the industrial machine, which, over the course of this century, has made it possible to rationalize work while decreasing the dependence on human skills" (2006, 310). Without the human capacity for decisions shaped by values that extend beyond profitability, more than money is likely to be lost.

Research with Kansas farmers—some of them among the most entrepreneurial operators of the largest farms—indicates that best practices incorporate a notion of stewardship that moderates the powerful market imperative, the drive to "stay current" and remain competitive (Gibson and Gray 2016). Despite the fact that farmers must think a lot about profitability given their narrow and unpredictable profit margins, still they consider long-run ecological health and perceived social obligations to the next generation of farmers to whom they believe they must leave the land healthier than they found it. But farming in digital agriculture is computer-mediated work (Zuboff 2006, 306), a restructuring and relocation of power in which the body ceases to bear the necessary knowledge, in which what farmers know from direct observation of the land is devalued in favor of data that are captured, distributed, and analyzed by sophisticated software and analysts. At issue is whether large-scale, industrial farmers, whose decisions may be influenced or even made by IT specialists, will be able to hold onto any long-run, nonmarket concerns for social and environmental health.

What, then, is to become of farmers' increasingly obsolete

skills and local ecological knowledge? The distance between a farmer in an air-conditioned tractor cab and thousands of acres of farmland demonstrates that we've been on this path since before digital technologies entered the field. Now that we've added experts, satellites, digital codes, and software to mediate farmers' relationship to the land, we can readily recognize the pattern that, taken to its logical extreme, will ultimately eliminate farmers' expertise based on their ability to see, smell, touch, and taste the natural world. Indeed, one must ask what additional effects accrue when natural systems are rendered as binary code.

One could argue that the diversity of nature, albeit radically reduced by industrial agriculture, may become more readily apparent because the success of precision farming depends on apprehension of variability. That is, if farmers once treated their fields uniformly, precision ag requires recognition that different areas have different characteristics and management requirements. This notion of biological diversity and ecological complexity, however, hides the fundamental reductionism of nature accomplished in large measure by the interaction of markets and technologies. Biologically diverse ecosystems, that have already been simplified and desacralized by capitalism (Heilbroner 1985, 134), yield to fragmentation as discrete commodity resources whose cash value tends to elide all others (Wieskel 1997). Nor do individual technologies recognize the complexity of integrated, dynamic, evolving biological systems, but rather capture information about a predetermined list of inert characteristics for which the market can supply remediation. When this information about nature is rendered in BITS, or binary code, one may ask: Does the soil need potassium, phosphorus, or nitrogen? Does it need additional moisture? Does it need lime? Does this part of the field hold enough water for this seed, or should the planter place drought-resistant seeds here instead? What and how much chemical is needed for geocoded locations of weeds and pests? Returning to the insights of Tom Goddard, "Conservation Agriculture . . . recognizes agriculture as a system of biologic processes first. [Precision farming] seems to recognize technologies first" (pers. communication, March 8, 2017).

The digital technologies of precision agriculture, including robotics, thus encode discrete characteristics to which the market can respond, and they do so while erasing dynamic, integrated, system characteristics with emergent properties. Remediation of disaggregated, isolated "problems" will inevitably produce unanticipated consequences. From the point of view of agribusiness, such effects guarantee future market opportunities, but they also point to the vulnerability and dependence of farmers trapped on an eco-modernist treadmill of debt-financed solutions to technology-induced problems—solutions that cause new problems that give rise to new technological solutions and new debt (Cochrane 1993).

While one must neither dismiss nor trivialize the important benefits of efficient resource use and reduced waste and environmental contamination promised by the latest agricultural technologies, an inescapable observation is that delivery occurs within the industrial production paradigm. This paradigm is arguably unsustainable for ecological, economic, and social reasons: it entails a set of practices dependent on nonrenewable resources; it destroys biodiversity, contributes to climate change, and compromises soil fertility with chemicals, salinization, and compaction; and it enables economies of scale dependent on farm failures and thereby hollows out rural communities (see chapter 9 of this volume). Fidelity to this system of production is not only consonant with the binary encoding of nature in agroecosystems; it also encodes a binary agricultural worldview. Successful farmers are those who "keep current" in education and technology; they are efficient and modern. Failed farmers do not stay abreast of the latest advances; they are inefficient and backward.[1] The choices farmers make in the production and management of their farms thus ideologically complement the economic imperatives that drive them. But the significant difference between a "smart farm" operated from a computer command center by an IT specialist, and a farm operated by a human farmer, is that the farmer can see the integrated system, recognize its dynamism, and make choices that reflect long-run cultural and environmental values as well as those that keep the farm in business in the short run.

Conclusions

From the beginning of agricultural industrialization, farmers were told by advertisers that machinery did not have to be fed and watered as draft animals did, that fossil fuel would be cheaper, and that work with machines could be done more easily and faster.[2] Agribusiness firms such as John Deere and International Harvester continued research and development of new technologies, building on this foundation of production claims that included ease of operation, speed, cost effectiveness, and efficiency. County agents, employed by state agricultural colleges and the federal government, carried out the marketing project, and farmers eventually came to equate state-of-the-art technologies with the highest efficiencies, increased competitiveness, and, above all, progress. Now, with advances in digital technologies that have exponentially increased computational power and connectivity, a whole new digital infrastructure has emerged, bringing with it a seismic shift in food production, the meaning and value of farm work, and the identity of farmers.

Schwab (2015) wrote that the Fourth Industrial Revolution will change not only what we do but also who we are. In the industrial farm world, farmers have already become growers or farm managers to survive, and in the digital farm world, they must either become or hire IT specialists. In an age of robotic agriculture, what will it mean to be a farmer? What will the work of farming entail? Will the pride farmers today take in autonomy and ownership be lost as control increasingly moves from the farmer to the technology specialist? How will future farmers be trained, by whom, and for what responsibilities?

Digital automation is transforming what it means to be a farmer, threatening farmers' value to society and the sense of identity that goes with farm work. Today's GPS-guided tractors and combines locate farmers in air-conditioned cabs, removed from the need to attend to soil conditions or even locations in the field. Soil sensors and variable rate applicators determine what inputs are needed where, and GPS guidance and autosteer functions mean farmers can go along for the ride, play video games, work crossword puzzles, or nap, until they are signaled by the equipment that it is time to turn around to start the next row. Even that requirement is disappearing with technologies that will take care of the turn. One can see what today's high-tech equipment requires of farmers who increasingly cede authority to IT specialists who know how to program, operate, and repair equipment, and who can interpret and respond to the massive amounts of data generated.

Despite their conservative tendencies to stay with "what works," and their worries about new vulnerabilities created by the digital revolution in agriculture, farmers' reverence for the technologies that drive their disempowerment is reflected in their view of the new skill requirements as "professionalization." These same farmers also predict that precision agriculture and robotic technologies will advance the ongoing transformation of rural society through further land consolidation and increasing average farm size as the "winners" gobble up the remains of the "losers." Still, an equipment dealer said that until they invent a robot "as scowly and frowny as a farmer who will show up at 10 a.m. at the café for coffee," he's not going to worry about robots replacing farmers. But revolution, by definition, signals a radical departure from the status quo. And while scholars cannot tell us how this Fourth Industrial Revolution will affect society, they are confident that it will be both profitable and disruptive. If mechanization has distanced industrial farmers from the soil, robotic and precision technologies incorporated into tomorrow's "smart farms" may remove him from the field altogether.

Notes

I wish to acknowledge the support and guidance of Don Stull, who reviewed an earlier draft of this chapter.

1. I am indebted to Simanti Dasgupta (2015) for this insight.

2. Contrary to this equipment advertisers' view, Stull and Broadway (2013, 59) reported that Tyson adopted chicken-catching machines to replace human chicken catchers who sought to unionize, and then, within a few years, abandoned those machines for human catchers. The mechanical catchers required more workers, did not save any time, cost too much to maintain, and often broke down. Human chicken catchers are contract workers, who work twelve hour shifts, and generally are not paid overtime. Their wages fell on average 15 percent over the first decade of the twentieth century. Robotics in meat and poultry processing plants has also lagged behind predictions—men are cheaper than machines, especially if they are migrant workers recruited from abroad; they require less maintenance; and if they break or become troublesome, they are easily replaced.

References

AgBot Challenge 2017a. "Seeding Competition 2017." http://www.agbot.ag/seeding-competition-2017/.

AgBot Challenge 2017b. "Weed & Feed Competition 2017." http://www.agbot.ag/seeding-competition-2017/.

Anderson, Lorena. 2016. "Robots and People Working Together to Save Water, Enhance Agriculture." *University of California News*, December 14. https://www.universityofcalifornia.edu/news/robots-and-people-working-together-save-water-enhance-agriculture.

Basler, Roy P. 1953. "Address before the Wisconsin State Historical Society. September 30, 1859." In *The Collected Works of Abraham Lincoln*. The Abra-

ham Lincoln Association. http://www.abrahamlincolnonline.org/lincoln
/speeches/fair.htm.

Bedord, Laurie. 2016. "Agbot Challenge Tests Robotic Planters." *Successful
Farming*, May 6. http://www.agriculture.com/technology/robotics/using
-robotics-to-test-power-of-broadb_581-ar51104.

Blue River Technology. n.d. "Equipping Every Farmer to Understand and
Manage Every Plant." Accessed May 31, 2017. http://www.bluerivert.com/.

Bosch. n.d. "Bonirob: Adaptable Multi-Purpose Robotic Platform." Accessed
March 2015. https://www.deepfield-connect.com/en/BoniRob.html.

Campbell-Kelly, Martin, and William Aspray. 1996. *Computer: A History of the
Information Machine*. New York: Basic.

CBS News. 2013. "Robot Lettuce Pickers in Salinas Point to Future of Farming."
July 14. http://sanfrancisco.cbslocal.com/2013/07/14/robot-farming/.

CNN Money. 2013. "The Fortune Interview with Geoff Colvin," September 3.
https://www.youtube.com/watch?v=IuXuZwx777E.

Cochrane, Willard W. 1993. *The Development of American Agriculture: A Historical Analysis*. Minneapolis: University of Minnesota Press.

Corsini, Lorenzo, Kim Wagner, Andreas Gocvke, and Torsten Kurth. 2015.
"Crop Farming 2030: The Reinvention of the Sector." Boston Consulting Group. April 30. https://www.bcg.com/publications/2015/crop
-farming-2030-reinvention-sector.aspx.

Dasgupta, Simanti. 2015. *Bits of Belonging: Information Technology, Water, and
Neoliberal Governance in India*. Philadelphia: Temple University Press.

Dejoia, Aaron, and Matt Duncan. 2015. "What is 'Precision Agriculture' and
Why Is It Important?," February 27. https://soilsmatter.wordpress.com
/2015/02/27/what-is-precision-agriculture-and-why-is-it-important/.

Edan, Yael, Shufeng Han, and Naoshi Kondo. 2009. "Automation in Agriculture." In *Springer Handbook of Automation*, 1095–96. Berlin: Springer.

Fitzpatrick, Alex. 2017. "Hand Me that Wrench: Farmers and Apple Fight
Over the Toolbox." *Time*, June 22. http://time.com/4828099/farmers
-and-apple-fight-over-the-toolbox/.

Gibson, Jane, and Benjamin J. Gray. 2016. "Regulating the Ogallala: Paradox
and Ambiguity in Western Kansas." In *The Economics Of Ecology, Exchange,
and Adaptation: Anthropological Explorations*, edited by Donald C. Wood.
Research in Economic Anthropology 36 (2016): 3–32.

Harper, Douglas. n.d. *Online Etymology Dictionary*. Accessed June 22, 2017.
http://etymonline.com/index.php?allowed_in_frame=0&search=robot.

Heilbroner, Robert L. 1985. *The Nature and Logic of Capitalism*. New York: W.
W. Norton.

IBM. n.d. "Precision Agriculture: Using Predictive Weather Analytics to Feed
Future Generations." IBM Research. Accessed March 15, 2017. http://
www.research.ibm.com/articles/precision_agriculture.shtml.

Jacobson, Howard B., and Roueek, Joseph S. 1959. *Automation and Society*. New York: Philosophical Library.

Kurfess, Thomas R. 2005. *Robotics and Automation Handbook*. Boca Raton FL: CRC Press.

Liu, Tessie P. 1994. *The Weaver's Knot: The Contradictions of Class Struggle and Family Solidarity in Western France, 1750–1914*. Ithaca NY: Cornell University Press.

Luddites. n.d. "The Luddites at 200." Accessed November 2017. http://www .luddites200.org.uk/theLuddites.html.

Ma, Kevin Y., Pakpong Chirarattananon, Sawyer B. Fuller, and Robert J. Wood. 2013. "Controlled Flight of a Biologically Inspired, Insect-Scale Robot." *Science* 340 no. 6132 (May 3): 603–7.

Marketsandmarkets.com. 2018. "Precision Farming Market by Technology (Guidance System, Remote Sensing, Variable Rate Technology), Offering (Hardware Automation & Control System, Sensor & Monitoring Device, Software, Services), Application, and Geography-Global Forecast to 2023." Report Code SE 2831. May. http://www.marketsandmarkets .com/Market-Reports/precision-farming-market-1243.html.

Marr, Bernard. 2016. "What is the Difference Between Deep Learning, Machine Learning and AI?" *Forbes*, December 8. https://www.forbes .com/sites/bernardmarr/2016/12/08/what-is-the-difference-between -deep-learning-machine-learning-and-ai/#1f0f0da326cf.

Martin, Philip. 2017. "Immigration and Farm Labor: Challenges and Opportunities." Giannini Foundation of Agricultural Economics. University of California Agriculture and Natural Resources. June. https://s.giannini .ucop.edu/uploads/giannini_public/dd/d9/ddd90bf0-2bf0-41ea-bc29 -28c5e4e9b049/immigration_and_farm_labor_-_philip_martin.pdf.

Patel, Prachi. 2016. "Agricultural Drones are Finally Cleared for Takeoff." IEEE Spectrum, October 19. http://spectrum.ieee.org/robotics/drones /agriculture-drones-are-finally-cleared-for-takeoff.

Phillips, Steve. 2016. "Precision Agriculture in the USA—Trends and Technologies." International Plant Nutrition Institute. IPNI Brazil Webinar. January 11. https://www.youtube.com/watch?v=SSyqg5fmqyM.

Rifkin, Jeremy. 1995. *The End of Work: The Decline of the Global Labor Force and the Dawn of the Post-Market Era*. New York: Putnam.

Sahi, Manoj Kumar and Clint Wheelock. 2016. "Driverless Tractors and Drones to be Among the Key Applications for Agricultural Robots." *AgriTech Tomorrow*. January 26, 2016. https://www.agritechtomorrow.com/article /2016/01/driverless-tractors-and-drones-to-be-among-the-key-applications -for-agricultural-robots/7566/.

Schimmelpfennig, David. 2016. "Farm Profits and Adoption of Precision Agriculture." USDA Economic Research Service. Economic Research

Report Number 217. October. https://www.ers.usda.gov/publications /pub-details/?pubid=80325.

Schnitkey, G. 2015. "Corn Seed Costs from 1995 to 2014." *farmdoc daily* 5: 214. Department of Agricultural and Consumer Economics. University of Illinois at Urbana-Champaign, November 17, 2015. http://farmdocdaily .illinois.edu/2015/11/corn-seed-costs-from-1995-to-2014.html.

Schnitkey, G., and S. Sellars. 2016. "Growth Rates of Fertilizer, Pesticide, and Seed Costs over Time," *farmdoc daily* 6: 130. Department of Agricultural and Consumer Economics. University of Illinois at Urbana-Champaign. July 12. http://farmdocdaily.illinois.edu/2016/07/growth-rates-of-fertilizer -pesticide-seed-costs.html.

Schot, Johan, and Adri Albert de la Bruheze. 2003. "The Mediated Design of Products, Consumption, and Consumers in the Twentieth Century." In *How Users Matter: The Co-Construction of Users and Technologies*, edited by Nelly Oudshoorn and Trevor Pinch. Cambridge MA: MIT Press.

Schwab, Klaus. 2015. "The Fourth Industrial Revolution: What It Means and How to Respond." Council on Foreign Relations, December 12. https:// www.foreignaffairs.com/print/1116143.

Stull, Donald D., and Michael J. Broadway. 2013. *Slaughterhouse Blues: The Meat and Poultry Industry in America*. Belmont CA: Wadsworth.

Taylor Farms. n.d. "Automated Romaine Harvester." Accessed May 2017. https://www.thesnack.net/article/future-tech/automated-romaine -harvester-taylor-farms-water-knife-bot/541/vol-28-chef-jet-tila-the-culinary -anthropologist/jessica-donnel/00545.

Temple, Robert K. G. 1991. *The Genius of China: 3000 Years of Science, Discovery and Invention*. London: Prion.

Tobe, Frank. 2015. "Service Robots get Multiple Positive Forecasts." *Robot Report*, July 19. http://www.therobotreport.com/news/service-robots -get-multiple-positive-forecasts.

Tractica. 2016. "Agricultural Robots." *ReportLinker*, Summary of Report ID 4540262, December. http://www.reportlinker.com/p04540262 /Agricultural-Robots.html.

———. 2017. "Deep Learning: Enterprise, Consumer, and Government Applications for Deep Learning Software, Hardware, and Services: Market Analysis and Forecasts for 112 Use Cases." Accessed May 30. https://www .tractica.com/research/deep-learning/.

United States Department of Agriculture. 2017. "Beginning Farmers and Age Distribution of Farmers." Economic Research Service. Updated April 13. https://www.ers.usda.gov/topics/farm-economy/beginning-disadvantaged -farmers/beginning-farmers-and-age-distribution-of-farmers/.

Widmar, David A. 2015. "The Aging American Farmer. Agricultural Economic Insights: Perspectives of Two Agricultural Economists," January 20. http://ageconomists.com/2015/01/20/the-aging-american-farmer/.

Wieskel, Timothy C. 1997. "Selling Pigeons in the Temple: The Danger of Market Metaphors in an Ecosystem." Occasional Papers Series No. 8. Harvard Divinity School. Center for the Study of Values in Public Life. July 6. http://ecoethics.net/OPS/OPS-008.HTM.

Wyatt, Sally. 2003. "Non-Users Also Matter: The Construction of Users and Non-Users of the Internet." In *How Users Matter: The Co-Construction of Users and Technologies,* edited by Nelly Oudshoorn and Trevor Pinch, 67–80. Cambridge MA: MIT Press.

Zuboff, Shoshana. 2006. "In the Age of the Smart Machine." In *Technology & the Future,* edited by Albert H. Teich, 304–11. Belmont CA: Thomson Higher Education.

5

Water to Wine

Industrial Agriculture and Groundwater Regulation in California

CASEY WALSH

Highway 101 between Santa Barbara and Salinas is a pretty stretch of road. This is the typical Central California landscape of rolling hills, grasslands and oaks, with occasional sandstone formations and quaint towns such as Solvang, Los Alamos, San Luis Obispo, and Paso Robles, that has attracted tourism for a century. During the last thirty years this region has become known as "wine country," as more and more of the land is dedicated to grape production and dozens of wineries have opened tasting rooms built in Tuscan-style architecture or some modality of the California ranch. Since about 1980, ever-larger patches of the hills and valleys of the Central Coast have been converted from golden brown grasslands to dark green vineyards. This landscape is nice to look at, and thousands of tourists come to the region each year; millions of bottles of wine flow out to consumers around the world.

This expansion of the wine economy in the Central Coast has been fueled by groundwater. Groundwater in California is governed by the "correlative rights doctrine," which recognizes the right of beneficial use (not ownership) of a "reasonable" amount of the substance. This right, and amount, can only be defined in relation to other uses and amounts. In practice, California landowners have been free in most cases to drill wells and extract groundwater for agriculture with just a ministerial building permit for the well emitted by a county government. There were no requirements to conduct an environmental impact report or register the quantity of water extracted, nor was there any cost assessed by any level of government for the use of this water. California was, in the words of one wine grower in Paso Robles, "the Wild West"—one of the least restrictive places in the United States to use groundwater.

Until the passage of the Sustainable Groundwater Management Act (SGMA) in 2014, groundwater use in California was only regulated when property owners brought lawsuits against neighbors overlying the same groundwater basin or aquifer, alleging that "their" water use rights were infringed on by the other's use. These lawsuits forced a process of adjudication by the state court that established limits to extraction and mechanisms to monitor it. Adjudication, however, is a notoriously lengthy and costly process that most overlying property owners are loath to embark upon, and only a tiny fraction of groundwater basins in California have been adjudicated, most of them in the urban areas of Los Angeles and the San Francisco Bay area (Landgridge et al. 2016).

In the Paso Robles region, the relentless extraction of groundwater to fuel the wine economy generated great prosperity, but also dry wells, protest, and conflict. There were contradictory responses: individual and collective. On the one hand, groundwater users squared off to protect their individual interests. As groundwater levels fell, those with deeper wells gained an advantage in access that favored the larger grape growers with deeper pockets. Shallow wells of rural residents ran dry during the hot summer irrigation season, forcing the deepening of wells or the construction of costly new ones, and putting property values in jeopardy. Small- and medium-size grape growers saw proportionally more of their profits erode as they dug deeper for water. At the same time, regardless of their own fortunes, most overliers recognized that everyone in the groundwater basin would eventually lose the race to the bottom of the aquifer. A number of people told me they reasoned that either costs of water extraction would get too high for even large growers to turn a profit, or the water would simply run out for everybody. Residents and growers certainly had their own private economic interests in mind, but in most cases, they also recognized that the only way to protect their individual interests was to create institutions to manage groundwater as a shared resource, a resource held in common by all users.[1]

Groundwater depletion and social conflict led to efforts among residents, agricultural users, and urban purveyors in Paso Robles to create a management plan to bring the groundwater basin into a sustainable balance between extraction and recharge. Despite the recognition by some that groundwater is a commonly held resource (and that correlative rights to groundwater are relational use rights), many others rejected any interference in the continued unlimited extraction of groundwater by individual overlying property owners. The rejection of the effort to create a plan to manage groundwater use was undergirded by a popular assumption that water rights are individual property rights, and by a libertarian distrust of government regulation and taxation. Distrust of collective management was also motivated by the idea that collective water management was a disguised water grab by corporate and financial capital. It was a response that harmonized at that moment with a nationwide insurgency most clearly represented by the Tea Party. However, both proponents and detractors of a hydro-commons in Paso Robles portrayed themselves as defenders of the region against outside forces.

In this chapter, I first discuss the wine industry and its effects on groundwater. Wine grapes are not a thirsty crop, but in Central California vines have been planted on grazing lands that were never previously farmed, leading to a large net increase in water use. Wine production is linked of course to consumption, and during the last thirty years there has been a restructuring and reconceptualization of social class (Roseberry 1996), in which consumers are encouraged to define themselves as sophisticated and elegant by quaffing one or another varietal or label that has an air of "prestige."

I then describe how wine production, groundwater depletion, and social conflict led the county government of San Luis Obispo to declare an emergency moratorium on new groundwater extraction in the Paso Robles groundwater basin in order to protect the resource while a more permanent management solution was devised. A new water district was proposed that rejected the "one-acre, one-vote" representational structure of water districts in California in favor of a complicated system that defined social groups by parcel size, and that balanced voting power among the groups. This "hybrid" water district was overwhelmingly voted down in a county election, and in the following section of the chapter I explain why. The chapter ends with a brief review of the California Sustainable Groundwater Management Act (SGMA), which emerged in parallel to the failed Paso Robles Hybrid Water District, and which is now in effect in all groundwater basins throughout the state. SGMA requires local actors overlying groundwater basins to form agencies and then to create and carry out, by 2040, sustainable management plans for groundwater. SGMA is thus also an effort to create a commons.

This research was conducted between 2013 and 2017 in the Paso Robles area of San Luis Obispo County, in the Central Coast region of California, as part of a comparative project on the production of high-value agricultural commodities, climate change, and groundwater management in California and Mexico.[2] To date, twenty-four formal interviews have been conducted with an array of people involved in groundwater politics in the region. Many dozens of informal conversations also produced information. Initial interviews and conversations were held with public figures who had been quoted in newspapers and whose contact information was available on the internet. Those I spoke with suggested further contacts, a standard procedure of "snowball sampling" that is not random, but in cases such as this one eventually leads to thorough coverage of the actors most relevant to the research problem. All those spoken with were provided with information about the research project and most consented to being part of the study. Given the highly politicized nature of groundwater management in Paso Robles, a few people refused to be interviewed. The personal names in this chapter are pseudonyms, an almost universal practice in anthropology that helps to ensure the anonymity and security of those involved with the research. Only a few quotations from those interviews were used in this chapter, but the information presented on the case reflects the cumulative knowledge offered by the informants.

Globalized Agriculture: The Wrath of Grapes

Growth in the market for "nontraditional" or "luxury" commodities such as berries, wine, exotic salad greens, and gourmet coffees has been spurred by increasing social inequality over the last thirty years and the re-imagination of social class among consumers (Bourdieu 1984; Harvey 1989; Klein 2002; Roseberry 1996; Schneider 1994; Stiglitz 2012; Watson and Caldwell 2005). The wine sections of Trader Joe's, Vons, Costco, or almost any other large supermarket chain in Southern California dazzle consumers with dozens of labels from the Central Coast and demand from them a decision about the kind of wine drinker they are: a fan of California zins, maybe a pinot lover, more of a white wine person, perhaps—chardonnay, reisling, viognier? Wine enables—requires, really—the consumer to make these sorts of distinctions no matter where they live.

Central Coast wines play a part in the identification of new consumers around the globe. One Paso Robles winemaker, Gary, when I asked him about the market for the record 2013 grape crush, said, "There are always more buyers for our wine in China" (pers. communication, October 17, 2014). And while some wine really is a luxury to purchase at fifty dollars or more a bottle, there is no shortage of labels that sell at five dollars. The enormous spread of price points in the wine industry enables virtually everybody in the developed world to identify as a sophisticated luxury consumer through the purchase of a bottle of wine at between ten and twenty dollars, what the wine industry calls "masstige" labels (mass + prestige).

Since the 1980s, individual and institutional investors have looked favorably upon vineyards and the possibilities for profit that are driven by the luxury drive among consumers. Wine production has soared; Paso Robles has been an important locus of interest. As John, one long-time small-scale farmer in the region explained to me, the region saw a huge influx of money when the federal tax laws were changed in the 1980s, enabling Wall Street investors to sell their holdings and reinvest in vineyards and houses, with very little lost to taxes (pers. communication, October 15, 2014). This led to a proliferation of small and large wineries and built the reputation of the Central Coast as an emerging premier vinicultural area. Large agribusinesses and institutional investors followed close on their heels, cashing in on the Central Coast reputation while producing larger volumes of low-cost wine.

Paso Robles wine production was soon part of a global market. Since the 1980s, free trade agreements and the globalization of agricultural commodity markets have stimulated the production of high-value commodities for distant consumption—part of a new "food regime" characterized by the mobility of capital, technology and labor, increasingly intensive manipulation of ecologies, and the impermanence of productive agricultural assemblages (McMichael 2009). In this context, agribusinesses have expanded operations globally. For example, Meridian Wines refocused operations from Napa and Sonoma Counties into the Central Coast in the 1980s, later expanding operations to Chile. In 2016 Australian wine giant Treasury Wine Estates bought Meridian's installations in Paso Robles (Buffalo 2016). Treasury Wine Estates, for its part, became a world player in the wine business when it bought most of the wine labels held by the UK alcoholic beverages giant Diageo. Although Paso Robles wines are produced in the region and convey a regional image, they are caught up in global markets.

The economic meltdown of 2008 has accentuated the presence of transnational capital in the wine industry. Finance firms, such as large insurance and investment banking companies, are buying agricultural land in a play to reduce portfolio risk through diversification and to increase returns. As Madeleine Fairbain (2014) puts it in the title of a recent article, in the eyes of capital, agricultural land is "like gold with yield" because it is a physical asset ("like gold") that both appreciates in value and generates profits from agricultural products ("yield"). Capital is attracted to exceptionally profitable luxury commodities, and in particular wine, the value of which is often accentuated by prestige, *terroir*, and other sometimes mystical factors of branding (Klein 2002).

Water and Agriculture in California

Despite these important global and consumer dynamics, the production of luxury agricultural commodities such as wine takes place in specifically local environmental conditions and principle among these in California is aridity. Irrigated capitalist agriculture was pioneered in California, and since the nineteenth century the river valleys of the state have been the site of the massification and technification of agricultural production based on complex water systems. In the early twentieth century, California's irrigation systems made the scalar jump from river to region, and consolidated landscapes and social formations controlled by agribusiness and the state. (Arax and Wartzman 2003; Worster 1985). State and federal government agencies built huge dams and thousands of miles of canals to capture, store, and distribute the water of the rivers that descend from the mountains to the valleys (Hundley Jr. 2001; Pisani 1984).

In addition, thousands of wells allow even more, and more flexible, access to the water of these regional drainages, especially in times of scarcity. California's water systems have given rise to complex social formations that include large and small producers, as well as a migrant agricultural working class in constant renewal (Goldschmidt 1978; Haley 1989; Holmes 2013). These infrastructures facilitate dramatic urban growth as well, and California's cities draw an ever-larger share of the water used by the rural sector (Hundley Jr. 2001; Zetland 2009).

In the 2000s and 2010s, California's irrigation infrastructure strained to confront a prolonged drought. Limits to the availability of surface water in California, as well as other arid and semi-arid areas around the world, led to the mining of aquifers and groundwater depletion for urban use and agriculture (Famiglietti 2014; Scanlon, Longuevergne, and Long 2012; Taylor et al. 2013; Voss et al. 2013). Evidence suggests that climate change is already affecting precipitation, with wet areas of the world foreseen to get wetter, and dry areas such as the Western United States and

Central-Northern Mexico to get drier (Durack, Wijffels, and Matear 2012). California straddles the line between relatively wet and dry areas, and so while wet and dry extremes will become more pronounced, overall precipitation in the state will likely remain somewhat steady (Berg et al. 2015). However, the southern end of California, including Santa Barbara County, is predicted to receive less precipitation, and increased temperatures will increase evaporation and reduce soil moisture, leading to more irrigation. For all these reasons, the drought that hit California between 2000 and 2015, and which still lingers in the Central Coast California wine region, seems to be a harbinger of a "new normal."

Groundwater is especially important to agribusiness as it seeks out favorable conditions of production (Budds 2004; Woodhouse 2012; Zlolniski 2011). Experts agree that groundwater extraction is a global problem for the sustainability of agriculture and society, but that it is largely unregulated and poorly understood (Giordano 2009; Glennon 2004; UC Center for Hydrologic Modeling 2014). By 2013, the lack of regulation, together with years of drought and a simultaneous expansion of certain high-value agricultural commodities—notably almonds and grapes—combined to provoke a grave over-extraction of groundwater resources in California: some thirty cubic kilometers between 2003 and 2009 (Famiglietti et al. 2011). Almonds, for example, use an extraordinary amount of water: one gallon for each almond. In 2014, more water in California was dedicated to almond trees, which are concentrated in the southern San Joaquin Valley, than to the urban and domestic use by humans in the entire state. Eighty percent of those almonds are exported, mostly to China, representing a huge loss of "virtual water" for the state (Fulton, Cooley, and Gleick 2014; Philpott 2015). The social effects of this overuse include the drying of the shallower wells of rural residents, and diminishing water quality as deeper, older, and more heavily mineralized water is brought to the surface.

In the Central Coast region of California, wine grapes are the commodity that is drying out the aquifers, and the Paso Robles American Vitacultural Area (PRAVA), in San Luis Obispo County, is a good example of this. Paso Robles and surrounding towns such as Creston, Atascadero, and Shandon lie in sandy hills that form the headwaters of the Salinas River, which flows north through San Luis Obispo and Monterrey counties, and eventually drains into the ocean south of Santa Cruz. The lower Salinas River valley, around the town of Salinas, has been producing high-value crops such as lettuce, artichokes, and strawberries for a hundred years. John Steinbeck's ethnographic novel about the region, *East of Eden*, made even more popular by James Dean in a 1955 movie, depicts life there in the first decades of the twentieth century and the emergence of vegetable production for national markets.

The upper Salinas River Valley, on the other hand, has much less water, and the hilly landscape is frequently made up of poor, rocky, and sandy soils. Until the wine boom, Paso Robles was more of a way station on Highway 101 than a destination in itself, although it did gain some fame in the late nineteenth century for hot springs baths. It is a region that is quite active geologically, with many faults, oil deposits, and thermal, mineral water that is not useful for irrigation. For all these reasons, the land around Paso Robles was primarily dedicated to ranching and oil until the rise of grapes, which are better suited to poor rocky soils and aridity. There were a few family vineyards in Paso Robles since the late nineteenth century, but until the 1950s, when high-voltage electricity was brought into rural areas of the county, there was very little pumping for irrigation. Even after the arrival of cheap electric centrifugal pumps, groundwater was generally used to nourish grains and alfalfa, which consolidated the existing ranching economy rather than transformed it into high-value agriculture.

Grape vines are capable of producing with very little water, and there are varietals that are well-adapted to the scant rainfall and hot summers typical of Mediterranean climates. Before groundwater pumping, "dry-farming" techniques were practiced such as spacing grape plants widely (a third of the number of plants that are found on irrigated land), training the plants into small trees that stand alone (rather than vines on a trellis), and sealing the moisture in the soil with a thin top layer of pulverized dirt (a "dust mulch") that does not conduct water to the surface through capillary action. Benito Dusi, for example, farms forty acres of "head-pruned" grapes that his father planted, some of them, like Benito himself, over eighty years old. A few other wineries, such as Tablas Creek, have planted dry-farmed vineyards more recently. Only a few such "dry-farmed" vineyards exist—two or three hundred of the more than 25,000 acres in Paso Robles that are dedicated to wine grapes—because the yield is, at best, one third of that of irrigated vineyards. This means that dry farmers either do not need to compete economically with conventional irrigated grapes because they own their land, or otherwise lower their production costs and income; or that they attract environmentally ethical, luxury consumers willing to pay three or four times the price of a bottle of conventionally produced wine—upwards of twenty-five dollars a bottle.

The explosion of wine grape production around Paso Robles since 1980 is almost entirely due to irrigation with groundwater. Between 1976 and 2006 wine grape production in the Central Coast grew from less than 20,000 tons to about 400,000 tons (Volpe et al. 2010). In the Paso Robles American Vitacultural Area, the number of wineries grew from 20 to 170 between 1990 and 2000. And the grape craze has expanded throughout the Central Coast of California.

PRO Water Equity, a citizens' group involved in the water conflict in Paso Robles, calculated the effects of grape production groundwater depletion and well-drilling this way:

2768 wells drilled in Paso basin from 1997 to 2011 = an average of *198* per year—during a period of significant residential and agricultural growth in the basin. 306 wells drilled in Paso basin from January to May 2014 = an average of *734* per year—during a time of essentially no residential growth and limited agricultural growth due to the urgency ordinance. This tells us that numerous wells have gone dry. Note that this data does not include well pumps lowered and people who can't afford to drill a new well and are trucking water. (Prowaterequity.org, n.d., italics in the original)

In 2010 the counties of Santa Barbara and San Luis Obispo produced about 1.7 billion dollars' worth of agricultural products, with wine grapes responsible for about a quarter of this number. To put this into perspective, "field crops" such as alfalfa, beans and grains—the mainstay of agriculture in the region before 1980—constituted a little more than 1 percent of the value of agriculture in 2010.

Farmers know that grape vines use far less water per acre than the alfalfa that was previously grown in the region. Bill, who farms grains and other staples, told me, "It isn't the grapes themselves, it's that so much acreage has been turned into vineyards" (pers. communication, February 24, 2015). Almost all the grape acreage in Paso Robles replaced grassland that was never irrigated. Grapes, while not thirsty like almonds, have nevertheless produced an enormous net increase in groundwater consumption. According to estimates made by a rural resident interviewed in 2014, over one hundred thousand acre feet of water has been extracted from the Paso Robles basin over the last thirty years. Rural residents report that the water levels in their wells have fallen 80, 100, even 150 feet since the 1990s. For some this means that their wells run dry in the summer months when irrigation peaks; for others it has meant drilling deeper wells at a price tag of at least $25,000.[3] Monitoring wells show that since 1981 water levels have dropped an average of 25, 60, and 110 feet in the three subdistricts of the basin, while annual precipitation has remained relatively constant.

Managing Groundwater Mining in Paso Robles

The growth of wine grape production in Paso Robles has generated a particular regional social formation with a diverse array of groups: small farmers with deep roots in the region; large commercial wineries; recently arrived boutique winery owners; growing numbers of Latino—mostly Mexican—agricultural workers; small organic family farmers; retired rural residents; and workers in the tourism industry. Wealthy people, attracted by the image of California wine country, cashed in securities such as stocks and bonds and bought land in Paso Robles, where they built luxury homes and established boutique wineries with tasting rooms. Most of this land was previously used for cattle ranching and had never been irrigated. Thus, a good number of groundwater-intensive wineries of less than one hundred acres were developed by these pioneering investors who focused on producing expensive high-quality products, raising the profile of the region among wine consumers and the general public.

Eyeing this success, commercial wineries and speculative investors followed, establishing larger vineyards. In the last decade, this expansion of wine production has brought with it a booming tourism industry, with new hotels and restaurants popping up to cater to visitors traveling the "wine routes" such as Union Road. Paso Robles is today a patchwork of different sized vineyards, some with wineries and some without. Scattered among these vineyards are rural residents, small vegetable and fruit farms, and horse ranches. The city of Paso Robles has also expanded, with thousands of new residents each decade since 1980. This influx doubled the population from 9,200 in 1980, to 18,600 in 1990 and increased it another 30 percent to 24,300 inhabitants in 2000. In the years since the economic crisis in 2008 (which was followed by the groundwater crisis a few years later) only five hundred new residents are registered—an increase of about 1.6 percent (Paso Robles Housing Division, 2018). When the depletion of the aquifers caused by all this growth finally caused alarm bells to ring, there were conflicting analyses of the cause of the problem and its solution. Groups blamed other groups; some accepted shared responsibility; others denied that a problem even existed.

Confronted with continual increases in water extraction and a conflict that showed no possibility of resolution in the short term, on August 27, 2013 the San Luis Obispo (slo) County Board of Supervisors passed an "urgency ordinance" that froze levels of groundwater pumping throughout the Paso Robles basin. On the face of it the ordinance was a drastic measure. California state law protects a property owner's right to make reasonable and beneficial use of water beneath his or her property—the "overlying right." And the only restriction slo County had on well drilling was a zoning code that a well could not be within ten feet of the neighbor's property line. Limits on groundwater extraction in California were only set by the quantity of recoverable water under the ground, the costs of extracting it, or the decisions reached by the judges in the twenty-six adjudicated water basins.

As water levels around Paso Robles dropped, however, it became clear that the groundwater "free-for-all" was not free at all, and the costs were distributed unevenly. There was the short term economic cost of drilling ever-deeper wells—even a small-bore well for residential use costs upwards of

$25,000. A large vineyard can assume the drilling of multiple wells as a cost of production with minimal effect on profit. But because Paso Robles had become home to many retirees and other rural residents who do not practice agriculture, as well as many small-scale farmers who operate with relatively small budgets, these people saw the depletion of groundwater and the well-drilling it required as a threat to their existence, rather than just another cost of production. Some of these rural residents and small farmers hold strong environmental values, and they saw aquifer depletion as an unacceptable environmental problem, beyond the economic costs it provoked. Springs might stop flowing and water quality would diminish. Mary, an environmental activist and rural resident, told me with sadness that "steelhead trout used to come all the way up here to the headwaters of the Salinas River. Now there is no water in the river" (pers. communication, April 10, 2016). For this resident, it was riverine ecology, including federally threatened species such as the California Red-legged frog and the Steelhead trout, that motivated efforts to reduce surface and groundwater use in the region.

Rural residents and small-to medium-sized farmers initiated the push for groundwater regulation in Paso Robles, and their actions were motivated by a strong if vaguely formulated notion of group inequality conceived in terms of small property owners versus large ones. There was a certain truth to it. The folks who began to press for a groundwater moratorium were not the biggest landowners, and their vineyards were often relatively modest. Nonetheless, at the current price of (about) $40,000 per acre for irrigated land, the proverbial forty-acre parcel of land around Paso Robles is worth $1.6 million dollars—much more with vines and buildings. So, these "small" farms are often multimillion dollar businesses. They look "small" next to the large commercial wineries, which sometimes cultivate thousands of acres. Some of the larger, commercial vineyards and wineries also spoke out against groundwater depletion, recognizing that their livelihoods were just as threatened as the others by unregulated groundwater use, despite their greater ability to absorb the high costs. In an initial moment, however, groundwater use resembled a "tragedy of the commons" scenario, where no one user would reduce pumping despite the fact that all would benefit if they all did.

Another divide was perceived by this amorphous social group of rural dwellers between themselves and the urban residents of Paso Robles. Urban dwellers far outnumber rural dwellers in the Paso Robles Groundwater Basin, but they are less wealthy. About 40 percent of urban residents in Paso are renters rather than property owners, and they are more often workers in the agricultural, service, and tourism industries, rather than owners of their own businesses. Furthermore, residents within city limits are provided water through the municipal water company—the "purveyor"—and it is the city rather than the individual property owners that holds "overlying rights" to the water. Race and ethnicity intersects with social class in the rural-urban divide, as more than one-third of residents of Paso Robles city are of Latino, mostly Mexican, descent, and many work in the vineyards (United States Census Bureau 2010). Rural residents tended to differentiate themselves from the urban residents by saying it was the wine grape agriculture that drove the economy, providing jobs to everyone else, and by claiming that they had the deepest roots in the region. Because rural dwellers were extremely aware of groundwater depletion and urban residents were far less so (they do not have their own wells), the push for groundwater sustainability in Paso Robles was led by white, relatively wealthy, rural dwellers. City water purveyors mobilized their own considerable resources behind the effort to economize and rationalize water use in the basin, but urban citizens in general did not mobilize, except for those with deep environmental values.

Once the problem of groundwater depletion was made visible by this mass of small farmers and rural dwellers, the regional press publicized the issue.[4] In March 2012, the county of SLO formed a "Blue Ribbon Committee" to study the problem of groundwater, made up of representatives of different social groups, each with longstanding presence in the region. In 2014, this committee was reformed as the Groundwater Advisory Board (GAB) and remained outside of the apparatus of county government while holding an official advisory role.

In addition to the GAB, various organizations formed to discuss, devise, and propose solutions to the problem before and after the declaration of the "urgency ordinance" that established the moratorium on groundwater extraction. The Paso Robles Alliance for Groundwater Solutions (PRAAGS) was a group that advocated for a "hybrid" water district model that ensures some representation of large landowners, small landowners, and rural residents. The board of this organization was made up of vineyard and cattle ranch owners, and others who own businesses related to agriculture. They tended to be from longstanding, economically strong families in the region. For example, PRAAGS board member, Matt Turrentine, came from a wine brokering family. Turrentine gained some dubious fame for brokering a series of deals by which large tracts of irrigated land, some planted in grapes, were sold to investment banking firms such as the Harvard University Trust (Philpott 2015). The PRAAGS organization backed the passage of Assembly Bill 2453 in the California State legislature, which was necessary to form a hybrid water district in Paso Robles that did not conform to the legal standard of the "one-acre, one-vote" formula of representation and cost distribution.

Pro Water Equity (PWE) was a parallel organization that

also emerged in this context to champion a model of managing groundwater with a regional "water district" that has equitable and proportional representation built into the board. The organization came into existence when fissures between people working on this issue led to a separation with the PRAAGS. PWE had some support from small-scale farmers and winery owners but gained the bulk of its membership among the rural residents in the Paso Robles groundwater basin. It was a volunteer organization that did not have the clear association with big agricultural interests that characterized PRAAGS. Its members argued for greater representation of small landowners in groundwater management than that contemplated in the hybrid water district approved by Assembly Bill 2453.

A third group, "Protect Our Water Rights" (POWR), rejected the water district model entirely, arguing instead for protecting the water rights of overlying property owners through the adjudication process in the courts. Adjudication is very costly and time-consuming; it can take decades and tens of millions of dollars in lawyers and court fees. PRAAGS and PWE both formed with the intention of reaching a political solution without entering the adjudication process. POWR, guided by a deep distrust of government and an exalted faith in property rights, rejected the hybrid, representational model of the water district outlined in the Assembly Bill 2435. Instead, POWR encouraged hundreds of landowners to file "quiet title" documentation with the courts that protected their water rights from encroachment.

Another key motivation of POWR was to defend its members and all residents of Paso Robles from water speculators, and in particular the large investors who might want to practice water trading or banking with Paso Robles' groundwater or aquifer. Water banking is a method of management of surface and groundwater in which an owner of physical water can store it in an aquifer for future use. The model assumes that in times of abundance, surface water would be used to recharge aquifers for use in times of scarcity. This storing cheap and selling dear would of course result in huge profits, as surplus water can be had for pennies per acre/foot and sold later for as much as $1,600 per acre/foot. According to a POWR organizer, Tracy, who farms five hundred acres of wine grapes, water banking and the creation of water markets mark a slow process of dispossession of the water rights of overlying property owners by big businesses working through government. "The only way to protect our water rights," she told a group convened to discuss groundwater management, "is to have them recognized by the courts" (pers. communication, September 3, 2014). Rights to aquifers, she insisted, are held by overlying property owners, and POWR defended these rights as a way to protect against water bankers and speculators who could gain control of the water district through electoral politics and could sell Paso Robles groundwater to urban developers in Southern California.

Maneuvers such as water banking are certainly not unheard of in California, where billionaire farming corporations exert constant pressure to control water. One company, Paramount Farms, owned by Stewart and Linda Resnick, holds enormous extensions of land in the dry Westlands irrigation district on the western side of California's southern Central Valley, where it grows almonds, pomegranates, and other crops. The Resnicks were instrumental in creating the Kern County Water Bank, inland from San Luis Obispo County, by buying up all the land over an aquifer and using it to store cheaply bought water for future use or sale. In 2011, their Fiji Water Company bought Justin Wineries in SLO, fueling speculation that they were making a water grab in the Paso Robles Groundwater Basin and perhaps trying to make a play for creating a water bank there ("Justin Vineyards" 2010). PRAAGS, with its Board of

Directors comprised of wealthy and powerful members of the region's wine industry, declared itself in favor of water banking. POWR's fears were perhaps not unfounded.

From Hybrid District to SGMA

The process of forming a water district to manage groundwater in Paso Robles was highly contested. One key problem was the representational structure of the district. California law enshrines water districts as organizations formed by landowners to build, maintain, and operate surface water storage and conveyance infrastructures. Usually these districts derive water from a river or canal, and distribute it among the landowners, but sometimes these districts also use settling ponds to recharge aquifers with water to be used later. California water districts operate like companies, and those who derive the most benefit from them pay the most for them, in a proportional manner. Thus, for example, if a landowner owns 5 percent of the land serviced by a water district, that landowner pays 5 percent of the costs and receives 5 percent of the water. This proportional principle also holds for the election of members to the Board of Directors of a water district: one acre, one vote. The landowner who owns 5 percent of the land has 5 percent of the votes.

The one acre, one vote mode of representation may make sense for traditional California water districts that manage surface water for irrigation, but it was seen as deeply problematic for overlying property owners and residents of the Paso Robles groundwater basin. In the first place, there was no conveyance and storage infrastructure to build, maintain, and operate in Paso Robles: the purpose of the proposed water district was to manage levels of extraction, with relatively minor costs for monitoring. Second, proportional voting would give the power to make decisions about extraction and conservation to the largest growers, seen by rural residents and small farmers to be the cause of aquifer depletion and dry wells in the first place. As one activist, Mary, put it, "proportional voting sends us back to the eighteenth century" when only property-owning white males could vote in the United States (pers. communication, April 27, 2014). When a prominent water lawyer drew up the plans for a traditional California water district in Paso Robles, overliers rejected it and demanded one that was more representative.

The GAB and San Luis Obispo County officials worked for years to design a representational format for the proposed groundwater water district that would be acceptable to the various groups in the groundwater basin. In the end, they came up with a complicated arrangement for electing directors to the Water District Board of Directors that gave votes to both overlying residents and to landowners (often the same person fit into both categories). There were nine seats in total: three to be elected by registered voters on a one person, one vote basis; and six to be elected by landowners on a one acre, one vote basis. However, these six landowner seats were divided into small landowners (less than forty acres), medium landowners (forty to four hundred acres), and large landowners (more than four hundred acres), each with two seats. Any landowner could only vote within their ownership category, and their vote was weighted by the number of acres they owned. Any registered voter within the district boundary could run for the registered voter seats, and any landowner could run for any of the landowner seats. This plan was thus a "hybrid" of representational and proportional voting systems. Because the hybrid district differed from the standard California water district, the California legislature approved it with Assembly Bill 2453. The hybrid water district proposal was approved by the San Luis Obispo County Local Agency Formation Committee, and it was put to popular vote.

The creation of the Paso Robles hybrid groundwater district was soundly rejected in an election held in February 2016. The San Luis Obispo County (SLO) government ran an extensive informational campaign about AB 2453 in the months preceding the election. SLO's Public Works Department held dozens of meetings with local residents to explain the details of the plan, but dissent increased as the election neared. Protect Our Water Rights (POWR) was especially vocal, fighting against any form of water district on the basis that groundwater was property of the landowner, and the political management of groundwater exposed landowners to the risk of dispossession by government and big business. POWR held informational meetings, social events such as barbeques and concerts, and advocated for adjudication as the only form of groundwater management that protected the individual property right to water. At the same time, critics on the left continued to voice that the proposed hybrid water district was fundamentally undemocratic and assigned the costs of operation disproportionally to the smallholders and rural residents. Despite the support of the local press and county government, 74 percent of the voters rejected the formation of a hybrid water district. Even more rejected a new tax to support regulation of the groundwater basin.

What made this resounding "no" vote especially interesting is that at the same time the Hybrid Water District process was unfolding in Paso Robles, the State of California was implementing a statewide regulatory framework for sustainably managing groundwater: the Sustainable Groundwater Management Act (SGMA). SGMA was passed into law in late 2014 and went into effect on January 1, 2015. For all but those few previously adjudicated basins, SGMA requires that overliers in each groundwater basin form Groundwater Sustainability Agencies (GSAs) by June 30, 2017, and that these GSAs create and carry out Groundwater Sustainability Plans (GSPs) by January 31, 2020 (or 2022, depending on the severity of overdraft in the groundwater basin). Any groundwater basin that does not meet these requirements will be put on probation by the California State Water Board, which then administers the basin and charges the overliers for the service, until the time when the overliers can file an acceptable GSA or GSP. Existing water agencies such as community service districts (CSDs), water districts (WDs), and county governments can be named GSAs, and it is the county governments that assume responsibility for all lands not covered by those other agencies.[5]

Paso Robles groundwater basin overliers, having rejected the hybrid water district, scrambled to comply with SGMA. Because water politics are so complicated, and many of the overliers reject the idea of water districts, only one such agency was formed before the GSA deadline of June 30, 2017: the Shandon-San Juan Water District, and another—the Estrella-El Pomar-Creston Water District—was in the formation process. Both of these water districts operate with the "one acre, one vote" proportionality principal and allow landowners within their boundaries to opt out of membership. Many have opted out, which has led to a highly fragmented, checkerboard pattern to the water districts and the need for the county government to cover groundwater sustainability activities in those areas not included in the water districts, paying for the services out of the county's general fund. Some of those resisting inclusion in the water districts cite fears of water banking; others simply do not want to pay both the charges assessed by the water district to run the GSA, and the county tax levied for the same reason. Whatever the reasons for resisting the creation of a basin-wide agency, Paso Robles enters the SGMA era with many of its groundwater users unconvinced of the need to treat groundwater as a common pool resource and with lingering suspicion about the aims of the state and capital in establishing such a hydro-commons.

Conclusion: Creating a Commons

In 2013, at the height of the recent extreme drought, the groundwater-fueled California wine crush was the biggest on record (CDFA 2015). In 2014 and 2015, farmers all over California were denied surface water allocations by the federal and California irrigation systems, and they increased groundwater pumping. The drought abated in most of California due to heavy rains and snow in the winter of 2016–2017, but the Central Coast is still relatively dry, and many areas such as Paso Robles that are not serviced by surface water irrigation systems continue to depend on groundwater. Although SGMA was passed in 2014, it will not be until the GSPs are submitted in 2020–2022 that any limits on groundwater extraction are likely to be set. And overlying groundwater users will have until 2040–2042 to restore groundwater levels to something like those of January 1, 2015 and reach equilibrium between extraction and recharge. A water manager, Tyler, in the Central Valley of California shared with me his opinion that many agricultural producers will simply ignore the regulations as long as possible, maximizing short term profits, and quit the business or declare bankruptcy when faced with sanctions. "If people are serious about reducing groundwater extraction, you will see property values falling," he told me in late 2016, "but for many parcels they aren't" (pers. communication, December 17, 2016). Agricultural land for orchards has indeed dropped in price in much of California, but vineyards have held their value (Rodriguez 2017).

While the twenty-year timeline for implementing state regulation of groundwater may seem very long, the SGMA legislation has already had effects. Growers in the Central Coast, driven by the profit motive and a strong market for wine, continue to maximize their individual benefit by perforating wells and even—as in the case of the North Fork

Ranch in Cuyama (actually an investment by the Harvard University Trust through the company Grapevine Capital)—converting hundreds of acres of grazing land to grapes. But in this changed legal and regulatory context, there are also signs that county governments are willing to take actions to protect groundwater as a public good. Paso Robles' urgency ordinance was copied by the Board of Supervisors of Ventura County to stop aquifer depletion in the Santa Clarita River drainage. Other counties, such as Santa Barbara and Modesto, failed to pass similar legislation, but the SLO Board of Supervisors approved ordinance 3308 that prohibits any new extractions from the Paso Robles aquifer until the GSP for that basin is formulated and goes into effect. This moratorium effectively locks existing water extractions in place and is supported by landowners (usually smaller producers and rural residents) wishing to protect their wells. Other county governments are considering implementing ordinances such as that passed in Paso Robles to avoid a rush of well-drilling before SGMA's GSPs go into effect and are fully implemented over the next two decades. Regardless of the mechanism by which overliers seek to regulate groundwater extraction, scarcity and the SGMA legislation have prompted government officials and landowners to begin to think about groundwater as a shared common-pool resource.

It is not at all clear how well groundwater regulation in the form of SGMA will work in California over the long term. At this early stage in the process, there is indication that local overliers of groundwater basins are taking the process seriously, under the threat that if they fail to comply with the law, the California Department of Water Resources (DWR) will take over the management of their basin and charge them for the service, with penalties. So, although the SGMA law was designed to minimize state involvement in the regulatory process, the DWR may need to expand its enforcement capacity greatly. It is also likely that some disgruntled overliers will push water management back into the courts through the adjudication process. A better outcome would be that the actual process of management will generate local enforcement capacity and positive values for groundwater that help consolidate the sustainable management of the resource. The conceptualization of groundwater as a common-pool resource will likely strengthen and spread as overliers participate in the formation of GSAs and GSPs, and in the daily activity of monitoring and ensuring the sustainability of their—and their neighbors'–water use.

This would be a positive outcome and would work against the efforts of individuals to elude and bypass regulation in order to realize short-term profits by draining the state's aquifers. And it would come none too soon, as climate change will most likely reduce precipitation in the southern half of the state of California, reduce the Sierra Nevada snowcap that works as the great storage mechanism for the state, and alter the timing of the snowmelt that feeds the reservoirs. But while California remains one of the world's premier agricultural producers, the water scarcity created by climate change and successful common pool resource management will certainly push capital toward investments in other places, where such management is lax or absent. The transnationalization of agriculture (Friedmann and McMichael 1989) has already morphed into a more sweeping tendency toward wholesale land and water "grabs" throughout the global south (Edelman, Oya, and Borras Jr. 2013). Unfortunately, the successful sustainable regulation of groundwater in California may depend on its unsustainable extraction elsewhere. The process of creating groundwater commons would have to proceed within hugely variable regimes of rights, customs, social institutions, and cultural values. At the very least, then, the future of SGMA cannot be understood independent from these other groundwater-fueled processes of agricultural development and management.

Notes

1. There is a vast discussion of "common-pool resources," "commons," "public goods," and other concepts used to understand how people share things. One scholar whose ideas have been applied to groundwater management in recent years in California is Elinor Ostrom (pers. communication, Seth, Paso Robles, January 31, 2017).

2. Funding for this research was provided by UC-MEXUS, through a collaborative grant to the author and Yanga Villagómez, to study "Groundwater Use and Management in the Context of Globalized Agriculture and Climate Change." UC-MEXUS is a research center of the University of California and Mexico's National Science and Technology Council, or CONACYT.

3. Prowater Equity, a group formed to argue for controlling on groundwater extractions, has collected testimonies about aquifer depletion and its effects on wells throughout the Paso Robles area. See: http://prowaterequity .org/stories/. Retrieved 2/27/2015.

4. A number of people active in water politics at the time cited a series of 2012 and 2013 articles in the *San Luis Obispo Tribune* for bringing the issue to the forefront of politics. See, for example, "Deep Trouble in North County." *San Luis Obispo Tribune*, June 16, 2013. http://www.sanluisobispo.com/news /special-reports/article39447159.html.

5. It is impossible to cover the details of the Sustainable Groundwater Management Act in this chapter. For more information see: http://www.water.ca .gov/groundwater/sgm/.

References

Arax, Mark, and Rick Wartzman. 2003. *The King of California: JG Boswell and the Making of a Secret American Empire.* New York: Public Affairs.

Berg, Neil, A. Hall, F. Sun, S. Capps, D. Walton, B. Langenbrunner, and D. Neelin. 2015. "Twenty-First-Century Precipitation Changes Over the Los Angeles Region." *Journal of Climate* 28: 401–21. DOI: 10.1175/JCLI-D-14–00316.1.

Bourdieu, Pierre. 1984. *Distinction: A Social Critique of the Judgement of Taste.* Cambridge MA: Harvard University Press.

Budds, Jessica. 2004. "Power, Nature and Neoliberalism: The Political Ecology of Water in Chile." *Singapore Journal of Tropical Geography* 25, no. 3: 322–42.

Buffalo, Sally. 2016. "Former Meridian Winery to Take on Treasury's 'Masstige' Wines." *Paso Robles Tribune*, June 8, 2016. http://www.sanluisobispo .com/news/business/article82606687.html.

California Department of Food and Agriculture (CDFA). 2015. "Grape Crush Report, Final 2014." Sacramento: CDFA.

Durack, Paul, S. E. Wijffels, and R. J. Matear. 2012. "Ocean Salinities Reveal Strong Global Water Cycle Intensification During 1950 to 2000." *Science* 336: 455–8. DOI: 10.1126/science.1212222.

Edelman, Marc, Carlos Oya, and Saturnino M. Borras, Jr. 2013. "Global Land Grabs: Historical Processes, Theoretical and Methodological Implications and Current Trajectories." *Third World Quarterly* 34: 1517–31.

Fairbairn, Madeleine. 2014. "'Like Gold with Yield': Evolving Intersections Between Farmland and Finance." *Journal of Peasant Studies* 41, no. 5: 777–95.

Famiglietti, J. S., M. Lo, S. L. Ho, J. Bethune, K. J. Anderson, T. H. Syed, S. C. Swenson, C. R. De Linage, and M. Rodell. 2011. "Satellites Measure Recent Rates of Groundwater Depletion in California's Central Valley." *Geophysical Research Letters* 38, no. 3.

Famiglietti, James S. 2014. "The Global Groundwater Crisis." *Nature Climate Change* 4, no. 11: 945–8.

Friedmann, Harriet, and Philip McMichael. 1989. "Agriculture and the State System: The Rise and Decline of National Agricultures, 1870 to the Present." *Sociologia Ruralis* 29, no. 2: 93–117.

Fulton, Julian, Heather Cooley, and Peter H. Gleick. 2014. "Water Footprint Outcomes and Policy Relevance Change with Scale Considered: Evidence from California." *Water Resources Management* 28, no. 11: 3637–49.

Giordano, Mark. 2009. "Global Groundwater? Issues and Solutions." *Annual Review of Environment and Resources* 34: 153–78.

Glennon, Robert Jerome. 2004. *Water Follies: Groundwater Pumping and the Fate of America's Fresh Waters.* Washington DC: Island Press.

Goldschmidt, Walter. 1978. *As You Sow: Three Studies in the Social Consequences of Agribusiness.* New York: Rowman and Littlefield.

Haley, Brian. 1989. "Aspects and Social Impacts of Size and Organization in the Recently Developed Wine Industry of Santa Barbara County, California." Vol. 2. Center for Chicano Studies, University of California, Santa Barbara.

Harvey, David. 1989. *The Condition of Postmodernity: An Enquiry into the Origins of Social Change.* Malden MA: Blackwell.

Holmes, Seth. 2013. *Fresh Fruit, Broken Bodies: Migrant Farmworkers in the United States.* Berkeley: University of California Press.

Hundley, Norris, Jr. 2001. *The Great Thirst: Californians and Water—A History.* Berkeley: University of California Press.

"Justin Vineyards Acquired by Fiji Water." *Wine Spectator*, December 5, 2010. http://www.winespectator.com/webfeature/show/id/44174.

Klein, Naomi. 2002. *No Logo: No Space, No Choice, No Jobs.* New York: Picador.

Langridge, Ruth, Abigail Brown, Kirsten Rudestam, and Esther Conrad. 2016. "An Evaluation of California's Adjudicated Groundwater Basins." Report for the California State Water Resources Control Board. http://www.waterboards.ca.gov/water_issues/programs/gmp/docs/resources/swrcb_012816.pdf.

McMichael, Philip. 2009. "A Food Regime Genealogy." *The Journal of Peasant Studies* 36, no. 1: 139–69.

Paso Robles Housing Division. 2018. "Housing: Demographics." http://www
.prcity.com/government/departments/commdev/housing/demographics
.asp#history.

Philpott, Tom. 2015. "Harvard is Buying Up Vineyards in Drought-Ridden
California Wine Country." *Mother Jones*, January 31, 2015. http://www
.motherjones.com/food/2015/01/wine-water-harvards-move-california
-farmland/.

Pisani, Donald J. 1984. *From the Family Farm to Agribusiness: The Irrigation Cru-
sade in California and the West, 1850–1931*. Berkeley: University of California Press.

Prowaterequity.org. n.d. "Stories." Accessed February 27, 2015.

Rodriguez, Robert. 2017. "Farmland Values in the Central San Joaquin Decline
in 2016 as Crop Prices Tumble." *The Fresno Bee*, March 30, 2017. http://
www.fresnobee.com/news/business/agriculture/article141831134.html.

Roseberry, William. 1996. "The Rise of Yuppie Coffees and the Reimagination
of Class in the United States." *American Anthropologist* 98, no. 4: 762–75.

Scanlon, B. R., Longuevergne, L., and Long, D. 2012. "Ground Referenc-
ing GRACE Satellite Estimates of Groundwater Storage Changes in the
California Central Valley, USA." *Water Resources Research* 48, no. 4. DOI:
10.1029/2011WRO11312.

Schneider, Jane. 1994. "In and Out of Polyester: Desire, Disdain and Global
Fibre Competitions." *Anthropology Today* 10, no. 4: 2–10.

Stiglitz, Joseph E. 2012. *The Price of Inequality: How Today's Divided Society Endangers our Future*. New York: W. W. Norton.

Taylor, Richard G., Bridget Scanlon, Petra Döll, Matt Rodell, Rens Van Beek,
Yoshihide Wada, Laurent Longuevergne, et al. 2013. "Ground Water and
Climate Change." *Nature Climate Change* 3, no. 4: 322–9.

UC Center for Hydrologic Modeling (UCCHM). 2014. "Water Storage Changes
in California's Sacramento and San Joaquin River Basins from GRACE:
Preliminary Updated Results for 2003–2013." Irvine: UC Center for Hydrologic Modeling, University of California, Irvine.

United States Census Bureau. n.d. 2010 Census: Apportionment Data Map,
CA—El Paso de Robles (Paso Robles) city. Accessed March 2, 2015. https://
www.census.gov/2010census/popmap/ipmtext.php?fl=06:0622300.

Volpe, R., Richard Green, Dale Heien, and Richard Howitt. 2010. "Wine-
grape Production Trends Reflect Evolving Consumer Demand over 30
Years." *California Agriculture* 64, no. 1: 42–6.

Voss, Katalyn A., James S. Famiglietti, MinHui Lo, Caroline Linage, Matthew
Rodell, and Sean C. Swenson. 2013. "Groundwater Depletion in the Middle East from GRACE with Implications for Transboundary Water Management in the Tigris-Euphrates Western Iran Region." *Water Resources
Research* 49, no. 2: 904–14.

Watson, James L., and Melissa L. Caldwell. 2005. *The Cultural Politics of Food and Eating: A Reader*. Malden MA: Blackwell.

Woodhouse, Philip. 2012. "Foreign Agricultural Land Acquisition and the Visibility of Water Resource Impacts in Sub-Saharan Africa." *Water Alternatives* 5, no. 2: 208.

Worster, Donald. 1985. *Rivers of Empire: Water, Aridity, and the Growth of the American West*. New York: Pantheon.

Zetland, David. 2009. "The End of Abundance: How Water Bureaucrats Created and Destroyed the Southern California Oasis." *Water Alternatives* 2, no. 3: 350–69.

Zlolniski, Christian. 2011. "Water Flowing North of the Border: Export Agriculture and Water Politics in a Rural Community in Baja California." *Cultural Anthropology* 26, no. 4: 565–88.

6

Forecasting the Challenges of Climate Change
for West Texas Wheat Farmers

SARA E. ALEXANDER

I've seen a lot of scary weather in my day. Lots of
tornadoes, passing right overhead. But nothing as
scary as what's been happening here the last few years.
Texas weather has always been unpredictable—there
are plenty of jokes about Texas weather—but I've never
felt anything like now. Hard rains, massive . . . brutal
flash floods and then nothin' . . . no rains at all, for
months on end. Summers are longer, hotter, drier, than
I remember my whole life. Makes me wonder what's
gonna happen to farming around here.

"Tim," seventy-four-year-old farmer, Taylor County, Texas

Globally, climate change is the most serious environmental threat affecting agricultural productivity. The relationship between climate change and agriculture is of particular
importance as the imbalance between world population
and world food production intensifies (IPCC 2014a, 6).
Based on projections for 2030, changes in temperature,
rainfall, and severe weather events are expected to reduce
crop yields in developing areas, particularly in sub-Saharan
Africa and parts of East Asia. Increased productivity is projected in select industrialized regions including Scandina-
via and the High Plains of North America (IPCC 2014b,
362; Yohannes 2016, 335). The consequences of climate

change for agriculture will be more severe for countries with higher initial temperatures, areas with marginal or already degraded lands, and lower levels of development, which in turn, may ultimately determine optimal adaptation capacity (Yohannes 2016, 337).

The nature of agriculture and farming practices in any particular location is strongly influenced by the long-term mean climate state—the experience and infrastructure of local agricultural communities are generally appropriate to particular types of farming and to a distinct variety of crops that are known to be productive under a present-day climate (Gornall et al. 2010, 2975). Changes in the mean climate away from current states will most likely require adjustments to existing practices to maintain productivity. In some cases, the optimum type of farming system will entail major alterations.

Climate change is projected to impact a range of human, social, and cultural resources, including infrastructure, transportation systems, and human health, as well as energy, food, and water supplies (IPCC 2014b). Populations that are most vulnerable, namely young children, pregnant women, the elderly, and the economically poor, will likely face greater challenges, especially those living in areas of developing countries most vulnerable to coastal storms, drought, and rising sea levels (Climate Change Science Program 2008). Certain professions and industries will also face considerable challenges, principally those closely linked to weather and climate conditions, such as construction, air travel, outdoor and wilderness recreation, ranching and farming, and some forms of tourism (U.S. Global Change Research Program 2009).

A changing climate will fundamentally alter many agricultural communities (Lal, Alavalapati, and Mercer 2010, 822). Crop productivity will not only be affected by abiotic elements (rising temperatures, declining water supplies, and increasing salinity and inundation levels), but also certain biotic stressors (higher incidence of pests or diseases) which will collectively impact soil conditions, water quality and supply, and could cause certain types of ecological contamination (Lal, Alavalapati, and Mercer 2010). Hence, a key challenge for future successful cultivation is for farmers to recognize the inter-relationships among key variables and to determine how specific varieties of crops can react to a range of stressors as they play out in certain changing climates.

Subsequently, farmers are challenged to secure the critical resources they need to cultivate crops, while the harmful consequences of agricultural production on our natural resource base is progressively more forceful. Intensifying these concerns are the risks associated with climate change and growing apprehension for how coping and adaptive strategies will affect life on the farm in its broader sense (Godfray et al. 2010, 812).

Godfray et al. (2010), von Braun (2007), and Pretty (2008) call for a "new agricultural revolution" to address these difficulties, with a comprehensive restructuring of the roles agricultural knowledge, science, and technology play in crop cultivation. Agriculture must not be thought of only in terms of production processes (Pretty 2008). Analyses must also consider how economics, social life, values, cultural norms, political decisions, and ecological services are synthesized and integrated into the broader system of which agriculture is a part (Crane et al. 2010; Godfray et al. 2010, 812).

In this chapter, I present findings from an ethnographic pilot study in West Texas wheat farmers in the context of the factors named above and the dire predictions for declines in wheat production in Texas over the near future. The study focuses on farmers' awareness of changing weather patterns, their use of climate forecasts in farm decision making, and subsequent implications for the viability of their choices in terms of successful production. Specifically, the research explores what motivates farmers and how they value those factors that contribute to secure livelihoods and fulfilled ambitions; their awareness of recent changes in local weather and their understanding of the potential impacts climate change can have on wheat cultivation; how they see themselves addressing climate risk in the context of their chosen lifeway, including configurations of norms, values, meanings, and knowledge; any mitigation measures they have adopted relative to recent weather patterns; and their acceptance of risks regarding changing climate conditions.

Scholars in an array of disciplines have researched the influence climate change is having and will continue to have on agricultural production globally and more pointedly here, in several areas of the United States—the Midwest, South, and Southwest (Barnett et al. 2008; Coles and Scott 2009; Gleick 2010). Much less research has addressed these impacts from the farmer's point of view, and in terms of how they respond to and plan for weather events and trends in their production systems (Brugger and Crimmons 2013; Buys, Miller, and van Megen 2012; Hu et al. 2006). Only a small body of literature addresses the farmers' understanding and use of climate (forecasting) information as part of their responses to certain weather predictions that could potentially have significant impact on their cultivation (Crane et al. 2010; Eakin 2000; McCrea, Dalgleish, and Coventry 2005). Farmers understand how particular weather events affect crop production, a critical factor in making longer-term farming system decisions that respond to climate change events.

The following section brings out key points from this literature and introduces the idea of "performative agriculture" as a critical concept serving as the basis for this study.

This discussion is followed by a brief summary of recent trends in Texas wheat cultivation relative to weather patterns, climate variability, political decisions, and the nature of recent developments regarding institutional support.

Farmers' Responses to Climate Change

There is no greater challenge to farmers worldwide than climate variability (Eakin 2000; Wilken 1987). Farmers obviously require particular environmental conditions to produce a high yield, which necessitates the management of risks associated with climate. These relatively few studies focus on a limited number of factors that can influence how farmers perceive risks associated with climate change and how they in turn act to mitigate climatic hazards. Eakin's study of the responses to climate variability on the part of small-scale maize farmers in Mexico indicates that their feelings of uncertainty relative to political-economic variables offset climate risks as the major determinant of production choices (2000, 20). Menzie's edited volume, which examines a range of communities along the Pacific Northwest Coast region, offers analyses of opportunities afforded by the local practice of traditional ecological knowledge (TEK) in response to unaccustomed climate risks, as well as the cultural importance of different subsistence practices using natural elements. The macro-level institutional reforms that were part of the restructuring of the North American Free Trade Agreement (NAFTA) in 1994 hindered the effectiveness of response strategies, especially for those farmers who were among the more "ecologically and economically marginalized" in the society (2006, 24).

From an economic standpoint, farming is a difficult, precarious, and expensive endeavor. Market and climate volatility may mean that farmers do not know their costs in advance, whether environmental conditions will favor production, or the price their yield will bring. An under-researched topic is that of the "performative element" of agriculture (Crane et al. 2010, 45), in which farmers engage in creative problem-solving in ways that draw on a pragmatic inventory of knowledge, skills, networks, and technologies connected by interrelated social and biophysical conditions (Crane et al. 2010, 46). Seen as performance, agricultural management is "a blend of planning, knowledge, experimentation, and circumstantial improvisation within an ever-shifting environment" (Batterbury 2001; Richards 1993). The result is a process whereby dynamic external conditions and available resources are to form a basic structure within which farmers apply their skills to leverage opportunities while working to minimize risks.

The range of impact levels caused by climate change can easily throw a wrench into the good intentions of performative agriculture. In Mozambique, both farmers and government workers disputed the seriousness of climate risks as well as the potential negative consequences of proposed adaptive measures (Patt and Schröter 2008). A program designed to educate these farmers about climate variation did little to change their beliefs, as their social and cultural backgrounds were disregarded in the approach used in the curricula. Therefore, these groups ultimately rejected the data presented supporting climate change as a serious threat to their livelihoods because it made little sense to them.

Basic obstacles to recognizing risks of changing weather and climate variability present themselves in the most obvious of cases. Climate change is projected to seriously impact agriculture in Australia by an overall decline of 17 percent by 2050, resulting from falloffs in productivity that brings into question the basic viability of family farms (Commonwealth of Australia 2008). Buys, Miller, and van Megen predicted improving adaptive capacity to climate change would become more prominent as a priority for rural Australia, given heavy dependence on natural resources for livelihoods, yet residents "remain[ed] skeptical about climate change" (2012, 251), citing drought and climate variations as a normalcy of rural life. Rooted in their position is the belief that local climatic changes are due to natural climate variability and not to anthropogenic causes (McDonald, Thwaites, and Retra 2006; Thwaites et al. 2008), a pronounced theme that may prove to endanger lives of entire populations.

In sum, in the face of climate uncertainty, we should expect farmers to seek to reduce their vulnerability by using multiple forms of knowledge and skills in combination with relevant technologies such as irrigation systems or improved seeds; institutional supports such as insurance credit and farm subsidies; and social networks comprising family and communities, but also extension and marketing groups—all of which, by the way, can lead to increased vulnerability of farms to the same forces that have been disenfranchising farmers for decades. Conceptualizing agriculture as performance emphasizes that risks, such as flooding or drought, are embedded within a complex system of interrelated biophysical and socioeconomic processes that are continuously being navigated by farmers. Agricultural practice is meant to be equally grounded in a landscape of shared worldviews, social identities, moral values, and cultural norms (Crane et al. 2010, 46; Jennings 2002). In this perspective, farming decisions acquire meanings and follow pathways that are far more complex than assumed when only considering agricultural productivity and economic principles. Rather, they engage farmers' subjectivity and socialization in addition to their technical skills and resource endowment (Lind 1995).

Will Wheat Production Wither in Texas?

Over the next century, Texas will experience significant climate change (USEPA 2007). Based on IPCC projections and the United Kingdom Hadley Centre's climate model

(HadCM2), by 2100 temperatures in Texas could increase by 3°F (~1.7°C) in spring and by approximately 4°F (2.2°C) in other seasons. Precipitation is estimated to decrease by 5–30 percent in winter and increase by approximately 10 percent in other seasons (USGCRP 2009). These changes have the potential to profoundly affect Texas crop production, including wheat.

Agriculture is a $12.6 billion per annum industry in Texas, and 86 percent of land is in some form of agricultural production. Texas leads the nation in the number of farms and ranches; there are 248,800 farms encompassing a total of 130.2 million acres; 98.6 percent of Texas' agricultural operations are family farms, partnerships, or family-held corporations. Approximately 25 percent of crop acreage is irrigated (Texas Dept. of Agriculture 2017).

Climate change is projected to reduce cotton and sorghum yields by 2–15 percent and wheat yields by 43–68 percent, leading to predicted adjustments in acres farmed and diminished production levels (USEPA 2007). In 2017, 86 percent of land sown in wheat in Texas was planted in the hard red winter varieties, as they are versatile for milling and for baking pan breads. Future projections suggest that irrigated acreage (wheat is on rotation with cotton in some cases, which requires irrigation) will decline due to decreased water availability and outright scarcity. A warmer and drier climate will lead to greater evaporation, as much as 35 percent decrease in streamflow, and less water for recharging groundwater aquifers (Gosling and Arnell 2013). Increased rainfall could mitigate these effects, but it could also contribute to localized flooding as occurred in late May 2015. Farmers replanted, but the delayed harvest led to bottlenecks all through the wheat supply chain that year. This most recent event gave wheat farmers a taste of potentially important climate-related challenges they may face in upcoming decades.

Institutional Support for Texas Wheat Production

The Texas Agricultural Extension System was instituted in 1914 as part of the Texas A&M University system. Federal appropriations matched by state, county, and local funds are used to educate farmers on input developments, technology improvements, new seed varieties, and scientific information on topics like climate change. The Texas Wheat Producers Association (TWPA), which handles all local, state, and federal farm policy issues, guides its members through policy resolutions that cover farm programs, foreign trade, crop insurance, taxes, research, water management, and property rights (Texas Wheat Producers Association 2016). Some of these resolutions may work indirectly to assist farmers in responding to climate-related challenges, while others may work counter to healthy production. For example, the TWPA supports maintaining a strong crop insurance program to manage risk but maintains that crop insurance should be a voluntary option available to all farmers and should not be tied to conservation compliance, an adjusted gross income (AGI) means test, or producer payments (Texas Wheat Producers Association 2016). However, if farmers who practice conservation compliance to mitigate the effects of climate change were to pay lower premiums, such a system might incentivize them to increase their knowledge and actions surrounding crop production in a changing climate.

The TWPA has a mixed record in acknowledging climate change as an acute issue. In June 2009, the organization was one of over one hundred agricultural associations nationwide to oppose HR 245, the American Clean Energy and Security Act, given the "lack of sound research illustrating the potential effect [of climate change] on the cost of production" for American producers and consumers" (TWPA 2009). HR 245, also known as the Waxman-Markey Bill, was proposed as a means of curtailing greenhouse gas emissions linked to climate change, but the bill never made it to the Senate for a vote.

The TWPA is currently lobbying for new regulations that would recognize and approve generally accepted cultural and seeding practices by regional areas; again, if these practices incorporated the effects of climate change, farmers could go a long way toward reducing the impacts on crop production. The TWPA also intends to secure subsidies for certain new drought-resistant wheat varieties (Texas Wheat Producers Association 2016), which could help some farmers with accessibility issues to ensure higher levels of crop production.

Research Framework and Methods

Given the distance in time and space involved in climate change, people are less likely to be personally involved and concerned about an environmental threat because they may fail to see how their actions, choices, and behaviors contribute to global environmental problems. Peoples' conceptualizations and mental or cultural models of climate change are based on their social values and belief systems—which are also reflected in their language choices and their understanding of knowledge and risk (Buys, Miller, and van Megen 2012). Thus, the first component of this research is to examine West Texas wheat farmers' understanding of weather and climate. The objective of this component is to explore how this population—one that is significantly dependent on a healthy resource base and ideal climate relative to the crop varieties cultivated—understands basic concepts related to environment, weather, and climate change.

Ascertaining and managing perceptions of climate risk is critical to understanding decision-making in response to an event or to longer-term environmental change, all in reference to developing a population's adaptive capacities (Valdivia, Seth, and Gilles 2010). The second component of this research focuses on perceptions of risk—in this case, specifically those risks associated with climate events or trends that impact (or potentially could impact) farm production. Perceptions of risk influence behavior, so it is important to identify what level of awareness farmers have in reference to climate change and what factors may be influencing these perceptions (Patt and Schröter 2008; Roncoli 2006).

The sociocultural perspective of risk studies argues that perceptions and management of risk are shaped by multiple social, cultural, and political factors, and are grounded in the experience of everyday life. These circumstances bring new and considerable challenges to Texas farmers. Understanding how wheat farmers perceive and respond to risk provides another clue as to how perceptions influence human behavior, and how they mediate vulnerability and resilience within broader social and environmental systems. Investigating what wheat farmers know about climate change and its effects on their decision-making processes provides critical understanding of the interrelationships between the sources of climate change information available to certain stakeholders, the extent to which they trust these sources, and their capacity to react to and use this knowledge.

Field Methods

The findings for this chapter are based on thirty-two semi-structured, qualitative interviews, conducted between May 2015–January 2016 in five Texas counties where wheat is one of the major crops grown (Brown, Coryell, Runnels, Tom Green, and Taylor) (see figure 14). Given time and resource constraints, I used a combination of purposive and snowball sampling strategies (Bernard 2011, 145–8) to identify farmers who include wheat production in their farming system and who were willing to spend roughly two–

three hours describing the history of their farm production, knowledge of climate-related issues, responses to changing weather patterns over recent years, and their decision-making processes as reflected in those parts of their lives that provide most meaning and satisfaction.

The interview was designed to gather basic demographic information, including land and property ownership, farm history (for those who have farmed the same plots for at least five years), community experience and civic participation, decisions pertaining to land and water management, awareness of relevant policies and institutional programs that could impact their production, use of weather information and perceptions of climate change, and their plans for the future of their farm.

An initial group of possible respondents was contacted via meetings at the Texas Farm Bureau and agriculture extension offices in each county, from which names were obtained and initial contacts made. The instrument is structured to tease out not only objective information but also to elicit a more qualitative understanding of the role of resource conservation measures and predictive information in management decisions influenced by weather and climate. The open-ended structure also allows unanticipated salient issues and insights to emerge during the course of the conversation. While some data can be quantified, the emphasis in this study remains on the qualitative information provided by each farmer. Interviews were audio-recorded, transcribed, and analyzed thematically using NVivo10.0 software (QSR International).

The Study Population

In the western part of Texas, where large farms average more than two thousand acres, wheat, grain sorghum, corn, and cotton are raised in fields adjacent to immense cattle feedlots. The majority of farmers live in cities and towns, earn-

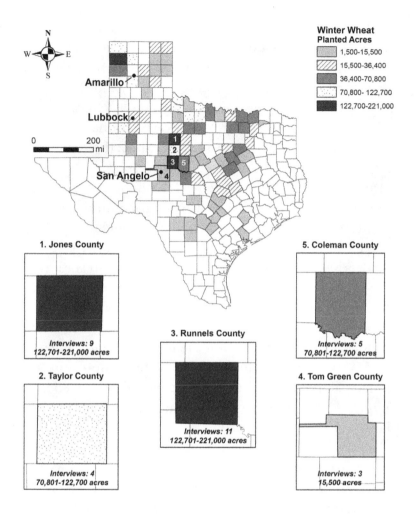

Amarillo

Lubbock

0   200
mi

San Angelo

1. Jones County

Interviews: 9
122,701-221,000 acres

2. Taylor County

Interviews: 4
70,801-122,700 acres

3. Runnels County

Interviews: 11
122,701-221,000 acres

5. Coleman County

Interviews: 5
70,801-122,700 acres

4. Tom Green County

Interviews: 3
15,500 acres

FIG. 14. Wheat production in study communities, 2013. Source:
Created by Claire Ebert, Northern Arizona University, 2018.

ing their primary income there, while commuting to their farms. Twenty-six respondents were male; twenty-one were Caucasian and the remaining eleven were Hispanic. The mean age was 54, with the eldest being 75 and the youngest 38. Education levels ranged from high school (eight) to Bachelor's degrees (nine) with one who had earned a Master's degree and one who had an M.D.; the remainder had "some college" education.

Despite a range of technological developments that have helped to improve the Texas wheat agricultural system in recent years, farmers still face challenges, including fluctuating environmental conditions and climate patterns (Smith 2010), as well as certain fungi and insect infestations—specifically the wheat streak mosaic virus, vectored by the wheat curl mite (*Aceria tosichella*) (Velandia et al. 2010). This threat has proven to be a major limiting factor in wheat production in this region. It is the most frequently encountered virus in these counties, affecting both shoot and root biomass; and consequently it has drastically reduced both forage and grain yield, as well as water-use efficiency of the plant (Velandia et al. 2010).

In the study region, the summers are hot and humid; the winters are short, cold, dry, and windy; and it is on average "partly cloudy" year-round. Over the course of the year, the temperature typically varies from 35°F to 96°F and is rarely below 24°F or above 102°F (Weatherspark 2017). Based on daily averages aggregated for the period from 1980–2016 for San Angelo, the hot season extends from mid-May to mid-September, with an average daily temperature above 89°F. The cool season lasts from late November to late February, with an average daily temperature below 67°F. The rainy season extends from late April to late October, with the chance of a wet day peaking at 31 percent on May 27. The drier season also lasts six months, from late October to late April.

Alexander

Today, as reported by the respondents, the most commonly cited constraints to their cultivation success are rising temperatures, increased number of "hot" days, erratic and changing rainfall patterns, and additional stress derived from insect and disease outbreaks. Though the application of scientific and technological practices could ameliorate some of these challenges, West Texas farmers across the region report feeling a sense of hopelessness when their crops are destroyed (USEPA 2007). The fear of being caught on the wrong side of the cost-price squeeze is ever present. As commercial operators depend on agribusiness suppliers, they report feelings of vulnerability in reference to any variation in costs or slippage in prices that can place them in jeopardy. Aside from the costs of crop production, those farmers who irrigate their cotton fear the threatened depletion of the Ogallala Aquifer (Hartmann 2017), which has made the region one of the most productive in the state. Despite such remedial efforts as the organization of water-conservation districts authorized by the Texas Legislature in 1949 (Texas State Historical Association 2017), the return of substantial watered acreage to dry land, the promotion of minimum tillage techniques, and the installation of more efficient equipment such as center-pivot sprinklers or low-energy pressure-application systems, concerns about aquifer depletion remain. Furthermore, though farmers recognize that both national and international incidents could influence their livelihood, an element of insecurity exists when political leaders make broad-ranging policy decisions that, in turn, affect the resources they may have available to them to secure their livelihoods (Smith 2010).

The farmers who participated in this study mostly come from either farming or farming and ranching families. Regardless of whether they work full- or part-time off-farm jobs, the majority identified themselves as farmers or ranchers. Most respondents who were working outside jobs were doing so to help support their farming business. Only two do not fit this description: an engineer and a physician. Three of the farmers working part-time jobs do so at businesses directly related to farming.

Twelve respondents are full-time farmers or full-time farmers and ranchers, and twenty are employed, part- or full-time, in nearby towns. Those respondents who have some form of off-farm employment either hire workers or farm as a hobby; the latter typically involves those with less than thirty acres. The physician sold 60 percent of his father's land while retaining two hundred acres for his own retirement. He currently rents this land out to someone who produces alfalfa hay. The average size of landholdings is 813 acres and ranges from 4,000 to 20 acres (the latter is an exception and involves someone farming contiguous land with a family member). Five respondents have holdings over 1,000 acres. A range of production systems were reported by the respondents as "used sometime over the last ten years," many of which were instituted in at least partial response to changing weather conditions. Operations vary from single wheat-only systems to more diversified rotations that oftentimes involve cultivating a small grain, followed by a fallow period(s), then cultivation of a different small grain or a crop that seeds directly such as sunflowers.

Wheat Cultivation in West Texas

The following brief synopsis highlights key basics of wheat cultivation in West Texas. Wheat is well-adapted to the deep, fertile fine textured clay or loamy soils of this region and is usually fall-sown. Spring-sown grains have lower yields and test weight given shallow root systems, heat, and the dry weather occurring in late spring (Warrick, Sansone, and Johnson n.d.). Farmers in this study acknowledge moisture as a critical limiting factor in West Texas for crop production in general; crop yield potentials vary widely within the region due to erratic rainfall distribution each year; and moisture management is considered the key element for increased production.

Wheat is the predominant small grain planted in the study region because of its versatility, winter-hardiness, ready market demand, and economic returns. Oats, barley, and rye are also winter-hardy small grains cultivated to a lesser degree and primarily for grazing purposes. Wheat is produced for grazing purposes, market, or for both, in many cases. Environmental conditions prevent many farmers from producing wheat continuously on the same land, as such a production system increases the probability of damage from winter grain mites, brown wheat mites (usually only a problem under drought conditions), soil borne diseases, and weed problems including mustards, ryegrass, and wild oats (Warrick, Sansone, and Johnson n.d.).

Wheat grown in sequence with other crops, or rotated with fallow fields, results in more stable production. As one example, dry winter wheat and grain sorghum are often cultivated using a wheat—sorghum—fallow (wSF) crop rotation where no-tillage or stubble-mulch-tillage residue management act to reduce evaporation and increase yield; but more runoff occurs with the no-tillage option compared to the stubble-mulch-tillage (Baumhardt and Jones 2002, 19). (Using a stubble mulch system is when the "blade plow or sweep plow, a common tillage implement in the High Plains, cuts weeds at the roots and leaves most of the residue anchored at the surface with minimum disturbance of the soil surface. Blade plowing is typically a summer fallow operation after small grain harvest. It kills weeds and loosens the surface. In moist soils, particularly those with higher clay contents, a blade plow may cause soil smearing below the blade, thereby limiting its use as a spring tillage implement" [https://cropwatch.unl.edu/tillage/stubble]).

The only operations that were irrigated by study respondents involved cotton production. Wheat, sorghum, sesame, sunflowers, and clover fields were rain-fed in every case. As is typical for roughly half of farms in Texas, these farmers manage a combination of owned and leased land, though in this sample, thirty respondents farm almost entirely land they personally own. Four farmers lease out part of their landholdings. Twenty respondents inherited the land they are farming; ten bought land to farm, usually after some schooling and working five to ten years prior; and two are leasing land.

Research Findings

The following presentation of findings begins with the heart of this study: the farmers' understanding of variations in weather patterns and climate change, and how they strive to minimize risk to maintain or improve yields, largely through the adoption of rotation systems. Relative to the ideas defining the notion of performative agriculture, I follow this discussion with an exploration of what gives meaning to farmers' lives, and whether the perceived uncertainty around climate change impacts their desired lifeway. The last section examines future prospective behaviors in terms of how these farmers presently elicit and interact with information systems relative to weather and climate, and, finally, how they envision using climate forecasts in their decision-making around crop production in the future.

Understanding Climate Change

By virtue of the nature of their work, farmers are closely tied to all natural elements that ultimately affect yields. Unless farmers or those close to them are personally and directly impacted by a climate-related threat, they do not usually acknowledge the hazard as important and assume no personal involvement. People normally fail to see how their understanding or behavior might influence a global environmental problem. The first objective of this component is to explore how this population—one that is significantly dependent on a healthy resource base and the abiotic and biotic factors that determine these conditions—understands basic concepts related to weather patterns and climate change.

Determining whether understanding climate change translates into feelings of risk to livelihoods comprises the second part of this element. Recent shifts in thinking about climate-related shocks and events have moved away from conceptualizing risks, hazards, and disasters as one-off events; to viewing them as longitudinal processes with diverse causes and consequences; to recognizing that climate events reveal the complex interrelationships between ecological systems and human societies; and to focusing on reducing social and ecological vulnerability and improving the capacity of human groups and environments to cope with the uncertainty in ways that promote security (Adger et al. 2009; Wisner et al. 2004).

An important component of these efforts has been the growing attention to "risk" itself. A few studies assess the range of climate-related risks to agriculture focusing specifically on how the farmer perceives the risk, and in turn, the response he or she makes to the more pragmatic threat or to the uncertainty of not knowing, to give an example, the precise consequences of a temperature or precipitation trend (Adger et al. 2009, 536–7; Valdiviaa, Seth, and Gilles 2010, 821).

Figure 15 indicates farmers' awareness levels of weather trends in these counties over the last ten years (2006–2016). High consensus is indicated for a number of trends that in fact are accurate depictions of weather patterns: higher temperatures, increased prevalence of heatwaves, fluctuations in when it rains (i.e., parts of which months), variations in types of rain, and flooding patterns.

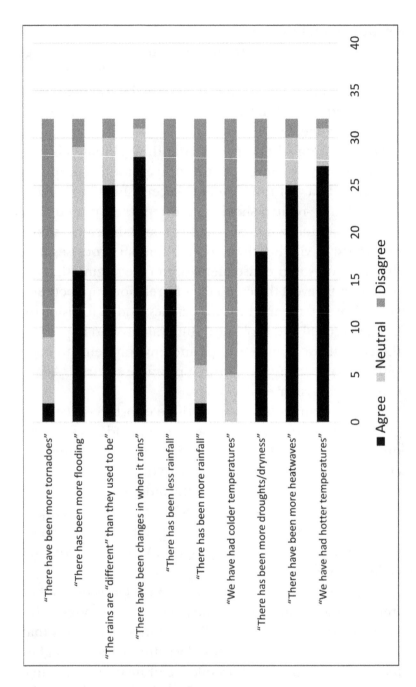

FIG. 15. Farmers' awareness of recent weather trends, 2006–2016.
Created by the author.

Farmers do accurately recount recent changes in weather patterns and are cognizant of how these patterns influence their decisions in terms of developing an effective response that secures a desired yield. Most have been farming a minimum of five years and understand the ideal abiotic factors for high wheat yields. Yet their explanations of what climate change is and their thoughts about the future of wheat farming in terms of climate change are less well defined. "Charles" describes how the weather has changed over the last ten to fifteen years, where the summer is longer with "hotter temperatures and the rainfall is not steady like it used to be." He describes climate change as "that thing about global warming where it's getting hotter and the sea is rising," yet he is not convinced of anthropogenic causation and expresses doubt as to long-term permanent changes. As he puts it, "I think this is all part of a regular up-and-down pattern. The temperatures are going to cool back down in a few years. I'm just going to wait it out."

"Mary" insists the weather is "Five to ten degrees higher now than when I was a child. It is hot, hot, hot, for at least six months out of the year." She is adamant that the summers are much longer and there is "no real winter." The weather is absolutely not like it was when she began farming roughly fifteen years ago in 2002. Yet Mary is reluctant to have any sort of conversation about climate change: "I'm not going to talk about that climate change. It's a four-letter word around here. I don't believe it is really happening. Some of those politicians are just trying to scare us so we'll change our farming and they can make money off of people like me." Her follow-up discourse does not effectively draw linkages relative to the means by which politicians will benefit financially from any adjustments she makes in her farming system, but she is adamant it will be so. "Carol" explains how she feels the weather has become more "haphazard" and "unpredictable." She says that it is not necessarily a new pattern that will be sustained and also expresses "that climate change is not real. I don't know why people wanna talk about that climate change." She explains that no recent changes in the weather are actually going to last the rest of her lifetime: "It's going to go back to normal here real soon." And finally, "Donnie" agrees with "Tim," the farmer whose sentiments are expressed in the epigraph; he explains there are "definite changes . . . higher temperatures, longer summers with more 'hot' days and big ups and downs in how much it rains." He is worried about the future of his farming and spends time trying to figure out the most cost-effective ways he can integrate revised methods because he does not have the financial means to start from scratch and initiate an entirely new system. He also provides a more formal definition of climate change, accurately outlining a number of causes—namely, increases in CO_2 from deforestation, methane, and air travel. Finally, he expresses concern about his own ecological footprint.

Livelihood Security and Management of Risk

Livelihood security embodies three fundamental attributes: the possession of human capabilities, access to other tangible and intangible assets, and the existence of economic activities (Drinkwater and Rusinow 1999). The interaction between these attributes defines what livelihood strategy a household may pursue at a given point in time. "Livelihoods are secure when households have adequate and sustainable access to resources to meet basic needs: adequate access to food, potable water, health facilities, educational opportunities, housing, and time for community participation and social integration" (Ghanim 2000, 3). Households have stable livelihoods when they can cope with and recover from stress and shocks, maintain or enhance capabilities and assets over time, and provide sustainable livelihood opportunities for the next generation (Chambers and

Conway 1992). In rural farming communities, livelihoods may consist of a range of activities that, when combined, provide a mix of procurement strategies for desired goods and services. Thus, an individual household may have a number of possible sources of entitlement that constitute its livelihood which are based on its resources and position in economic, political, and social realms of society (Drinkwater and McEwan 1992).

A handful of the respondents in this study stated that their main goal as farmers was to produce enough agricultural output to cover their input costs. In Coleman County, "Javier" explained his cropping choices in terms of his preference for a yield result that provides economic security but also allows him to be more relaxed and not constantly worry about his farm:

> I don't grow cotton because it's too much work. And it can be expensive, what with the irrigation system and all. And even if I insure it, you have to prove you've done absolutely everything you can do before the insurance company pays, so you have to water, water, and water! I know all about the way that crop insurance works and I don't like it. We all water even though you know the field is dead. I want to be able to relax and enjoy my life. Cotton is too much work. Farming takes enough of my time as it is.

In explaining their decision to make a living from farming, despite the associated costs and risks, respondents talk about the pleasure of working outdoors, the feel of the soil, the freedom of being self-employed, and the ability to take time off for hunting and fishing when the farming season is over. They also emphasize the close connection between rural life, family values, and moral character. As "Kevin" from Tom Green County says, "I love the feel of the soil, being out on the land, and making something from it. I love when the harvest comes in and I know that I did 'that.' There's a completeness about it that I know I could never get working some office job." In his interpretation of agricultural intensification in the High Plains, Spear (1997) reminds us of the moral dimensions of the struggles various culture groups experienced as they settled land and set up farming households and agrarian-based communities. His study explores how thriving economies developed despite harsh environmental conditions and within the context of distinct cultural traditions. Even though most of the farmers in West Texas regard their operation as a "business," the need for additional money from a non-farm source is often rationalized in terms of being a good provider for one's family and being financially able to send their children to college or trade school, as this is how we define success in our society. This outlook is exemplified by "Stephen," who explains why he and his wife feel forced to take off-farm work: "I prefer to only farm, but when our children were young, we didn't want to live with the chance of not always being able to provide for them, so we both took work off the farm. I worked part-time as a mechanic and "Millie" cleaned houses. We earned enough to provide for ourselves so that we could relax a little about the return off the farm." Multiple livelihoods seem to be the rule rather than the exception these days. He admits that he is frustrated with his losses due to the flooding in 2014 and having to replant, but he is willing to take the occasional loss as long as he can produce steady returns over at least a five-year period.

It has been well documented, since the farm crisis of the 1980s, that farm foreclosure not only indicates economic failure; it also has profound emotional and social implications for farmers, particularly when they are forced to sell family land or home equity (Crane et al. 2010). In these counties, however, not a single respondent expressed unhappiness when their adult children pursued careers outside of farming. A recognition that perhaps the family farm is to be lost was evident and voiced with little to no regret. The concern they have for their children is represented by "Allen," who wants them to be "happy, have a good education, stable employment, and be successful enough in their careers to support a family, if they choose to have one." At the same time, thirteen of the respondents expressed a personal desire to retain land ownership for themselves. Several relayed how difficult they were finding this to be in an environment of escalating costs, unstable markets with shifting prices, and chronic droughts. "Robert" explained the steps he took when he and his brother first started working the 165 acres they bought when they finished college and saved enough money for a down payment. They initially relied heavily on the Soil Conservation Service and the local agricultural extension agents to guide them through the process of having their soil tested to help build the correct components required for the rotation farming system they intended to manage. Their rotation comprises wheat, fallow, and cotton; the latter requires irrigation and has necessitated diverting water from nearby streams. They are required to water their cotton fields even during drought cycles, or crop insurance payments will be abrogated.

The commitment to farming as a livelihood and a lifestyle implicitly entails an acceptance of living and working in an environment characterized by risk—sometimes a high degree of risk—because of the variability of climate, inputs, markets, and policy (Hendrickson, Howard, and Constance, chapter 1 of this volume). Vulnerability is further magnified by the high capital investments and heavy debt burdens that are required to make a farm operation viable. Risk management is not simply a technical calculation; it is central to farmers' ability to hold on to their land, their lifestyle, and their sense of self. Even when not explicitly articulated in farmers' accounts of agricultural decisions, these values epitomize the high stakes farmers have in risk management, as well as the deep-seated meanings and far-reaching aspirations that may be destabilized by potential yield or income losses (Crane et al. 2010).

Twenty-two of the farmers in this study conceded that they cannot manage their farm operations in ways that completely eradicate weather-related risk. Rather, they understand that the means by which they are able to respond to risks will vary over time and by nature of the risk. It is a give-and-take process where farmers acknowledge "failure and success," typically over any number of growing seasons. Acknowledging that occasional bad years are inevitable, they anticipate choices that have to be made based on personal and collective experience. Wheat farmers in West Texas diligently utilize management strategies that have strong probability of producing a healthy yield under most conditions most of the time (Hartmann 2010). The rationale for this approach, as evidenced from practice in other locales, is that consistency eventually pays off, so in the long run it is safer to "stay steady" than adjust cropping patterns seasonally to maximize short-term gain (Crane et al. 2010; Eakin 2000; Ingram, Roncoli, and Kirshen 2002; Luseno et al. 2003). The following statement exemplifies this long-term perspective on climate uncertainty and agricultural outcomes, supported by overall confidence in farming as a viable livelihood option:

> My farming system is never going to be perfect. In Texas, the weather is crazy man—some years it floods, other years we have drought. I'm always going to have some bad years, but I can't have too many of them. So, I mostly stay steady because I feel like you can't change things up too often, or else you won't really know what's working or what's helping the soil. But I do consider different options if I've had too many bad years all at once. Then I go ask for help and then I have to make some big decisions. ("Carl" from Runnels County)

As with rural producers in other parts of the world, diversification is gaining popularity with some Texas wheat farmers, specifically as a means to manage environmental and climate risk. Having fields in various rotations allows for experimentation in terms of micro-level variation in soil types and rainfall conditions. Planting different crops and varieties also spreads risks over different operations. As "Charles" from Jones County says, "I heard about some others deciding to try two or more crops together, one after the other, and sometimes on fields next to each other and at the same time, so I decided to try part of my land— about two hundred acres—in that way. And I think it's goin' pretty good. My wheat yield is higher and the sunflowers are producing real fine." The farmers in this study contemplate these alternative strategies when making decisions as to a possible new system structured to respond to changing environmental conditions. Table 6 indicates rotation systems used by farmers over the ten-year period extending from 2006–2016.

Both the TWPA and AgriLife (the Texas agricultural extension agency out of Texas A&M) generally recommend all these rotations in terms of recent weather patterns and consequential soil conditions. The stronger recommendation from AgriLife is to use a small grain–fallow–small grain system in these counties. The data indicate more than twenty of the farmers have tried this system. "Billy" relays how he was nervous about cultivating anything except wheat, but he decided to initiate a system more of his farmer friends were also trying: to add a fallow period and sorghum to create a basic rotation. His results are positive in terms of wheat, with a roughly 15 percent increase in yield over the last three years. Less farmers are using a rotation that includes a "seeds directly" crop, but they are motivated to take the risk for economic gain. Early reports indicate mixed results that may influence their risk-taking behav-

Table 6. Farming systems, 2006–2016

General (rotation) system	Specific example(s)	Frequency
Small grain only	Wheat for market only	24
Small grain only	Wheat for hay and market	19
Small grain–fallow–small grain	Wheat–fallow–sorghum	14
Small grain–fallow–seeds directly	Wheat–fallow–sesame	9
Small grain–fallow–seeds directly (2x)	Wheat–fallow–sesame–sunflower	7
Small grain–fallow–cotton	Wheat–fallow–cotton	6
Small grain–cotton–small grain	Wheat–cotton–sorghum	6
Small grain–cover–seeds directly	Wheat–clover–sunflower	5
Small grain–fallow–cotton–small grain	Wheat–fallow–cotton–sesame	4

Note: Farmers may report more than one system as they adjust their production systems over time.

Source: Created by the author.

ior in the future. Rotations that require double cropping generally are not desirable in the dryland area, and fallow practice may not increase yields enough to justify operation; hence, farmers in these counties are not adopting this type of farming system.

Crop insurance is another risk management tool that guarantees farmers a minimum financial return on their yield. Farmers choose the highest level of insurance they can negotiate and still afford, with coverage ranging between 40–65 percent of their established average yields. The highest incidence of crop insurance was held by those farmers producing cotton, wheat, or a combination of both. The availability of different insurance products may influence crop choices because coverage is more favorable for some crops such as corn than for others—namely, cotton. In sum, although farmers routinely deploy ways of dealing with risk, they operate in a decision-making environment that is conditioned by a host of considerations, including climate but also economic, institutional, and policy-related uncertainties, as well as what personally gives their life meaning.

The Social and Cultural Life of Farming

While a subsistence-based economy has long been abandoned in this part of Texas (Hartmann 2010), traces of some of the characteristics of what is understood as "house-holding" (Brown 1971; Polanyi 1944) persist in these counties. This depiction is especially accurate in reference to the notion of the family homestead, where at least partial economies are organized around community groups and kin relationships (Sahlins 1972). In these counties, house-holding is not based solely on economic variables as they are normally conceived, but rather as an economy also defined by social, cultural, and kinship dimensions. In his longitudinal study of Beech Creek in eastern Kentucky, Brown portrays the homestead as the "focal point," where kin-based relationships were most important, even over friendships with neighbors. The house and owned land were conceived by themselves as "their place" (1971, 20–2). As Gudeman so aptly describes, "Our value domain . . . consists of a community's shared interests, which include lasting resources . . . produced things, and ideational constructs such as knowledge, technology, laws, practices, skills and customs. The base comprises cultural agreements and beliefs that provide a structure for all the domains. These locally defined values—embodied in goods, services, and ideologies—express identity in community" (2001, 6–7).

In the case of rural West Texas, house-holding typifies a class group with a strong local orientation around farming and also a defined set of social and cultural norms of behavior. In these counties, life centers on farming and family first, with local community second, where family is incomplete without community, but where it is the family that must first be successfully supported by work and agriculture. "Producers today emphasize different moral dimensions of economic behavior, such as producing quality human beings than during earlier eras, when moral-economic actors pressed for state intervention in economic crises" (Griffith 2009, 432). Moral-economic principles are not limited to foreign or pre- or historical groups; they guide economic production and exchange systems and ideology in industrial capitalist locales even today (Griffith 2009).

The farmers who participated in this study mostly grew up in the small towns that comprise these counties, with the exception of seven who were raised within or in close proximity to San Angelo, which has a current population of 100,702 (U.S. Census Bureau 2017). In these towns, many adults still live in close proximity to parents, grandparents, and extended family members; farming practices and "know-how" are passed down through the generations. After working long weekday hours, Friday nights are spent at local high school football games or other sporting events. Folks spend time together at the local farmers' markets on Saturday morning and then migrate out to nearby lakes for fishing or picnics. Many attend church services on Sunday, followed by visits with extended family members to watch televised football games.

When asked where they draw meaning in their lives, the most frequent responses comment on their social life, being drawn to the small-town way of life, spending most of their leisure time at family get-togethers, and sometimes at community sporting events and church activities. Farmers also talk about finding satisfaction in working their land and accepting the challenges of producing a "full-on crop" designed specifically to provide for their family.

It is a commonplace experience to grow up or spend significant parts of a childhood on a farm helping with chores and learning various skills. "John's" father died when he was young; he was raised by his paternal grandparents who owned a farm. Every summer he enjoyed helping his grandfather with farm work. He eventually attended Texas A&M after high school, earning a BS degree in agronomy. He then returned to San Angelo to work in a farm supply business, to continue to help his grandfather on the weekends, and to eventually inherit the family farm. "I just like being outside, especially after working at the store in town. And I also like the challenge—finding the time to do it right, even farming forty acres—it takes time to get it right, to farm smart." John also spends some of his leisure time at the mills with other farmers, where they gather to relax and tell stories; this is where he also collects information about different techniques, seeds, and possible rotations to address the challenges he and some of his farmer friends may be facing. In Taylor County, "David" inherited 1,400 acres that he began to farm when he returned to his hometown after serving in the military. Roughly five years later he was able to purchase 1,100 acres to add to his farm operation. He talks about his deep roots in this region: "I never gave it a second thought to move somewhere else when my military service was over. I have deep roots right here and I like working the land and getting a good crop." Any motivation for a different life is non-existent given his strong family roots and his desire to be back on the land.

"Connie" is one of a small number of female farmers in this study. She works roughly twenty acres adjacent to her brother's larger farm, on a part-time basis, and is a full-time nurse practitioner. While she admits that she sometimes struggles with a lack of energy and low motivation to work on her farm after a full day at her job, she adamantly talks about her inheritance: "This land has been in our family for many generations and I won't give it up." She feels a sense of belonging with her individual piece of land, as if it is a part of her being, her family. "This land is like a mother to me. I've worked it for many years and I know what it will do and what it can't do." There is a strong sense of place, of emotional connection, and feeling of security with their particular land that these farmers want to protect. While thirteen of the respondents commented that they did not always have leisure time, given the demands of their farm work, eleven made strong statements about how they would not want any other life, regardless of long-term prospects about the weather. At the same time, seven explained that they would accept their children not wanting to hold on to the farming tradition in their respective families despite their own strong sentiment to do so for themselves.

Forecasting: Using Weather and Climate Information

A critical step in identifying the social processes whereby scientific information is accessed and processed is essential to understanding how such information is ultimately assimilated into the knowledge base that supports adaptive adjustments in agricultural planning and performance (Meinke et al. 2006). Research shows that attitudes toward climate predictions, including beliefs and feelings, are as important as comprehension in determining whether farmers use the information (McCrea, Dalgleish, and Coventry 2005). Such attitudes are grounded in personal experience (as when someone has suffered losses because of a "wrong" forecast) but also in the way people relate culturally and socially to the means and the messengers that deliver predictive information (Sherman-Morris 2005). Table 7 indicates respondents' frequency of reference to sources of scientific forecasts, with television being the most common, followed by information accessed via cell phone, websites, and friends. In addition, four farmers, all over 68 years of age, mentioned the *Farmer's Almanac* and folk knowledge based on environmental indicators. Interviewees reported using at least two sources of information, not including interpersonal exchanges. This process of triangulation, whereby farmers cross-check information from different sources and from their observations, is exemplified by the following comment:

I sometimes spend a good thirty to forty-five minutes in the morning and some at night checking the weather, watching the weather channel, talking with friends who are also farmers, and then sometime during the day, going by one of the farmer offices in town. It's a constant thing on my mind during the season and I can't ever get it out of my mind . . . every day, what's the weather going to be tomorrow, and the next day, and the next week. And we talk amongst ourselves, sometimes trying to make the same decision, so we're not out on our own, doin' something different. ("Bill" Jones County)

This passage also highlights the magnitude of social networks for the processing of this particular information. Weather and climate are often discussed with other farmers at the mills in San Angelo or at social gatherings; with extension agents during conferences at the Texas Farm Bureau or at more informal farmer get-togethers; and with suppliers, buyers, and brokers during business transactions.

Although farmers are highly attuned to weather forecasts, their use of such information is impeded by uncertainties relative to the information's accuracy. Even while conceding that weather forecasting has improved considerably over recent decades, the farmers' conversation is often characterized by jokes about the unreliability of predictive information (especially since one of the more established meteorology programs in Texas is at Texas A&M, a school that is infamous for Aggies jokes pervasive throughout the United States). Joking about Texas weather is prevalent

Table 7. Farmers' sources for weather and climate information

Source of Information	Frequency
Weather channel (national)	23
Weather channel (local)	30
Online sources (general)	18
NOAA and National Weather Service	19
Cell phone (Accuweather, weather.com)	28
Neighbor friends	12
Farmer's Almanac	4
Local news	11

Note: Respondents were requested to indicate all sources they regularly use.

Source: Created by the author.

throughout the state, in all kinds of social groupings. All but two of these farmers talked about the unpredictability of Texas weather, as well as the forecasts. "You can never count on what you hear on the TV about what our weather is going to be," explains "Winston."

Among interviewed farmers, thirteen do not clearly distinguish between "climate" and "weather," often using the terms interchangeably. This inconsistency is important as it indicates that attitudes toward ENSO- (El Niño Southern Oscillation) based seasonal climate forecasts are influenced by their perceptions of weather forecasts. Farmers interviewed are not in the habit of actively seeking seasonal climate forecasts for reference in management decisions. Of the seven who acknowledged encountering seasonal climate forecasts, only two farmers mentioned using the information: the first while responding to a heavy thunderstorm season forecast and the second during a warning for an intense tornado season. The other farmers typically say that, although they do not rely on the forecasts to make farm decisions, they appreciate having the information when they remember to look for it. As also found in other studies of climate applications in agriculture (Ingram, Roncoli, and Kirshen 2002; Klopper, Vogel, and Landman 2006; Luseno et al. 2003; Ziervogel and Calder 2003), the timing and distribution of rainfall events, particularly during periods when crops are most vulnerable, is more useful information than a relative measure of total quantity of seasonal rainfall, such as that provided by ENSO-based seasonal climate forecasts. The lead time of forecast delivery is equally important because farmers arrange for seed purchases as early as possible to ensure the availability of their preferred varieties. Even more than forecast parameters and lead time, the forecasts' past performance emerges as a key issue, mentioned by twenty-seven of the farmers interviewed, for determining whether they would consider trusting and using the information. The two most frequently cited reasons for not using seasonal climate forecasts are lack of accuracy (mentioned by eleven farmers) and reliability (cited by nine). In sum, moving seasonal climate forecasts from a "conversation piece" to a risk-management tool requires not only assimilating them into farmers' habitual information flows but also framing forecasts in ways that allow for learning and judgment in farmers' own terms.

Conclusion: Future Wheat Farming in Texas

Farmers' foremost goals include preserving their lifestyle, and nurturing social networks and economic linkages. These aspirations are a fundamental part of farmers' decision-making logic, even as they struggle to "make a crop" each season. The multi-dimensional perspective means that farmers' time horizon for coping with climate uncertainty exceeds the seasonal framework of climate predictions. Risk management is framed as a multi-year process, during which farmers accept that both gains and losses will occur but aim to ensure the long-term stability of their farm. Furthermore, even as farmers strive to minimize their vulnerability to climate shocks and financial shortfalls, their experience has led them to perceive uncertainty as inherent to agricultural livelihoods, stemming not only from climate variability but also from economic and institutional milieus. The perceived relevance of seasonal climate forecasts is thus determined by the importance of climate uncertainty vis-à-vis other decision drivers. Because of this, assessment efforts must consider the multi-variate nature of farming decisions to determine whether and how climate-based decision support systems serve the different goals that influence farmers' risk-management strategies (Hayman 2007; Moser 2009).

As with most of humankind, farmers do not prefer change. If these West Texas wheat farmers could have their way, they would stay the course, "stay steady," preserving both their familiar farm practices along with the social and cultural lifeway they are accustomed to and to which they are emotionally tied. Yet central to farmers in these rural counties is the idea that a successful livelihood means "making the crop." In an age of varying weather patterns and, for these farmers, less so climate change, the central question presents itself: "Can I 'stay steady' and still make my crop given these recent changes in the weather, or do I have to do things differently?" John's response to this question, as relayed above, was to learn how to "farm smart"—to adjust to both the changing abiotic trends as they influence the biotic stressors that ultimately determine the efficacy of his agricultural system, and to devise adjustments so he does not have to abandon house-holding as his way of life, which ultimately defines meaning for himself and his family.

The time frame reference for these farmers is a shorter-term future, perhaps ten to fifteen years. None of the younger farmers made any reference to how wheat farming in West Texas would be twenty to thirty years from now. In their discourse, there was no evidence of even the general ideas around the proposal (Godfray et al. 2010) for a

Alexander

"new agricultural revolution" and all of the changes such a movement would entail. Rather, without apparent acknowledgement, wheat farmers in Texas have begun to "live with climate" which involves the recognition that weather is changing and that, over periods of time, adjustments must be made (Brugger and Crimmons 2013, 1834). Former mono-cropped systems of wheat or corn are being transitioned to diversified rotation systems as farmers opt to take risk in a new and different structure to address larger-scale risks and to ultimately retain their capacity to "make the crop." Where I feel this group of farmers has not yet gone is to take their basic tenet one step further and to orient pursuit of their desired livelihood around "living with climate *change*" (Brugger and Crimmins 2013, 1836). The basic premise would be to learn to understand climate change more fully, not to fight against it or to attempt to control the biotic factors impacted by the changes.

For West Texas wheat farmers, an important first step will be to understand and accept the scientific information that supports climate change and not to fight against it or to attempt to control the biotic factors impacted by the changes. Given the conservative orientation of most of these farmers, this task will not be easy, but farmers do not necessarily need to know highly technical information regarding why the climate is changing, nor exactly how it will change, but rather to feel confident of available forecasting information relaying upcoming climate projections. This assurance would help address the uncertainty felt by the majority of these farmers, which has created doubt as to the longer-term effects of recent fluctuating weather patterns. Building on this basic awareness—and knowing the options farmers have in terms of crop rotation, system diversification, more effective water management, and addressing any climate-related challenges to their operations—can come from established technological advancements of geographically specific climate-smart farm practices that are deemed feasible given cost, environmental, and policy constraints. The positive, long-standing relationships these farmers have with AgriLife and the TWPA should bode well for continued willingness to initiate perhaps increasingly impactful reform. Having access to information, technology, inputs, and resources are all critical to making adjustments in these farmers' agricultural systems. Their feelings of risk can be ameliorated through education, knowledge, and practice. As conveyed in their conversations, they are not unsympathetic to taking a certain degree of risk in their cultivation system to do so.

The idea of Climate-Smart Agriculture (CSA) was put forward a number of years ago and has since been advanced with specific knowledge, skill sets, and technologies to reorient agricultural systems to support production under the realities of climate change (Lipper et al. 2014; Scherr, Shames, and Friedman 2012, 13). The main ideas around CSA have not yet reached the county extension offices in this study region. As research and policy links between climate change and agriculture advance, Climate-Smart Agriculture will strengthen as an approach to capture the concept that agricultural systems can be developed and implemented to simultaneously improve economic security and preserve rural livelihoods; it can also facilitate climate change adaptation while offering mitigation benefits.

I wish to thank all the farmers who participated in this study; the offices of the Texas Farm Bureau and AgriLife in each of the respective study counties for their assistance in identifying wheat farmers; Heidi Marcum for her insightful comments on early drafts; and the C. Gus Glasscock, Jr. Endowed Fund for Excellence in Environmental Sciences, College of Arts and Sciences, Baylor University, for funding the research.

References

Adger, W. N., S. Dessai, M. Goudden, M. Hulme, I. Lorenzoni, D. Nelson, L. O. Naess, J. Wolff, and A. Wreford. 2009. "Are there Social Limits to Adaptation to Climate Change?" *Climatic Change* 93: 335–54. DOI: 10.1007/s10584-008-9520-z.

Barnett, Tim P., David W. Pierce, Hugo G. Hidalgo, C. Bonfils, B. D. Santer, Tapash Das, G. Bala, Andrew W. Wood, Toru Nozawa, Arthur A. Mirin, Daniel R. Cayan, and Michael D. Dettinger. 2008. "Human-induced Changes in the Hydrology of the Western United States." *Science* 319, no. 5866: 1080–83. DOI: 10.1126/science.1152538.

Batterbury, S. P. J. 2001. "Landscapes of Diversity: A Local Political Ecology of Livelihood Diversification in South-western Niger. *Cultural Geography* 8: 437–64.

Baumhardt, R. L., and O. R. Jones. 2002. "Residue Management and Para-tillage Effects on Some Soil Properties and Rain Infiltration." *Soil and Tillage Research* 65, no. 1: 19–27. DOI: 10/1016/S0167-1987(01)00273-2.

Bernard, H. Russell. 2011. *Research Methods in Anthropology: Qualitative and Quantitative Approaches.* Lanham MD: AltaMira.

Brown, James S. 1971. *Beech Creek: A Study of a Kentucky Mountain Neighborhood.* Berea KY: Berea College Press.

Brugger, Julie, and Michael Crimmins. 2013. "The Art of Adaptation: Living with Climate Change in the Rural American Southwest." *Global Environmental Change* 23: 1830–40. DOI: 10.1016/j.gloenvcha.2013.07.012.

Buys, Laurie, E. Miller, and K. van Megen. 2012. "Conceptualizing Climate Change in Rural Australia: Community Perceptions, Attitudes and (In)actions." *Regional Environmental Change* 12: 237–48. DOI: 10.1007/s10113-011-0253-6.

Chambers, R., and Conway, G. 1992. *Sustainable Rural Livelihoods: Practical Concepts for the 21st Century.* IDS Discussion Paper 296. Brighton, UK: Institute of Development Studies.

Climate Change Science Program (CCSP). 2008. *The Effects of Climate Change on Agriculture, Land Resources, Water Resources and Biodiversity in the United States.* A Report of the U.S. Climate Change Science Program and the Subcommittee on Global Change Research. Washington DC: U.S. EPA.

Coles, Ashley R., and Christopher A. Scott. 2009. "Vulnerability and Adaptation to Climate Change and Variability in Semi-arid Rural Southeastern Arizona, USA." *Natural Resources Forum* 33: 297–309. DOI: 10.1111/j.1477–8947.2009.01253.x.

Commonwealth of Australia. 2008. *Australia 2020 Summit: Final Report,* April 2008. http://www.apo.org.au/system/files/15061/apo-nid15061-10481.pdf.

Crane, Todd, C. Roncoli, J. Paz, N. Breuer, K. Broad, Keith T. Ingram, and Gerrit Hoogenboom. 2010. "Forecast Skill and Farmers' Skills: Seasonal Climate Forecasts and Agricultural Risk Management in the

Southeastern United States." *Weather, Climate and Society* 2: 44–59. DOI: 10.1175/2009WCAS1006.1.

Drinkwater, M., and McEwan, M. 1992. "Household Food Security and Environmental Sustainability in Farming Systems Research: Developing Sustainable Livelihoods." Paper presented to the Adaptive Research Planning Team (ARPT) Biannual Review Meeting, Mongu, Zambia, April.

Drinkwater, M., and Rusinow, T. 1999. *Application of CARE's Livelihoods Approach: Presentation for NRAC 1999.* Atlanta: CARE-USA.

Eakin, Hallie. 2000. "Smallholder Maize Production and Climatic Risk: A Case Study from Mexico." *Climatic Change* 45: 19–36. DOI: 10.1023/A:1005628631627.

Ghanim, I. 2000. "Household Livelihood Security: Meeting Basic Needs and Fulfilling Rights." Atlanta: CARE Discussion Paper.

Gleick, P. H. 2010. "Roadmap for Sustainable Water Resources in Southwestern North America." *Proceedings of the National Academy of Sciences of the United States of America* 107, no. 50: 21300–05.

Godfray. H. C. J., J. R. Beddington, Ian R. Crute, L. Haddad, D. Lawrence, J. F. Muir, J. Pretty, Sherman Robinson, Sandy M. Thomas, and Camilla Toulmin. 2010. "Food Security: The Challenge of Feeding 9 Billion People." *Science* 327, no. 5967: 812–18. DOI: 10.1126/science.1185383.

Gornall, Jemma, R. Betts, E. Burke, R. Clark, Joanne Camp, Kate Willett, and Andrew Wiltshire. 2010. "Implications of Climate Change for Agricultural Productivity in the Early Twenty-first Century. *Philosophical Transactions of the Royal Society B: Biological Sciences.* DOI: 10.1098/rstb.2010.0158.

Gosling, Simon N., and Nigel W. Arnell. 2013. "A Global Assessment of the Impact of Climate Change on Water Scarcity." *Climatic Change* 134, no. 3: 371–85. DOI: 10.1007/s10584-013-0853-x.

Griffith, David. 2009. "The Moral Economy of Tobacco." *American Anthropologist* 111, no. 4: 432–42.

Gudeman, Stephen. 2001. *The Anthropology of Economy: Community, Market and Culture.* Malden MA: Blackwell.

Hartmann, Clinton P. 2010. "Wheat Culture." In *Handbook of Texas.* Austin: Texas State Historical Association. https://tshaonline.org/handbook/online/articles/afw01.

Hayman, P. J. Crean, J. Mullen, and K. Parton. 2007. "How Do Probabilistic Seasonal Climate Forecasts Compare with other Innovations that Australian Farmers are Encouraged to Adopt?" *Australian Journal of Agricultural Research* 58: 975–84.

Hendrickson, Mary K., Philip H. Howard, and Douglas H. Constance. 2019. "Power, Food and Agriculture: Implications for Farmers, Consumers and Communities" (herein).

Hu, Qi, Lisa M. Pytlik Zillig, Gary D. Lynne, Alan J. Tomkins, William J. Walyman, Michael J. Hayes, Kenneth G. Hubbard, Ikrom Artilov, Stacey J.

Hoffman, and Donald A. Wilhite. 2006. "Understanding Farmers' Forecast Use from Their Beliefs, Values, Social Norms, and Perceived Obstacles." *Journal of Applied Meteorology and Climatology* 45: 1190–1201.

Ingram, K. T., M. C. Roncoli, and P. H. Kirshen. 2002. "Opportunities and Constraints for Farmers of West Africa to Use Seasonal Precipitation Forecasts with Burkina Faso as a Case Study." *Agricultural Systems* 74: 331–49.

IPCC. 2014a. *Climate Change 2014: Synthesis Report.* Contribution of Working Groups I, II and III to the Fifth Assessment Report of the Intergovernmental Panel on Climate Change. Core Writing Team, R. K. Pachauri and L. A. Meyer, editors. IPCC, Geneva, Switzerland.

———. 2014b. *Climate Change 2014: Impacts, Adaptation, and Vulnerability.* Working Group II Report to the Fifth Assessment Report of the Intergovernmental Panel on Climate Change. Core Writing Team Field, C. B., V. R. Barros, D. J. Dokken, K. J. Mach, M. D. Mastrandrea, T. E. Bilir, M. Chatterjee, K. L. Ebi, Y. O. Estrada, R. C. Genova, B. Girma, E. S. Kissel, A. N. Levy, S. MacCracken, P. R. Mastrandrea, and L. L. White, editors. Cambridge: Cambridge University Press.

Jennings, T. L. 2002. "Farm Family Adaptability and Climate Variability in the Northern Great Plains: Contemplating the Role of Meaning in Climate Change Research." *Culture and Agriculture* 24: 52–63.

Klopper, E., C. H. Vogel, and W. A. Landman. 2006. "Seasonal Climate Forecasts—Potential Agricultural-Risk Management Tools?" *Climatic Change* 76: 73–90.

Lal, P., J. R. Alavalapati, and E. D. Mercer. 2011. "Socio-economic Impacts of Climate Change on Rural United States." *Mitigation and Adaptation Strategies for Global Change* 16, no. 7: 819–44. DOI: 10.1007/s11027-011-9295-9.

Lind, Christopher. 1995. *Something's Wrong Somewhere: Globalization, Community and the Moral Economy of the Farm Crisis.* Halifax: Fernwood.

Lipper, Leslie, Philip Thornton, Bruce M. Campbell, Tobias Baedeker, Ademola Braimoh, Martin Bwalya, Patrick Caron, Andrea Cattaneo, Dennis Garrity, Kevin Henry, Ryan Hottle, Louise Jackson, Andrew Jarvis, Fred Kossam, Wendy Mann, Nancy McCarthy, Alexandre Meybeck, Henry Neufelt, Tom Remington, Pham Thi Sen, Reuben Sessa, Reynolds Shula, Austin Tibu, and Emmanuel F. Torquebiau. 2014. "Climate-smart Agriculture for Food Security." *Nature Climate Change* 4: 1068–72.

Luseno, W. K., J. G. McPeak, C. B. Barrett, P. D. Little, and G. Gebru. 2003. "Assessing the Value of Climate Forecast Information for Pastoralists: Evidence from Southern Ethiopia and Northern Kenya." *World Development* 31: 1477–49.

McCrea, R., L. Dalgleish, and W. Coventry. 2005. "Encouraging Use of Seasonal Climate Forecasts by Farmers." *International Journal of Climatology* 25: 1127–37. DOI: 10.1002/joc.1164.

McDonald, T. R. Thwaites, and K. Retra. 2006. "Climate Change Impacts and Adaptation in North Central Victoria: Landholders' Perceptions." *Institute for Land, Water and Society Report No. 27.* Albury: Charles Sturt University.

Meinke, H., R. Nelson, P. Kokic, R. Stone, R. Selvaraju, and W. Baethgen. 2006. "Actionable Climate Knowledge: From Analysis to Synthesis." *Climate Research* 33: 101–10. DOI: 10.3354/cr033101.

Menzies, Charles R. 2006. *Traditional Ecological Knowledge and Natural Resource Management.* Lincoln: University of Nebraska Press.

Meza, F. J., J. W. Hansen, and D. Osgood. 2008. "Economic Value of Seasonal Climate Forecasts for Agriculture: Review of Ex-ante Assessments and Recommendations for Future Research." *Journal of Applied Meteorology and Climatology* 47: 1269–86.

Moser, S. 2009. "Making a Difference on the Ground: The Challenge of Demonstrating the Effectiveness of Decision Support." *Climatic Change* 95: 11–21. DOI: 10.1007/s10584-008-9539-1.

NAFTA. 1994. *The North American Free Trade Agreement: A Guide to Customs Procedures.* Washington DC: Dept. of the Treasury, U.S. Customs.

Neumann, P., H. Krahn, N. Krogman, and B. R. Thomas. 2007. "My Grandfather Would Roll Over in his Grave: Public Perceptions of Poplar Plantations." *Rural Sociology* 72: 111–35.

O'Brien, K. 2009. "Climate Change and Values: Do Changing Values Define the Limits to Successful Adaptation?" In *Adapting to Climate Change: Thresholds, Values, Governance,* edited by W. N. Adger, I. Lorenzoni, and K. O'Brien, 164–80. Cambridge: Cambridge University Press.

Patt, Anthony G., and Dagmar Schröter. 2008. "Perceptions of Climate Risk in Mozambique: Implications for the Success of Adaptation Strategies." *Global Environmental Change* 18, no. 3: 458–67. DOI: 10.1016/j.gloenvcha.2008.04.002.

Polanyi, Karl. 1944. *The Great Transformation: The Political and Economic Origins of Our Time.* Boston: Beacon.

Pretty, Jules. 2008. "Agricultural Sustainability: Concepts, Principles and Evidence. *Philosophical Transactions of the Royal Society B: Biological Sciences* 363: 447. DOI: 10.1098/rstb.2007.2163.

QSR International. 2014. *NVIVO Qualitative Data Analysis Software.* QSR International Pty Ltd. Version 10.

Richards, P. 1993. "Cultivation: Knowledge or Performance?" In *An Anthropological Critique of Development: The Growth of Ignorance,* edited by M. Hobart, 61–78. London: Routledge.

Roncoli, C. 2006. "Ethnographic and Participatory Approaches to Research on Farmers' Responses to Climate Predictions." *Climate Research* 33: 81–99.

Sahlins, Marshall D. 1972. *Stone Age Economics.* New York: De Gruyter.

Scherr, Sara J., Seth Shames, and Rachel Friedman. 2012. "From Climate-smart Agriculture to Climate-smart Landscapes." *Agriculture and Food Security* 1: 12–26. http://www.agricultureandfoodsecurity.com/content/1/1/12.

Sherman-Morris, K. 2005. "Tornadoes, Television and Trust—A Closer Look at the Influence of the Local Weathercaster during Severe Weather." *Global Environmental Change* 6B: 201–10.

Smith, Ron. 2010. "Climate Change Will Affect Crop Production." *Southwest Farm Press*. Accessed September 7. http://www.southwestfarmpress.com /management/climate-change-will-affect-crop-production.

Spear, Thomas. 1997. *Mountain Farmers: Moral Economies of Land and Agricultural Development in Arusha and Meru.* Berkeley: University of California Press.

Texas Department of Agriculture. 2017. *Texas Agriculture Statistics.* http://www .texasagriculture.gov/About/TexasAgStats.aspx.

Texas State Historical Association (TSHA). 2017. "Underground Water Conservation Districts." Accessed October 14, 2017. https://tshaonline.org /handbook/online/articles/mwund.

Texas Wheat Producers Association (TWPA). 2009. "Committee Discusses Pending Climate Legislation." Texas Wheat Producers News.

———. 2016. "Texas Wheat Producers Board: Roles and Responsibilities." http://texaswheat.org/about-2/association.

Thwaites, R., A. Curtis, N. Mazur, and D. Race. 2008. "Understanding Rural Landholder Responses to Climate Change." *Institute for Land, Water and Society Report No. 48.* Charles Sturt University, Albury NSW.

U.S. Census Bureau. 2017. "Population and Housing Unit Estimates." https:// www.census.gov/programs-surveys/popest.html.

U.S. Environmental Protection Agency (USEPA). 2007. "Climate Change and Texas." Office of Policy, Planning and Evaluation. EPA 230-F-97-008qq.

U.S. Global Change Research Program (USGCRP). 2009. *Global Climate Change Impacts in the United States,* edited by Thomas R. Karl, Jerry M. Melillo, and Thomas C. Peterson. New York: Cambridge University Press.

Valdivia, Corinne, A. Seth, and J. Gilles. 2010. "Adapting to Climate Change in Andean Ecosystems: Landscapes, Capitals, and Perceptions Shaping Rural Livelihood Strategies and Linking Knowledge Systems." *Annals of the Association of American Geographers* 100, no. 4: 818–34. DOI: 10/1080/00045608.2010.500198.

Velandia, M., D. M. Lambert, A. Jenkins, R. Roberts, J. Larson, B. English, and S. W. Martin. 2010. "Precision Farming Information Sources Used by Cotton Farmers and Implications for Extension." *Journal of Extension* 48, no. 5, article 5. https://www.joe.org/joe/2010october/rb6.php.

Von Braun, J. 2007. "The World Food Situation: New Driving Forces and Required Actions." Washington DC: International Food Policy Research Institute.

Warrick, Billy E., Chris Sansone, and Jason Johnson. n.d. "Small Grain Production in West Central Texas." Texas A&M AgriLife Extension, San Angelo. Accessed May 14, 2015. https://sanangelo.tamu.edu/extension /agronomy/small-grain-production-in-west-central-texas/.

Weatherspark. 2017. "Average Weather in San Angelo, Texas, 1980–2016." https://weatherspark.com/y/5240/Average-Weather-in-San-Angelo -Texas-United-States-Year-Round.

Wilken, G. 1987. *Good Farmers: Traditional Agricultural Resource Management in Mexico and Central America.* Berkeley: University of California Press.

Wisner, Ben, Piers Blaikie, Terry Cannon, and Ian Davis. 2004. *At Risk: Natural Hazards, People's Vulnerability and Disasters.* New York: Routledge.

Yohannes H. 2016. "A Review on Relationship between Climate Change and Agriculture." *Journal of Earth Science and Climatic Change* 7, no. 2: 335–42. DOI: 10.4172/2157-7617.1000335.

Ziervogel, G., and R. Calder. 2003. "Climate Variability and Rural Livelihoods: Assessing the Impact of Seasonal Climate Forecasts in Lesotho." *Area* 35: 403–17.

7

From Partner to Consumer

The Changing Role of Farmers in the Public Agricultural Research Process on the Canadian Prairies

KATHERINE STRAND

When driving past the Mutschler Farm on Highway 21 northeast of Fox Valley, Saskatchewan, the small farmstead nestled between the wheat and lentil fields of this gently rolling landscape reveals nothing of its historic role in building a scientific community in the Canadian Prairies. The farmstead stands out only because it shows signs of life in a region where every other collection of buildings and trees scattered along these roads confirms the telltale signs of human abandonment. Older residents of the region still call this piece of land the Experimental Farm and, when asked, they offer stories about social events held at the farm including dances and field days. This chapter delves into the history of the Mutschler Farm as part of a broader examination of knowledge transfer between public science and farmers in the Canadian Prairies. I use the historic example of knowledge transfer at illustration stations to draw a comparison with the modern relationship between public scientists and farmers within the federal research context of Saskatchewan.

The Mutschler Farm was part of a network of illustration stations organized by the Research Branch of Agriculture Canada (now known as Agriculture and Agri-Food Canada or AAFC), which is the federal department of agriculture similar to the USDA in the United States. In this chapter I propose that while the Mutschler Farm operated as an illustration station between 1928–1959, Agriculture Canada used the network of illustration stations and its larger branch stations to build a science community with farmers based on mutually beneficial alliances. Since this early period, the relationship between farmers and researchers within federal stations has changed dramatically. In the second part of the chapter, I use ethnographic research conducted at the Swift Current Research and Development Centre (SCRDC) and the Indian Head Agricultural Research Foundation (IHARF) to conclude that public research now focuses on building alliances with private sector employees who, in turn, act as consultants for farmers. The role of farmers has shifted from active participants in the research process at illustration stations into passive consumers of agricultural science through private crop consultants and producer groups. As farmers and public research scientists face an indeterminate future with the effects of climate change looming, they lack a key resource that helped them resolve difficulties during the last monumental environmental crisis: the 1930s Dust Bowl. This resource is the farmer-scientist collaborative research model that proved indispensable to refining methods and technology to halt large-scale soil erosion and improve dryland agriculture on the Canadian Prairies.

Methods

In July 2014, I arrived in Swift Current, SK to begin my ethnographic project focusing on the "boundary" between science and community in agricultural research. I chose the location because the Swift Current Research and Development Centre (SCRDC) is one of the oldest and largest remaining public, federal research stations in the prairies and historically maintained a close relationship with the non-scientific community (Gray 1967). For this project, I conducted seventeen recorded interviews with scientists and technical staff at SCRDC, fifty-six recorded interviews with farmers in Swift Current and around southwestern Saskatchewan, three recorded interviews with provincial extension staff, five recorded interviews with private crop consultants and industry representatives, and twenty-two additional interviews with individuals who did not wish to be recorded (including farmers, scientists, and crop consultants). Most of my research participants prefer to remain anonymous; therefore, I use pseudonyms for those individuals in the chapter.

I lived in the community of Wymark with a former grain elevator agent for sixteen months and carried out participant observation with members of the farm community as well as those working within SCRDC. I attended all the extension events held at the station, including six field days over three years. Two of the field days focused on forage research, two on alternative crops including pulses, and two on "low-input" cropping practices, which basically meant organic. The research station is primarily known for its soft white wheat and durum wheat breeding program led for many years by Dr. Ron DePauw. Known as the "billion-dollar man," DePauw has developed close to sixty new cultivars with his colleagues and by 2011 had generated $8.8 million in royalties for the Canadian government (Dawson 2015). The wheat breeding division of SCRDC never offered a public field day during my research, but I was informed of several private field tours for industry affiliates, including SeCan, and individuals from Western Grains Research Foundation, which is an NGO that controls the wheat check-off money.

I also attended the field days of two producer managed research groups: the Indian Head Agricultural Research Foundation (IHARF) in Indian Head, SK and the Wheatland Conservation Area (WCA) in Swift Current, SK. As I will explain in greater detail later in the chapter, these research groups provide an interesting comparison to the older, federal research stations because for many public researchers at SCRDC, they represent the next step in the federal government's strategy to extricate itself from agricultural research. Although managed by an elected board of local farmers, WCA and IHARF blur the lines between three groups that during the earlier period under examination in this chapter (late 1920s through the 1950s) remained separate: public agricultural research institutes, private agrochemical businesses, and farmers.

The area of southwestern Saskatchewan is primarily composed of dryland farms ranging in size from one thousand to forty thousand acres. The primary cash crops include soft white spring wheat, durum wheat, lentils, canola, peas, and flax. Secondary crops include mustard, barley, alfalfa, and oats. According to Pulse Canada, Saskatchewan accounts for 99 percent of the country's lentil production, while Canada leads the world in lentil exports. For this chapter I focus on chemical farmers, although I interviewed seven organic farmers in the area. Chemical farmers typically use air drill systems between forty to seventy feet in length to seed and fertilize their crops with mixtures of nitrogen, phosphorus, potassium, and other micronutrients. They operate tractors and combines with GPS guidance systems that fully automate steering and many other seeding and harvesting functions. Most chemical farmers direct cut their crops and eliminate the need for swathing through the use of desiccants including glyphosate. Ten of my interview participants stated that their high clearance sprayers are the most frequently used piece of equipment on their farms. They spray herbicides (primarily glyphosate and glyphosate cocktails) before seeding (pre-burn), during the growing season, prior to harvest as a desiccant, and oftentimes after harvest. This large acreage, minimum tillage, input-dependent system differs drastically from what was utilized during the earlier period under examination in this chapter.

Between 1920 and 1950, farmers had not expanded their cropped land much beyond the 320 acres acquired through the Dominion Lands Act and subsequent pre-emption (Bennett 1969; Friesen 1987). Bennett recorded the average Saskatchewan farm in 1940 at 432 acres and only rising to an average of 686 acres by 1960 (1969, 45). Farmers during this period primarily relied on a two-year rotation of spring wheat and summer fallow; however, unlike their twenty-first century counterparts, they diversified their farms by including livestock, pasture, and forage crops into their production systems. Farmers seeded with drill attachments behind cultivators and discs, and during rotations of summer fallow they spent the entire growing season keeping their fallow ground free from weeds by using multiple methods of cultivation. Some phosphate fertilizers came into use during this period; however, overall, crop inputs of any kind remained minimal. Although tractors, harvesting equipment, seeding equipment, crop varieties, and herbicides changed dramatically between the two periods under examination, farmers continued including a summer fallow rotation into the 1980s and 1990s. It took many years before farmers in this semi-arid environment believed that crops could be grown continuously without periods of summer fallow for moisture conservation. With the exception of four farmers I interviewed or spent time with during my ethnographic data collection, all continue to farm the land of their families' original homesteads. They are multi-generational farmers, but the scale and type of operation that dominates the region would be unrecognizable to their homesteader ancestors.

Community Science

For this chapter, I rely on Shapin's (1984) account of Robert Boyle's pneumatics experiments from mid-seventeenth century England to explain the importance of a "scientific public." In this work, Shapin argues that Boyle shifted knowledge production in science toward the creation of "matters of fact" through the public witnessing of experiments. Witnessing in the seventeenth century meant gathering gentlemen observers to view an experiment and verify the results. This contrasted with the practices of alchemy, which purposefully obscured experimental practices and kept the material conditions of the work private. Boyle argued that the combination of multiple witnesses and experimental devices such as the air pump (used in pneumatics research) provided "unclouded and undistorted mirrors of nature" (Shapin 1984, 497) that could be replicated by other scientists. Witnessing evolved into the system of scientific writing familiar to us all in which the various parts of the process (hypothesis development, methods, results, and conclusion) reproduce the effect of witnessing by giving full accounts of the material conditions and practices. Boyle relied on witnessing to authenticate his knowledge as an alternative to his epistemological opponents in alchemy and religion.

Witnessing scientific experiments (either through in situ observers or scientific writing) is a practice designed to build alliances with individuals sharing common interests (Shapin 1984). Latour (1983, 1988) highlights this point as he chronicles the work of Louis Pasteur in creating an anthrax vaccination for livestock in late nineteenth-century rural France. Latour credits Pasteur's ability to enlist outsider interest in his work from the farm community and the government as key to his success in creating the vaccine and becoming the authoritative spokesman for these hidden and sometimes virulent microscopic organisms. Pasteur was able to "translate others' interests into his own language" (Latour 1983, 144) by staging performances of the vaccination process before an assembled public. Farmers witnessed the effect of the vaccinations on livestock and eventually replicated the process by inoculating their own herds. Henke (2008) explores how field trials staged on farmer land from agricultural research in California work in similar ways. As Henke explains, "authenticity makes field trials a powerful demonstration for growers" because the trials are "intended to be place-bound" (2008, 114). Farmers cannot accept universalizing practices and knowledge claims that sometimes characterize data generated in other areas of science, so field trials offer an opportunity to witness testing on soils and in conditions similar to their own (Henke and Gieryn 2008). Researchers bring the science onto the field, thereby translating the experiment into terms familiar and relevant to the growers. The farmers become conversant in the experimental process, which makes them powerful allies. Overall, the process of witnessing is key to building alliances across the institutional boundaries of agricultural science, which brings the scientific process onto fields and into farm communities.

Illustrating Science on the Canadian Prairies

The Mutschler Farm was part of a network of illustration or sub-stations that extended across Canada beginning in 1915 (Canada Experimental Farms Service 1939). The illustration stations were connected to larger branch stations where scientists managed their operations and organized the leasing agreement with families like the Mutschlers. "The Dominion Experimental Farms System may be loosely compared to the hub and spokes of a wheel. The hub is the headquarters at the Central Farm. . . . The branch farms and stations and branch laboratories of certain divisions are the main spokes, while carrying the influence still further afield are the sub-stations and 195 illustrations stations. The branch farms and other outlying units are in contact with the public continually, co-operate with extension men and serve in many ways. They are close to the farmer and the farmer uses them" (Canada Experimental Farms Service

1939, 25–6). Today, the Central Farm continues to oversee agricultural research from Ottawa; however, many of the branch stations have closed in recent years. In Saskatchewan, only two of the original seven branches remain open as independent stations. The closed stations operate as outlets for Branch Station Swift Current (SCRDC) and Saskatoon, which direct most of the federal research carried out in the province.

SCRDC, the closest federal branch station, directed the work carried out on the Mutschler Farm while it operated as an illustration station. Illustration stations began in Saskatchewan in 1915 as outlets for the branch station at Indian Head (Johnson and Smith 1986). The goal of these early stations was to rent a portion of a "farmer's publicly placed farm . . . so that a systematic rotation of crops, using suitable seed and judicious cultural methods, might be followed and then to direct the attention of neighbors in the community to this illustration station in the hope that they might emulate the work being done there" (Canada Experimental Farms Service 1939, 87). In a seminar addressing the scientific staff at SCRDC in 1937, E. C. Sackville, the illustration station supervisor based in Swift Current, listed three criteria to consider when opening an illustration station. First, they needed a "practical and progressive farmer" who was interested in experimental work (Sackville 1937, 1). As Sackville explained, "He should be a man in whom the people of the district have implicit confidence and should be public spirited and have the ability to meet people well" (1937, 1). Second, they needed a farm in a "prominent location and on a road which is well travelled" (Sackville 1937, 1). The land should be typical of the region in terms of topography and soil type, and the farmstead "should be neat and attractive" (Sackville 1937, 1). Finally, Sackville explained that the work, both experimental and demonstrational in nature, should be geared toward the problems of the local community. In the seminar, he highlighted the importance of testing new seed varieties and fertilizers, practices to limit soil erosion, and plants for the home garden. He also emphasized how the ideal station would build shelterbelts around the farmstead, keep well-bred livestock, and develop dugouts and dams to secure water. Sackville closed his seminar with a brief discussion of annual field meetings that should be educational but also "somewhat of a social event and the picnic feature should be a part of the programme" (1937, 5).

Sackville's seminar intended illustration stations to provide the basis to build a scientific community on the prairies. Drawing on Shapin's account of scientific witnessing, the illustration stations built alliances with the community by choosing a well-regarded operator, or local farmer, and by locating the experiments in ideal locations for "roadside farming" (Burton 2004). "Roadside or hedgerow farming" are terms Burton (2004) uses to describe how farmers gather knowledge about their neighbors and their practices through constant observation, from vehicle cabs, along well-traveled routes. Shapin explains that in experiments conducted for the Royal Society of London, the qualifications and community standing of the witnesses contributed to the credibility of the work as much as Boyle's rigorous attention to method and his experimental tools. Burton (2012), in reference to Bourdieu (1984), uses the phrase "cultural capital" to describe how farmers build prestige in their communities through the visible manifestation of productivist agriculture (e.g., yield, minimal weeds, and new machinery). In Fox Valley, the Mutschlers were well-known in the community. According to Marvin Mutschler, the grandson of the original operator, his father (who inherited the farm and illustration station agreement from his grandfather) kept the grounds of the farmstead in near perfect condition and meticulously tended to the weeds on his land. A tidy farmstead and attention to weeds are traits that farmers still use to categorize "good" and "poor" farmers. No doubt this contributed to their cultural capital in the region, which mattered a great deal when they discussed the efficacy of various practices on "coffee row." The phrase "coffee row" is used by farmers all over Saskatchewan to describe their off-season ritual of gathering at cafes, grain elevators, and homes to drink coffee and discuss their own and their neighbors' farms and families. Farmers in Saskatchewan have gathered for coffee row, in some cases at the same location, for multiple generations. When well-regarded farmers attend coffee row, their opinions matter to the decisions of others. Sackville's attention to the characteristics of the operator indicates that the opinions of highly regarded farmers carried weight in the community, for as he said, "The success of a sub-station depends on the personality of the operator more than anything else" (1937, 1).

Farmers in Saskatchewan display a great talent for roadside farming, and the grid-pattern of their roads affords them ample opportunity to observe new practices and machinery throughout the growing season. Most of the farmers who participated in this research cited the success of a neighbor's experience with a crop, input, implement, or practice as the primary motivation for their decision to change operations. Sackville understood the importance of location in terms of the illustration stations because he knew that farmers needed to observe new practices or inputs for one or more growing seasons before they risked their own time and money. Illustration stations relieved the farmer of the experimental financial burden (Moynan and Tinline 1939) while providing powerful demonstrations within conditions similar to their own (Henke 2008) along routes accessible to roadside farming. Overall, the choice of operator and location allowed farmers to fully assess the value of any given practice. As a current researcher at SCRDC explained to me, "Knowing the ability of the operator and the quality of land is what mattered. They knew the land, they knew the man, and could predict their own success accordingly."

Illustration stations also built a scientific community by providing a central hub for researchers from Swift Current and other branch stations, local farmers, and Agricultural Improvement Associations (AIAS) to meet, identify regional problems, and mobilize the local community to take action (Palmer 1939). In 1935, the Parliament of Canada passed the Prairie Farm Rehabilitation Act (PFRA) in response to severe soil erosion, large-scale crop failures, and mass farm abandonments throughout the prairie provinces in the 1920s and 1930s (Canada Department of Agriculture 1961). The PFRA provided additional resources to expand extension activities under the existing research network and to intervene where necessary to stabilize severely eroded land. As part of the PFRA, some illustration stations expanded to encompass entire farms up to 640 acres (known then as sub-stations), and branch stations organized Agricultural Improvement Associations to mobilize community-based action (Moynan and Tinline 1939). As Dr. Asael Palmer, a proponent of stubble farming and key soil researcher at the Lethbridge Branch Station, explained, "It was clearly recognized that the causes of wind erosion and the nature of damage done by drifting soil were problems of the community as well as of the individual since drifting not only injured the field from which the soil moved but the drift soil blew over adjoining fields, covered up fences and roads and filled the air with dust. . . . This situation made it imperative that organized effort be adopted" (1939, 35).

Agricultural Improvement Associations (AIAS) fulfilled this need for organized effort. Gray (1967) credits Shorty Kemp, one of the original staff members at SCRDC, with the idea of officially organizing groups of farmers around each sub-station to form AIAS. The AIAS, under farmer leadership and with the guidance of researchers at the branch stations, acted as conduits of communication to mobilize labor for emergency actions, organize farm meetings at the sub-stations, and distribute seed to create additional pasture on badly eroded land (Gray 1967).[1] By 1937, there were 109 AIAS across the prairies with official membership at 14,000 individuals. Some AIAS extended the work of sub-stations onto the fields of their members, with financial assistance from the government, to provide additional demonstration plots for practices such as seeding crested wheatgrass in pastureland (Murray 1940; Shirriff 1939). The PFRA intended sub-stations to function as "community centres," where farmers could meet regularly and exchange information (Moynan and Tinline 1939, 83). Overall, AIAS, organized around the sub-stations, sought to fulfill the third point made above by Sackville. They were designed to address community problems collectively and allow farmers to discover for themselves the "practical means within their power of controlling their drifting soil even under severe conditions" (Shirriff 1939, 34).

Many aspects of social and farm life fell within the purview of illustration stations. Thus, these outposts disregarded the institutional boundaries that create stark divisions between science and society (Gieryn 1999). While researchers such as Latour (1983) question the reality of such boundaries for all science, illustration stations clearly differ from contemporary public research in regard to the breadth of their concerns. Sackville (1937) touches on this when he discusses the importance of the social picnic, the attractiveness of the farmstead, and the home garden to the effectiveness of the illustration stations. Part of the PFRA's intent behind expanding the illustration stations into sub-station outposts and mobilizing resources for AIA projects, such as planting thousands of trees around farmsteads, was to "give permanence" to prairie communities (Jacobson 1939, 58). Permanent communities in the prairies suited the interests of the federal government as much as the local farmers (Jones 2002). Thus, particularly through PFRA funding for sub-stations, they encouraged operators to devote time to planting shelterbelts (Moynan and Tinline 1939), updating houses (Sackville and Janzen 1939), and expanding the home garden. Sub-station annual reports to the branch station at Swift Current between 1935 and 1957 included sections devoted to the activities of each illustration or sub-station with details on home improvements; the condition of orchards; the yield of home gardens; the number of eggs collected from laying hens; the purchase of new appliances (e.g., washing machines); and home and farm expense reports. Some of this information was made available to farmers; thus, neighbors could assess the economics and usefulness of practices from initial cost to final profit (in the case of crops and livestock).

Overall, the illustration stations were at least initially designed to demonstrate how to make life possible in this unforgiving environment. A major part of that work involved organizing social events to be held at the stations each year. When asked about the Fox Valley Station, Marvin Mutschler remembers the field days more than anything else. He described for me the huge tents they set up each year for the crowds of people who would travel to his family farm to observe the demonstration plots, listen to speakers from the Swift Current Branch Station, and eat food prepared by the women of Fox Valley. Ellen, a ninety-year-old woman who grew up a short distance from the Fox Valley Station, described her experience at the field days and dances during an unrecorded conversation. She remembered large crowds of people and a banana cake that was served at one of the field days. Ellen explained to me that she had never before tasted this cake and still remembers it as being one of the most delicious foods she ever ate as a child in Fox Valley. In addition to viewing demonstration plots, testing new equipment, and speaking to the scientists from Swift Current (see figure 16), each field day around the province included a speaker for the women attendees. Topics included choosing color schemes for home décor, canning garden produce, and understanding the cuts of meat from hogs. Ellen's son, a sixty-year-old farmer, remembers attending an event at the Fox Valley Station in the 1950s where men demonstrated farmyard safety with newly installed electric lines. Overall, Sackville (1937) recommended the inclusion of a picnic at each illustration field day. Based on archival reports and the recollections of those around Fox Valley, operators and branch station scientists went beyond this recommendation to create a "mixed cultural space" similar to what Diser describes of the Belgian agricultural laboratories from the mid-nineteenth century. She describes these research stations as a "porous and informal sphere [where] the laboratories exercised authority, while absorbing and accommodating lay people and their practices" (Diser 2012).

Powerful Allies

Taking Diser's (2012) point one step further, I suggest that illustration stations built alliances with farmers in which local communities became well versed in the experimental process and contributed information to their scientist allies from Swift Current. Marvin Mutschler, the grandson of the original operator at Fox Valley, remembers "constantly checking that damn rain gauge" for his father and recording daily measurements. This example is the tip of the iceberg in terms of the information generated and recorded by illustration operators for branch station scientists. Scattered across the province in various soil types and climatic enclaves, the illustration stations provided the per-

FIG. 16. A farm safety presentation given by NA Korven, a research
scientist from Swift Current, at the 1956 Fox Valley Illustration Station
field day. Photo courtesy of SCRDC Archives, Agriculture and Agri-
Food Canada.

fect opportunity for branch scientists to test seed varieties, tillage methods, forms of weed control, harvest practices, forage production, and livestock management using comparison as an experimental technique. Each operator's knowledge and skill in creating and managing the demonstration plots ensured meaningful results on a yearly basis. Their intimate relationship with the land meant that researchers could introduce a new practice (such as the Noble Blade for weed control in 1949), give the operators a crash course on its use, then allow them to figure out the best way to incorporate the new technology into their existing operations (Janzen and Korven 1949). The illustration station operator's long-term history on the land provided scientists with a readily available comparative resource. In the case of the 1949 Noble Blade experiment, operators reported on its effectiveness in killing thistle on their soil type when compared with other methods such as the one-way disc. Perhaps moisture levels differed between these comparative years; but farmers more than anyone else could isolate those factors as meaningful to the comparison. As Henke explains from his research on field trials in California, farmworkers "help standardize the collection of data . . . At the same time, their skills make the trial seem relevant to the current standards and practices of the local farm industry" (2008, 127). The operators' full immersion in variables such as soil moisture, weed pressure, and crop diseases that constitute producing yearly crops gave them an advantage over branch scientists in terms recognizing the factors that made a difference on any given trial.

W. M. (Bill) Harding (assistant to Shorty Kemp at Swift Current) presented a seminar on December 12, 1938. He described his frustrations when applying the experimental process to improving wheat yields on test plots at the Swift Current Station. He found it almost impossible to isolate any given variable when testing various "treatments," leading him to conclude that the best solution is cooperative experiments:

> Cooperative experiments with farmers would seem like the most satisfactory arrangement for this type of work and it may be best carried out by agricultural improvement associations. Work of this kind would likely be beneficial in a double way. We would, in the first place, obtain a more thorough understanding of the value of our various treatments under different conditions. At the same time we would have at our disposal the advice of individual farmers in respect to various treatments. This phase is most important. In most cases the farmer himself has established the principles by which we conduct our farming activity. By working together both experimentalist and farmer should certainly benefit. (Harding 1938, 16)

Twelve years later, Joe Ficht, from the Field Husbandry Section at Swift Current, expressed a similar sentiment in his seminar at the station: "The talent for invention, and the gift of philosophy are never found wanting among farm people. The direct contact with groups of farmers will always be a useful source of guidance and inspiration to the research worker" (Ficht 1950, 6). More than sixty years later, the public research scene in Saskatchewan looks very different from the historic period of the early twentieth century. Turning now to ethnographic research conducted in Saskatchewan from July 2014 through April 2017, the next section highlights key points of divergence from the model of building a science community described above.

Modern Agricultural Witnessing

For this section, I draw on two ethnographic examples of field days to show how witnessing in contemporary agricultural research remains key to building a science community in Saskatchewan. Although some field testing on producer land still occurs through the federal research stations (primarily for new cultivars in breeding programs), scientists at SCRDC and provincial extension agents cite field days at the station as the activity most frequently used to build relationships with farmers and distribute research findings. Many groups around the province host field days, including private seed companies and distributors of agricultural chemicals. Here, I examine only those hosted by SCRDC and the contemporaneous events hosted by producer-directed, applied research groups in cooperation with the federal stations. I limit the discussion to these events because I want to compare how the process of witnessing has changed within the public context of federal research institutions. Thus, I focus on field days hosted by SCRDC and affiliated producer-directed groups including the Indian Head Agricultural Research Foundation (IHARF) and the Wheatland Conservation Area (WCA). WCA shares facilities with SCRDC in Swift Current, while IHARF has largely taken over what remains of the federal research farm in Indian Head (known as The Indian Head Research Farm). The next section examines public field days at SCRDC to highlight the key role of private crop consultants as mediators between scientists and farmers. I also use this ethnographic material to explain how funding models for federal research have changed since the days of illustration stations and how this can be seen through these witnessing events.

Swift Current Field Day

In July 2015, I attended the Swift Current Research and Development Center's (SCRDC) Alternative Crops Field Day cohosted by the federal station and WCA (the affiliated producer-directed research group). At this point in my research, I had already attended two field days at the station and was well-acquainted with the scientists and technical staff at SCRDC, as well as numerous farmers, provincial extension employees, and private crop consultants in attendance. One of the scientists in charge of organizing the field day later told me that about eighty people attended the event with less than half categorizing themselves as producers or farmers on the sign-up sheet. Large air-conditioned buses drove us to the test plots located about eight minutes south of the SCRDC station, where we circulated around ten stations in small groups. Hundreds of one-meter by three-meter test plots bordered by neatly mowed, grassy pathways created a patchwork pattern with signs describing different treatments for visual comparison. At each stop, at least one individual used a microphone to address the audience, explaining the details of the trial, the results since spring seeding, and the primary funding source. Presenters gave attendees the opportunity to ask questions at each stop but time constraints limited discussions to only a few minutes. Presenters held individual conversations with attendees while walking or driving between stops. WCA hosted the first five stops in the morning, which included topics on mustard variety tests, weed control for mustard, soybean and fava bean testing, and an update on the crop disease fusarium head blight. We took a short lunch break and spent the afternoon touring the SCRDC plots led by scientists and postdoctoral researchers. Topics from these stops included intensifying pulse rotations, testing minor crops including quinoa and hemp, testing new lentil varieties, and pulse inoculant testing.

Three points stood out in my field notes from the day and later conversations with farmers, scientists, and crop consultants about the event. First, private industry in the form of agrochemical companies including Monsanto and FMC, seed companies, input distributors such as Pioneer Co-op, and crop consultants or professional agrologists working independently or through input distributors played a large role in the witnessing event that day. According to the same scientist reporting on farmer attendance, close to half of the eighty participants fell into one of the categories listed above. I found them easily recognizable through what I began to call the "chem. rep." (an abbreviated phrase for chemical representative) uniform. Almost all in attendance and those at the Indian Head Field Day (discussed below) wore colored polo T-shirts with company names embroidered on the chest and back, as seen in figure 17. Between the Swift Current and Indian Head field days, I spotted Koch Agronomic Services, BASF, Monsanto, Bayer CropScience, Seedmaster, Dupont, and several other companies represented on their polo uniforms. These individuals socialized amongst the other attendees, and they asked and answered questions during discussion. At one point the FMC representative took over a presentation given by Barbara Ziesman (a provincial government specialist in plant disease) to update everyone on the status of Authority, a residual herbicide manufactured by FMC, as a potential herbicide for weed control in mustard. Some plot signs displayed company and product names in use during the trial, although this signaling of corporate presence was more of a feature at the Indian Head Field Day.

In conversations after the field day with one of the presenting scientists, he explained to me that the provincial and federal governments anticipate and encourage a large industry presence at the field days because they recognize these individuals as the primary mechanism of technology transfer to farmers. Crop consultants attend to keep updated on the latest research, obtain the educational credits necessary to maintain their "professional agrologist" status through the Saskatchewan Institute of Agrologists, and meet potential new customers. Most farmers above the 4,000-acre mark in southwest Saskatchewan use the services of crop consultants to test their soils for nutrients; scout their fields for disease and weed issues; and write "prescriptions" that include fertilizer and seed rates, and herbicide and fungicide recommendations. Of the farmers I interviewed, those who use the services of consultants remarked on their trust that consultants will attend informational events that they have no time or desire to attend themselves. They see this feature as part of the services offered through consultant packages and, as we saw above, the scientists also understood that these individuals become the primary translators of their research to the farm community.

The other category of attendees whose presence was felt at the Swift Current event through test plot signage, funding declarations, and polo T-shirts was made up of producer groups, including the Sask Mustard and the Saskatchewan Pulse Growers. Within the first five minutes of arriving at the event, I ran into Dwight Debruyn (see figure 17), a farmer near Hazlet, sk and a board member of Sask Mustard. I had helped him with seeding earlier that spring and had interviewed him over the previous winter. On this July morning, Dwight wore a black and yellow polo T-shirt displaying Sask Mustard and a hat with the same logo. Dwight told me that morning that he has attended all of the Alternative Crops Field Days as scrdc and wca since becoming a board member of Sask Mustard because he "checks on the plots to report back to the other members" (Strand field notes 2015). Sask Mustard provided the funding for many of the wca and scrdc plot trials that we viewed later in the day. Dwight grows mustard, so he has a personal interest in the research. As he explained to me, his job that day was to "see how these folks were spending the group's research money" (Strand field notes 2015). As Gray explains, "producer check-offs are created through government policy that gives industry the ability to introduce a 'check-off,' 'a levy,' or 'a tax' on the sale of a product. Proceeds are typically put into a fund controlled by producers who decide how to invest it in agricultural research"

FIG. 17. The "chem. rep." uniform on display at the Alternative Crops field day in Swift Current. Dwight Debruyn is pictured on the left wearing a Sask Mustard polo T-shirt. Photo by Katherine Strand.

(2014, 10). Sask Mustard began in 2004 when the Saskatchewan Mustard Development Commission (comprised of mustard growers) voted to collect a 0.5 percent refundable levy on gross sales of mustard. An elected board of members, including Dwight, reviews research applications and contributes money for projects at SCRDC, WCA, and other research groups around the province.

Some producer groups like Saskatchewan Pulse Growers and Sask Canola (a provincial producer group linked to the national "industry association," the Canola Council of Canada) accept additional funding from Agriculture and Agri-Food Canada, the federal department of agriculture, AAFC, and private industry partners to supplement their research funds. This funding arrangement is called a "science cluster," and it is through these clusters (i.e., Canola/Flax Science Cluster, Beef Science Cluster, and Pulse Science Cluster) that most public SCRDC scientists fund their projects. For the year ending August 31, 2015, Sask Pulse Growers recorded an "industry revenue" of $18,327,882 on the levy, $225,280 from industry partnerships, and $168,860 from AAFC (Saskatchewan Pulse Growers Annual Report 2014-2015). The first four "core funders" listed on the Canola Council of Canada (2017) include ADM, Alberta Canola, BASF, and Bayer Crop Science. Thus, producer groups form powerful relationships with AAFC, the Saskatchewan Ministry of Agriculture, and agrochemical companies through their collection and distribution of research money.

Producer groups distribute research findings through their own publications, websites, Twitter accounts, and conferences. Using Saskatchewan Pulse Growers as an example, this group posts daily updates on their Twitter account alerting followers to new publications offered on their website (which include research findings from federal stations), links to the provincial government's agricultural reports, and agronomic advice on issues such as insect damage in crops. Without access to academic publications, farmers cannot read the results of research done at federal stations unless they contact scientists directly or look up those trials sponsored by Sask Pulse on their website. For example, the Sask Pulse website offers a summary of research findings for Dr. Yantai Gan's project *Biological Tactics of Tackling Field Pea Yield Declining in the Semiarid Southwest* (Gan n.d.). Dr. Gan is a federal research scientist at SCRDC who received $294,225 for his project from Sask Pulse, which offers his research findings on their website and hosted a 2015 conference in Swift Current featuring Dr. Gan as a speaker. Additionally, the Sask Pulse website offers webinars on agronomic topics like crop disease and weeds. They remain in constant contact with individuals on their mailing lists through newsletters, videos, and two magazines, *Pulse Point* and *Pulse Research*, that circulate once per year electronically and through the mail to give short descriptions of all the research projects Sask Pulse funds each year, including those at federal research stations. Their website blends contributions from public research with promotions for private products such as the Clearfield Production System for Lentils (which includes the non-GMO, herbicide tolerant seed and associated herbicide system) sold by BASF. A judicious observer of the website will note that the public research and private product promotions blend seamlessly together to present an integrated website that occasionally credits the public institute or scientists for their contributions. Every page on the website is branded with the Saskatchewan Pulse Growers logo, thus making their name (and not Agricultural and Agri-food Canada-AAFC) the one predominantly associated with new agronomic information. Overall, Sask Pulse, as one example of a producer group, has a media platform to connect with farmers and distribute research findings through electronic resources as well as public events. Farmers I interviewed expressed a greater familiarity with these sources of information than they did of those distributed by AAFC or the Saskatchewan Ministry of Agriculture, even though many of the federal and provincial informational materials circulate through the media platforms of Sask Pulse and other producer groups.

Thus, although significantly fewer producers attend events hosted by federal researchers than historically occurred through illustration stations, a small number of elected farmers control a significant portion of the research money that keeps SCRDC projects afloat. However, some producer groups, such as Sask Canola, are closely linked to national-level industry associations such as the Canola Council of Canada. The industry associations allow non-farming, "industry" members on their boards and present a united image of the canola industry that blurs the line between farmers and agribusinesses such as Bayer CropScience. What we see at events, such as the Alternative Crops Field Day, are representatives from all segments of the "industry" who, through these funding schemes, exert their influence on the public research agenda. Farmers, if elected by other growers to the Sask Pulse Growers Board, attend these events to monitor the public scientists and their projects. These board members made decisions on funding that led to the projects. Thus, those scientists hosting the field day present their results as a mechanism to build alliances with one of their major funders. WCA, as a farmer-directed research group, also applies for funding through producer groups such as Sask Mustard. Their board votes on projects, obtains funding, and uses hired technicians (mostly retired SCRDC employees) to carry out test plots. The original idea behind farmer-directed research was to work in cooperation with the federal research stations. At Swift Current, none of the scientists I interviewed played a significant role in any of the WCA experiments; thus, it increasingly seems as though the producer groups with check-off money can fund farmer-directed research groups without involving the federal station. One scientist I interviewed at SCRDC explained that this model is what the federal government hopes to achieve at a national level as they slowly step away from public research altogether. The Indian Head Agricultural Research Foundation gives us a good idea of what this model of research might look like if all the remaining branch stations follow its lead.

Indian Head Agricultural Research Foundation

In July 2015 and 2016, I attended the annual IHARF Field Day located on what remains of the federal branch station at Indian Head in southeastern Saskatchewan. This site is significant because the Indian Head Research Farm was one of the original federal stations established in Canada in 1886, but in 1992 it lost its administrative independence to SCRDC (Lafond and Gehl 2013). As the IHARF website explains (IHARF n.d.), in 1990 local farmers formed an alliance with federal researchers to "promote profitable and sustainable agriculture by facilitating research and technology transfer activities." Currently, only one member of the scientific staff at the federal station remains at Indian Head, while IHARF employs around eight individuals including a full-time research manager and multiple technicians. IHARF receives funding from the federal and provincial governments (31 percent in 2016), as well as industry partners including BASF, Koch Agronomic Services, Bayer Crop Science (32 percent in 2016), and various producer groups (37 percent in 2016). In 2015, 217 people attended the July field day, which significantly outnumbered any event I attended at SCRDC. Saskatchewan is home to eight Agri-ARM (a program managed by the Saskatchewan Ministry of Agriculture), producer-directed research centers, five of which are located at the sites of operational or defunct federal research stations (Indian Head included). Indian Head is considered by farmers and researchers alike as the crown jewel of this program, so I attended two of their field days. The IHARF Field Day in 2015 followed the model at Swift Current with a morning and afternoon session organized around stations to display field plots with speakers. During the IHARF portion, a mini grandstand pulled by a tractor weaved through the nearly perfect patchwork of test plots to provide seating for the participants (see figure 18). The morning session toured plots with IHARF's research manager Chris Holzapfel, while the afternoon focused on plots cared for by the remaining federal employees and directed from SCRDC. Of all of the field days I attended during this research, Chris Holzapfel stands out as the most gifted presenter of scientific experiments. His breadth of knowledge became clear as he explained each experiment without using scientific jargon, answered questions from the audience with ease, and offered advice producers could directly implement on their own fields. His presentations contrasted sharply with those given by the scientists at SCRDC, who find it difficult to answer technical questions because they do not participate in fieldwork and are discouraged by their superiors in Ottawa from giving agronomic advice to farmers unless first receiving written approval. The IHARF test plots mostly involve tinkering with the existing zero tillage, high input system to make it more efficient. They test seed and fertilizer placement, different cocktails and application timing of herbicides, fertilizer blends and amounts, and new crops such as carinata. IHARF conducts field scale experiments using the latest technology in precision agriculture and drones to remain relevant to the needs of large-scale farmers; thus, even farmers around Swift Current (close to 314 kilometers away) follow their work. IHARF is the oldest farmer-directed research group, and as a provincial extension agent in Swift Current explained, it is "the model" that other groups are encouraged (by the provincial and federal governments) to achieve.

Fig. 18. The mini grandstand at the IHARF field day in Indian Head, SK.
Photo by Katherine Strand.

The agribusiness and producer group presence at the IHARF Field Day integrated many of the same features as the one in Swift Current. Industry representatives, wearing the polo uniform, participated and led discussions. Each plot we visited included a sign with funding information and some featured input information from specific companies. On the drive back to the main station for lunch, I sat next to an older man wearing a Koch Agronomic Services polo. He introduced himself as an agronomist working for Koch in Canada. I later learned that he is the senior agronomist for Koch and used to work as a professor at McGill University in Montreal. I asked why he decided to attend the field day, and he explained that he was there "to check his plots" (Strand field notes 2015). Koch hired IHARF to test Agrotain, which is a product designed to stabilize urea for controlled, slow release. The Koch (n.d.) website cites AAFC and IHARF as research sources in their promotional material. A technician working for WCA (the farmer-directed research group in Swift Current) explained in an interview later in the summer that a major funding source for both WCA and IHARF is the agrochemical industry. He referred to these companies as WCA's "clients" and suggested that their funded projects consume the majority of the group's research space and time. It became clear by the end of the field day that IHARF promotes, not always explicitly, only a zero tillage system, which relies solely on herbicides for weed control. From the presentations I heard, synthetic fertilizers are the only mechanisms of nutrient management included in their trials.

On our third stop of the day the tractor driver pulled the mini grandstand alongside a collection of canola plots with a sign reading "Bayer Invigor L140P." The plots looked impressive with high densities of canola in neon yellow bloom. The ongoing trial tested various rates of phosphorus fertilizer placed directly with the seed or in a band 3.8

cm alongside the seed (side-banding). The idea behind the trial was to test how much phosphorus could be added to the soil before it damaged the emergence of the crop. Our tour guide Chris explained that canola is very "plastic" and, as such, "we don't fully know how far current fertilizer recommendations can be pushed to increase yield" (Strand field notes 2015). He explained how the plots each received one round of glyphosate to "burn-off" weeds prior to seedling emergence. They were sprayed again on June 15 with a different mixture of herbicides. Within a few days after the field event, they planned to spray the crops with a round of fungicide to prevent the disease sclerotinia. The plants showed no signs of the disease, but they spray to reduce the risk. Finally, prior to harvest, they planned to spray another round of glyphosate on the crop to desiccate the plants in preparation for harvest. Chris explained that glyphosate is not technically a desiccant but will "do the job by slowing down plant growth and cleaning up any remaining weeds" (Strand field notes 2015). The crowd listened intently, only asking questions regarding the timing of each chemical input. What struck me as particularly curious was that all of the test plots looked identical. Chris acknowledged this as well, laughing and explaining that the audience needed to wait for the report to see how the various levels of phosphorus impacted the yield. The control plot received no phosphorus, and the plants clearly looked shorter, less abundant, and with less vegetation than the other plots. Chris laughed again as he directed our attention to the control plot explaining, "Here's what we get with no phosphorus as I'm sure you could all guess" (Strand field notes 2015). Aside from seeing the result of no phosphorus, it was visually impossible to assess the results of the other treatments, which made me wonder why IHARF included this trial on their field tour. After a few more stops with trials testing fertilizer, herbicide, or fungicide treatments, I realized that very few test plots showed visual results. However, the control plot, which always excluded the chemical input under study, could easily be picked out each time. The plot always looked slightly stunted next to the other plots, which handily communicated the unequivocal, visual message: "This is what you get when you eliminate our inputs."

As discussed earlier in regard to Sask Pulse, IHARF distributes information through their website, Twitter account, and email newsletters. They offer easily accessible fact sheets for agronomic information, yearly reports on research, and downloadable presentations given by IHARF employees and AAFC scientists (i.e., Yantai Gan from SCRDC). Everything is branded with the IHARF logo, which blends contributions made by public science, private industry, and IHARF employees.

Discussion

Based on this brief review of AAFC research, field trials, and extension services from two different time periods, four salient points deserve further discussion. First, witnessing field trials to build alliances is a practice we see from both periods, although the major players and roles have changed considerably. The Mutschler Farm served as a community center for farmers and public researchers to exchange information and work cooperatively to stabilize farms and families during the 1930s Dust Bowl. The SCRDC and farmer-directed field trials continue to build alliances but create different types of relationships with private industry and producer groups. Second, as the federal and provincial governments scale back their extension work and research money, a critical gap is created for private agribusinesses to fill. We see this as agrochemical companies fund more research and crop consultants take on the role as the primary extension agents. Of the fifty-six farmers I interviewed during this research, roughly half expressed

concern about how this relocation of both funding responsibility and expertise impacts their access to information.
The other half did not seem concerned and, as one farmer
explained, "With consultants, I just pay for what I used to
get free" (pers. communication, February 2015). Unfortunately, the lack of events and nonacademic publications coming directly from SCRDC has created distance between the
farming community and the scientists. During the period
of illustration stations, AAFC and its scientists led communities as the sole providers of scientific information. Nowadays, farmers either claim to have no knowledge of the work
done at SCRDC or, even worse, believe that public research
is falling behind its private counterparts.

Third, producer groups and farmer-directed research
groups blur the line between multinational agribusinesses
and farmers in local communities. The overlap serves the
interests of the multinational companies because farmers still maintain a level of trust in the eyes of consumers
and provide a friendlier face to represent the industry as a
whole. Some farmers recognize why this seeming endorse-
ment is problematic and call the producer groups "Astro-
turf." This term is in reference to the lack of grassroots
organization with producer groups that characterized the
now defunct Saskatchewan Wheat Pool and the Canadian
Wheat Board. Some see producer groups as "storefronts"
for government policies that support the interests of large
agribusinesses over farmers and consumers. What is clear
is the role of these groups in funding research and dis-
seminating agronomic information. Crop consultants and
chemical representatives blur the line even further because
these individuals typically come from farm families and work
in their home communities. As a large-scale farmer near
the Cutbank area southwest of Swift Current explained to
me, "There is a network that exists in farm communities
between farmers and everyone else. Most everyone I know

is related to a chem. rep., P. Ag. (professional agrologist), or someone with insider knowledge" (pers. communication, April 2015).

Finally, although it is difficult to pull apart the source of money that funds certain projects and to understand how this impacts research agendas, it speaks volumes when the only public events held at SCRDC include a large private and producer group presence. Early illustration stations were funded either with federal money from the research branch in Ottawa or federal money through the PFRA. Although high rates of return on public investment in Canadian agricultural research have been well-documented (Zentner 1982; Brinkman 2004; Gray and Malla 2007), in 1995 the funding model for public research farms like SCRDC switched from "A-base" to the Matching Investment Initiative (Martel 2013; SCRDC scientists and staff, pers. communication). A-base is money given for research from the federal government. Until 1995, the federal government gave each station a sum of A-base money to be used at the discretion of the branch director and the scientists. Funding for contemporary SCRDC scientists is much more complicated. What started out as a matching investments initiative in which scientists secured private funds to be matched by the government for projects has since evolved into a complicated (and perhaps intentionally obscure) model where scientists apply for grants provided by private industry, the provincial government, the federal government (including A-base), non-government organizations, and producer groups with check-off money. In interviews with seventeen scientists and technical staff from SCRDC, they estimated that between 75 percent to 90 percent of their time each year was spent applying for external sources of funding. Needless to say, this demand on their schedule to secure funding did not leave much time to engage in extension and alliance-building activities with the local farming community.

Scientists at SCRDC find this situation troubling, particularly as it concerns the need for long-term research related to climate change and environmental sustainability (SCRDC scientists, pers. communication). As a SCRDC scientist nearing retirement who works in climate research explained to me, "The government is modeling its research on private industry. This [approach] influences timing, measurable results, products, and budgets" (pers. communication, March 2015). He went on to explain how the protocol of writing grants for science clusters must include a typical three-year timescale; procedures to reduce risk to the field plots and data collection (e.g., herbicides, fungicides, and insecticides); and explanations for how results will be relevant to agriculture beyond the Swift Current region. Applications that include the elements listed above are more likely to receive funding from the clusters, particularly if the result is a marketable product. Scientists that fall outside of these parameters find it difficult to get funding from the clusters, although they often spoke of ways to get money for the "product proposal" and use it for their long-term, more environmentally-focused research.

Conclusion

Part of my ethnographic research in southwestern Saskatchewan focused on the long-term relationship between public agricultural science and local farming communities. The foundation of this relationship is public witnessing, which helps to disseminate information as well as build alliances between science and farmers. However, between the two periods under study in this chapter, new stakeholders including private consultants, agrochemical businesses, producer groups, and producer-directed research organizations now play an increasingly important role in mediating the relationship between farmers and public scientists. Farmers must assume the role of consumers of private products to make this new farming industry (which includes multiple private and public-private blended organizations) continue to function and support public research. The category of farming has broadened to include profit-driven stakeholders who make every attempt to present a unified image of the farming industry, which includes farmers, public scientists, crop consultants, and agrochemical businesses. This unified farming industry is very different than what existed in the early twentieth century example under study in this chapter. During this period, farmers and public scientists each played a clearly defined role in a collaborative research process that helped to address the environmental challenges of soil erosion. The goal of the cooperative effort was to build permanent communities on the Canadian Prairies, which undoubtedly included a profit incentive on the part of farmers but did not place them in the role of consumers supporting a bloated agrochemical economy. What is most troubling in terms of this new farming industry is how it has deteriorated the process of public science and the relationship between public agricultural research institutes and local farming communities. This comes at a time when scientists at SCRDC confront the reality of climate change, with its obvious effects on moisture levels and on soil and plant diseases. As I discussed above in the case of IHARF, the new model is moving us toward a single, input-dependent system for the entire Canadian Prairies. During the Dust Bowl, numerous strategies to address soil erosion evolved from the collaboration between farmers and scientists. This resulted in a bloom of new practices: strip farming (Hopkins, Palmer, and Chepil 1946); equipment such as blades (Fulton 2009; McInnis 2004) and discers (Isern 1988); and conservation organizations such as Agricultural Improvement Associations (Awada, Linwall, and Sonntag 2014). Without the network of stations to facilitate collaboration between farmers and scientists on a local level, it is difficult to imagine how a second bloom in farming technology in response to climate change could ever occur. We may need to find inspiration from the century-old illustration station model to prepare for the next hundred years of agricultural research and farming on the Canadian Prairies.

Notes

I would like to thank all of my research participants including the staff and scientists from the Swift Current Research and Development Centre. Thank you to the many farmers and residents of southwest Saskatchewan who generously donated time to my ethnographic work.

1. Gray (1967) uses listing bees as an example of emergency action during the 1930s. Listing bees primarily involved gathering equipment (tractors and listing implements) and people together on wind eroded land. Listers worked the surface of the soil into a series of troughs that disrupted the velocity of wind, collected snow in the winter, and provided protection from water erosion in the spring.

References

Awada, L., C. W. Lindwall, and B. Sonntag. 2014. "The Development and Adoption of Conservation Tillage Systems on the Canadian Prairies." *International Soil and Water Conservation Research* 2, no. 1: 47–65.

Bennett, John W. 1969. *Northern Plainsmen; Adaptive Strategy and Agrarian Life.* Chicago: Aldine.

Bourdieu, Pierre. 1984. *Distinction: A Social Critique of the Judgement of Taste.* Cambridge MA: Harvard University Press.

Brinkman, George L. 2004. "Strategic Policy Issues for Agricultural Research in Canada." *Current Agriculture, Food, and Resource Issues* November: 131–47.

Burton, Rob. 2004. "Seeing Through the Good Farmer's Eyes: Towards Developing an Understanding of the Social Symbolic Value of Productivist Behavior." *Sociologia Ruralis* 44, no. 2: 195–215.

———. 2012. "Understanding Farmers' Aesthetic Preference for Tidy Agricultural Landscapes: A Bourdieusian Perspective." *Landscape Research* 37, no. 1: 51–71.

Canada Department of Agriculture. 1961. *Prairie Farm Rehabilitation Act: What It Means to the Prairie Provinces.* Ottawa: Queen's Printer and Controller of Stationary.

Canadian Experimental Farms Service. 1939. *Fifty Years of Progress on Dominion Experimental Farms 1886–1936.* Ottawa.

Canola Council of Canada. 2017. "Core Funders." Accessed April 12, 2017. https://www.canolacouncil.org/what-we-do/canola-council-of-canada /core-funders.

Dawson, Allan. 2015. "Wheat Breeder Extraordinaire Ron DePauw Retires from Agriculture and Agri-Food Canada." AGCanada.com.

Diser, Lyvia. 2012. "Laboratory versus Farm: The Triumph of Laboratory Science in Belgian Agriculture at the End of the Nineteenth Century." *Agricultural History* 86, no. 1: 31–54.

Ficht, J. P. *Public Relations*, January 30, 1950. Seminar Paper. Swift Current Research and Development Centre Library.

Friesen, Gerald. 1987. *The Canadian Prairies: A History*. Toronto: University of Toronto Press.

Fulton, Fred. 2009. "Early Roots of Conservation Tillage: Recognizing the Need and the First Steps." In *Landscapes Transformed: The Quiet Triumph of Conservation Tillage and Direct Seeding*, 1–6. Saskatoon: Knowledge Impact in Society.

Gan, Yantai. n.d. "Biological Tactics of Tackling Field Pea Yield Declining in the Semiarid Southwest." Accessed September 22, 2017. http://saskpulse .com/research/research-project-listings/dr-yantai-gan-3.

Gieryn, Thomas. 1999. *Cultural Boundaries of Science: Credibility on the Line*. Chicago: Chicago University Press.

Gray, James H. 1967. *Men Against the Desert*. Saskatoon: Modern.

Gray, Richard. 2014. "Solutions to the Agricultural Research Funding Conundrum." *Canadian Journal of Agricultural Economics* 62: 7–22.

Gray, Richard, and Stavroula Malla. 2007. "The Rate of Return to Agricultural Research in Canada." *Canadian Agricultural Innovation Research Network* 11: 1–11.

Harding, W. M. *Cultural Experiments, Past Results and Future Experiments to Meet a Changing Agriculture*. December 12, 1938. Seminar Paper. Swift Current Research and Development Centre Library. Accessed September 2, 2016.

Henke, Christopher. 2008. *Cultivating Science, Harvesting Power Science and Industrial Agriculture in California*. Cambridge MA: MIT Press.

Henke, Christopher, and Thomas Gieryn. 2008. "Sites of Scientific Practice: The Enduring Importance of Place." In *The Handbook of Science and Technology Studies*, edited by Edward Hackett, Olga Amsterdamska, Michael Lynch, and Judy Wajcman. Cambridge MA: MIT Press.

Hopkins, E. S., A. E. Palmer, and W. S. Chepil. 1946. "Soil Drifting Control in the Prairie Provinces." *Farmers' Bulletin* 32, Publication 568. Ottawa: Dominion of Canada, Department of Agriculture.

IHARF. "About Us," Indian Head Agricultural Research Foundation. Accessed April 12, 2017. http://iharf.ca/about-us.

Isern, Thomas. 1988. "The Discer: Tillage for the Canadian Prairies." *Agricultural History* 62, no. 2: 79–97.

Jacobson, W. L. 1939. "Progress of Small Water Development Projects." In *Prairie Farm Rehabilitation*, edited by C. Gordon O'Brien, 58–63, 84. Ottawa: Canadian Society of Technical Agriculturalists.

Janzen, P. J., and N. A. Korven. *Report of the District Experimental Substations in Southwestern Saskatchewan*, 1949. Annual Report. Swift Current Research and Development Centre Library. Accessed March 10, 2015.

Johnson, W. E., and A. E. Smith. 1986. *Indian Head Experimental Farm 1886–1986*. Ottawa: Research Branch Agriculture Canada.

Jones, David C. 2002. *Empire of Dust : Settling and Abandoning the Prairie Dry Belt*. Calgary: University of Calgary Press.

Koch Agronomic Services. n.d. "We've Dug Up Some Dirt on Nitrogen Loss." Accessed April 12, 2017. http://kochagronomicservices.com/us/products /agriculture/agrotain/shallowband.

Lafond, Guy, and David Gehl. 2013. "Indian Head Research Farm." In *The Innovators Rooted in Science: The History of Research Branch 1986–2011*, edited by Yvon Martel, Jean-Marc Deschenes, and Nathalie Corbeil, 310–16. Ottawa: Minister of Agriculture and Agri-Food Canada.

Latour, Bruno. 1983. "Give Me a Laboratory and I Will Raise the World." In *Science Observed: Perspectives on the Social Study of Science*, edited by Karin Knorr-Cetina and Michael Mulkay, 141–70. London: Sage.

———. 1988. *The Pasteurization of France*. Cambridge MA: Harvard University Press.

Martel, Yvon. 2013. "The Management of Research Branch from 1986 to 2011." In *The Innovators Rooted in Science: The History of Research Branch 1986–2011*, edited by Yvon Martel, Jean-Marc Deschenes, and Nathalie Corbeil, 19–42. Ottawa: Agriculture and Agri-Food Canada.

McInnis, Amy. 2004. "The Development of Better Farm Practices in Saskatchewan." Western Development Museum: Saskatoon SK. http://www.wdm .ca/EdPrograms/discoveryboxes/20.htm.

Moynan, J. C., and M. J. Tinline. 1939. "Sub-Stations and Their Relation to Rehabilitation." In *Prairie Farm Rehabilitation*, edited by C. Gordon O'Brien, 78–84. Ottawa: Canadian Society of Technical Agriculturalists.

Murray, J. A. *The Objects and Achievements of the A.I.As.* January 8, 1940. Seminar Paper. Swift Current Research and Development Centre Library. Accessed March 9, 2016.

Palmer, Asael E. 1939. "Organized Methods of Soil Drifting Control." In *Prairie Farm Rehabilitation*, edited by C. Gordon O'Brien, 35–37. Ottawa: Canadian Society of Technical Agriculturalists.

Sackville, E. C. *The Set-Up For An Ideal Experimental Sub-Station*. February 15, 1937. Seminar Paper. Swift Current Research and Development Centre Library. Accessed February 20, 2015.

Sackville, E. C., and P. J. Janzen. *Report of the District Experiment Sub-Stations in Southwestern Saskatchewan for 1939*. Annual Report. Swift Current Research and Development Centre Library. Accessed March 10, 2015.

Shapin, Steven. 1984. "Pump and Circumstance: Robert Boyle's Literary Technology." *Social Studies of Science* 14, no. 4: 481–520.

Shirriff, C. 1939. "Agricultural Improvement Associations." *In Prairie Farm Rehabilitation*, edited by C. Gordon O'Brien, 32–34, 42. Ottawa: Canadian Society of Technical Agriculturalists.

Zentner, R. P. 1982. "The Social Value of Public Investment in Canadian Wheat Research." Agriculture Canada Research Station, Swift Current Seminar Paper, 1–32.

8

Transmission of the Brazil Model of Industrial Soybean Production

A Comparative Study of Two Migrant Farming Communities in the Brazilian Cerrado

ANDREW OFSTEHAGE

Until 30 years ago, the Cerrado, the vast tropical
savanna of Brazil, was sparsely inhabited and generally
considered to have little value for agriculture. Some
agriculture was practiced along the margins of streams
on strips of alluvial soils which were less acidic and
where there had been an accumulation of nutrients. In
addition, there was some cattle production although
the natural savanna/brush flora characterized by
poor digestibility and nutritive quality resulted in low
carrying-capacity. Today, a great agricultural revolution
is under way in the Cerrado, the result of a long process
of research and development that began more
than 50 years ago.

"The Acid Lands," N. E. Borlaug and C. R. Dowswell (1997)

The soybean boom of South America—the rapid expansion of soybean production into Brazilian Amazonia, the
Argentinian and Uruguayan Pampas, the Chaco of Paraguay
and Bolivia, and the Brazilian Cerrado—has transformed
the region and formed a "Soybean Republic" (Turzi 2011).
Soy covers fifty-seven million hectares of South American
farm land, and South American farmers and agribusinesses
account for 54 percent of global soy production (Oliveira
and Hecht 2016). The expansion of soy production has

extended and consolidated "highly capital and chemical intensive agroindustrial practices" across savannah, woodlands, pastures, and areas that formerly practiced small-scale agriculture (Oliveira and Hecht 2016, 251). The Brazil Model—a subset of capital and chemical intensive practices, including no-till; intensive application of herbicides, pesticides, and fungicides; dependence on fertilizers; and use of hybrid and genetically modified (GM) seed—was designed specifically for the Brazilian Cerrado and has been credited with transforming a "region with little agriculture" into a global and national breadbasket (Borlaug and Dowswell 1997). Proponents celebrate the model as a sustainable development package to be implemented in similar ecological regions (Economist 2010), a trend that is now nascent in Mozambique (Wolford and Nehring 2015). Critics of the model, however, find it to be destructive of local communities and the Cerrado ecosystem (Sawyer 2008; Klink and Machado 2005; Campelo 2017; Klink and Moreira 2002).

The transmission of the Brazil Model and the relation between the model and its implementation have remained relatively unexamined. Recent work has shown heterogeneity within Brazilian soy production, suggesting that farm scale and farming styles produce difference in practices (Mier y Terán Giménez Cacho 2016; Ofstehage 2016; Vennet, Schneider, and Dessein 2016). Using ethnographic evidence, this chapter asks how this agroindustrial and managerial model of farming becomes transmitted across landscapes, and how is it in turn transformed by the on-the-ground farming realities, both material (e.g., soil qualities, pest pressure, and climatic conditions) and social (e.g., values of good farming, knowledge, and know-how). I analyze two encounters with the Brazil Model. The first began when a colony of Holdeman Mennonites, a conservative branch of Anabaptism, settled in rural Goiás in the late 1960s and began converting the Cerrado land to soy production. The second began when a disarticulated group of Midwestern farmers migrated to Western Bahia in the 1990s and 2000s and adopted many aspects of the Brazil Model of industrial soy production (Ofstehage 2017a; Ofstehage 2017b).

Farmers' decision-making processes of adoption or non-adoption of agricultural practices are neither simple nor solely economic-minded. Rather, they emerge out of the engagement between values, agroecology, competing agronomic know-how, and political economy (Gray and Gibson 2013). North Carolina farmers reject water conservation programs partially because of unbalanced long-term risks and short-term rewards, as well as moral logics that deflected responsibility to urban residents (O'Connell et al. 2017), a moral logic shared by Maryland farmers (Paolisso and Maloney 2000). A study of Washington farmers demonstrates that while years of farming experience, education, and full-time status of farmers mattered little to conservation practices, effectiveness of those practices did affect their adoption (Tosakana et al. 2010). Transmission of farming practices is dependent on both social and material acceptability to the farmer.

This chapter analyzes the emerging encounters between land, soy, and farmers as a meshwork (Ingold 2011) that has come into being through planned actions but also thwarted plans, improvisation, and engagements. Where a network is a set of interconnected points, a meshwork is "a tangled mesh of interwoven and complexly knotted strands" (Ingold 2011, 151) in which humans and non-humans act on each other to create emergent realities together. Two aspects of this framework guide this chapter: encounters and movement. First, I approach farmers' adoption, adaptation, or non-adoption of farming practices as an encounter between farmers and other humans (e.g., researchers, other farmers, family members, government agents, and investors), as well as encounters between farmers and soil, landscapes, pests, and climate. Second, I incorporate movement by understanding this encounter not as a moment in time but as a transformative and ongoing relationship in which both the land and farmer transform each other and become something new.

I find that the Brazil Model is not transmitted easily or intact across landscapes of practice, values, and ecologies but rather is subject to careful negotiation and constant improvisation. This finding challenges articulations of models as realizable matters of fact without internal fragmentation and local context. Additionally, encounters with the Brazil Model do not end with complete transmission of the model, but rather with a reworking of the model that enables new formations of work, value, and land. This process of working with models reveals the contingent and emergent qualities of farming practices as local producers adapt to physical landscapes and social communities. After reviewing my research methods, I will outline the emergence of the Brazil Model and its critics and opponents before describing two encounters between transnational farmers and the Brazil Model. After my discussion of these findings, I conclude that the transmission of industrial farming is subject to socio-ecological contingencies that modify the model, the land, and the farmers themselves. This model is not easily and seamlessly transmitted; it is contingent on social and material factors, and this has implications for the transmission and adoption of industrial farming.

Research Methods

I conducted this research over a two-month period in 2012 and a twelve-month period in 2014–2015. Participant observation of farm work in the field and in the office, conducted alongside Mennonite and non-Mennonite American farmers in Western Bahia and Southwestern Goiás, enabled me to experience the everyday realities of transnational soy farming. I also conducted ethnographic interviews with farm families in Brazil; in the United States (some farm owners lived primarily in the United States and many farm families had family members in both the United States and Brazil, often moving across borders); and with their associates (workers and community members) in Brazil. Interviews with farmers and their families and associates necessitated my own mobility. While interviewing in person whenever possible, I spoke with Brazilian farm owners in Iowa and Indiana because they rarely visited Brazil and instead Skyped with investors and farmers when face-to-face meetings were impossible. In total, I met with twenty Midwestern farmers in Bahia out of a total that ranges from thirty to forty and met with twenty Mennonite farmers out of a total of seventy farm families. Due to the lack of information on the respective groups, I used snowball sampling, asking farmers to refer me to others. I designed the study as a comparative ethnography to capture different capital, social, and ecological factors in the two sites and study groups, and to address the perceived socio-ecological homogeneity of Soylandia. While both sites lie within the Brazilian Cerrado, Goiás and Bahia differ in rainfall patterns, and the two groups differ significantly in cultural characteristics and access to capital. The group of Midwestern farmers is primarily young, educated, and well-capitalized thanks to either farm sales or outside farm investors. Many received post-graduate education. The group of Mennonite farmers have an eighth-grade education, are of mixed age, though tend to be older, and are not well-capitalized.

Emergence of a Brazil Model

The Cerrado, referred to as "infertile" by the kindest of writers and as a "wasteland" by others, has some of the oldest soils on earth. Soil scientists write that, due to non-extreme soil and climate factors, "Once established, the Cerrado

FIG. 19. Brazil soybean production by municipality. Goiás and Bahia are among the new centers of soy production in Brazil. USDA 2017.

tends to maintain itself with more tenacity than other vegetation formations" (Motta, Curi, and Franzmeier 2002, 13). The earliest record of "Cerrado-type vegetation," by analysis of plant pollen, dates to 32,000 YBP, while vegetation that closely resembles present-day Cerrado occurred 7,000 YBP in central Brazil and 10,000 YBP in northern Brazil (Ledru 2002, 47). Archaeological evidence shows thriving hunter-gatherer societies dating to 9,000 YBP and at the beginning of European colonization in the fifteenth century; Xavante and Xerente cultures thrived in the Cerrado before dramatic population decreases brought about by disease and enslavement (Klink and Moreira 2002). Before agricultural development and industrialization beginning in the 1970s, production systems included extensive pastoralism on common land (100–150 cattle per 500–700 hectares); small agricultural areas (3–4 hectares cultivated per 50 hectares of land); traditional farming systems in wetlands that mixed crop production (potato, maize, and beans) with fishing; and traditional farming systems in valleys, similar to that of wetlands, but with higher productivity (Diniz 1984). The emergence of the Brazil Model, coupled with capital and "agents of modernization" (Diniz 1984), transformed this social and ecological landscape into vast hectares of soy.

The Brazil Model emerged in the 1970s out of engagements among scientists, farmers, and the Cerrado. The "miracle of the Cerrado" (Economist 2010) is often attributed to two major breakthroughs: innovation of soil management practices to coax commercial crop production out of the "barren" land, and then the development of hybrid soybean seeds to adapt to the climate of the Cerrado. The *Empresa Brasileira de Pesquisa Agropecuária* (Brazilian Agricultural Research Corporation), henceforth EMBRAPA, led this agricultural transformation and built upon Brazilian President Juscelino Kubitschek's determination to "rationalize agriculture" and extend the presence and visibility of the Brazilian state into the interior of Brazil (including the Cerrado and Amazonia) (Kubitschek 1955; Nehring 2016).

Cerrado soils have very low levels of phosphorus and a low pH associated with high levels of aluminum toxicity (Kiihl and Calvo 2008). Researchers found that fertilizing with high levels of lime (Calcium carbonate) could, as local agronomists and farmers say, "correct" the pH of the soils and, with heavy applications of phosphorous fertilizers, drastically increase soil productivity. Inoculation of Cerrado soils with *Bradyrhizobium* and biological nitrogen fixation by soybean plants eliminated otherwise necessary and costly nitrogen fertilization (Alves, Boddey, and Urquiaga 2003). Further, farmers widely adopted no-till soy production (production that substitutes herbicide applications for field cultivation) to maintain soil moisture, reduce soil erosion, and reduce production costs (Kiihl and Calvo 2008).

Fertilization and tillage practices increased Brazilian soybean yields by an average of 0.8 bushels per acre annually from 1984–2005, due primarily to improvements in hybrid seeds that were resistant to plant diseases and pests, as well as developed for the low latitudes and high acidity of the Cerrado (Almeida et al. 1999). More recently, Brazil has allowed the planting of GM seeds, and Monsanto's RoundUp Ready soybean and Bt Cotton seeds have become commonplace (Motta 2016). GM seeds and no-till practices have further encouraged the use of pesticides as the primary form of weed and pest management.

The Brazil Model incorporates high rates of fertilization and pesticide use, no-till practice, and hybrid and GM seeds (Motta 2016). However, Gudynas characterizes this system of production by its cultural practices as much as its agronomic ones, recognizing its contribution to the "great transformation" of rural Latin America (2008). These cultural practices include a shift from farmers of land to managers of farms; full commodification of the production process;

and the use of the latest agricultural technologies (for example, GPS-guided planting, harvest, and spraying). We can therefore identify the Brazil Model of industrial soy farming as two-sided. Agronomically, it is defined by the use of no-till, hybrid and GM seed; new kinds of production machinery; and intensive use of pesticides and fertilizers. Socially, it is defined by the new farmer subject who lives in the city, manages the farm sometimes in person and often at a distance by email or phone, and hires farm laborers.

Similar to narratives of progress common in the Nacala Corridor of Mozambique (Wolford and Nehring 2015), commodity frontiers in Eastern Colombia (Jenns 2017), and the United States prairie (Cunfer 2005), agronomists, farmers, and scientists have viewed the Brazilian Cerrado as an exemplar of the promise of agricultural science to convert a valueless wasteland into a global breadbasket. To Nelson Borlaug, father of the Green Revolution and Nobel Peace Prize laureate, the Cerrado began as a land that could barely support an insignificant number of cattle aside from a few streamside patches of fertile land. Through the application of new and intensive fertilization, newly developed hybrid seed varieties, and an emerging set of best agricultural practices, Green Revolution proponents defined the area as a contributor to the reduction of national and global hunger in the world's growing population and as the economic lifeblood of the Cerrado region (Borlaug and Dowswell 2003; Hosono, da Rocha, and Hongo 2016). The president of the Japan International Cooperation Agency claims, "Brazil achieved an epoch-making breakthrough to become a net exporter of grain by converting barren land into one of the most productive agricultural areas in the world" (Tanaka 2016, x). The volume goes on to argue that this "epoch-making breakthrough" converted the Cerrado into a source of local employment and impetus to regional development (Hosono, da Rocha, and Hongo 2016). The "miracle of the

Cerrado," the authors argue, was accomplished with little environmental destruction and little social displacement by the complex of business and farming practices that make up Brazilian industrial soy production; they conclude that the development of the Cerrado should be "regarded as a sustainable development model" (Hosono, da Rocha, and Hongo 2016, 2). *The Economist* celebrated the miracle of the Brazil Model for providing work, modernizing agriculture, increasing production, and feeding the hungry, all with little government support and no deforestation. EMBRAPA's greatest achievement was "to turn the Cerrado green"—a feat that led the author to recommend the model's export as a model for development in Africa (Economist 2010).

Meanwhile, ecologists have criticized this model as environmentally destructive of a fragile ecology. At the same time, activists, social scientists, and environmental scientists have argued that the model provides little local benefit at best and endangers the health and livelihoods of local communities at worst. The Cerrado is a highly endemic tropical savannah with a diverse population of plants, birds, fishes, reptiles, insects, and amphibians unique to the ecosystem. With only 2.2 percent of its land legally protected, nearly half of the Cerrado was converted to agricultural use from 1970 to 2005 (Klink and Machado 2005). Environmental effects are concentrated in hotspots of agricultural development and have led to the rapid decline of the Cerrado biome, the second-largest biome in Brazil (Brannstrom et al. 2008). Furthermore, land use changes in the Cerrado, even early in the historical process, have provoked the influx of "agents of modernization" (capitalized farmers, economic groups, and the state) and led to social and violent conflicts between local communities and newcomers (Diniz 1984). These conflicts have continued into the present, including poor working conditions for farm workers (Silva Coutinho, Germani, and de Oliveira 2013) and dispossession of land from indigenous and peasant groups (Top'Tiro 2009). For Eduardo Gudynas, the Brazil Model of farming is indicative of the great transformation of rural South America, which entails a shift from socio-ecologically integrated agricultural systems to monocultures, from partial to strong commodification of labor and agricultural products, and from locally-consumed to export-oriented production (2008). Genetically modified seed, no-till farming, precision fertilizer and pesticide application, and cutting-edge farm machinery serve as a technological package, while the farm itself is packaged as a hierarchically organized and highly capitalized business in which the "classic image of poor farmers and rich ranchers is replaced by one of rural managers, most of them with university-level education, living in cities, and specialized in business management" (Gudynas 2008, 515). Neoliberal hegemony is also reflected in the transformation of business organization and practices: large-scale soybean farmers come to see themselves as pioneers and heroes of market-oriented export agriculture and rely on the market as legitimation of their work (Peine 2009). At the same time, growing consolidation of agribusiness power and control has shrunken farmers' field of options in acquiring land, choosing seeds, and determining commodity sale decisions (see Hendrickson, Howard, and Constance, chapter 1 of this volume).

Encounter No. 1: Mennonites and the Cerrado

In 1968 a small group of Holdeman Mennonite men traveled to rural Brazil to scout for fertile, cheap farmland. The men were representatives of Mennonite communities in the United States who had become fearful of social change. The Vietnam War draft threatened their pacifist theology. Changes in educational curriculum standards suggested they would have to teach human evolution and sex education in their classrooms. Even the ubiquitous television brought uncensored "worldliness" into their homes and, along with it, a perceived immediate threat to their cultural reproduction. Scattered across the country, Holdeman Mennonites worked in a variety of industries. Those from Georgia operated small-scale farms and were accustomed to farming rice.

Holdeman Mennonism was founded in the United States by John Holdeman in 1859 and split off from the conservative Old Order Mennonites. Holdeman believed that Mennonism had strayed too far from its roots and Mennonites needed to rededicate themselves to non-resistance, the idea of one true church, shunning, evangelism, and traditional dress. Holdeman Mennonites are somewhat of an anomaly, as most Mennonites are not evangelistic (Hiebert 1971). As seen in this group's migration to Brazil, and in other cases (Pemberton-Pigott 1992), Holdeman Mennonites consider education exceptionally important and have demonstrated willingness to work toward educational autonomy through civil action and migration. Bottos frames this work not as resistance and conservatism, but as political action meant to bring about imaginations of the future (2008). He writes, "The repeated migrations and schisms . . . can be interpreted as the concrete ways in which different imaginations of the future were being accepted and rejected, what conditions were deemed suitable for the appropriate reproduction of the Old Colony moral order, and which were not" (Bottos 2008, 192). In Rio Verde, Goiás, the group of men did not find the most fertile land, nor the cheapest, but they saw an infrastructure and space that could support their future visions of autonomy. Guided by an auspicious omen in the form of a flooded roadway that blocked their tour route, emotional and spiritual appeals by members of the group, and strong local infrastructure, they chose Rio Verde as the site of their new colony. The men purchased ten thousand hectares of Cerrado land from a single local landowner.

Locals, according to interviews with Mennonites, thought the buyers had been fools. Aldo Claasen recounted the difficult early years to me at his son's kitchen table. Aldo's family had 960 hectares at the start. Holdeman Mennonites hold land as individual property and operate in family units or, as one farmer said, "Every man for himself." Aldo remembered the locals' prediction: "They're gonna die of hunger," but as he said, locals were happy to sell so that they wouldn't have to pay taxes on the land anymore. Brazilians said the land wasn't worth anything but pasture for anteaters and armadillos.

In the early 1960s, 44 percent of Goiás land was under agricultural production and that was primarily an extensive cattle production system. The region was at the frontier of agricultural production and limited by poor land and lack of capital (Estevam 2004). In the mid-1970s, the government's *Programa de Desenvolvimento dos Cerrados* (PRODECER) provided rural credit and agricultural research to encourage agricultural development. The program increased the amount of land under production, the use of tractors, and the economic development of the region. It induced a shift in production from predominantly rice in 1960 (5 percent of total value of agricultural production), to a more mixed production system in 1993, including only 3.7 percent rice and 16 percent soybean. These changes attracted outsiders from southern Brazil and Europe (Estevam 2004).

In the first years, as Aldo recounted, the Mennonites added a large amount of lime and nitrogen fertilizer to plant rice, practices they had learned to use for rice production on Georgian soils. The rice grew well, only "you can't make a living on rice." They tried to grow corn, but it came up with yellow streaks and only grew to knee-high before dying. Then they added more lime and fertilizer, and the corn grew well. As Aldo explained to me, a year later, one local Brazilian told another about the yields Mennonites were getting on corn, but the listener didn't believe the story. Aldo remembered the Brazilian farmer visiting the farm and saying, "They'll never grow corn here," but later saw that it had grown well. The Mennonite colony started planting soy some years after that, when the organic matter and nutrient level of the soil had improved and soybeans were more marketable at the time. Then and now, market prices were the primary motivation for planting soy. Reflecting on the colony's history, a member of the original search party stated, "The good lord picked us up and set us down in the Promised Land." The Mennonites had fled a society deemed unsupportive of their cultural and religious values, but they found a climate amenable to farming, productive land (once soil amendments were applied), and semi-autonomy over educational and cultural life.

With a laugh, Aldo's son remembered locals thinking they were taking advantage of the Mennonites but resenting it when the Mennonites did well. One Brazilian farmer was so offended that he wouldn't talk to the Mennonites, but he later became an admirer. The Mennonites, Aldo remembered, "really were leading things" until 1975, when Southern Brazilians began to outcompete the Mennonites. As Aldo recounted, locals thought Mennonites weren't better farmers, just bigger liars; locals were mad about the land deal and getting "beat out." Farming practices, primarily the intensive use of fertilization and beginning their rotation with rice and transitioning later to soy, allowed them to thrive economically, but later on Mennonites "got passed up" by southern Brazilians and Dutch migrants, who came later, bringing with them more advanced technology and more capital after 1975. The Holland Dutch came "by hook and by crook," as Aldo put it, implying that they overpaid for land and entered the scene not through hard work, but by any means necessary. As the region filled up, the price of land increased from $2.50 per acre in 1968, to $600 in the late 1970s, to $4,000–$5,000 per acre today, according to interviews. Indigenous populations were excluded from this land rush altogether, having been expropriated of land by Goiás elites in the nineteenth century (Estevam 2004; McCreery 2006).

Members of the Mennonite colony expressed both agreement with productivist models of progress and opposition to them. Aldo claimed that Mennonites "aren't so materialistic" and therefore are more conservative in their pursuit of profit and progress, yet they recognized land accumulation, technology, and machinery acquisition as markers of progress. They refer to outsiders "passing them up" in terms of capital, land, and technology. In one farmer's words, "They stole a march on us," meaning they outcompeted the Mennonite farmers by adopting technology early and taking advantage of government credit. Aldo, his son, and other Mennonites claim some credit for developing the practices that converted the formerly "worthless" Cerrado into a productive global breadbasket. Aldo also gives some credit to newly developed hybrid seeds that increased yields as well. They were only "passed up" years later when PRODECER provided rural credit to farmers to expand into the Cerrado. Gauchos from the south of Brazil used this credit, and the practices developed by Mennonites, to expand soy production in Goiás.

In the 1970s and 1980s, the Mennonite colony provided the model of farming that was widely adopted by soy farmers in the region. By the early 2000s, the relationship between local Brazilian farmers and Mennonites had changed and production practices diverged. Brazilian farmers adopted no-till in order to reduce production costs and to preserve soil moisture and organic content. Mennonites continued to use tillage. Brazilians adopted improved seed varieties to improve yields, while Mennonites continued to save non-GM seed for planting from year to year. Brazilians began to implement a *safrinha* (a short-season crop of corn after soybeans) to increase profits and, in conjunction with no-till, to increase soil organic matter. Mennonites continued to plant soy only, believing that rotation was not necessary. Now Mennonites have decided to emulate selected practices employed by Brazilian farmers.

In the last fifteen years the Mennonites have almost wholly adopted no-till, genetically modified seeds, and the use of *safrinha.* They have also begun to engage more with field research demonstrations to understand new seed varieties and farming methods. Holdeman Mennonites model what Roessingh and Boersma call "selective modernization" (2011), adopting aspects of modern agriculture that they find supportive of their economy, community, and theology, and forsaking those that they do not find supportive. Thus, they found that working with the Cerrado land required certain agronomic practices of fertilization and crop rotation, then later found that supporting their household economy required lowering production costs using GM seeds, no-till, and, for some, *safrinha.* No-till greatly reduced machinery costs and time needed in the field but called for the implementation of RoundUp Ready soybeans to improve weed control. They also became convinced that GM seeds were worth the extra cost in terms of production yield and costs of production.

Yet farmers in the Mennonite colony have not adopted all aspects of Gudynas's "great transformation" (2008). While they incorporate genetically modified seeds, no-till, and *safrinha,* they do not use advanced farming technology such as GPS-guided tractors, nor have they fully embraced full commodification of labor. They are integrated into the market economy yet see work as multifunctional: it is necessary to support one's family, an effective way to teach children the benefits of hard work, and a demonstration of one's work ethic. Many insisted in interviews that the most important function of farming is to provide for the family. Having learned about the importance of hard work to Mennonite theological practice, I often asked farmers about the importance of work. One morning a farmer expressed dismay at my obsession with the subject. "Does my brother work hard?" he asked of his brother who worked for the colony printing press. He went on to explain that the method of work is far less important than the ability of a man to provide for his family. The ability to provide sets an upper limit to livelihoods in a way as well. Not only are the use of advanced technology and hired workers often regarded as unnecessary luxuries; they are regarded as leading to a loss of humility for farmers. I was told several stories of American or Brazilian Mennonites in the colony losing sight of God and community after becoming materialistic and overly dependent on technology. Colony members found materialism, expressed though brand-new pickups, dependence on farm workers, or even brightly colored T-shirts, antagonistic to community life. Further, the Mennonites believe that the use of technology and hired labor separates farm managers from "real farmers." The difference, Mennonites believe, is that farm managers cannot properly call themselves farmers because they are not, in fact, farming. This differentiation implies that real farmers should be in the field and conduct farm work. Yet, while Mennonites distinguish between real farmers and farm managers, they also note that Brazilians have "passed them up" in terms of profits, technology, and acreage. Mennonites also valorize productivist measures of development and technology acquisition as demonstrations of progress.

The story of the Holdeman Mennonites' encounter with the Brazil Model is a winding one. They consider themselves foundational in implementing the practices that were necessary to produce soybeans in Goiás, as they developed fertilization practices that intensified production. The influx of southern Brazilians, along with government support, brought more advanced technology and new farming practices to the region, leaving Mennonites to see themselves as "passed up." Finally, the group began selectively adopting aspects of these farming practices. At different stages, then, they have been pioneers, resistors, and adopters of selected elements of the Brazil Model as the model itself has been co-constructed by farmers. Their contribution to and later adoption of the Brazil Model was always with religion and other Mennonite values. Their very presence in Goiás is an action taken to preserve a measure of cultural and religious autonomy. Their subsequent refusal of certain farming technologies and work practices (hiring labor) supported their values but, in their view, also placed them at an economic disadvantage in comparison to Brazilian farmers in the region. However, Holdeman Mennonite farmers did not concern themselves with competing against Brazilian farmers; their concerns centered on economically and spiritually supporting their families.

Encounter No. 2: Family Farmers and the Cerrado

Midwestern family farmers migrated to Brazil in two phases in response to much of the same economic and social markers of dying U.S. farming communities (Bell 2010). They originated primarily in Iowa, Illinois, Missouri, and Indiana, though individuals came from upstate New York, Idaho, and North Dakota as well. The first group migrated in the 1980s in response to farm financial stress in the United States. The second migrated in the early 2000s in response to land inaccessibility caused by rising farmland values (Ofstehage 2017b). Both groups recall having a sense of excitement about the idea of going to the agricultural frontier of Brazil—often explicitly connecting this journey to their families' migration histories from Northern Europe to the Great Plains. These groups primarily settled in Western Bahia, which at the time was an active site of frontier expansion. They often state that they chose Bahia due to its cheap land, good infrastructure, and cheap labor, but a tour guide who directed farmers to Bahia, and the presence of a growing expat community, also attracted farmers to the area.

Centered on the "City of Agribusiness," Luis Eduardo Magalhães, the soy frontier of Western Bahia, has experienced rapid demographic and agricultural change after soybean production began in the region in 1979. Native Cerrado vegetation land accounted for 73 percent of land cover in 1986 and only 40 percent of land cover in 2002 (Brannstrom et al. 2008). Luis Eduardo itself has grown from a rural outpost to a town of seventy thousand people. In my interviews there, several farmers reported that when they first arrived there was "nothing," a view that reflects their dismissal of indigenous communities that preceded them and continue to dwell in the region. Western Bahian agricultural production increased from 2.05 km^2 in 1979, to 1,615 km^2 in 1986, then to 5,743 km^2 in 2000, and to 7,259 km^2 in 2005 when agricultural production accounted for 55 percent of total land (Brannstrom 2009). Meanwhile, the introduction of capital and self-identified "agents of modernization" provoked a transformation toward agricultural capitalization, *technification* and, in farmers' words, modernization (Diniz 1984).

Coming twenty years after the Mennonite colony, Midwestern family farmers migrated to Bahia at a time when farmers and agronomy researchers had generally come to a consensus regarding the "best practices" of soy farming in the Cerrado. These included a cotton–soy–corn rotation, use of genetically modified seed, and no-till. They generally embraced these practices, with few exceptions, and their reliance on Brazilian farm workers and managers considerably eased their transition while also "chickenizing" their farms (see Stull, chapter 2 of this volume).

In contrast to the small Mennonite farms (30–160 ha)

which employ few laborers, large-scale North American farmers manage farms of 10,000 hectares or more and employ 50–100 workers. Their business model is a hybrid of production agriculture and speculative landholding. Using investment capital, they purchase land at low cost, work to gain a profit through production agriculture, and then have the option to sell the improved land at a profit. Whereas Mennonites have cash flow from production agriculture and occasional wage labor, large-scale American farmers in the Bahia have capital flowing from investors, production agriculture, and possible future income from the sale of land. Additionally, their business model incorporates farm workers, as their acreages are too large to manage as a family, and many claim that to run the farm as a business (rather than a hobby) requires office work. With this business model, they depend on Brazilian know-how and know-what to implement farming practices. I often asked farmers what their most difficult challenge was with farming in Brazil. All responded that the main obstacles were governmental regulations concerning labor, or the environment, or both. One farmer brought up worker regulations almost immediately after we began the interview:

> Labor laws are unbelievable, they're so invasive . . . it's a way to regulate, to increase income to the government without raising taxes. To give you an example, we're required to provide shoes, you know full clothes and shoes for all the employees. . . . Well, two years ago we were out hoeing and the ministry of labor shows up and there are two guys out of the 102 out there that did not have their shoes on. . . . So that's a fine of, it's 5,000 [Brazilian Reals] for infraction and it's up to the auditor out there for the minister of labor, whether they want to multiply that times the number of infractions or the number of employees working for you, so they took 5,000 times 102. So that's a half million. That's insane!

Midwestern farmers found agricultural practices, on the other hand, easy to manage. One farmer recounted thinking the biggest challenge of farming would be learning plant names, insect names, and best practices, "but that's easy. You have crop scouts, agronomists, managers, and farmworkers that know everything here and tell you all you need to know, know how to operate machinery. The most important thing is city work—paperwork, legalese, culture. You need a good scout, a couple tractors, a couple good tractor drivers, and everything else is easy."

This group of farmers did encounter a much different agroecology in Brazil and had to adjust. Accustomed to fertilizing with only nitrogen, phosphorous, and potassium on their Midwestern farms, they learned to incorporate micronutrient fertilization and lime fertilization in Brazil. Micronutrients, they explained, were necessary for the "infertile" soils of the Cerrado, while lime was necessary to modify the soil pH. They also increased the amount of pesticides used, especially fungicides, to address increased pest pressure, and they adopted no-till to reduce costs of production and retain soil moisture. While now popular in the United States, no-till at the time was less common among Midwestern farmers. The introduction of cotton into their rotations was perhaps the most significant change. One farmer commented, "It's a lot more difficult to farm [in Brazil]. The level of technology that is applied at the agronomic level is much higher in terms of just balancing the soil, micronutrients, and then we're doing multiple applications of chemical, of fungicide. We're doing foliar fertilization. We're doing stuff that, here, the top end guys are experimenting with and it's a fact of business in Brazil that you have to do it." That farming in Brazil is at once "easy" and "difficult" indicates that this group recognizes the inherent difficulties of farming in the Bahia's particular agroecology, but they also are able to manage this difficulty by incorporating local agricultural know-how by hiring experienced farm workers and managers.

Midwestern family farmers embrace aspects of the Brazil Model that Mennonites shun. Nearly all interviewees held bachelor's degrees or above; all lived in the nearby town of Luis Eduardo Magalhães and travelled to the farm; and all personified the shift from owner operators to farm managers. When asked how they would farm in the United States if they returned, all stated that they would employ a more managerial role and spend their time in the office rather than the field. Following Gudynas, they often explained this decision in terms of commodified labor. They could earn more money per hour in the office—staying on top of regulations, managing investors, negotiating contracts, and managing their workforce—than working in the field. Indeed, North American farmers in Bahia spend 50–60 percent of their working day in the office, and the remaining time is spent checking up on workers. The rare minutes spent on a tractor are often to impress visiting agricultural tourists or farm investors. Both groups of visitors are made up primarily of Midwestern farmers—agricultural tourists looking for answers about the characteristics of their competition and farmer-investors checking in on the state of their investments (see Ofstehage 2017b). In the office, they manage workers, contracts, and regulatory paperwork for the farm. They also produce farm updates and progress reports for investors, in addition to corresponding with investors over email, Skype, and phone.

Despite the farmers' warm embrace of the Brazil Model, some do find space to distinguish themselves from Brazilians. They do not do this by claiming that they are better farmers; rather, they say that they are better managers. An example can be seen in their preferred measurement of value. It is common in Brazil to quote prices for land, machinery, and high-expense items in units of sacks of soy.

FIG. 20. A transnational farmer's daily commute. A U.S. farmer's personal airplane, useful for commuting from Luis Eduardo Magalhães to his farm on the escarpment at the border of Bahia and Tocantins. Photo by Andrew Ofstehage.

Thus, if the price of soy changes, so does the price of the good in question. On paying, the buyer can provide the listed quantity of soybeans or their cash value. Some North Americans interpret the use of crop quantities instead of cash as bartering, a type of exchange they regard as backward and unwelcome in business. They argue, then, that they are indeed better at managing farms than other farmers under the Brazil Model. This adept turn from students of the Brazil Model to evangelists of the model has the effect of reframing the deskilling of farming associated with technified agriculture as a skilling of business know-how and know-what. They minimize deskilling of farm practices, and increasing dependence on technology (see Gibson, chapter 4 of this volume) and workers, by framing these skills as romantic notions of older farmers and hobby farmers. In turn, they highlight their ability to manage workers, regulations, and investors as skilled work. They praise Brazilians for their ability to run a farm as a business and counter that they can run it as an even more streamlined business, referring to what they argue are superior accounting skills. Migrant North American family farmers quickly adopted the Brazil Model in broad measure, then made an interesting turn: they became Brazil model evangelists. Much like Gaucho soy farmers' claims to be "missionaries of modernity" in Santarem (Adams 2008), these farmers hope to bring this model back with them to the United States and implement an improved, modern approach to farming.

Discussion

For detractors and proponents alike, the set of farming, business, and cultural practices of industrial soy production in Brazil constitutes a model to be either fiercely resisted or liberally disseminated. Models of farming serve as both heuristic devices in debates over farming ideals and values, and as generalizations of observed realities of farming. In his 1977 critique of industrial farming, Wendell Berry discusses the "South Dakota State Model" of farming (Berry 1977). Designed by agricultural engineering students, the South Dakota State model is a vision, set in the year 2076, of an enclosed farming system with livestock housed in a fifteen-story building and crops grown year-round under plastic covers. Planting, tillage, and harvest would be conducted by machines. Pest control would be unnecessary due to the strict phytosanitary controls of the system. The Brazil and South Dakota models overlap in their conceptualizations of control and common good. Each presupposes a direct relationship between a set of agricultural practices and a desired social and agronomic outcome, absent friction between the complex, sometimes chaotic, biological and chemical relations of agroecosystems and cultural practices of tillage, planting, and harvesting. Additionally, proponents of each model envision panaceas for local economies and communities, as well as a neutral or positive impact on local ecologies. Berry argued that visions of futuristic farming lacked an understanding of the contingencies of community, land, and ecosystems. By the time his work was published, he worried that it was already out of date—the agricultural secretary and the administration he served were out of office—yet the extent of the transformations in farming he foresaw then are perhaps just coming into focus now.

Development unfolds uneasily across social and physical landscapes. Socio-ecological difference gives friction to top-down development, both supplying traction to the process of change and obstructing the process (Tsing 2011). Friction at the level of socio-ecological encounters shapes processes of development as much as the dissemination of farming models. Berry argues that the South Dakota State model is an attempt to impose control on rural ecologies and communities. Along the same lines, the Brazil model is imagined as control and domination by capital, science, and the state over the Cerrado and its human and nonhuman inhabitants. Yet, we see ecology and culture have profound effects on the implementation of the Brazil Model and, through these effects, we can see how farmers engage with the model.

Sharing space in the Brazilian Cerrado, Goiás and Bahia have similar soil compositions, climate, and elevation, but some small differences change the ways farmers implement the Brazil Model. For example, Western Bahia receives lower annual precipitation compared to Goiás and does not support a *safrinha* due to insufficient moisture. On the other hand, the climate in Western Bahia does support growing cotton, which has become a major crop in the area. Nearly homogeneous *Latossolo Vermehlo Amarelo* (red-yellow oxisol in USDA nomenclature) soil of Luis Eduardo Magalhães allows extensive, uninterrupted fields to be cultivated continuously, while the more mixed soil makeup of Rio Verde discourages this kind of practice.

More important in these two encounters are the cultural values at play. The Mennonite farmers engaged with the agronomic aspects of the Brazil Model with thoughtful attention to how necessary each practice was, and to how they would impact the rest of the farm and community. Thus, they adopted lime fertilization early on, but delayed use of *safrinha*, no-till, and hybrid and GM seeds until they found themselves unable to compete with local Brazilian farmers. They disregarded the cultural aspects of the Brazil Model altogether, eschewing high-tech machinery, dependence on farm-workers, and disconnection with farm life. The large-scale American farmers in Western Bahia, on the other hand, quickly and seamlessly took up the cultural practices of the Brazil Model. They visited farms a few times per week from their base in Luis Eduardo Magalhães, depended heavily on farm workers, and took pride in advanced machinery.

Ofstehage

Further, they prided themselves on running their farms as businesses, going as far as saying they were better at implementing this business approach to farming than their Brazilian counterparts.

In each of these cases, the encounters go beyond transmission of aspects of the Model. Mennonites frame themselves as real farmers in contrast to farm managers; they stand against the farm management set of practices. They farm for the family and community, not for investors or for capital accumulation. They also take pride in their early role in developing the Brazil Model and perhaps feel resentment at being "passed up" by it in later years. Large-scale industrial farmers from the Midwest have adopted several aspects of the Brazil Model in the Bahia and have used this to frame themselves, especially to investors, as good businessmen who know how to run a farm as a profitable enterprise without romantic agrarian notions. In each case, the Model is modified as it becomes integrated into the farmers' narratives of themselves and of others.

Conclusion

Two encounters between migrant soy farmers and the Brazil Model of farming demonstrate the importance of sociomaterial relations in the transmission of industrial farming. In our first case, transmission is a dynamic process in which the Mennonite colony members engage first with the biophysical properties of the soil in the Cerrado and second with Brazilian farmers in the area. Mennonites then shared their adapted farming practices with Brazilian farmers. This process of dynamic transmission continued in the 2000s when Mennonites turned to no-till, *safrinha*, and genetically modified seeds. This process was mediated by the colony members' social values, which led them to reject certain aspects of the Brazil Model. In the case of Midwestern family farmers, transmission was relatively seamless yet similarly mediated by social values. Farmers adopted the business and farming practices of the Brazil Model, yet they claim to be improving upon the model by focusing their energies on management for profit.

These differences in transmission processes suggest that the Brazil Model is not as unified and dominant as often suggested in discussion of the soy boom. The encounter between the model and the socio-material realities of farming result in not only the transmission of a model of farming and business practices, but also the counter-tendency of farmers inserting their own sets of knowledge, practices, and values into soy farming. The Brazil model is commonly framed as the transfer of knowledge from agricultural scientists to farmers and as a smooth transformation. In reality, the process is an entangled encounter between people, plants, and soils that proceeds in fits and starts across varied landscapes and communities. The model itself is disambiguated into parts to be adopted, rejected, adapted, or created.

This ethnographic narrative of the transmission of an industrial model of farming reveals the contingent and emergent realities of farming models. The agronomic aspects of the Brazil model—no-till, high rates of fertilization, high rates of pesticide use, and crop rotations—are not directly transmitted from scientific researchers to farmers, but are imagined, tried out, and adapted as well by farmers on the ground. The social aspects of the model—living off farm, valuing agribusiness, and using advanced technology—can either be adopted or rejected. More interestingly, their adoption or rejection can become the basis for pride in production practices. Mennonites take pride in avoiding being "hitched to the satellite," while American family farmers take pride in outdoing not only their one-time neighbors in the U.S. Midwest, but even the Brazilians in their use of business principles in farming. Together, this comparative case study indicates that the Brazil model, as Wendell

Berry argued decades ago in relation to the South Dakota State Model, is subject to the physical and social realities of everyday farming.

The contingencies of the transmission of the Brazil Model suggest some parting notes. First, it is transmitted unevenly over both physical landscapes and social meaning. It does not come with a set of preconfigured social meanings but is adapted to farmers' vision of themselves in relation to their world. Mennonites use the model to celebrate their innovation and ingenuity as well as their steadfast beliefs. Large-scale American farmers incorporate the Brazil Model into visions of themselves as the next generation of modern, high-tech farm managers. The model is also implemented in relation to the physical contexts of farming (e.g., soil, climate, and topography).

Second, the transmission of the Brazil Model, especially in the case of Mennonites, is not an object bound in time nor one transmitted without feedback. The colony continually worked with the Model, helping to define it in the early 1970s, then adopting new characteristics of it thirty years later. They worked with government agronomists throughout this process as they coproduced the Model.

Third, these cases stand as a warning. Despite the cultural and agronomic differences, this model and soybean production have spread rapidly through the Brazilian Cerrado, dispossessing landowners and deforesting the Cerrado as it progressed. Both groups of American farmers escaped socio-ecological crises in the United States only to find themselves creating the same conditions from which they fled in Brazil. Mennonites have already founded new communities in more isolated parts of Brazil, and several large-scale American farmers have left their Brazilian farms as they see profit margins falling and opportunities elsewhere. Further, Brazilian agronomists, farmers, and capitalists are now exploring agricultural expansion in Mozambique and plan to implement elements of the Brazil Model (Wolford and Nehring 2015). As noted by Tsing (2011), friction can act as an impediment, but it can also provide traction. In these cases, difference has limited, altered, and magnified aspects of the Brazil Model, and we should expect its diffusion to farmers in other parts of the world to do likewise.

In his work on the U.S. farming crisis, Michael Bell describes the "treadmill of production" that traps many American farmers (2010, 41). As farmers gobble up each other's land, and as land becomes scarce or excessively costly, individual farmers are left with few other options. They can adopt new technologies or production practices to reduce production costs or increase yield, but any solution only makes a difference in the short-term until neighbors adopt the same technology. On the production treadmill, production-based solutions are short-term and serve to intensify the struggle (Bell 2010). The two transnational soy farming communities in Bahia and Goiás escaped this treadmill by finding another answer to the land question: instead of reducing production costs or increasing yields, they found cheaper land elsewhere. Yet, they escaped one struggle for another. In escaping crisis in the United States, they helped advance the soy commodity frontier in Brazil (Moore 2010). The farm families left established and expensive farmland of the Midwest in search of cheap land at the soy commodity frontier of Brazil only to find years later that farmland values have risen to nearly match values in Iowa or Indiana. Mennonites have now branched out to Tocantins State and Mato Grosso State in Brazil to find even cheaper land, and many Midwestern family farmers are actively considering selling land in Western Bahia.

Opponents and supporters alike cite the set of agricultural and cultural practices that I call the Brazil Model for the expansion of soy production in South America. However, this chapter demonstrates that the power of this model to "turn the Cerrado green," or in turn to dispossess people and deforest the Cerrado, is a credit to its flexibility, not rigidity (Ofstehage 2017a, 2017b). The two groups differed in accumulation strategies, values of farming, and farming expertise. Specifically, Mennonites pursued a strategy rooted in community and theology that emphasizes family over profit accumulation; they eschew many of the cultural aspects of the model (living off the farm and dependence on farm workers) and, while claiming a pioneering role in soy production on the Cerrado, self-identify as conservative and skeptical adopters of new practices and technologies. Midwestern family farmers pride themselves on their ability to manage a farm in-person, or from afar, and readily adopt new farming practices and technologies in search of competitive advantage and labor-saving tactics. Yet, they share a basic set of practices, including no-till, fertilization practices, and use of GM seeds. At a more basic level, they share a role in expanding and establishing the soy commodity frontier of Brazil. In these two cases, transmission of industrial agriculture is mediated by farmers' values and experiences but transmitted, nonetheless. This may hold lessons for the continued expansion of the model to Mozambique and elsewhere in Africa. It is going to be adapted, improved, reworked, and mediated, but it will continue to advance the commodity frontier, expand the influence of capital, and deforest especially undervalued grasslands.

I would like to thank our editors, Jane Gibson and Sara Alexander, for organizing the original panel on industrial agriculture at the Society for Applied Anthropology meetings and diligently and tirelessly bringing this volume to fruition. I also want to thank Rudolf Colloredo-Mansfeld and the anonymous reviewers for comments on this chapter. I also thank my research interlocutors in Brazil and the United States for patiently answering my questions. Finally,

I thank the Wenner-Gren Foundation, Fulbright-IIE, and the University of North Carolina at Chapel Hill Graduate School for funding this research.

References

Adams, Ryan. 2008. "Large-Scale Mechanized Soybean Farmers in Amazônia: New Ways of Experiencing Land." *Culture and Agriculture* 30, no. 1–2: 32–7.

Almeida, Leones Alves de, Romeu Afonso de Souza Kiihl, Manoel Albino Coelho de Miranda, and Gilson Jesus de Azevedo Campelo. 1999. "Melhoramento Da Soja Para Regiões de Baixas Latitudes." In *Recursos Genéticos e Melhoramento de Plantas para o Nordeste Brasileiro*, edited by M. A. de Queiroz, C. O. Goedert, and S. R. R Ramos, 129–43. Mimeo: EMBRAPA.

Alves, Bruno J. R., Robert M. Boddey, and Segundo Urquiaga. 2003. "The Success of BNF in Soybean in Brazil." *Plant and Soil* 252, no. 1: 1–9.

Bell, Michael Mayerfeld. 2010. *Farming for Us All: Practical Agriculture and the Cultivation of Sustainability*. University Park: Penn State University Press.

Berry, Wendell. 1977. *The Unsettling of America: Culture and Agriculture*. San Francisco: Sierra Club.

Borlaug, Norman E., and Christopher R. Dowswell, 1997. "The Acid Lands: One of the Agricultures Last Frontiers." In *Plant Soil Interactions at Low pH: Sustainable Agriculture and Forestry Production*, edited by A. C. Moniz, A. M. C. Furlani, R. E. Schaffert, N. K. Fageria, C. A. Rosolem, and H. Cantarella, 5–15. São Paulo: Brazilian Soil Science Society.

Bottos, Lorenzo Cañás. 2008. *Old Colony Mennonites in Argentina and Bolivia: Nation Making, Religious Conflict and Imagination of the Future*. Boston: Brill.

Brannstrom, Christian. 2009. "South America's Neoliberal Agricultural Frontiers: Places of Environmental Sacrifice or Conservation Opportunity." *AMBIO: A Journal of the Human Environment* 38, no. 3: 141–9.

Brannstrom, Christian, Wendy Jepson, Anthony M. Filippi, Daniel Redo, Zengwang Xu, and Srinivasan Ganesh. 2008. "Land Change in the Brazilian Savanna (Cerrado), 1986–2002: Comparative Analysis and Implications for Land-Use Policy," *Land Use Policy* 25, no. 4: 579–95.

Campelo, Lilian. 2017. "Cerrado Perde Metade Da Vegetação Nativa; Agronegócio Acelera O Processo." *Brasil de Fato*, February 8, 2017. https://www.brasildefato.com.br/2017/02/08/cerrado-perde-metade-da-vegetacao-nativa-agronegocio-acelera-o-processo/index.html.

Cunfer, Geoff. 2005. *On the Great Plains: Agriculture and Environment*. College Station: Texas A&M University Press.

Diniz, José Alexandre Felizola. 1984. "Modernização E Conflicto Na Fronteira Ocidental Do Nordeste." *Revista GeoNordeste* 1, no. 1: 12–20.

Economist. 2010. "The Miracle of the Cerrado." *The Economist*, August 26, 2010. http://www.economist.com/node/16886442.

Estevam, Luís. 2004. "O Tempo Da Transformação: Estrutura E Dinâmica Da Formação Econômica de Goiás." PhD diss., Universidade Católica de Goiás.

Gibson, Jane W. 2019. "Automating Agriculture: Precision Technologies, Agbots, and the Fourth Industrial Revolution." In Gibson and Alexander 2019, 123–56.

Gray, Benjamin J., and Jane W. Gibson. 2013. "Actor—Networks, Farmer Decisions, and Identity." *Culture, Agriculture, Food and Environment* 35, no. 2: 82–101.

Gudynas, Eduardo. 2008. "The New Bonfire of Vanities: Soybean Cultivation and Globalization in South America." *Development* 51, no. 4: 512–18.

Hendrickson, Mary K., Philip H. Howard, and Douglas H. Constance. 2019. "Power, Food and Agriculture: Implications for Farmers, Consumers and Communities." In Gibson Alexander 2019.

Hiebert, Clarence Roy. 1971. "The Holdeman People: A Study of the Church of God in Christ, Mennonite, 1858–1969." PhD diss., Case Western Reserve University.

Hosono, Akio, Carlos Magno Campos da Rocha, and Yutaka Hongo. 2016. *Development for Sustainable Agriculture: The Brazilian Cerrado.* London: Springer.

Ingold, Tim. 2011. *Being Alive: Essays on Movement, Knowledge and Description.* New York: Taylor and Francis.

Jenss, Alke. 2017. "Control, Utility and Formalization at the 'Frontier': Contested Discourses on Agriculture in Eastern Colombia." *Alternautas* 4, no. 2: 128–47.

Kiihl, Romeu, and E. Calvo. 2008. "A Soja no Brasil: Mais de 100 Anos de História, Quatro Décadas de Sucesso." In *Agricultura Tropical: Quatro Décadas de Inovações Tecnológicas, Institucionais E Políticas*, edited by A. Albuquerque and A. Silva. Brasilia: EMBRAPA Tecnologia Da Informação.

Klink, Carlos A., and Adriana G. Moreira. 2002. "Past and Current Human Occupation, and Land Use." In *The Cerrados of Brazil: Ecology and Natural History of a Neotropical Savanna*, edited by Paulo S. Oliveira and Robert J. Marquis, 69–88. New York: Columbia University Press.

Klink, Carlos A., and Ricardo B. Machado. 2005. "Conservation of the Brazilian Cerrado." *Conservation Biology* 19, no. 3: 707–13.

Kubitschek, Juscelino. 1955. "Diretrizes Gerais do Plano Nacional de Desenvolvimento." http://www.fau.usp.br/cursos/graduacao/arq_urbanismo /disciplinas/aup0270/4dossie/kubi tschek-plano55/kubit-1a-parte.pdf.

Ledru, Marie-Pierre. 2002. "Late Quaternary History and Evolution of the Cerrados as Revealed by Palynological Records." In *The Cerrados of Brazil: Ecology and Natural History of a Neotropical Savanna*, edited by Paulo S. Oliveira and Robert J. Marquis, 33–50. New York: Columbia University Press.

McCreery, David. 2006. *Frontier Goiás, 1822–1889.* Stanford: Stanford University Press.

Mier y Terán Giménez Cacho, Mateo. 2016. "Soybean Agri-Food Systems Dynamics and the Diversity of Farming Styles on the Agricultural Frontier in Mato Grosso, Brazil." *The Journal of Peasant Studies* 43, no. 2: 419–41.

Moore, Jason. 2010. "Cheap Food and Bad Money: Food, Frontiers, and Financialization in the Rise and Demise of Neoliberalism." *Review* 33, no. 2–3: 225–61.

Motta, Paulo E. F., Nilton Curi, and Donald P. Franzmeier. 2002. "Relation of Soils and Geomorphic Surfaces in the Brazilian Cerrado." In *The Cerrados of Brazil: Ecology and Natural History of a Neotropical Savanna*, edited by Paulo S. Oliveira and Robert J. Marquis, 13–32. New York: Columbia University Press.

Motta, Renata. 2016. "Global Capitalism and the Nation State in the Struggles over GM Crops in Brazil." *Journal of Agrarian Change* 16, no. 4: 720–7.

Moura Schwenk, Lunalva, and Carla Bernadete Madureira Cruz. 2008. "Conflitos Socioeconômicos-ambientais Relativos ao Avanço do Cultivo da Soja em Areas de Influência dos Eixos de Integração e Desenvolvimento no Estado de Mato Grosso." *Acta Scientiarum Agronomy* 30, no. 4: 501–11.

Nehring, Ryan. 2016. "Yields of Dreams: Marching West and the Politics of Scientific Knowledge in the Brazilian Agricultural Research Corporation (EMBRAPA)." *Geoforum* 77: 206–17.

O'Connell, Caela, Marzieh Motallebi, Deanna L. Osmond, and Dana L. K. Hoag. 2017. "Trading on Risk: The Moral Logics and Economic Reasoning of North Carolina Farmers in Water Quality Trading Markets." *Economic Anthropology* 4, no. 2: 225–38.

Ofstehage, Andrew. 2018. "Financialization of Work, Value, and Social Relations among Transnational Soy Farmers in the Brazilian Cerrado." *Economic Anthropology* 5, no. 2: 274–85.

———. 2018. "Farming out of place: Transnational family farmers, flexible farming, and the rupture of rural life in Bahia, Brazil." *American Ethnologist* 45, no. 3: 317–29.

———. 2017a. "Encounters with the Brazilian Soybean Boom: Transnational Farmers and the Cerrado." In *Food, Agriculture and Social Change: The Vitality of Latin America*, edited by Stephen Sherwood, Alberto Arce, and Myriam Paredes, 60–72. London: Earthscan.

———. 2017b. "From US Farm Crisis to the Cerrado Soy Frontier: Financializing Farming and Exporting Farmers." In *Land Justice: Reimagining Land, Food and the Commons in the United States*, edited by Eric Holt-Jimenez and Justine Williams, 174–90. Oakland: Food First Books.

———. 2016. "Farming Is Easy, Becoming Brazilian Is Hard: North American Soy Farmers' Social Values of Production, Work and Land in Soylandia." *The Journal of Peasant Studies* 43, no. 2: 442–60.

Oliveira, Gustavo, and Susanna Hecht. 2016. "Sacred Groves, Sacrifice Zones and Soy Production: Globalization, Intensification and Neo-Nature in South America." *The Journal of Peasant Studies* 43, no. 2: 251–85.

Paolisso, Michael, and R. Shawn Maloney. 2000. "Farmer Morality and Maryland's Nutrient Management Regulations." *Culture & Agriculture* 22, no. 3: 32–9.

Peine, Emelie. 2009. "The Private State of Agribusiness: Brazilian Soy on the Frontier of a New Food Regime." PhD diss., Cornell University.

Pemberton-Pigott, Andrew. 1992. "Conflicting Worldviews in the Classroom: The 'Holdeman' Mennonite School Trial 1978." *Past Imperfect* 1, no. 1: 49–75.

Roessingh, Carel, and Kees Boersma. 2011. "'We Are Growing Belize': Modernisation and Organisational Change in the Mennonite Settlement of Spanish Lookout, Belize." *International Journal of Entrepreneurship and Small Business* 14, no. 2: 171–89.

Sawyer, Donald. 2008. "Climate Change, Biofuels and Eco-Social Impacts in the Brazilian Amazon and Cerrado." *Philosophical Transactions of the Royal Society B: Biological Sciences* 363 (June): 1747–52.

Silva Coutinho, Elen da, Guiomar Inez Germani, and Gilca Garcia de Oliveira. 2013. "Expansão da Fronteira Agrícola e Suas Relaçõs com o Trabalho Análogo a de Escravo no Oeste da Bahia." *Brasiliana-Journal for Brazilian Studies* 2, no. 2: 236–63.

Stull, Donald. 2019. "Chickenizing American Farmers." In Gibson and Alexander 2019, 59–89.

Tanaka, Akihiko. 2016. "Foreword." In *Development for Sustainable Agriculture: The Brazilian Cerrado*, edited by Akio Hosono, Carlos Magno Campos de Rocha, Yutaka Hongo, and Naohiro Kitano, x—xi. New York: Palgrave Macmillan.

Top'Tiro, Hiparidi. 2009. "My Cerrado." *Cultural Survival Quarterly*. https:// www.culturalsurvival.org/publications/cultural-survival-quarterly/my -cerrado.

Tosakana, Naga S. P., Larry W. Van Tassell, J. D. Wulfhorst, Jan Boll, Robert Mahler, Erin S. Brooks, and Stephanie Kane. 2010. "Determinants of the Adoption of Conservation Practices by Farmers in the Northwest Wheat and Range Region." *Journal of Soil and Water Conservation* 65, no. 6: 404–12.

Tsing, Anna Lowenhaupt. 2011. *Friction: An Ethnography of Global Connection.* Princeton: Princeton University Press.

Turzi, Mariano. 2011. "The Soybean Republic." *Yale Journal of International Affairs* 6: 59–68.

USDA. 2017. "Brazil-Crop Production Maps by Municipality." Brazil: Soybean Production by Municipality." https://www.pecad.fas.usda.gov/rssiws/al /br_cropprod_m.htm?commodity=Soybean&country=Brazil.

Vennet, Bert Vander, Sergio Schneider, and Joost Dessein. 2016. "Different Farming Styles behind the Homogenous Soy Production in Southern Brazil." *The Journal of Peasant Studies* 43, no. 2: 396–418.

Wolford, Wendy, and Ryan Nehring. 2015. "Constructing Parallels: Brazilian Expertise and the Commodification of Land, Labour and Money in Mozambique." *Canadian Journal of Development Studies* 36, no. 2: 208–23.

9

The Price of Success

Population Decline and Community
Transformation in Western Kansas

JANE W. GIBSON AND BENJAMIN J. GRAY

> The reason we get less people, and I kind of hate to
> agree with them, is because we got only one main
> industry out here. That's agriculture.
>
> Interview with a northwest Kansas farmer, summer 2011

> Interviewer: What do you predict for the future of your
> community?
> Farmer: I'd say ten to fifteen years, [it] will no longer be
> here. It'll be a ghost town.
>
> Interview with a central Kansas farmer, summer 2011

Many of the small towns that dot the plains of western Kansas are in trouble. With rare exceptions, these towns have fewer than five thousand people and are often the only incorporated municipalities in their depopulating counties. Gas stations, fast food restaurants, farm equipment dealers, and one-story motor inns mark some town limits. In downtown business districts, there might be a bank, a diner, a grocery store, and a few retail shops alongside city hall and the county courthouse. People who live in and near these towns appreciate their amenities and services but are forced to drive considerable distances to larger towns to buy clothing and furniture, or to see a movie. These residents remember a time when they could satisfy all their material needs in local communities. The empty storefronts down-

FIG. 21. Mom and daughter walking down Main Street, Pretty Prairie, Kansas, May 2012. Photo by Larry Schwarm.

town remind them of the economic contraction that has encouraged people to move away.

Western Kansas is no stranger to economic hardships. The Dustbowl and Depression of the 1930s, the Farm Crisis of the 1980s, and numerous smaller crises in the intervening years are part of the shared memories of the people who live there. Many of these same people, who laud their parents' and grandparents' courageous tenacity in the face of these disasters, are preparing to face their own challenge in the looming depletion of the Ogallala Aquifer and the economic hardship that event will bring (Buchanan et al. 2009). Although not all farms are irrigated, water from the Ogallala has helped many farmers in this semi-arid stretch of America's heartland turn the vast plains into waves of grain that stretch from horizon to horizon. Isolated houses dot the landscape and occasional lines of scraggly trees, planted as windbreaks, interrupt uniform fields.

The western Kansas agricultural landscape is unlike the relatively dense farming communities of the eastern United States. West Kansas farms have expanded in size, as if trying to fill the landscape in which they are situated. Following national patterns (United States Department of Agriculture 2017a), farms in Kansas have grown from an average of 272 acres in 1920 to 754 acres in 2014, while the number of farms has dwindled. Only 61,000 farms operate in Kansas today compared to 161,000 farms in 1920 (Institute for Policy & Social Research 2016).

Many western Kansas farmers are over sixty years old and are the second or third generation of their families to farm in the region. Their work anchors them firmly in place, unlike occupations that allow for, or even require, mobility. As a result, older farmers have a deep perspective on the ways in which place-based communities have changed. This chapter explores farmers' experiences of demographic decline in rural western Kansas, a pattern they attribute to farm-size expansion. We offer an alternative theory, one that contextualizes farmer decision-making, reframes "decline" as "transformation," and redefines community as performative symbolization that is born of individuals' interpretations and interactions at particular times and places. This reframing of the notion of community and its decline allows us to see how western Kansas farmers come to naturalize change and risk while adjusting to neoliberal norms of capitalist competition, personal responsibility, and the need for resilience.

Our research shows that farmers have naturalized community decline as an inevitable outcome of their own necessary pursuit of efficiencies, a pursuit manifested in land consolidation for which farmers blame themselves. We see this self-blaming as part of neoliberalism's ideological pattern, which works to remove sources of friction that would otherwise interfere with the acceleration of transactions and the accumulation of profit. In this case, we refer primarily to interactions between agribusiness firms and the large-scale industrial farms that comprise their main market. This situation has come about as farmers have been ideologically colonized by the values of industrial agriculture and materially rewarded or punished by the workings of the competitive capitalist economic system. Although farmers see the loss of face-to-face community as the price they must pay for survival within this system, we show how they have mitigated social loss by using new technologies to perform and reproduce their communities, which are becoming increasingly deterritorialized as competition in a scale-biased game relocates members to other places. This transformation heralds the future of rural communities, interwoven and maintained by qualitatively different ties, ones that are weakened in the absence of the daily, social performances and material reinforcement that face-to-face relationships entail. Yet within new performances, we can see how farmers discursively preserve those values and norms that distinguish the rural from the urban as they construct them, and as a form of resistance against modernization. We argue that this transformation protects the system of capitalist accumulation by providing access to a social and material world that farmers and their families require. It does so in ways that undermine the possibility of a shared critique of the political economy that drives many farmers off the land.

We begin with a description of the methods we used in our research with Kansas farmers to elicit conversations about their communities and land consolidation. We then set this factor in the larger context of the globalization of the American industrial food system, following ethnographers, historians, sociologists, and others who have situated farmers' decisions in response to forces beyond their control. Next, we take up theories of community to examine both farmers' experiences of the decline of place-based communities and support for an alternative view we propose. In our discussion and analysis of the data on demographic decline in farmers' communities, we draw from work on the colonization of consciousness as well as the political economy of capitalism. We conclude with a summary of our findings and speculation about the future of community in rural western Kansas.

Methods

We conducted our research as part of an interdisciplinary team, funded by the National Science Foundation's Experimental Program to Stimulate Competitive Research (NSF EPSCOR) to study Kansas farmers' decision making under conditions of climate change and growth of the biofuel industry. Our group of seven researchers (including the authors of this chapter) interviewed 151 farmers across the state during the summer of 2011. Of these interviews, 149 were recorded, transcribed, and coded using NVivo software. Though insights come from across the state, most of the data for this chapter are derived from interviews with the thirty-eight farmers from western Kansas, the area west of the 100th meridian, and from observations of the communities they identify as their own. The sample was drawn from a subset of those who responded to a survey and indicated that they were amenable to being contacted for a request to be interviewed. Researchers met farmers, usually in their homes, and carried out interviews that lasted from thirty minutes to six hours for an average of about two hours. Interviews covered a wide range of subjects such as farm histories, water management issues, and community life. Additional interview data from Gray's (2016) doctoral dissertation research, conducted in the same area of Kansas in 2014, are also included in data presentation and analysis.

All of the individuals in our western Kansas sample were white men, consistent with the general profile of Kansas farmers. They ranged in age from 25 to 85 and had farmed an average of thirty-five years (from six to sixty-nine years). As a group, western Kansas farmers have the same amount of farming experience as their central and eastern Kansas counterparts, but they are about five years older (who have a mean age of 58.2 years) (Kansas Department of Agriculture 2017). They most commonly grow corn, milo, soybeans, and wheat, and they have a mean farm size of 2,232 acres, triple the state mean, with the smallest operation consisting of twenty-six acres and the largest with 13,237 acres. A few farmers also raise cattle, but this is not a primary focus of most operations.

In semi-structured interviews that we recorded and later transcribed, we invited farmers to identify and describe the places they recognized as their communities. Farmers usually responded with the names of incorporated municipalities and occasionally unincorporated townships. While we have included community names and we use farmers' words to convey their experiences and views, we have not associated town names with quotes to protect the identities of those individuals who taught us about community life and its transformation.

The places farmers named average just under 1,900 people, ranging from 29 to 26,658. The largest community, Garden City, is an outlier with over four times the population of the next largest town. Interestingly, most towns were larger in 2010 than they were in 1910, though demographic trends can be described as generally flat or declining in recent years. Garden City and a few other communities have experienced population increases because of the influx of recent immigrants seeking work in dairies, feedlots, and meatpacking plants that have opened in southwest Kansas since the 1980s (Stull and Broadway 2013; Sulzberger 2011).

Although they identified their communities as particular towns, few farmers we interviewed lived within city limits. Instead, they lived on well maintained, but infrequently travelled, county roads along which demographic decline has emptied the countryside. The populations of counties have diminished dramatically, raising the question of what farmers mean by "community." To answer this question, we draw from interviews that asked farmers about the places they identified as their communities, how they had changed, and what farmers thought the future might hold. In the course of these conversations, we learned how farmers explain the community transformation they described.

Land Consolidation and Demographic Decline

I mean, you have to be realistic that this community is dying. I mean we brought it on ourselves. And it'll continue that way because we can talk about it here, and it's going to be the same thing. I mean, these guys with 80-foot sprayers (a large piece of equipment that can apply agricultural chemicals to an 80-foot swath of ground in one pass). And they can do a section (640 acres) of ground in a day. And so it's more efficient for them to buy another quarter (160 acres), you know, and that's one less family that has the opportunity to be here. And I don't know how to stem that tide. And I don't think we can.

The farmers we interviewed, like the one quoted above, link decisions to expand their operations to the demographic decline of their counties. Yet farmers choose to grow their farms given the opportunity and ability to do so. Opportunity arrives when another farmer needs to sell land to raise money, to retire, or when the bank presents him with a foreclosure notice. Farmers often rent land as well, sometimes when circumstances make it available. Although these are not permanent arrangements, rental agreements can be of very long duration. Ability depends on the banker's willingness to finance the purchase and the farmer's ability to operate the additional acreage. Agricultural mechanization helped farmers realize the interdependent goals of farm size expansion and increased production. It did so by reducing the need for farm labor and encouraging land consolidation, thereby reducing the number of farmers on the land, as well as the number of families sending their children to school and shopping in local businesses. An examination of this process makes clear that the depopulation of the countryside results from members' decisions made in the context of powerful external forces.

As Adams noted, the U.S. policy of becoming the "breadbasket of the world" (2007, 3) during post-World War II reconstruction meant that American farm production had to increase significantly. But mechanization and the lure of higher urban incomes contributed to the cycle of rural outmigration and labor shortages, problems to which policy makers responded with cheap credit for the purchase of land, machinery, fertilizers, hybrid seed varieties, and chemicals. The consequences of the adoption of such technology packages were seen early in the rapid capitalization of agriculture after World War II and, as we discuss below, the dramatic changes seen in rural American communities.

As the policy of postwar agricultural expansion continued, farmers were admonished by Secretary of Agriculture Earl Butz to "Get big or get out!" (Thompson 1988, 69). Butz's announcement signaled a reduction in the perceived relative value of small and midsized farms in favor of the large-scale, industrial production model. Critics of this and other expansionary policies charged that, at the expense of smaller farmers, the country's largest farms, with more assets to leverage, were the main beneficiaries because they could afford the fertilizers, pesticides, new hybrid seeds, and advances in labor-saving machinery that encouraged farm-size expansion and monoculture specialization (Hazell 2002).

As farms expand, operators need to be able to farm more acres more quickly. The capacity of modern farm machinery allows this feat, but it is also more sophisticated, complex, and expensive. As farmers try to maximize production efficiencies, they find themselves on a treadmill of investments in high-capacity equipment that requires them to spread costs over as many acres as possible, continuing the cycle of farm expansion, investments in labor-saving technologies, and indebtedness (Gray and Gibson 2013).

The need to seek economies of scale results not simply from technological investments. Rather, it stems fundamentally from what Marx called the crisis of capitalism—the fact that profits tend to fall (Marx [1894] 2001). Farmers, like all capitalists, must counter this tendency if they are to remain in business. Thus, the word efficiency, and the myriad ways farmers seek it, permeates their talk about the practices and technologies they employ. As Marx explained, contributors to falling profit include, paradoxically, investments in new technologies that create economies of scale, reduce need for labor, and increase yields that depress crop prices and perpetuate the need for even greater efficiencies. An additional downward pressure on profits is the fact that the market for crops grown in western Kansas is a monopsony. With only a few buyers, farmers are price takers, caught between dealers who set prices for farm inputs such as equipment, seeds, and chemicals, and buyers who dictate how much they will pay for farmers' crops. Not surprisingly, farmers' share of food dollars has been in decline.

Between 1993 and 2008, farmers received 24¢ of every dollar spent on food (Canning 2011, iv). In 2018, the farmers' share had declined to 14.8¢ (National Farmers Union 2018), while inflation drove up input costs and the prices farm families have to pay for food, transportation, and other commodities and services. Declining farm incomes lead farm families to try to maintain their standard of living with off-farm work and debt-financed investments in land and large-scale machinery to increase production. Once on the treadmill of debt and the search for efficiencies, the goals and incentives provided by the USDA and the Farm Credit Association, among other institutions, and farmers' disadvantaged market position, make farm expansion one logical response to the national policy for abundant, cheap food, and farmers' need for income they hope at least keeps up with inflation.

Noneconomic considerations also play a role in encouraging land consolidation that contributes to outmigration from rural communities. Prestige flows, in large measure, from visible markers of success, such as operating a large farm. One farmer with one of the largest farms in our sample offered this observation: "So that's the beginning history of the farm that I currently operate and have expanded immensely, from 160 acres up to 10,000 acres today, see. But I say I've expanded it; my sons have participated in the expansion through ownership, which I coached them into, owning land early on. And you can't be a farmer substantially unless you own land."

A "substantial" farmer is one whose operation reflects its considerable importance, especially in size and wealth. The other side of this coin is that a farmer who sells land is likely to be perceived as one who has fallen on hard times, often due to his own missteps. And while farmers are keenly aware of risks beyond their control—fluctuating global markets for inputs and commodities, government regulations, and capricious weather—they define the successful farmer as one who is still farming despite such challenges. He does his work in a timely way, stays current in the latest technologies and production practices, and minimizes waste by increasing efficiency. In this framework, substantial farmers succeed and grow their operations; others fail, sell their land, and move away.

To protect their farms, most farmers, some willingly and others less so, have pursued land acquisition and industrial production strategies that promise increased efficiencies. At the same time, they acknowledge that the way farming has changed is to blame for the emptying of the countryside. If being a successful farmer means owning a lot of land, and farm expansion depends on the financial crises and failures of other farmers, those aspects of the identity of a modern farmer that are rooted in production success exist in tension with community membership as farmers define it.

Theorizing Community and Rural Depopulation

Anthropologists have long engaged in community studies with special interest in community change. Drawing from Ferdinand Tönnies's conceptualization of *gemeinschaft* ([1887] 1955), scholars continue to debate what community is and how it ought to be studied. In his youth, Robert Redfield observed social changes that transformed wilderness into commercial farmlands near industrial cities. As a professional anthropologist, he constructed a folk-urban continuum to enable analysis of such changes (Redfield 1941). Redfield understood community to be a small-scale, face-to-face traditional, homogeneous, territorially based, closed corporate group. Similarly, Arensberg and Kimble ([1940]

1968) took a structural functionalist approach to the study of rural communities in Ireland, describing a social system of mutuality built around kinship and self-sufficiency. Economic and technological changes impinged on these communities, but the authors observed that the pace of change was slow, locally controlled, and adapted to beliefs and values in place.

Inspired by the community studies of the first half of the twentieth century (particularly Robert and Helen Lynd, and W. Lloyd Warner and his coauthors), the capitalization of agriculture after World War II led scholars to focus on rural American communities (Adams 2007). Consistent with earlier place-based models, Walter Goldschmidt's comparative study of Arvin and Dinuba, California, related farm scale to the quality of community life (Goldschmidt 1948). Arvin—dominated by large, nonfamily operated farms—had a smaller middle class, more hired workers, higher poverty rates, lower family incomes, poorer quality schools and public services, and fewer civic organizations, retail businesses, and churches. Civic participation in public decisions was low. Dinuba, by contrast—with locally owned farms operated by families—enjoyed greater civic participation, a diversified economy, and a higher standard of living. The United States Department of Agriculture (USDA) first suppressed Goldschmidt's controversial report, but it was eventually entered into the Congressional Record, published as a book, and confirmed by the Small Farm Viability Project's restudy (Lobao and Stofferahn 2008).

Other early approaches to the study of rural communities emphasized the importance of locality, whose characteristics present common challenges that give rise to a certain social homogeneity (Minar and Greer 1969). As individuals work to overcome obstacles, they develop shared perspectives, identity, interdependence, common attachments, commitments, and goals. In her review of social science contributions to the study of rural life, Adams (2007) identified a hiatus in attention to rural America that lasted until the oil, debt, and farm crises of the 1970s and 1980s inspired significant research published in the 1980s and 1990s.

Inspired by Goldschmidt's example, more recent scholars have also shown how rural communities are affected by farm and corporate industrialization. Kendall Thu and Paul Durrenberger (1998) show the consequences for rural North Carolina and Iowa communities of concentrated animal feeding operations (CAFOs) in pork production: community disruption, economic displacement, noxious odors, health effects on facility workers, and environmental harm. Similarly, Don Stull and Michael Broadway (2013) detail the impact of the meatpacking and poultry industries on workers, growers, animals, and communities.

More recently, studies that hold communities as place-based, bounded entities, have yielded to views of community as symbolic systems of meaning that arise from social interaction and relationships. Cohen ([1985] 2001, 14), for example, sees boundaries as "symbolic constituents of community consciousness," revealing the "essential symbolic nature of the idea of community itself." His work illustrates how communities exist as systems of meaning in the consciousness of their members, and how relationships between members and their actions signify social bonds and community boundaries, even when those boundaries are changed by circumstances.

In *The Trouble with Community*, Amit and Rapport (2002) build on these ideas in their dialogue on the meaning and production of communities. Amit notes that in the history of scholarship, community tends to signify the location of research rather than its subject. Those with ontological concerns for the existence of the subject have focused on matters of locality and identity, arguing that locality is insufficient to establish relationships that signify social bonds.

"People might live alongside each other, cheek by jowl, but the social distance separating them could still be a chasm of class, ethnic, occupational and age differences" (Amit and Rapport 2002, 47). Taking this position another step, one may conclude that while close proximity is insufficient to produce the relationships and performances that constitute community, distance is insufficient to dissolve those relationships. How, then, are communities reproduced?

Giddens described how the actions of individuals produce and reproduce the structures of social systems in the context of historically defined forms of socially acceptable conduct. He writes that "the production of society is a skilled performance, sustained and 'made to happen' by human beings" (Giddens 1976, 15). Community members reproduce the structures of their social systems by following norms and rules of conduct (Giddens 1984, 3) but, following Cohen (1989, 300), always retain the ability to do otherwise, to modify, or to transform the social world (Cohen 1989, 300). Social systems are constantly reproduced through social practice, but they are also subject to change when individuals choose to change them.

West's place-based study of Plainville, Missouri (West 1945) and Gallaher's subsequent restudy fifteen years later (Gallaher 1961), illustrated community resistance and contestation over changes in agriculture introduced and advocated by the U.S. government. The Agricultural Adjustment Administration—renamed under President Eisenhower the Agricultural Stabilization and Conservation Service (ascs)—discovered that "positive inducements and compulsions" were more effective influences over farmers who earlier rejected the information and advice delivered by government representatives seeking control over production and marketing. Cash incentives led farmers to cooperate in some ways, though they continued to berate the ascs committees as "meddlin' too much in the private affairs of us farmers" (Gallaher, 37). The U.S. Agricultural Extension Service and the Farmers Home Administration (FHA) met with similar resistance by older farmers who barely survived the Great Depression and came away with commitments to independence and preservation of a simple, debt-free way of life. Not so their children, however, who, to their parents' dismay, embraced mechanization and other opportunities to elevate their standard of living with the material rewards of credit and an approach to farming "more as a business enterprise than as a way of life" (Gallaher 1961, 43; Danbom 1979).

Writing about rural communities in the midwestern United States, Ronald Kline anticipated the theories of Cohen, Giddens, and Amit and Rapport when he described how farm families resisted the introduction of electrification and television in the 1950s. Kline argued that farmers contested modernization aimed at urbanizing rural life when they initially refused to adopt new technologies, later "weaving [them] into existing cultural patterns to create new forms of rural modernity" (Kline 2003, 51). Kline, unlike Gallaher, saw farmers who refused these new technologies not as ineffectual in understanding the values of modernity, nor as signs of market failure, but as agents who shaped their own social worlds in ways that opposed the patterns of modernization. He identifies these "decisions to do otherwise" as transformative resistance. As Kline wrote, "Throughout the twentieth century, middle-class farm people made decisions about whether to accept new technologies and how to use them in the context of such enduring, yet historically contingent, rural practices as making do with the materials at hand, sharing work, visiting, avoiding debt, distrusting urban culture, and defending property rights" (2003, 65–6).

Communities, then, are performative, "the subjective realizations of those who symbolically articulate and animate them at particular times and places" (Amit and Rapport 2002, 8). Such insights help us see communities as fluid, dynamic performances in which individuals can adjust, transform, and relocate as changing conditions require. The farmers we interviewed are mindful of the symbols and meaning of localized demographic decline: empty store-fronts, closed schools and post offices, and the absence of kin and friends. We can also see in their answers to questions about the experiences of community how they perform community relations, transforming them as adjustments require, while discursively preserving those elements that matter most to them.

Performing Community

The farmers we interviewed described their remembered communities as people dedicated to place, who enjoyed a shared sense of identity and the familiarity that comes from a relatively small, historically homogeneous population. Whether the past was as pleasant as they remember, they still long for their remembered lives. Small town life, they said, engenders feelings of closeness, trust, and security. They talked about neighborliness, of being able to stay abreast of current events, and of being connected, for better or worse, to other community members, as these two farmers did. The first said, "Well, it's a small community and you know most of the people most of the time, and if anyone's doing something wrong everybody learns about it fairly quickly." The fact that community members know about each other's lives was repeated by the second farmer: "Most of the time it's a pretty tight-knit community. You know, if something happens to somebody, they help each other out, you know. Small communities are like that."

Farmers also feel that close relationships, low crime rates, and a shared work ethic make their hometowns ideal places to raise families. Levels of trust are so high for some, who feel they know almost everybody, that they leave their doors unlocked and their keys in their vehicles. The distance between small towns and the nearest metropolitan areas, sometimes up to several hours' drive, contributes to this sense of security that stems from the perception that families are insulated from big city problems like crime, drugs, and traffic. As one farmer said, "There's a lot of messed up people out there. I'm thankful that in the agricultural environment that tends to be very, very minor."

Family relationships are keys to understanding the importance of place in the culture and meaning of western Kansas communities. Farmers in our sample often constructed genealogies that linked them and their farms to an original homesteader. Through these relationships, farmers identify closely with their farms, families, and the communities of which they are a part. This identification extends into the past with a generations-long relationship to the land, and it extends across communities in kinship, and in shared experiences and memories with other families. Most grew up in and around the places where they currently live, giving them a sense of rootedness absent in more mobile populations. As one farmer explained,

My great-grandfather homesteaded in [this county] in 1888, and he had a couple of boys that stayed on the farm, and my grandfather ended up at the homestead site and then my dad was born and was a farmer and he farmed the ground, and now I'm farming the ground and own it now, since my dad passed in '06. My brother, who was killed in a vehicle accident in '04, built a house there on that property, and his wife, my sister-in-law, lives there, but my son also built a house there north of [town]. So, we've been here awhile.

Another farmer created a similarly unbroken connection between his place on the farm today and that of his grandparents: "I'm a third-generation farmer. Basically, my grandpa lived here in this house and his grandpa bought him the place. He started it. Then, dad farmed and I'm farming, too. I just grew up a mile and a half south of this place. Been here forever. This is where I've always been at, I guess."

Despite these deeply rooted sentiments, farmers' observations of community decline reveal lost opportunities to reproduce face-to-face community relationships through their enactment. Instead, they report that they have experienced a loss of neighborliness and its replacement with a business-like detachment. One farmer was disappointed that the land his family had rented from a neighbor for decades would no longer be available because the neighbor had found someone who would rent it for a better price.

This abandonment of formerly stable relationships sometimes implicates the involvement of formal institutions to mediate close relationships and communications. A farmer told a story about a cow that wandered onto his neighbor's property. In the end, the farmer had to call the county sheriff to get his cow back: "I call her up and she answers the phone and she said, 'We really don't have any time to help you.' I says, 'I know you don't have any time, but I want permission to go in there and get my cow.' 'Well we still don't have time to help you.'"

Consistent with this change in the nature of relationships, farmers noted that reciprocal labor and equipment exchanges are now uncommon. Today, they told us, farmers prefer to hire help rather than ask for it, and the cost of equipment discourages its sharing. Commenting on this situation, one farmer observed, "Everybody does their own thing. Used to be when I was younger in the fifties and sixties, people would go, 'Oh, I want to borrow your disc,' and they just don't do that no more. But if anybody was wanting to come in and borrow it, well, I would let them. It just don't happen no more." Another farmer offered his theory for this change: "It's not as much done as it used to be in the past. There's a lot of custom farming going on. They always want to charge. . . . When farming turned into a business, that's 90 percent of it."

Examples like those above could be taken to suggest that the moral economy of western Kansas has receded in the face of time and labor demands imposed by industrial agriculture. Ties have indeed weakened, and norms of generalized reciprocity have waned as farmers increasingly emphasize the business aspects of their operations. However, the farmers in our sample also cited examples of how the community came together to help a person or family in crisis. The business norms Walter Goldschmidt (1948, 182–3) described almost seventy years ago for industrial agriculture are suspended in such cases, and families enact the older closeness they value and miss: "My brother got sick, and the men out there—I was trying to do his milking and do his chores and everything and farm his ground—and the community all got together, and they come and helped me farm it. Did it all in one day." This collective response indicates that conceptions about the right to subsistence and the obligations of reciprocation (Scott 1977), and the social norms and responsibilities of living in a community (Thompson 1971)—which are often termed "moral economy" and set theoretically in opposition to the market economy—still operate in western Kansas. Indeed, recent perspectives on moral economy note that it has always been concerned with the "practices, meanings and institutions that regulate social formations in a world increasingly dominated by the principles of capital accumulation" (Palomore and Vetta 2016, 428). It is also true, however, that as farm families have left western Kansas, fewer and fewer people are left to ensure the right to subsistence of individuals and families who experience hardship, or to support local businesses and institutions that enable individuals and families to gather, socialize, produce, and reproduce localized community.

> This town had two movies. We had one, two, three, four, clothing stores, one shoe store, two hardware stores, and umpteen gas stations. And all of that's gone. I mean, Main Street U.S.A. is closing down, and there's talk of bringing a Walmart to town, which I'm not sure will be good or bad. I think everybody's got their own opinions on that. But Main Street U.S.A. is not what it used to be. And that's sad sometimes to think back to where we actually were then. Are we ahead now or behind? You know, I think sometimes we're behind.

The sense of "getting ahead," as this farmer uses it, indexes a view of life in motion, one that changes and makes progress as it moves toward a better future. But the prospect of getting ahead again seems dim, creating nostalgia for a better past. As a farmer lamented, "I long for those individual, family-owned businesses that are gone now and I'm sure will never return." Another farmer pointed to the importance of the off-farm jobs those businesses might have provided as the source of income that supplements farm earnings for so many. But modestly paying jobs disappear when service-oriented businesses close, and small towns can support even fewer professional jobs. Thus, farmers complain that their college-educated children cannot return to their communities, even if they want to, because there are no employers left to hire them. One farmer expressed his desire to change this situation: "If I could change anything about my community, it would be to get some type of economic activity. Something that would stymie the population decline. Population decline is the killer for all of northwest Kansas, literally."

Even if returning children could find employment in their hometowns, some farmers note that the condition of the

FIG. 22. Post office in Belvidere, Kansas. Photo by Larry Schwarm.

housing stock has deteriorated, or that there are no houses available for newcomer families. Many farmers' children do not return to their natal communities because they are not interested in taking over the farm, and the lack of alternative employment, adequate housing, amenities, entertainment, and services dissuades them from coming back. This is a lament expressed by many farmers, including this one: "I have two daughters, one mid-thirties and one forty, and neither of their families won't come back here. There's no reason to. We have a very substantial farm, but either one won't come back to take that over. It's very difficult in attracting and keeping young people here."

Farm failures that promote land consolidation, business closures, and out-migration have reduced the property taxes necessary to fund schools. Schools, primary sites for the performance and reproduction of community, signify connections to the past and the future, and to the social world. When they close, remaining parents send their children to schools in other towns or move away altogether. The tradition has been that kids grow up together in schools where they later send their own children, so families feel the loss of more than classrooms.

One farmer noted that when the school closed, he and others who grew up in the area lost a part of their identity. Sports teams, theatrical performances, and band concerts all disappeared. These events were available at the newly consolidated schools in other towns, but the opportunities to socialize, affirm, and reinscribe community membership in places that embodied shared memories were lost. Under these circumstances, individuals begin to lose touch with each other if they cannot find new ways to perform community ties as they did in the past. In need of jobs and schools for children, young families leave and have little reason to return or relocate to rural towns that cannot meet their needs.

FIG. 23. Laurence and Pauline Schwarm in front of their one-hundred-year-old farm, June 2011. Photo by Larry Schwarm.

The loss of young people to opportunities available in larger urban areas leaves an older population behind in rural ones. Therefore, there are fewer people to volunteer in various public and private organizations, and to serve in city government. Many of our respondents have long, active histories as leaders in civic organizations such as the school board, sports clubs, Lion's Club, Rotary, water resources board, and church groups. Some reduced their participation in these groups for a variety of reasons: their children grew up, they encountered health problems as they aged, they burned out, or they simply lost interest. Others explained that they reduced their commitments to civic participation as they expanded their farm operations and found more of their time was needed to manage the responsibilities of increased acreage. Now too few remain with both time and inclination to reproduce the civic life of community organizations and governance. Farmers recognize the challenges this void creates: "I wish there were more leaders. You know, fifty years ago when the community would lose a business of significance there were town fathers that would say, 'We got to change this,' and then they would make things happen. There's still that community involvement but there's not that core group of people that can make things happen anymore. It's not to say that they aren't there. Most of those types of individuals are fully immersed in running something successful."

Some say it is time for young folks to step forward, but few young adults remain these days. Concern about their absence from community life is matched by farmers' worries about whether any of their children will want to take over the farm someday, or whether they will be able to afford the costs of doing so, even if they would like to remain in the places they call home. If a farmer wants to retire, he can sell or rent land to another farmer at market prices. But if a farmer would like his children to take over the farm, the high cost of land and equipment means it is unlikely that a daughter or son would be able to pay as much as the operation is worth. Such a farmer is caught between pursuing full market value for the farm, the proceeds of which may be necessary to care for the farmer in later years, and ensuring that his children have an opportunity to farm.

New Community Performances

While farmers define their communities as bounded, localized groups whose historic decline signifies the end of community, they still perform community locally through expressions of residual mutualism and reciprocity when opportunities or needs arise. Beyond the local, their need to defragment and stabilize the relationships that anchor their lives has led them to innovate new ways to create, reproduce, and redefine their communities. One predictable approach responds to the disappearance of grocery stores, gas stations, clothing stores, farm implement and parts dealers, banks, and other businesses that meet families' material needs. As life gets a little harder for farm families who now must go farther afield for supplies and services, they expand the physical boundaries of place-based community, using ubiquitous cars, trucks, and roads and highways to connect with others. As this farmer said, traveling for necessities is routine: "People in this country are very mobile. Going to Garden City . . . they go there to shop. It's kind of a social thing to go there and get away. They have a nice park over there and a zoo. Fifty miles is less than an hour's drive, so that's a hop, skip, and a jump."

Farmers have also found substitutes for many local, face-to-face relationships by joining virtual networks that offer regional, national, and even global resources. They use smart phones and other computers to reach the Internet where they track commodity and input prices; check the weather; stay abreast of agricultural innovations; communicate with suppliers, business associates, and other farmers; find equipment dealers and repair shops; and stay in touch with distant family and friends. One farmer on an Internet discussion group recounted a story in which he was stuck in his tractor in the middle of a field waiting for a remote repairperson to download changes to his tractor's operating system. Another talked about how his sister accessed his desktop computer from halfway across the state to manage his farm's finances. Such patterns are still young, but indications are that these new social networks are the wave of the future: dynamic, symbolic, performative, and free of the limitations of locality and face-to-face interactions. Farm families can extend their reach great distances and across geopolitical boundaries.

The creation of virtual communities that we detected among western Kansas farmers is evident in statewide and national data as well. Biennial studies of farm-based computer use by the USDA/NASS (United States Department of Agriculture 2017b) show that U.S. farms with computer access had increased to 73 percent by 2015, despite the greater challenges of access in rural areas, and that 71 percent of farmers owned or leased computers. Data are similar in Kansas where 72 percent of farmers reported access in 2015, and 70 percent owned or leased computers.

Having computers and Internet access hasn't translated for all farmers into use for farm business, however. But these numbers, too, are growing at both state and national levels. Only 39 percent of Kansas farmers used their computers in 2015 for farm business compared to 43 percent nationally. Nor is this innovation in communication distributed evenly by farm sales class. Those farmers nationally in 2015 with sales of $250,000 and more were most likely to have access to computers (85 percent), and the Internet (82 percent), and to use them for conducting farm business (73 percent) (United States Department of Agriculture 2017).

USDA/NASS biennial reports collected data on the use of the Internet to purchase farm inputs and access government reports. Our interest in farmer use of the Internet includes but goes beyond its facility to help farmers cope with the loss of local business and government resources. Farmers meet a diversity of other needs such as accessing parts suppliers, family members who manage farm budgets from distant locations, nongovernment sources of information, and family and friends who have left rural communities. Because farmers are using the Internet in these additional ways, we believe the data underestimate the importance of these trends for reshaping, redefining, and reproducing communities that include rural farm families.

Discussion

The social evolution of food production systems has come a long way from swidden horticulture to today's various farming systems of which capitalist industrial agriculture is the dominant, globalizing form. Given the extraordinary price this model of production has exacted against millions of farm families and rural communities over the past century, we must ask why farmers participate in it, and of what consequence is the social pattern that results for the future of those communities. We begin with insights drawn from the theory of the colonization of consciousness (Comaroff and Comaroff 1989; Mander 2012; Mies and Bennholdt-Thomsen 1999; Mitchell 1988; Norberg-Hodge et al. 2002; Shiva 2015; Steppling 2012), a view that allows us to see the ideological mechanisms of modernization.

Colonization of consciousness refers to the control of "the signs and practices of everyday life" (Comaroff and Comaroff 1989) that form the basis for economic and political domination. In this instance, domination does not refer to physical force, but to the promotion of a production system within a particular political economic formation in which options for thinking and acting outside the system are limited ideologically and materially. Capitalist industrial agriculture relies on costly modern inputs such as patented seeds, synthetic fertilizers and pesticides, irrigation, and high-capacity equipment to achieve the highest possible crop yields. Production efficiencies reward economies of scale achieved through land consolidation, which, with large-scale machinery, replaces labor with capital, encourages competitive relations instead of cooperative ones, and elevates profitability over other values. Industrial agriculture bestows prestige and defines success in terms of crop yields and acreage, trading financial rewards enjoyed by a shrinking pool of substantial farmers for the fragmentation, destabilization, and transformation of the social worlds of all. Colonization of farmer consciousness can be seen in the ways farmers naturalize such losses, even as they grieve for them.

The transformation of communities in western Kansas has been a long, multi-generational process whose causes cannot be reduced to the decontextualized decisions of individual farmers, nor to any single cause. As we discussed earlier, land consolidation, which farmers see as the root of the changes in their communities, is a process that has been ongoing since about 1900 (Institute for Policy & Social Research 2016; United States Department of Agriculture 2003). We argue that the historical logic that informs industrial production practices and encourages land consolidation is the result of a dialectic between the colonization of farmers' consciousness with the values of modern agriculture, and the material and ideological rewards and punishments of competitive capitalism.

Mitchell (1988), in his analysis of the colonization of Egypt, wrote:

> Colonizing refers not simply to the establishing of a [colonial] presence but also to the spread of a political order

that inscribes in the social world a new conception of space, new forms of personhood and a new means of manufacturing the experience of the real. . . . The new controls of the nineteenth century attempted not just to appropriate a share of the agricultural surplus but to penetrate the processes of rural production, manipulate its elements, and multiply . . . 'the productive power' of the country. The effectiveness of disciplinary methods, as Michel Foucault has termed these modern forms of power, lay not in their weight or extent, but in the localized ability to infiltrate, rearrange, and colonize. (ix)

We see this kind of colonization, the multiplication of productive powers, and social rearrangement in Adams's (2007) post-World War II history, cited earlier. Underscoring the mechanisms of the national modernizing project, she points to the state's demand for farmers to intensify production and expand the sizes of their operations. Cheap credit and selected crop subsidies accomplished the transformation of production practices from diversified, family-operated, small-scale systems to large-scale, technology-dependent, monocultural grain crops.

Drawing further from Foucault, Mitchell considers disciplinary power as a force working to transform consciousness from "within local domains and institutions, entering into particular social processes, breaking them down into separate functions, rearranging the parts, increasing their efficiency and precision, and reassembling them into more productive and powerful combinations." Disciplinary power is also internalized by individuals, not restricting them and their actions, but rather producing them "as isolated, disciplined, receptive, and industrious political subjects" (Mitchell 1988, xi). In our interviews, Kansas farmers reveal how they have enshrined the modern values of individualism and autonomy among the most valued rewards of farming, and how the greatest rewards come to those who do their work in a timely way and stay current regarding the latest production technologies and practices. Farmers see themselves as the loci of responsibility for their farms' successes or failures, both outcomes of the result of farm management that conforms, or fails to conform adequately in their views, to the industrial agriculture paradigm. This is true even though very little—input costs, crop prices, lending rates, farm policies, environmental conditions, and weather—is under their control.

Going beyond Foucault, Mitchell takes up a second consequence of disciplinary power—one that yields insight into Kansas farmers' consciousness of who they are and how they relate to one another. As power relations become internal, "they now appear to take the form of external structures." Using the Egyptian military as his example, Mitchell notes that groups of armed men come to see themselves as part of a military apparatus that is "greater than the sum of its parts, as though it were a structure with an existence independent of the men who composed it. Older armies suddenly looked formless, composed of 'idle and inactive men,' while the new army seemed two-dimensional" (Mitchell 1988, xi). By the same method, individual farmers see themselves as part of one social construct within another—the farm sector nested within the larger economy—with both constructs seen to operate independently of those who constitute them. Many scholars (Mies and Bennholdt-Thomsen 1999; Norberg-Hodge et al. 2002; Shiva 2015), and others have written about the material and class transformations of colonization that manifest the goals of modernization. From this perspective, colonization has affected the restructuring of agriculture from an orientation in which food is the end, to one in which commodities serve as the means to accumulation of wealth and participation in the agricultural sector, the larger economy, and consumer culture.

Gibson and Gray

This disciplined understanding locates farmers in a subordinate position to "the market," and it produces farmers who naturalize the system of competition in which they participate. The farmers we interviewed see farm failures, signified by bank foreclosures, as indicative of individuals' production inefficiencies and their failure to "stay current." They view community depopulation as a sad but inevitable consequence of individual successes that leave many rural families without work, schools, groceries, repair services, a post office, goods and services, and the nearness of kin and friends.

Writing against tendencies to romanticize America's farming communities, Dudley affirms that farming communities have been successfully colonized with key elements of what it means to be modern: they are "as shot through with the logic of the market as their urban, industrial counterparts" (1996, 47). She argues that individualism and profit maximization are values that emerge from a certain type of community that "cannot be understood apart from the distinctive cultural logic that orders social relations in a market-oriented society" (Dudley 1996, 49). Drawing from Mary Douglas's concept of the "normative debate," Dudley explains that arguments about the organization of social relations and how to rationalize decisions within those relations gives rise to a "context of accountability" (1996, 49) wherein people expect to reap the punishments and rewards of their actions. The context of accountability emerges, however, within a system that promotes a deepening sense of insecurity about a future in which the only certainties are risk, instability, and change.

In their critique of neoliberal discourses of community resilience, Evans and Reid (2013) view instability, risk, and change as normalized conditions within capitalist discourses such that community leaders are assigned responsibility for their lack of preparedness in the face of economic contraction, population decline, and other crises. Competition between cities, like competition between individuals, produces winners and losers and so rends the social fabric of community.

According to Davis (1992, 126), this is not an unintended consequence, but rather a feature of capitalism—to break apart the social ties that bind people together so workers can be exploited more efficiently and with fewer threats to capital's profits. Colonization of those relationships by capitalist values and norms appropriated and reshaped relationships to the ends of the accumulation of wealth. In this light, the marginal persistence of cooperation and neighborliness that farmers affirm in their interviews can be seen as resistance against the socially destructive nature of capitalism and the project to modernize rural America (Kline 2003). Yet, despite the fact that farmers naturalize the political economy within which they have lived all their lives, Davis echoes Mitchell when he argues that "a free market, in classical terms, is always the product of political control rather than the automatic outcome of unrestricted exchange. . . . It is the case that conditions approaching perfect competition have only been achieved where governments intervene to maintain them" (Davis 1992, 126). Thus, there is nothing natural about the demographic decline of rural communities because there is nothing natural about competitive capitalism in rural Kansas. Farmers have been convinced of the virtues and persuaded to participate in a system that pits them against each other, culls the inefficient, and transforms their social worlds.

Conclusions

Western Kansas farmers grieve over the emptying of the counties in which they live, and over the loss of traditions and face-to-face relationships they and previous generations enjoyed. Yet they naturalize risk and blame themselves and local government leaders for demographic decline and its localized consequences. While we agree that farmers' decisions to acquire more land play an important role, we have situated land consolidation in the larger political economy of capitalist industrial agriculture to show an assemblage of historical, economic, structural, and ideological conditions that drive such decisions. We have further shown how farmers have been led to accept the loss of their face-to-face social worlds as the inevitable price of success, and the risks of farm failure as necessary to preserving the way of life to which they are committed. Colonization of consciousness with free market ideology, interacting dialectically with the material rewards and punishments of market competition, make the endless pursuit of efficiencies, including farm-size expansion, the logical response necessary to keep farms off the auction block.

In the face of depopulation and the loss of localized social, emotional, and material support, farmers have begun to act in new ways on what Davis identifies as the social need for community relations. Farmers, who readily name their communities of remembered, localized relations, and who experience the consequences of capitalist competition in weakened social bonds and reciprocal relations, respond with increasing use of material highways and virtual ones to counter the fragmentation, dislocation, and destabilization inherent in the neoliberal regime of capital. Thus, following Giddens, who points to the power of individuals to change their social worlds, and Amit and Rapport, who see such changes as the result of new performances, we argue that farmers are actively transforming their communities. They increasingly reach out through the Internet to businesses and experts who can provide the material and informational resources farmers can no longer acquire locally, and to family and friends to maintain affective ties at a distance. In these new performances of community, farmers work to preserve those values and norms that distinguish the rural life they admire from the modern urban project toward which political, economic, and ideological forces impel them.

What will these processes of transformation mean for the future? The high probability is that the search for efficiencies will continue to drive farmers to seek new high-capacity technologies and more land, decisions that will continue to drive the depopulation of western Kansas. Many of those farmers who have survived the century-long pattern of rural modernization and economic culling find themselves more and more physically isolated yet, ironically, a growing number are newly connected to a virtual social world that extends beyond county, state, and national borders. The significance of this deterritorialization of social relationships is that the new community idiom—anchored in remembered places, relationships, and needs—stabilizes and preserves the livelihoods of surviving farmers and the market they constitute for agribusiness corporations that must also meet the crisis of capitalism in the tendency of profits to fall. But we believe that the absence of daily performances of face-to-face ties and the reinforcement of strong social bonds these performances engender, while discursively preserved at a distance, will further undermine the possibility of a community critique of the conditions that give rise to struggle induced by forces beyond farmers' control. Thus, the transformation of rural communities from face-to face relations to virtual ones, on the one hand, produces a new form of community of farm families' making while, on the other, it enables the ongoing process of capital accumulation on farms that remain to compete and by the corporations that supply the inputs farmers need.

These relationships and processes may well preserve some key values of rural life, production of grains and soybeans for international markets, and the market that growers constitute for agribusiness industries, but the larger economic system engenders a process of attrition that will leave a lonely landscape. Here, fewer and fewer farmers will remain to perform community and remember what rural modernization's ideological commitment to competitive capitalism has cost them.

Funding for this project was provided by the National Science Foundation's Experimental Program to Stimulate Competitive Research (EPSCOR), No. EPS-0903806. We are grateful to the National Science Foundation, our colleagues at the Kansas Geological Survey, the University of Kansas, K-State University, and Emporia State University. We wish to thank the reviewers for their thoughtful and insightful comments and suggestions, Don Stull for his editorial advice and comments on an earlier draft, and the Kansas farmers who invited us into their homes and taught us about community.

References

Adams, Jane. 2007. "Ethnography of Rural North America." *North American Dialogue* 10, no. 2: 1–6.

Amit, Vered, and Nigel Rapport. 2002. *The Trouble with Community: Anthropological Reflections on Movement, Identity and Collectivity.* London: Pluto Press.

Arensberg, Conrad M., and Solon T. Kimball. (1940) 1968. *Family and Community in Ireland.* Cambridge MA: Harvard University Press.

Buchanan, Rex C., Robert R. Buddemeier, and B. Brownie Wilson. 2009. The High Plains Aquifer. Public Information Circular 18. Kansas Geological Survey, Lawrence KS.

Canning, Patrick. 2011. *A Revised and Expanded Food Dollar Series: A Better Understanding of Our Food Costs.* (ERR-114).

Cohen, Anthony P. (1985) 2001. *Symbolic Construction of Community.* New York: Routledge.

———. 1989. *Whalsay: Symbol, Segment and Boundary in a Shetland Island Community.* Manchester: Manchester University Press.

Comaroff, Jean, and John L. Comaroff. 1989. "The Colonization of Consciousness in South Africa." *Economy and Society* 18, no. 3: 267–96.

Danbom, David. 1979. *The Resisted Revolution.* Ames IA: Iowa State University Press.

Davis, John. 1992. "Trade in Kufra (Libya)." In *Contesting Markets: Analyses of Ideology, Discourse and Practice*, edited by R. Dilley, 115–27. Edinburgh: Edinburgh University Press.

Dudley, Kathryn Marie. 1996. "The Problem of Community in Rural America." *Culture & Agriculture* 18, no. 2: 47–57.

Evans, Brad, and Julian Reid. 2013. "Dangerously Exposed: The Life and Death of the Resilient Subject." *Resilience* 1, no. 2: 83–98.

Gallaher, Art, Jr. 1961. *Plainville Fifteen Years Later*. New York: Columbia University Press.

Giddens, Anthony. 1976. *New Rules of Sociological Method: A Positive Critique of Interpretative Sociologies*. London: Hutchison.

———. 1984. *The Constitution of Society: Outline of the Theory of Structuration*. Berkeley: University of California Press.

Goldschmidt, Walter Rochs. 1948. "Down on the Farm: New Style." *The Antioch Review* 8, no. 2: 179–92.

Gray, Benjamin J. 2016. "Going With the Flow: Southwest Kansas Farmers and the Ogallala Aquifer." PhD diss., University of Kansas.

Gray, Benjamin J., and Jane W. Gibson. 2013. "Actor-Networks, Farmer Decisions, and Identity." *Culture, Agriculture, Food and Environment.* 35, no. 2: 82–101.

Hazell, Peter B. R. 2002. *Green Revolution: Curse or Blessing*. Washington DC: International Food Policy Research Institute.

Institute for Policy & Social Research. 2016. Kansas Statistical Abstract 2015, edited by G. M. Hurd. Lawrence KS: Institute for Policy and Social Research, the University of Kansas.

Kansas Department of Agriculture. 2017. "Who is Kansas Agriculture?" Manhattan KS: Kansas Department of Agriculture. http://agriculture.ks.gov /about-kda/kansas-agriculture.

Kline, Ronald. 2003. "Resisting Consumer Technology in Rural America: The Telephone and Electrification." In *How Users Matter: The Co-Construction of Users and Technology*, edited by N. Oudshoorn and T. Pinch, 51–66. Cambridge MA: MIT Press.

Lobao, Linda, and Curtis W. Stofferahn. 2008. "The Community Effects of Industrialized Farming: Social Science Research and Challenges to Corporate Farming Laws." *Agriculture and Human Values* 25, no. 2: 219–40.

Mander, Jerry. 2012. "Privatization of Consciousness." *Monthly Review* 64, no. 5: 18–41.

Marx, Karl. (1894) 2001. *Capital. Volume III*. London: Electric.

Mies, Maria, and Veronika Bennholdt-Thomsen. 1999. *The Subsistence Perspective: Beyond the Globalized Economy*, translated by P. Camiller. London: Zed Books.

Minar, David, and Scott Greer, eds. 1969. *The Concept of Community: Readings with Interpretations*. New York: Routledge.

Mitchell, Timothy. 1988. *Colonising Egypt.* Berkeley: University of California Press.

National Farmers Union. 2017. "The Farmer's Share, 2017."

Norberg-Hodge, Helena, Todd Merrifield, and Steven Gorelick. 2002. *Bringing the Food Economy Home: Local Alternatives to Global Agribusiness.* Bloomfield CT: Kumarian.

Palomera, Jaime, and Theodora Vetta. 2016. "Moral Economy: Rethinking a Radical Concept." *Anthropological Theory* 16, no. 4: 413–32.

Redfield, Robert. 1941. *The Folk Culture of the Yucatan.* Chicago: University of Chicago Press.

Scott, James C. 1977. *The Moral Economy of the Peasant: Rebellion and Subsistence in Southeast Asia.* New Haven CT: Yale University Press.

Shiva, Vandana. 2015. "We Must End Monsanto's Colonization, Its Enslavement of Farmers." EcoWatch. https://www.ecowatch.com/vandana-shiva-we-must-end-monsantos-colonization-its-enslavement-of-fa-1882075931.html.

Steppling, John. 2012. "Colonizing Consciousness." http://john-steppling.com/2012/10/colonizing-consciousness/.

Stull, Donald D., and Michael J. Broadway. 2013. *Slaughterhouse Blues: The Meat and Poultry Industry in North America.* Belmont CA: Wadsworth.

Sulzberger, A. G. 2011. "Hispanics Reviving Faded Towns on the Plains." *New York Times,* November 13, 2011.

Thompson, E. P. 1971. "The Moral Economy of the English Crowd in the Eighteenth Century." *Past & Present* 50: 76–136.

Thompson, Paul B. 1988. "Of Cabbages and Kings." *Public Affairs Quarterly* 2, no. 1: 69–87.

Thu, Kendall M., and E. Paul Durrenberger. 1998. *Pigs, Profits, and Rural Communities.* Albany: State University of New York Press.

Tönnies, Ferdinand. (1887) 1955. *Community and Association.* New York: Routledge.

United States Department of Agriculture. 2003. *Agriculture Fact Book 2001–2002.* Washington DC: U.S. Government Printing Office.

United States Department of Agriculture, National Agricultural Statistics Service. 2017a. *Farms and Land in Farms 2016 Summary.* Washington DC: U.S. Government Printing Office.

United States Department of Agriculture, National Agricultural Statistics Service, Kansas Field Office. 2017b. *Farm Computer Usage and Ownership.* Washington DC: U.S. Government Printing Office.

West, James. 1945. *Plainville, U.S.A.* New York: Columbia University Press.

10

An Alternative Future for Food and Farming

JOHN IKERD

The Failure of Agricultural Industrialization

When anticipating the future, many people tend to examine trends of the past and simply project them into the future, as if current trends are destined to continue indefinitely. Many futurists forecast the future of farming in this way. They foresee a continuing trend toward fewer and larger agricultural operations that rely on increasingly sophisticated electronic and biological technologies. However, trends never continue, at least not indefinitely.

In 1991, in the journal *Science*, several scientists proposed a list of "top twenty great ideas in science" (Pool 1991, 267). The article invited scientists from around the world to comment on the ideas in the proposed list. Among the top twenty were such ideas as the laws of gravity, motion, and thermodynamics. The top twenty also included the idea that *everything* on the earth operates in cycles—including everything physical, biological, social, and economic.

No respondent suggested removing the idea of "universal cycles" from the top-twenty list (Culotta 1991, 1308). Some scientists suggested that things "tend" to cycle. They pointed out that many cycles are not precise in terms of timing, amplitude, or pattern. This characteristic is particularly true of biological, social, and economic cycles. Regardless, all trends eventually run their course. Admittedly, some cycles are extremely long, as are cycles in global climate due to natural causes. However, most social and economic cycles are sufficiently short to be of significant consideration in projecting future trends. All trends eventually stall out, change course, and the future evolves in a fundamentally different direction from the past.

We might logically conclude that recent trends in farming and food production eventually will stall out and come to an end, particularly given the growing list of unintended negative consequences. And at some point, the future of the agrifood system will begin to evolve in a fundamentally different direction. We might also logically suggest that the emergence of the organic, local, and sustainable food movements are early indicators of a fundamental shift away from the historic trend toward fewer, larger industrial operations that has characterized farming and food production for the past several decades.

Perhaps more significant, modern society as a whole appears to be in the midst of a "great transformation." I believe the current postindustrial revolution could be at least as important as the Industrial Revolution of the late 1700s, perhaps as great as the beginning of science in the late 1600s. This transformation is being driven by the basic question of sustainability: *How can we meet the needs of the present without diminishing opportunities for the future?* The sustainable agrifood movement is but one part of a far larger sustainability movement. The organic and local food movements are but different dimensions of the larger sustainable food movement. The question of sustainability could well be the defining question of the twenty-first century—for agriculture, food production, economic development, societal advancement, and for the future of humanity.

There is no indication the current trend of global industrialization of agriculture will be abandoned voluntarily or will be easily reversed. A popular myth—"American Farmers Must Feed the World!"—is perpetuated by the "agricultural establishment" in an attempt to maintain public support for the current industrial system of agricultural production.[1] Most agricultural academics and agribusiness professionals seem to have bought into the idea that only a bio-tech, info-tech industrial approach to agricultural production will be capable of meeting the biofuels and global food demands of the future. Americans are led to believe that farmers in the United States will need to double agricultural production by 2050 to meet increasing food demands from the world's "developing economies" (Food and Agricultural Organization, United Nations 2009).

A similar myth is being promoted in the international agricultural arena as well. The Food and Agricultural Organization of the United Nation's (FAO-UN) *Climate Smart Agriculture* also touts high tech, industrial agriculture as the key to feeding the world in the era of global climate change (Food and Agriculture Organization, United Nations 2017). Genetic engineering of crops and livestock, and GPS-controlled "precision farming," are just a couple of technological fixes promoted as essential for future food security. The Bill and Melinda Gates Foundation also is a major financial supporter and promoter of a high tech, market-driven agriculture as the key to eliminating global hunger (The Gates Foundation 2012).

These organizations are supporting, perhaps unwittingly, the economic agenda of transnational corporations to dominate and control global food production. Recent and ongoing corporate mergers will leave three agribusiness corporations in control of 60 percent of the world's seeds, 70 percent of the agricultural chemicals and pesticides, and nearly all of the world's patented genetic traits for crop production (The Guardian 2016). A new wave of investor and corporate "land grabbing" is giving industrial agriculture access to vast acreages of farmland in Africa, South America, Southeast Asia, and elsewhere—much of which had previously provided food for indigenous small family farmers (GRAIN 2016). In most cases, control of land also means control of water. Wherever industrial agriculture goes, it inevitably replaces small, multifunctional, diversified, independent family farms with large, specialized, mechanized, corporately-controlled agricultural operations, as we have seen in the United States over the past several decades.

I understand the industrial agriculture myth—perhaps better than most—because I spent half of my thirty-year academic career promoting it. I grew up on a small dairy farm in southwest Missouri. After high school, I attended the University of Missouri (MU). In those days, a poor farm kid of modest intelligence could still work his or her way through their state university. I earned my BS, and eventually my MS and PhD degrees in agricultural economics from MU. Between my BS and MS degrees, I worked for three years for Wilson Packing Company, the fourth-largest meat packer in the country at that time. My academic career spanned thirty years, including faculty positions at North Carolina State University, Oklahoma State University, and the University of Georgia, before returning to the University of Missouri, where I eventually retired in early 2000.

I spent the first half of my academic career as an extension livestock marketing specialist. I did research and taught courses, but I spent most of my time working with farmers. I helped start the hog industry in North Carolina and worked with the big feedlots in western Oklahoma. During those times, I was a very traditional agricultural economist. I told farmers they had to treat farming as a *business*, rather than a *way of life*, if they expected to survive. If they had a family farm, I warned that "family business" should not be allowed to interfere with "farm business." I advised farmers to either "get big or get out." Farms of the future would need the economic efficiency that comes with large-scale production. I taught the things I had been taught—things I believed.

This was not a popular message in rural America at the time, but I believed the potential benefits for greater economic efficiency outweighed the inevitable *inconveniences* of losing traditional family farms. Most important, I believed that the industrialization of agriculture could provide domestic food security or eliminate hunger. We were going to help farmers make agriculture more economically efficient by reducing production costs. This ultimately would reduce food costs for consumers, making good food affordable and accessible for everyone. The profits made by progressive farmers who reduced production costs would support viable rural economies and communities. It was a well-intended experiment—but it failed.

In 2015, the USDA classified nearly 13 percent of U.S. households as "food insecure," and nearly 17 percent or one-in-six of American children lived in food insecure households (Economic Research Service, USDA 2017). Food insecurity means uncertainty regarding whether enough food will be available to meet the nutritional needs of the household at all times. Nearly all the food insecure households were relying on food stamps or other government food assistance for survival. Five percent of these households had "very low food security," meaning that someone or everyone in these households had to do without food at various times during the year. In 1967, when CBS-TV aired its classic documentary, "Hunger in America," only 5 percent of the people in the United States were estimated to be hungry. Back then, 5 percent of Americans going hungry was considered a national emergency; today 13 percent food insecurity is not even a political priority. Sixty years of industrial agriculture has done nothing to alleviate hunger in the United States

Furthermore, the industrial food system is linked to a new kind of food insecurity, meaning foods that lack the nutritional value essential to support healthy lifestyles. The United States is confronted with a growing epidemic of obesity and related diseases, such as diabetes, high blood pressure, heart disease, and a variety of diet-related cancers. While the percentage of income spent for food dropped by nearly half, the percentage of GDP spent for health care in the United States more than tripled, from 5 percent in 1960 to nearly 18 percent in 2015 (CMS.gov 2016). A large portion of these increases was linked to diet-related illnesses. Also, there is growing evidence that today's diet-related health problems are not limited to poor food choices or the prevalence of "junk foods" but begin with a lack of nutrient density in food crops produced on industrial farms (Ikerd 2013).

Any concerns today's agrifood corporations have about providing safe, nutritious food for people extend no further than concerns for their economic bottom lines. Their priorities are production and profit, not nutrition and health. Wealthy people can pay more for food they waste than poor people can pay for food to feed their children. About 40 percent of total U.S. food production is wasted and another 20 percent of it is exported (Economic Research Service, USDA 2017a). However, only 0.5 percent of U.S. agricultural exports go to the nineteen countries of the world with the highest levels of hunger (Share, World Resources 2016). How can people elsewhere in the world take U.S. farmers' proclaimed commitment to "feeding the world" seriously while 40 percent of the U.S. corn crop has been used to make ethanol to fuel our cars and more than one-third is fed to animals rather than people (Foley 2013).

My first realization that something was fundamentally wrong came during the mid-1980s. I had just moved from Oklahoma to Georgia to take a position as Head of the Department of Agricultural Economics Extension at the

University of Georgia. This was during the time many of us remember as "the farm financial crisis." Many farmers had borrowed heavily at record high interest rates during the 1970s, which was an inflationary, but still profitable, time for farmers. American farmers were going to "feed the world" back then as well, and farming would remain profitable until everyone in the world was "well fed." Farmers planted "fencerow to fencerow," then ripped out and farmed the fencerows. Farms got bigger as big farmers bought out their neighbors at record high land prices—many using money borrowed at record high interest rates.

But then came the early Reagan-era domestic economic recession, which triggered a global economic recession. U.S. export markets dried up; farm commodity prices fell dramatically; and many farmers couldn't even make interest payments on their loans, let alone keep up with payments on principals. Farm foreclosures and bankruptcies were regular fare on the evening TV network news programs, and reports of farm suicides were not uncommon. Suicides were particularly high in Georgia, where the FMHA had been pushing big farm loans to impress the Carter administration. My department at UGA had the responsibility of trying to help Georgia farmers find some way to survive— pay off their loans, sell out while they still had equity, or at least not kill themselves.

We traveled around the state holding face-to-face meetings with farmers and going over their financial records. During these meetings, it dawned on me that the farmers who were in the biggest financial trouble were those who had been doing what we so-called experts had been telling them they should do—they "got big rather than getting out." What we didn't tell them was that for some farmers to get bigger other farmers inevitably had to get out. There is only so much farmland and a limited market for food that farmers must share. I knew farm failures were an inevitable result of agricultural industrialization. As a "good econo-mist," I had rationalized that displaced farmers would find better opportunities elsewhere. However, many farmers who lost their farms had no other opportunities. In depression and despair, some killed themselves. I simply didn't under-stand that the farm and the farmer are inseparable on a true family farm. Losing the farm didn't mean just losing a job; it meant losing an important part of themselves.

Something was fundamentally wrong with the economics I had been taught. I then began to see that forcing families off their farms was also destroying farming communities. It takes people to sustain rural communities, not just pro-duction (see Alexander, chapter 6 of this volume). I also began to understand what industrial agriculture was doing to the land—the erosion of soil, and pollution of air and water with agricultural chemical and biological wastes from factory farms. Industrial agriculture was destroying the ulti-mate sources of its own productivity; it was not sustainable.

Fortunately for me, the sustainable agriculture move-ment was emerging on the national scene during the late 1980s. I first understood sustainable farming as balanced farming: balancing the need to make an economic living for the family with the need to take care of the land and to be a socially responsible community member. The chal-lenge of sustainability is really quite simple. Everything of value to us, including our food, ultimately comes from the earth, and beyond self-sufficiency, comes to us by way of other people, by society. The economy allows us to meet our needs by buying and selling rather than gifting or bar-tering with other people. If we destroy the productivity of the land and people, we cannot sustain the economy. With-out the impersonal economy, we cannot provide enough food for even current levels of population. If we cannot sustain food production, we cannot sustain our economy, society, or humanity. Sustainable farming requires balancing the need to make a living with caring for the land and caring about people.

In 2014, I was commissioned by the Food and Agricultural Organization (FAO) of the United Nations to write the regional report, "Family Farms of North America," in recognition of the International Year of Family Farming (Ikerd 2016). In the process, I became convinced the negative ecological, social, and rural economic impacts of agricultural industrialization are much the same globally as in the United States—just less advanced in most other places.

A 2016 United Nations study by an International Panel of Experts in Sustainability (IPES) described the scientific evidence against industrial agriculture as "overwhelming" (Germanos 2016). They cited more than 350 studies that document the failures of industrial agriculture and call for fundamental change. The study concluded, "Today's food and farming systems have succeeded in supplying large volumes of foods to global markets, but are generating negative outcomes on multiple fronts: widespread degradation of land, water and ecosystems; high GHG emissions; biodiversity losses; persistent hunger and micro-nutrient deficiencies alongside the rapid rise of obesity and diet-related diseases; and livelihood stresses for farmers around the world" (International Panel of Experts, Sustainability 2016, 3). The failures of industrial agriculture are well-documented and widespread.

The IPES report also provides extensive scientific confirmation that alternative nonindustrial approaches to farming and food production hold the greatest promise of future global food security. The report states, "What is required is a fundamentally different model of agriculture based on diversifying farms and farming landscapes, replacing chemical inputs, optimizing biodiversity and stimulating interactions between different species, as part of holistic strategies to build long-term fertility, healthy agroecosystems and secure livelihoods. Data shows that these systems can compete with industrial agriculture in terms of total outputs, performing particularly strongly under environmental stress, and delivering production increases in the places where additional food is desperately needed. Diversified agroecological systems can also pave the way for diverse diets and improved health" (International Panel of Experts, Sustainability 2016, 3).

More than 70 percent of the people in the world today are still being nourished by small, family farms—not by industrial agriculture (Food and Agricultural Organization 2014). Various studies funded by the United Nations confirm that agroecology and other nonindustrial approaches to farming could double or triple the yields on such farms (Kirschenmann 2012). This scientific evidence suggests that small family farms could provide enough food to meet global food needs using nonindustrial approaches to farming. They could provide sustainable food security for themselves and others in their nations. To do so, farmers in the "less-developed" countries would need protection from economic extermination by industrial agriculture and would need the kinds of public assistance afforded industrial agriculture in the "developed" countries.

The primary challenge of the future for farmers in the United States is not to increase agricultural productivity but instead to achieve agricultural sustainability. U.S. farmers already produce more food than is needed for food security, and more could be produced—sustainably. Current production just isn't getting to the people who need it most. History has confirmed that reducing farm-level production costs and increasing total agricultural production are not effective means of providing domestic or global food security. The American agrifood system needs to refocus on domestic food security, rather than producing feed for livestock, biofuels for automobiles, and exports for global markets.

The focus of agricultural sustainability in the United States tends to be on the ecological degradation and social disruption resulting from agricultural industrialization. However, the first requisite of agrifood sustainability is to meet the basic food needs of the present. It is difficult for parents to show concern about factors that affect the well-being of future generations when their own children are hungry. For sustainability, everyone must have enough good food, regardless of his or her ability to earn enough money. The challenge of eliminating hunger and ensuring agrifood sustainability ultimately is a social and ethical challenge. The great transformation must be rooted in a social and ethical transformation in personal values.

The Necessity for Fundamental, Systemic Change

The IPES report concludes, "What is required is a fundamentally different model of agriculture" (IPES 2016, 3). The report identifies biological diversity, holistic management, and mutuality as key characteristics of sustainable farming systems. In other words, what is required is a fundamentally different system of farming. Merriam-Webster defines a system as "an organized set of doctrines, ideas, or principles usually intended to explain the arrangement or working of a systematic whole" (Merriam-Webster 2017). The multiple negative ecological and socioeconomic outcomes linked to industrial agriculture in the IPES report are inevitable consequences of the set of doctrines, ideas, and principles that explain the arrangement and working of industrial organizations—including the working of industrial agriculture.

Perhaps industrial agriculture can be made "less bad" with new technologies, practices, and methods that allow it to use resources more efficiently and mitigate its negative impacts on nature and society. However, many of its negative impacts are inherent consequences of the doctrines, principles, and ways of thinking that characterize industrialization as a model or paradigm of economic development. Such problems cannot be prevented or solved without replacing industrial agriculture with a fundamentally different agricultural system. Industrial agrifood systems are simply not sustainable. New production technologies, practices, and methods will naturally evolve from the new principles and ideas that characterize the new systemic whole of sustainable agriculture.

Government policies can either aid or hinder this evolution, just as farm and food policies aided and continue to support the industrialization of agriculture. However, without the supportive ideology of industrialization, government policies supporting industrial agriculture would not likely have succeeded in transforming American agriculture. A fundamental challenge today is that industrialization has allowed corporate agribusiness to gain dominant influence, if not outright control, of the public policy agenda for agriculture. Strong ideological support for sustainable agriculture—among farmers, consumers, and citizens in general—will now be required to shift government farm and food policies from an industrial to a sustainable agenda.

Healthy living ecosystems, such as those of farms, are inherently diverse polycultures, not specialized monocultures. Living things cannot be standardized; each is a unique creation. Living organisms are self-making and thus cannot be fully replicated or precisely controlled. In agriculture, industrialization inevitably had, and still has, major unanticipated and unintended consequences. The negative impacts are not limited to agroecosystems but are also felt by the human communities and societies that support and are supported by agriculture.

The problems associated with industrial agriculture are what social scientists call "wicked problems." They are called wicked not because they are evil, but because they are difficult to clearly identify, isolate, and solve. The negative impacts of industrial agriculture are of the same kind or nature as those of other industrial production processes—steel mills, oil refineries, power plants, and chemical factories. The problems of industry are wicked because of the complexity, interconnectivity, and dynamic nature of the ecological and social systems within which the problems arise. They are impossible to solve partially or sequentially because of the inability to collect and analyze enough data to include all of the interconnected variables needed to draw irrefutable conclusions. Different scientists draw different conclusions from different subsets or series of data. This challenge leads to conflicting "scientific" conclusions because of the virtual impossibility of isolating specific cause and effect relationships. Apparent causes often are also the effects of other causes somewhere in the system. Efforts to solve one aspect of wicked problems may reveal or create other problems, as we have seen with the diet and health problems that arose from trying to make farming more efficient and food more affordable.

Wicked problems can be solved only by choosing different systems. Wendell Berry—philosopher, author, and farmer—refers to systems solutions as "Solving for Pattern." He writes, "A good solution is good because it is in harmony with those larger patterns—and this harmony will, I think, be found to have a nature of analogy. A good solution acts within the larger pattern the way a healthy organ acts within the body" (Berry 1981, 3). The pattern of industrial agriculture is that of a large, complex machine or mechanism. The natural ecosystems and social cultures within which farms function are living systems, not machines—organisms, not mechanisms. The mechanistic pattern of industrial agriculture conflicts with the organismic pattern of nature and society.

A further problem in the case of agriculture is that the

farm itself is a living, organismic system rather than an inanimate, mechanistic system. Organisms are unique wholes composed of unique organs or parts. Living organisms have emergent properties that are not present in their parts—the most important being "life." A healthy farm is a unique living system made up of the soil, plants, animals, and people that constitute an integral whole. Problems such as the inhumane treatment of animals and destruction of biological diversity are inherent consequences of managing farms as factories. A farm is not a factory and animals are not machines—and cannot be treated as such without negative consequences.

In summary, the failures of industrial agriculture in general are an inevitable consequence of the inherent disharmony between industrial agricultural systems and the social and ecological environment within which agriculture must function. The internal mechanistic industrial agricultural paradigm conflicts with its external organismic social and ecological context. The only way to solve the wicked ecological, social, and economic problems of industrial agriculture is to abandon the mechanistic paradigm of industrial agriculture in favor of a paradigm that treats agriculture as a resourceful, resilient, regenerative living system.

New Patterns for the Future of Food

Thousands of new farmers all across America and around the world are rising to the challenge of creating a replacement for the failed industrial system of farming. They may call themselves organic, ecological, regenerative, holistic, biodynamic, or family farmers. All of these alternative approaches share a common philosophy of farming as a social and ethical way of life, as well as a way to make a living. Sustainable farmers accept the responsibility of caring for the land and caring about their communities and society, as well as caring for themselves and their families. They understand that a farm is a living system and, to be sustainable, it must be managed as a living ecosystem. These new farmers are in the process of creating a new future of farming.

Sustainable agriculture is fundamentally different from industrial agriculture. Sustainable farms are diverse, rather than specialized; individualistic, rather than standardized; and interdependently operated, rather than hierarchically controlled. Industrial agriculture is a linear system in that it extracts and exploits the resources of nature and society and turns them into useful products but also useless or harmful wastes. Sustainable agriculture is a circular system that produces useful products but turns wastes from one production process into inputs for other processes or nourishment for nature. Sustainable farms rely on the inflow of solar energy and the resilience and regenerative capacity of healthy living systems to meet the basic food needs of the present without diminishing opportunities for the future.

The resilience and regeneration essential for sustainable productivity requires some sacrifice in short-run efficiency. Investments in the resilience and regenerative capacity essential for sustainability require the use of resources that could instead be used for current productivity. Thus, sustainable farming requires attention to balance and harmony among resourcefulness, resilience, and regenerative capacity to renew and regenerate the ecological, social, and economic sources of agricultural productivity. This challenge is very similar in concept to the challenge faced by farmers throughout history. The key is to focus on long-run economic viability rather than maximum economic efficiency.

The principles, values, and ideas that characterize sustainable farming have characterized agriculture throughout much of human history. Agricultural history is punctuated by cycles—the flourishing of nations when agriculture flourished and the fall of nations when agriculture failed. These cycles reflect times in history when human civilizations have alternately embraced and abandoned the values, principles, and ideas essential for agricultural sustainability. Returning to those core principles and ideas of farming in the past does not mean that farms of the future will rely on the farming methods, practices, or technologies of earlier agrarian times. Instead, farms of the future must respect the basic principles of nature that have been necessary for farms of the past to be sustainable. Nature's principles include those of human nature such as the need for love, purpose, and meaning in life. Whenever farming has deviated from this path, farming systems have failed. In many respects, sustainable farms of the future must have the same basic characteristics as "traditional family farms."[2]

The primary motivation or purpose for farming is perhaps the most important difference between today's industrial farm businesses and traditional family farms. Family farms, traditionally, were not just family businesses but also were an integral part of the farm family's social and ethical way of life (see Alexander, chapter 6 of this volume). The farm and the family are inseparable. The same farm with a different family would have been a different farm, and the same family with a different farm would have been a different family. The positive or negative impacts of family farms on the health of the land and their communities were reflections of the ethical and social values of the farm family.

Using contemporary agricultural terminology, traditional family farms were multifunctional farms. They provided multiple economic, social, ecological benefits for farm families, farm workers, communities, consumers, and society in general—not just profits for farm businesses. This multifunctionality is reflected in the etymology of root words used for farm and farmer. Historically, the word "farmer" has been defined as one who cultivates land, cares for livestock, or otherwise operates a farm. The English word farmer has varied origins: from Middle English, *fermer, fer-*

mour ("steward"); from Old French *fermier* ("husbandman"); and from Medieval Latin *firmarius* ("one who rents land") (Wiktionary, n.d). The English word *farm* comes from Middle English, *ferme, farme* ("rent, revenue, produce, stewardship, meal, feast"); from Old English, *feorm, fearm, farm* ("meaning provisions, food, supplies, possessions, stores, feast, entertainment, haven"); from Proto-Germanic *fermō* ("means of living, subsistence"); and from Proto-Indo-European *perkw-* ("life, strength, force"). It is related also to Old English words such as *feormian* ("to provision, sustain") and *feorh* ("life, spirit") (Wiktionary, n.d.).

These historic meanings of the words farmer and farm suggest that economics has always been an important motivation for farming. Farming has always been a way to make a living. Farming also was a means of providing more food for communities and societies than could be provided by hunting and gathering. The root words also suggest that farms historically have met the noneconomic as well as economic needs. Farming philosophies, methods, and practices were linked to the social and spiritual values of farmers and people in farming communities. The etymology of farming also suggests that sustainable farming is a timeless phenomenon; it is of the past as well as the present and future. Historical meanings such as "stewardship, security, and sustain" clearly confirm an historical ethical commitment to the ideal of sustainability.

Interestingly, the root words for farmer and farm have all tended to be positive or beneficial. This is consistent with farmers historically being held in high esteem in the United States and in much of the rest of the world. Thomas Jefferson, for example, believed strongly that the "yeoman farmer" best exemplified the kind of "independence and virtue" that should be respected and supported by government. Adam Smith, an icon of capitalism and author of the classic, *The Wealth of Nations*, observed that farmers ranked among the highest social classes in China and India, and he suggested that it would be the same everywhere if the "corporate spirit" did not prevent it. Smith never trusted businessmen in general and corporate managers in particular, and he suggested that the legitimate role of corporations was very limited.

Smith's reference to China was to the philosopher Confucius who ranked Chinese farmers second only to Chinese scholars. Workers ranked below farmers, and businessmen ranked last. Jefferson didn't trust financiers, bankers, or industrialists to be responsible citizens and suggested they should not be encouraged by government. These and other respected historical figures have placed farmers at or near the top of society and those involved with business and economics at the bottom. The farmers extolled by Jefferson, Smith, and Confucius were multifunctional family farmers. They were respected not just as businessmen but as honorable people making positive contributions to society and humanity.

The farmers valorized by past cultures obviously were intentionally multifunctional farmers. Their farms produced multiple benefits for natural ecosystems, communities, and societies, thus justifying their high esteem. Had the benefits been an inherent consequence of farming, there would have been no reason to consider farmers to be uniquely worthy. The lowly ranked businesses and corporations were also multifunctional. However, the detrimental social and ecological impacts of their businesses apparently weighed heavily against their economic benefits. There would have been no justification for condemning the owner or manager of businesses if their negative impacts were inherent rather than a consequence of the intent, or perhaps neglect or indifference.

The question of functionality is just as relevant today as it was in the days of Jefferson, Smith, or Confucius. An

Ikerd

International Assessment of Agricultural Knowledge, Science and Technology for Development report, *Agriculture at a Crossroads*, focused on multifunctionality and sustainability (IAASTD 2009). The authors of the report observed that all agriculture is inherently multifunctional: "It provides food, feed, fiber, fuel and other goods. It also has a major influence on other essential ecosystem services such as water supply and carbon sequestration or release. Agriculture plays an important social role, providing employment and a way of life. Both agriculture and its products are a medium of cultural transmission and cultural practices worldwide. Agriculturally based communities provide a foundation for local economies and are an important means for countries to secure their territories" (IAASTD 2009, 3).

The fundamental question is whether these multiple functions and their ecological, social, economic consequences result in positive or negative net benefits for global society and the future of humanity. As decades of real-world experience has confirmed, negative ecological and social consequences are inevitable whenever farms are managed mono-functionally for the single economic bottom line. When farms are managed multifunctionally, they can be managed for ecological, social, and economic sustainability (Ikerd 2016a). The IAASTD report called for governments to give more attention to small-scale multifunctional farmers and sustainable farming practices.

The industrial farms that dominate U.S. agriculture today are intentionally mono-functional rather than intentionally multifunctional. Their success is measured in terms of economic performance rather than by the multiple economic, social, and ecological benefits associated with traditional family farms. Farm business managers rationalize their decisions by relying on the now-discredited belief that the market economy will somehow transform their mono-functional pursuit of economic self-interests into benefits for society as a whole. The fundamental problem with industrial agriculture is that its mono-functional focus on economic performance invariably has detrimental ecological, social, and economic consequences—even if unintended. These consequences are inherent within the industrial system. An industrial agrifood system is inherently unsustainable.

In summary, the global food system of the future must balance the need for greater productivity and resource efficiency with the resilience to thrive under uncertain climatic conditions and the capacity to regenerate the soil, water, air, energy, and other resources needed to sustain productivity. Rather than being mechanistic, specialized, standardized, and centrally controlled, farms of the future must be diverse, individualistic, and interdependent. They must be multifunctional farms that are ways of life, as well as means of making a living (Ikerd 2016a, 23). This is a timeless pattern for sustainable farming.

New Sustainable Agrifood Systems

The realization of the new multifunctional food system of the future is emerging from the sustainable agrifood movement. The organic food movement probably has been the most popular indicator of the transformation in food production. Organics has grown from a fringe movement in home gardening to become a significant sector of the mainstream food economy. However, the local food movement is probably a more accurate expression of the new pattern for the sustainable food system as a whole—although local foods have proven more difficult to monitor. The local food movement is transforming the industrial and global food system of today into the sustainable and local food system of the future. To understand the significance of the local food movement, it is important to understand the birth of the modern organic movement.

The current organic movement has its roots in the natural food movement of the early 1960s, which was a rejection of the industrialization of American agriculture. When the mechanical and chemical technologies of World War II were adapted to industrial agriculture, the people of the "back to the earth" movement decided to create their own food system. They grew their own food, exchanged food with each other, and formed the first cooperative food buying clubs and natural food stores. Concerns about the health and environmental risks associated with synthetic fertilizers and pesticides were important but were not the only reasons these people chose to grow food organically. They were also creating "organic communities" and nurturing a sense of connectedness and commitment to taking care of each other as well as caring for the earth. These organic values were deeply embedded in the philosophy of organic farming as well as in their intentional communities. Organic was as much a way of life as a way to produce food.

Organic farming and food production remained on the fringes until the environmental movement expanded into the mainstream of American society during the 1980s. The market for organic foods then grew at a rate of more than 20 percent per year from the early 1990s until the economic recession of 2008. Growth in organic food sales have since stabilized at around 10 percent per year. The organic food market reached $43.3 billion in sales in 2015: about 5 percent of the total U.S. food market (Organic Trade Association 2016). Organic fruits and vegetables claim more than 10 percent of their markets (Gelski 2015). As they grew in popularity, organic foods eventually moved into mainstream supermarkets. However, the only value of organic foods respected by the industrial food system was its economic value. Organics was a new and growing opportunity to make money.

By the late 1980s, several of the early natural foods cooperatives had expanded into small chain operations of between three and twenty stores. In 1991, Whole Foods, at the time a six-store operation, initiated a consolidation process that ultimately reshaped the natural foods market (Whole Food Market, n.d.). In 1993, Wild Oats followed the lead of Whole Foods in acquiring other stores (Wild Oats, n.d.). During the 1990s, prospects for profits from the rapidly growing organic food market eventually attracted the attention of the large industrial food corporations. With overall demand for food limited by population growth of roughly 1 percent per year, the fast-growing organic market represented a rare opportunity for economic growth. Mainstream supermarkets, including Kroger, Safeway, and Walmart, added lines of organic foods and began promoting organic foods in their ads.

The large corporate food retailers, and the large food processors who supplied them, found it difficult to deal with large numbers of small organic farms. In addition, a diversity of organic standards and certification programs existed among different groups of farmers in different regions of the country at that time. So, organic farmers were encouraged to adopt uniform standards for national organic certification to access mainstream markets. In 2002, the USDA launched its National Organic Program (NOP) of uniform national standards for certification of organic foods. By standardizing the specification of organic foods, national organic standards opened the door to specialization and corporate consolidation of control of organic production and distribution (Kirschenmann 2000; Ikerd 1999).

The new USDA organic standards were limited primarily to identification of lists of allowable "organic" fertilizers, pesticides, and other production inputs and materials. Typical organic production practices such as crop rotations, cover crops, and access of livestock to pastures were included in the standards, but such practices were difficult to define in terms that could be monitored and enforced. In the quest for greater productive efficiency, many organic producers began to adapt the industrial system of farming to accommodate the new organic standards. They simply substituted organic for nonorganic inputs and materials and modified production practices to accommodate industrial production, while meeting minimum requirements for organic certification. The resulting simplification allowed consolidation or management to achieve the economic efficiencies of large-scale, industrial organic production.

With its industrialization, the organic market share held by natural food chains and mainstream retailers continued to grow. The share held by independent natural foods and health foods stores fell from 62 percent in 1998 to 31 percent in 2003 (Ruiz-Marrero, 2004). By 2006, the Whole Foods chain had grown to 186 stores in North America and the UK, while Wild Oats operated 110 stores in the United States and Canada. Whole Foods acquired Wild Oats in 2007 and continued adding stores to more than 450 stores by 2015 (Statista 2015). Mainstream corporate supermarkets had gained 47 percent of the organic foods market by 2007, with natural foods stores and specialty retail chains accounting for another 46 percent (Ruiz-Marrero 2004). These trends left direct sales at farmers markets and cooperative food-buying clubs with just 7 percent of the organic market. In spite of the growth in local or direct sales of organic food, a 2016 USDA report still quoted an earlier Organic Trade Association estimate of 93 percent of organic sales going through natural food chains and mainstream supermarkets (Economic Research Service, USDA 2016). In 2017, Amazon .com acquired Whole Foods, adding a completely different dimension to the organic evolution (Bhattara 2017).

The industrialization of organics reflects the inevitable results of a quest for ever-greater economic efficiency. The basic economic motivations for moving organics into mainstream markets were prospects for reduced prices for consumers, increased profits for producers, and greater affordability and availability of organic foods for more people in more places. While organic foods became available to more people in more places, organic processors and retailers captured much of the increase in economic efficiency, leaving organic consumers with high prices and independent organic producers often striving to break even. Furthermore, with the new national standards in place, organic food was no longer defined by a commitment to historical ecological, social, and economic values that had characterized the earlier natural and organic food movements. The metrics for success were purely economic: increased sales and profitability. The organics movement had shifted from a multifunctional food revolution to just another mono-functional business opportunity. Organic farmers who refused to compromise historical organic values were forced to rely on direct markets where consumers were willing and able to pay the economic cost of ecological and social integrity.

Consumers who were concerned about the ecological and societal consequences of industrial agriculture responded by looking to local farmers to ensure the integrity of their foods. Small organic farms that were being abandoned by industrial organics were quick to respond to growing demand from local customers. Sales of local foods grew from $5 billion in 2008 to an industry estimated $12 billion in 2014 and were projected to hit $20 billion by 2019 (Blue Book Services 2016). Farmers markets increased in number from 1,755 to 8,476 between 1994 and 2015 (Economic Research Service, USDA 2016a). The number of community supported agriculture farms or CSAs had grown from virtually none in the early 1990s to 12,000 in the 2012 Census of Agriculture (U.S. Department of Agriculture 2012). The number of farmers reportedly selling directly to consumers by all means—on-farm, roadside stands, farmers

Ikerd

markets, and CSAs—was estimated at 50,000. Many farmers who used organic production practices didn't bother with the expense and paperwork of organic certification. Their local customers trusted them personally more than they trusted the USDA standards, and their success depended on their social embeddedness in the community.

A more recent and perhaps more significant development in the local food movement has been the growth in multiple-farm networks of local farmers. Most of these began as multi-farm CSAs, where several farmers shared the task of supplying a wide variety of local food products during local growing seasons. These multi-farm networks may be called food alliances, cooperatives, collaboratives, or food hubs. *Grown Locally, Idaho's Bounty, Viroqua Food Coop*, and *Good Natured Family Farms* are examples of food multi-farm local food networks. The Oklahoma Food Cooperative provides a directory of fifteen similar cooperatives in other states. These alliances range in size from a couple dozen to a couple hundred farmers. The *National Good Food Network* lists more than 300 "food hubs" (2017). However, the local food movement is so decentralized and dispersed that it is impossible to accurately estimate the size or importance of the movement. Local foods may now be the fastest growing as well as the most innovative and progressive sector of the American food system.

The local food movement is also so diverse that it is difficult to distinguish between networks that are committed to principles and values of sustainability and those who simply see local foods as another opportunity for profits. Food hubs are organizations that allow farmers to aggregate individual production to serve markets that are larger than they can serve alone. Some simply serve as collective assembly operations for the industrial food system. Others are made up of local farmers committed to responding to local demand for foods that have ecological and social integrity. The future of the local food movement depends on being able to "scale up" to serve increasing numbers of consumers. However, if producers compromise their ecological and social integrity in the process of scaling up, their local food networks will become little different from the unsustainable industrial food system that ultimately must be replaced.

The Role of Government in the Future of Food

Local food networks can continue to grow in spite of the lack of government support. However, markets alone cannot create a sustainable agrifood system, no matter how committed individual consumers and farmers may be. Economic value is a reflection of scarcity, not human necessity. Air and water have no economic value until they become scarce through pollution or overuse. Efficient markets can allocate scarce resources among competing uses more effectively than any other system of economics that has yet been tried. However, markets alone cannot meet the basic food needs of all in the present or ensure equal opportunities for those of the future.

Sustainability is based on the premise that everyone has a basic human right to enough safe, nutritious food to meet their basic human needs—including those of future generations. Markets will only provide enough food for those who can earn enough money to compete with others who need or want food. Those of future generations have no means of competing in markets for the land, water, and other resources of nature that will be needed to produce their food. A fundamental flaw in current agrifood policies is their reliance on markets to provide food security. A fundamental purpose of government is to ensure the rights of the people governed. The creation of a new sustainable agrifood system ultimately will require effective governance.

The American Declaration of Independence proclaims that all people are created equal and endowed with certain unalienable rights, including life, liberty, and the pursuit of happiness—and "to secure these rights, governments are instituted among men." What can possibly be more essential for "life" than clean air, clean water, and safe, nutritious food? To create a sustainable food system for the future, people must be willing to work through government to secure the "right to food" as a basic human right. The mission of government farm and food programs must shift from food security through market-driven, industrial agriculture to food sovereignty through values-driven, agricultural sustainability.

Contrary to claims by its advocates, the industrialization of agriculture was not a natural consequence of free markets—at least not solely. Instead, it is the consequence of a premeditated shift in agricultural policies during the 1970s. As I have suggested above, the political justification for agricultural policy has always been domestic food security. No nation, at least until recently, has been willing to trust its food security to the global marketplace. U.S. farm policies from the 1930s through the 1960s were premised on the proposition that food security could best be ensured by keeping independent family farmers on the land. Family farmers had been the cultural foundation of American society and were committed to maintaining the productivity of their land, not only for the benefit of their own families and communities but also for the food security of their nation.

U.S. farm policy was fundamentally changed during the early 1970s. The policy objectives shifted from supporting family farms to promoting the industrialization of agriculture. Food security would then be ensured not by family farms but by reducing the cost of food production and making good food affordable for all—also known as the "cheap food policy." Food would be cheap enough for everyone to buy enough safe, healthful food to meet their basic nutritional needs. The markets would ensure food security more efficiently than could government. Government food assistance programs would be limited to filling in gaps for the young, old, and disabled.

The farm policies of this era were designed specifically to support, subsidize, and promote specialization, standardization, and consolidation of agricultural production into ever-larger farming operations. Every major farm policy since the 1970s—price supports, farm credit, crop insurance, disaster payments, farm tax credits, and depreciation allowances—in one way or another has supported the industrial paradigm. Soil and water conservation and more recent organic and sustainable farming programs were adopted due to public pressure and are under constant threat, with funds often diverted to subsidize industrial farming practices. "Plant fencerow to fencerow" and "Get big or get out" remain the watchwords of U.S. farm policy. The mandate of U.S. farm and food policy—to provide safe, nutritious, appetizing food for all Americans—remains unfulfilled (Ikerd 2016a).

The challenge of agrifood sustainability simply adds to that mandate the responsibility of ensuring opportunities for the food security of future generations. The "right to food" is not as radical an idea as it might first seem. Current USDA food assistance programs are a reflection of the unwillingness of Americans to let other people starve. However, public food assistance is treated more as an act of charity than a public responsibility. Some have argued that government food security programs are motivated more by preventing social disruption than alleviating hunger (Piven and Cloward 1993).

The right to food already is explicitly recognized in many other parts of the world. Food sovereignty is a term coined in 1996 by Via Campesina, an organization of 148 international organizations advocating family farm-based, sustainable agriculture (Via Campesina, n.d.). The initial call for food sovereignty was a response to the failure of the Green Revolution to provide food for the poor. The movement is a clear rejection of the industrial agriculture polices that were forced upon "lesser-developed" nations under the guise of promoting food security. During a global Forum for Food Sovereignty in Mali in 2007, about five hundred delegates from more than eighty countries adopted the "Declaration of Nyéléni." Food sovereignty was defined as "the right of peoples to healthy and culturally appropriate food produced through ecologically sound and sustainable methods, and their right to define their own food and agriculture systems. It puts the aspirations and needs of those who produce, distribute and consume food at the heart of food systems and policies, rather than the demands of markets and corporations" (Nyelini Forum on Food Sovereignty 2007).

A basic premise of the food sovereignty movement is that people of the world must have food sovereignty to achieve true food security. The food sovereignty movement places a high priority on sustainable local food systems that allow local consumers and farmers to control their own choices in foods and production practices to meet their physical and cultural needs, at least to the extent that local needs can be met locally. People in local communities would have the right to protect local farmlands from degradation and development through local autonomy and authority for land use planning. Local control also would give communities the ability to control water for irrigation and to maintain free access to crop and livestock genetics adapted to local growing conditions. Trade policies that threaten local agricultural economies would be dismantled and replaced with policies to protect local agricultural economies from corporate exploitation. People in local communities would need to accept the responsibility for restoring the integrity of local, democratic governance and protecting local agencies from corporate corruption.

The kind of local democracy suggested by food sovereignty is not new in American history. Alexis de Tocqueville, a French diplomat, visited America and wrote his classic book, *Democracy in America*, in 1835—some fifty years after American independence. De Tocqueville believed the American democracy was sustained by a widespread commitment to the common good because of a belief in what he called "self-interest rightly understood" (de Tocqueville 1836, 646–9). Early Americans did not deny the right of everyone to pursue his or her self-interest, "but they endeavored to prove that it is in the interest of every man to be virtuous" (de Tocqueville 1836, 647). De Tocqueville believed also that decentralization or localization of government authority had been critical to the success of early American democracy. Federal and state laws were enforced in large part within local communities. Local administrators of laws and regulations were respected as responsible representatives of the people rather than government enforcers. The local township was the central focus of formal government administration in early America. There was no sense that big government was imposing its will on the people. The people were simply using local government to enforce a community consensus. It was in the common interest to be virtuous.

Government policies supporting food sovereignty cannot be imposed on the American people. It must be supported by a consensus that enough safe, nutritious food to meet basic human needs is a fundamental right, to be secured for current generations and preserved for those of the future. Such a consensus is only possible if Americans return to the time-honored principle of self-interest rightly understood. Food sovereignty ultimately will require a new "social contract" among the people within the United States, as well as between the United States and the rest of the world. Global food sovereignty explicitly calls for freedom from economic oppression and inequality at all levels. It calls for a new, deeper sense of equality and respect between men and women, among racial and ethnic groups, among social and economic classes, and within and across generations. Policies supporting food sovereignty would empower the local food movement to grow and evolve to create a new community-based, sustainable food system.

Creating "Trim Tab" Food Communities

The seeds of change in the global agrifood system have emerged and are growing. Growth of the sustainable, agrifood movement will be hastened or hindered by the economic and political environment in which it grows. The agrifood corporations will continue to be formidable defenders of the economic status quo of industrial agriculture. These corporations gain their economic power through predatory competition and corporate consolidation, then use their economic power to exert political power in shaping farm and food policies. Corporations are masters at defending the status quo by distracting and depleting the resources of their opponents in arguments over rules and regulations. To shift the policy agenda to food sovereignty and sustainability, we ultimately must reclaim political and economic power from the corporations.

Admittedly, the challenge of transforming the agrifood system is formidable, but it is not unsurmountable. Yet we need not wait for changes in policy to begin transforming the food system. We instead can bring about changes in the food system that ultimately will change agrifood policy. In fact, fundamental, systemic change often must begin by finding points of leverage where small, practical actions can lead to large, seemingly impossible effects—like the small trim tab that turns the rudder of a ship, which in turn causes the whole ship to change direction.[3] For example, progressive local communities might well accept the challenge of food sovereignty as a local responsibility, much as some communities in the United States have accepted the challenge of global climate change. Cultural change always begins small, in communities where new ventures succeed in solving problems and realizing opportunities; over time, these changes evolve to become accepted as new norms.

One means of solving the problems of industrial agriculture and realizing the opportunities of food sovereignty might be through "community food utilities" or CFUs. People in the United States tend to be very skeptical of government interference in private markets. However, public utilities are widely accepted as a means of providing specific "public services." Public utilities typically are used to provide water, sewer, electricity, natural gas, communication systems, and other essential services. Public utilities are granted special privileges that protect them from market competition and are subject to special governmental regulation to protect public interests. Governments grant local monopolies to public service providers.

Public utilities typically ensure universal access to essential services. Utilities do not ensure that everyone can afford adequate access of those services but often have special programs to continue services in life-threatening situations regardless of ability to pay. Community Food Utilities would not only ensure universal access to food but would also ensure enough good food to meet the basic needs of all—not as an exception or act of charity but as an essential public service. The CFU could fill in the persistent gaps that have been left by markets, charities, and impersonal government programs to ensure food security for every household in a community.

The American culture is unlikely to accept food as a publicly-secured right unless recipients accept corresponding responsibilities. One possibility would be to require recipients to provide public services of equivalent value to the food received. However, public services of both economic and non-economic values would need to be accepted as payment. Those without food are frequently hungry because they are incapable of producing enough economic value to meet their needs. To address this challenge, contributions by recipients could be based on hours of service rather than economic value, giving everyone an equal opportunity to contribute. Those choosing not to contribute anything would be opting out of the program by choice. Those who could not contribute would not be asked to contribute anything. CFU payments for services could be made in local currency or Community Food Dollars (CF$s). CF$s could be used only to buy food provided by the CFU.

Priority in procuring food for the CFU could be given to local farmers willing to meet locally-determined standards for food safety, nutrition, freshness, and sustainable means of production. Organic, ecological, biodynamic, regenerative, holistic, and other sustainable approaches to farming provide useful models for CFUs. A logical organization for a CFU would be a vertical cooperative with a board of directors that includes local farmers, consumers, processors and distributors, taxpayers, and local government officials. Under the current system of vertical integration, large corporate food retailers essentially control the other levels in the vertical food supply chain through outright ownership, formal contractual arrangements, strategic alliances, or through sheer market power. In such cases, the dominant corporations decide what is to be produced, when it is to be produced, how it will be produced, and who will produce it—and take most of the profits. Vertical integration is a corporate version of "central planning."

Cooperative relationships are neither competitive nor exploitative; instead, they are mutually beneficial. Within a vertically cooperative CFU, economic costs and benefits would be shared fairly and equitably among consumers, retailers, processors, and farmers. The vertical system would be coordinated through cooperation rather than competition or integration. The board of directors, representing the local community, would decide what to produce, where and when it would be available, how it would be produced and processed, and who would produce and process it. They also would agree on pricing arrangements to ensure that farmers would be able to cover cost of production, plus a reasonable profit, and that consumers would be able to obtain the products they need and want at affordable prices. The local officials on the boards of CFUs would represent the interest of local taxpayers in the negotiation process.

Producers within the vertical cooperative would receive an economic return adequate for a sustainable livelihood without exploiting the natural and human resources that must sustain the economic viability of the system over the long run. Thus, fair and equitable economic returns would be sustainable for all participants. Sustainable benefits for such CFUs would depend on cooperative members consistently expressing their shared social and ethical commitments to the long-term sustainability of their common venture. The key to sustainable livelihoods in food systems is for farmers, processors, retailers, and consumers to form vertical cooperatives with like-minded friends, or to make friends of like-minded people with whom they choose to cooperate.

A CFU could serve as a "food grid" by procuring foods from non-local producers when necessary to fill in gaps in local production. Priority for non-local procurement would be given to regional suppliers who are willing and able to meet locally-determined quality standards—the standards of food sovereignty. CFU foods would be made available to participants by means that ensure physical access to food for everyone. The needs of children, the elderly, and the disabled would be given special consideration. The CFU would coordinate its functions with local charities and impersonal government programs, such as "food stamps" and "school lunches," to avoid duplication. The CFU might also operate a "community food market" where those without special needs could buy CFU food using CF$. For those who lack ready access to transportation or refrigeration, delivery options could include periodic deliveries of individually selected CSA-like "food boxes." Home delivery of foods for specific meals could be provided for those who cannot be accommodated with other options. Meal preparation guidelines, along with basic refrigeration and storage, would be provided to minimize food wastes, to accommodate various delivery options, and to meet participants' specific needs.

Nutrition education could be integrated into all CFU programs to help participants learn to select nutritionally balanced diets for their families and to prepare appetizing meals from the raw and minimally processed foods provided by the CFU. More than 80 percent of foods purchased in supermarkets and 90 percent of the cost of restaurant meals are associated with costs of processing, packaging, transportation, energy, taxes, insurance, and services provided by food retailers (Economic Research Service, USDA 2017b). By spending CF$s on raw and minimally processed local foods provided by the CFU, even the lowest income consumers would be able to afford more than enough good food.

Food security could be provided for everyone by making nutritious, minimally processed, un-packaged, and unadvertised food available locally. Additionally, it is important to help people learn to select foods for nutrition and to prepare food for themselves. Most people would find ways to spend quality time with their families by preparing food from scratch if they understand the true costs of quick, convenient, and cheap industrial foods.

The CFU would operate as efficiently as possible, but the CFU would require continuing commitments of local tax dollars to ensure the local right to food. The key difference between the CFU and existing food assistance programs would be that government officials in caring communities would feel a personal sense of connection with their community, and community members would feel a personal sense of responsibility for each other. A sense of self-interest rightly understood would be needed to support the CFU program.

As local production expands beyond levels needed to address hunger, the CFU could offer food to the general community at prices covering full costs plus a profit for the CFU. The CFU would provide a secure economic foundation from which commercial local food systems could grow. The assurance of a stable market for a portion of their production and access to scale-appropriate facilities for processing and distribution provided by CFUs would remove major obstacles to further commercial development of local food systems. CFU communities would develop connections with other CFU communities to secure foods that cannot be produced locally. These connections could evolve into regional, national, and even global food networks of local food systems linked with other food systems through a shared commitment to the principles of sustainability and values of food sovereignty.

Returning to historic principles does not mean a rejection of new technologies. The business of retailing—including food retailing—is changing fundamentally and rapidly. The total value of Amazon stock recently surpassed the total stock value of Walmart, although Walmart is still far larger in total retail sales. Virtually every major retailer, including food retailers, are scrambling to develop web-based markets. Food home-delivery programs—such as Blue Apron and Hello-Fresh—may be paving the way for the post-industrial food assembly and distribution system. The purchase of Whole Foods by Amazon.com could signal the end of food retailing as we have known it for the past fifty years (Bhattara 2017). However, local food networks would seem to have a natural economic advantage over regional or national distribution systems in local home delivery of locally grown foods. Regardless, the challenge will remain to develop and maintain the personal relationships of trust essential for a community commitment to the common good—to self-interest rightly understood.

As Americans respond to national and global challenges such as natural resource depletion, climate change, dying oceans, species extinction, social injustice, and economic inequity, we will create the environment for fundamental changes in our systems of farming and food production. The historic basic patterns of agricultural cycles have been for trends to be built to a climax and then collapse with disastrous results, only later to be rebuilt on a foundation of depleted natural and human resources. We now have the knowledge and uniquely human capacity for thoughtful, intentional actions to avoid a similar fate for ourselves and our current industrial agricultural cycle.

As "trim tab" communities meet the challenges of ensuring food as a basic human right, the "rudder" of public policy may begin to shift and the "ship of state" may begin turning away from industrial agriculture toward a commitment to sustainable agriculture and global food sovereignty. With supportive public policies, the transition from global to local, and from industrial to sustainable, could move from gradual to explosive. A disastrous collapse in global agriculture will have been avoided and agricultural production eventually will stabilize at sustainable levels. There would still be future cycles, even great transformations, but they need not be cycles characterized by explosive growth followed by periodic collapse. We can choose to embrace the current great transformation and help move humanity toward a fundamentally better future. We can each do our part in transforming the future of food and farming from industrial and global to sustainable and local.

Notes

1. The "agricultural establishment" includes large agribusiness corporations, major commodity groups, the American Farm Bureau Federation, the USDA, and most state Departments of Agriculture and agricultural colleges.

2. Much of the following section is adapted from "Family Farms of North America," a working paper by John Ikerd, published by the Food and Agriculture Organization of the United Nations and the International Policy Centre for Inclusive Growth of the United Nations Development Programme. Working paper number 152. December 2016. ISSN 1812-108x. http://www.ipc-undp .org/pub/eng/WP152_Family_farms_of_North_America.pdf.

3. Much of the section is adapted from: Ikerd, John. 2016. "Enough Good Food for All: A Proposal." *Journal of Agriculture, Food Systems, and Community Development.* 7, no. 1, 3–6.

References

Alexander, Sara E. 2019. "Forecasting the Challenges of Climate Change for West Texas Wheat Farmers." In Gibson and Alexander 2019, 186–226.

Berry, Wendell. 1981. "Solving for Pattern." In *The Gift of Good Land: Further Essays Cultural & Agricultural.* New York: North Point.

Bhattaral, Abha. 2017. "FTC Clears Amazon.com Purchase of Whole Foods." *Washington Post,* August 23, 2017. https://www.washingtonpost.com/news /business/wp/2017/08/23/ftc-clears-amazon-com-purchase-of-whole -foods/?utm_term=.d647f2a0c8fe.

Blue Apron. n.d. "Food Is Better When You Start from Scratch." Accessed October 18, 2017. https://www.blueapron.com/.

Blue Book Services. 2017. "Vetting Suppliers." Accessed April 19, 2017. https:// www.producebluebook.com/blog/2017/04/19/vetting-suppliers/.

CMS.gov. 2016. "Center for Medicare and Medicate Services National Health and Expenditure Data. 2015." December 06, 2015. https://www.cms .gov/research-statistics-data-and-systems/statistics-trends-and-reports /nationalhealthexpenddata/nationalhealthaccountshistorical.html.

Culotta, Elizabeth. 1991. "Science's 20 Greatest Hits Take Their Lumps." *Science* 251, no. 4999 (March): 1308–9.

De Tocqueville, Alexis. (1835) 2000. *Democracy in America.* New York: Bantam, 646–9.

Economic Research Service, USDA. 2016. "Organic Market Overview." https:// www.ers.usda.gov/topics/natural-resources-environment/organic -agriculture/organic-market-overview.aspx.

Economic Research Service, USDA. 2016a. "Number of U.S. Farmers Markets has Nearly Tripled Over Last 15 years." https://www.ers.usda.gov/data -products/chart-gallery/gallery/chart-detail/?chartId=78388.

Economic Research Service, USDA. 2017. "Food Security Status of U.S. House-holds in 2015." Accessed October 4, 2017. https://www.ers.usda.gov/topics /food-nutrition-assistance/food-security-in-the-us/key-statistics-graphics/.

Economic Research Service, USDA. 2017a. "Frequently Asked Questions." https://www.ers.usda.gov/faqs/.

Economic Research Service, USDA. 2017b. "Food Prices and Spending." April 2017. https://www.ers.usda.gov/data-products/ag-and-food-statistics -charting-the-essentials/food-prices-and-spending/.

Foley, Jonathan. 2013. "Time to Rethink America's Corn System." *Scientific American*, March 5, 2013. https://www.scientificamerican.com/article /time-to-rethink-corn/.

Food and Agriculture Organization. United Nations, High Level Expert Forum. 2009. "How to Feed the World–2050." October 2009. http:// www.fao.org/fileadmin/templates/wsfs/docs/Issues_papers/HLEF2050 _Global_Agriculture.pdf.

Food and Agriculture Organization, United Nations. 2014. "State of Food and Agriculture, 2014 In Brief." Accessed October 18, 2017. http://www .fao.org/3/a-i4036e.pdf.

———. 2017. "Climate Smart Agriculture," http://www.fao.org/climate-smart -agriculture/en/.

Gates Foundation. 2012. "Helping Poor Farmers, Changes Needed to Feed 1 Billion Hungry: Bill & Melinda Gates Foundation." https://www .gatesfoundation.org/Media-Center/Press-Releases/2012/02/Helping -Poor-Farmers-Changes-Needed-to-Feed-1-Billion-Hungry.

Gelski, Jeff. 2015. "U.S. Organic Food Sales Rise 11% in 2014." *Food Business News*, April 15, 2015. http://www.foodbusinessnews.net/articles/news _home/Consumer_Trends/2015/04/US_organic_food_sales_rise_11 .aspx?ID=%7B0C1920D3-1822-4467-9FF0-F1EE00E53F54%7D&cck=1.

Germanos, Andrea. 2016. "'Overwhelming' Evidence Shows Path is Clear: It's Time to Ditch Industrial Agriculture for Good." *Common Dreams*, June 02, 2016. http://www.commondreams.org/news/2016/06/02/overwhelming -evidence-shows-path-clear-its-time-ditch-industrial-agriculture-good.

Good Natured Family Farms. n.d. "Nature's Best from Local Family Farms." Accessed October 18, 2017. http://www.goodnaturedfamilyfarms.com/.

GRAIN. 2016. "The Global Farmland Grab in 2016: How Big, How Bad?" June 16, 2016. https://www.grain.org/article/entries/5492-the-global -farmland-grab-in-2016-how-big-how-bad#.

Grown Locally. n.d. "Fresh, Local, Sustainable Food." Accessed October 18, 2017. http://www.grownlocally.com.

Guardian. 2016. "Farming Mega-mergers Threaten Food Security, Say Cam-paigners," September 26, 2016. https://www.theguardian.com/global -development/2016/sep/26/farming-mega-mergers-threaten-food -security-say-campaigners.

Hello Fresh. n.d. "Get Cooking." Accessed October 18, 2017. https://www
.hellofresh.com/tasty/.

Idaho's Bounty. n.d. "Your Local Farm Delivered." Accessed October 18, 2017.
http://www.idahosbounty.org/.

Ikerd, John. 1999. "Organic Agriculture Faces the Specialization of Production Systems; Specialized Systems and the Economic Stakes." Paper
presented at the Organic Agriculture Faces the Specialization of Production Systems Conference, Lyon, France. December 6–9, 1999. http://
docplayer.net/27895757-organic-agriculture-faces-the-specialization-of
-production-systems-specialized-systems-and-the-economical-stakes-john
-ikerd-university-of-missouri.html.

———. 2013. "Foreword." In *Soil Fertility & Human and Animal Health,* edited
by William A. Albrecht, xv–xxvi. Austin TX: Acres U.S.A.

———. 2016. "Family Farms of North America." Food and Agriculture Organization of the United Nations and the International Policy Centre for Inclusive Growth of the United Nations Development Programme. Empowered
Lives. Resilient Nations. *Working Paper 152.* December 2016. http://www
.ipc-undp.org/pub/eng/WP152_Family_farms_of_North_America.pdf.

———. 2016a. "How Do We Ensure Good Food For All?" *Journal of Agriculture, Food Systems, and Community Development* 6, no. 4: 3–5.

International Assessment of Agricultural Knowledge, Science and Technol-
ogy for Development. 2009. *Agriculture at a Crossroads.* Washington DC:
Island Press. http://www.fao.org/fileadmin/templates/est/Investment
/Agriculture_at_a_Crossroads_Global_Report_IAASTD.pdf.

International Panel of Experts, Sustainability. 2016. "From Uniformity to
Diversity: A Paradigm Shift from Industrial Agriculture to Diversified
Agroecological Systems." June 2016. http://www.ipes-food.org/images
/Reports/UniformityToDiversity_FullReport.pdf.

Kirschenmann, Fredrick. 2000. "The Hijacking of Organic Agriculture . . .
and How USDA is Facilitating the Theft." Organic Consumers Association. http://www.organicconsumers.org/Organic/kirschenmann.cfm.

———. 2012. "The Challenge of Ending Hunger." Leopold Center for Sustainable Agriculture, Winter 2012. http://lib.dr.iastate.edu/leopold
_letter/59/.

Merriam-Webster. 2017. "System." Accessed October 18, 2017. https://www
.merriam-webster.com/dictionary/system.

National Good Food Network. 2017. "US Food Hubs, Full List." Accessed
October 18, 2017. http://www.ngfn.org/resources/food-hubs.

Nyelini Forum on Food Sovereignty. 2007. "Declaration of Nyeleni." February 27, 2007. http://nyeleni.org/spip.php?article290.

Oklahoma Food Coop. n.d. "Directory of Local Food Cooperatives in Other
States." Accessed October 18, 2017. http://www.oklahomafood.coop
/Display.aspx?cn=otherstates.

Organic Trade Association. 2016. "U.S. Organic Sales Post New Record of $43.3 Billion in 2015," May 19, 2016. https://www.ota.com/news/press-releases/19031.

Piven, Frances, and Richard Cloward. 1993. *Regulating the Poor: The Functions of Public Welfare*. New York: Vintage.

Pool, Robert. 1991. "Science Literacy: The Enemy is Us." *Science* 251 (March 15): 4991.

Pulitzer Center. 2010. Africa's Hunger Hardships Spur Biotech Debate." July 10, 2010. http://pulitzercenter.org/reporting/africas-hunger-hardships-spur-biotech-debate.

Ruiz-Marrero, Carmelo. 2004. "Clouds on the Organic Horizon: Is Organic Farming Becoming the Victim of Its Own Success?" *Us*, December 2004. https://www.indybay.org/newsitems/2004/12/22/17108771.php.

Share, World Resources. 2016. "Think U.S. Agriculture Will End World Hunger, Think Again?" http://www.sharing.org/information-centre/reports/think-us-agriculture-will-end-world-hunger-think-again#sthash.qnWMlVhz.dpuf.

Statista. 2015. "Number of Stores of Whole Food Markets Worldwide 2008 to 2015." https://www.statista.com/statistics/258682/whole-foods-markets-number-of-stores-worldwide/.

U.S. Department of Agriculture, Census of Agriculture. 2012. "Table 43. Selected Practices," http://www.agcensus.usda.gov/Publications/2012/Full_Report/Volume_1,_Chapter_2_US_State_Level/st99_2_043_043.pdf.

Viroqua Food Coop. n.d. Accessed October 18, 2017. http://viroquafood.coop/.

Whole Foods Market. n.d. "Our History." Accessed October 18, 2017. http://www.wholefoodsmarket.com/company/history.html.

Wikipedia. 2017. "Via Campesina." Accessed October 18, 2017. http://en.wikipedia.org/wiki/Via_Campesina.

Wiktionary. n.d. "Farmers." Accessed October 18, 2017. http://en.wiktionary.org/wiki/farmer.

Wiktionary. n.d. "Farm." Accessed October 18, 2017. http://en.wiktionary.org/wiki/farm.

Wild Oats. n.d. "Our Story." Accessed October 18, 2017. http://wildoats.com/about-us/our-story/.

CONTRIBUTORS

Sara E. Alexander is professor of anthropology at Baylor University. Her current research interests focus on the dynamics of human populations, and environmental and climate change, specifically in reference to risk perceptions and resulting adjustments in human behavior. She also studies the relationships between resource use and conservation, and livelihood, food, and nutritional securities in rural areas of developing countries. Her current research projects take her to Belize, Ethiopia, the Republic of Georgia, West Texas, and Eastern Appalachia. Alexander consults for TANGO International in its work on building resiliency to natural hazard events in developing regions. She has served on the World Hunger Relief board of directors for over ten years, as a steward on the Seeds Council (hunger awareness), and as an activist for the Texas Drought Project.

Douglas H. Constance is professor of sociology at Sam Houston State University in Huntsville, Texas. His degrees are in forest management (BS), community development (MS), and rural sociology (PhD), all from the University of Missouri–Columbia. Constance's research focuses on the impacts of the globalization of the conventional agrifood system on rural communities and on alternative agrifood systems. He has numerous journal articles, book chapters, and books on these topics. His most recent coedited book is *Contested Sustainability Discourses in the Agrifood System* (Earthscan, 2018). He is past president of the Southern Rural Sociological Association (2003) and the Agriculture, Food, and Human Values Society (2008), and past editor in chief of the *Journal of Rural Social Sciences*.

Jane W. Gibson is associate professor of anthropology at the University of Kansas. Her degrees are in anthropology (BA and PhD) and environmental studies (BA and MS). Her research focuses on the interface between economic and ecological systems and has included studies of the development of fishery and wildlife management institutions; the conversion of rural environments for tourism and state protection; and, most recently, farmer engagement with land and groundwater. She is the author of *Skin and Bones: The Management of People and Natural Resources in Shellcracker Haven, Florida* (2004). In addition she has produced applied project reports in the United States and Costa Rica and published articles on alligator and fisheries management, conservation and development, and Kansas agriculture.

Benjamin J. Gray is a postdoctoral researcher in the Department of Society and Conservation at the University of Montana. His research, centered on the North American Great Plains and Intermountain West, focuses on agricultural issues, attitudes about climate change, community resilience, and the governance of water resources and wildfire risk. The overarching theme of his work is the ways people and institutions navigate change and risk in an uncertain world.

John K. Hansen is the president of Nebraska Farmers Union and serves on the board of directors of the National Farmers Union, the Organization for Competitive Markets, and the Coalition for a Prosperous America. His research and policy interests include farm policy, trade policy, market concentration, antitrust enforcement, and renewable energy development including biofuels, wind and solar energy, climate change, soils, rural development, and conservation.

Mary K. Hendrickson is an assistant professor of rural sociology in the Division of Applied Social Sciences at the University of Missouri. Her research focuses on understanding the structural issues in the food system and finding ways for farmers, eaters, and communities to create profitable and sustainable alternatives. For over fifteen years she worked with the University of Missouri Extension, helping create community food systems across the state. She serves as the undergraduate advisor for sustainable agriculture and teaches courses on sustainable food and farming systems.

Philip H. Howard is an associate professor in the Department of Community Sustainability at Michigan State University. His research and teaching interests focus on changes in food systems and responses to these trends. He is the author of *Concentration and Power in the Food System: Who Controls What We Eat?* (Bloomsbury Academic, 2016) and is a member of the International Panel of Experts on Sustainable Food Systems.

John Ikerd is an emeritus professor of agricultural and applied economics at the University of Missouri–Columbia. Since retiring, he spends most of his time writing and speaking on issues related to sustainability with an emphasis on economics and agriculture. He is author of six books plus numerous journal articles and scholarly papers on agrifood issues. In 2014 Ikerd was commissioned by the Food and Agricultural Organization of the United Nations to write the regional report, "Family Farms of North America," in recognition of the International Year of the Family Farm.

Sarah Kollnig is currently finishing her PhD dissertation titled "The Coloniality of Taste: An Analysis of Socio-Biophysical Inequalities in Bolivia Through the Lens of Food" at the Human Ecology Division at Lund University, Sweden. She is passionate about studying social inequalities and their relationship to sustainability. She has studied these issues through the lens of food culture in Bolivia where she lived for many years, conducting ethnographic research among food vendors, farmers, and middle-class residents of the city of Cochabamba.

Andrew Ofstehage grew up on a small farm in South Dakota. He is now a postdoctoral fellow in the Department of Development Sociology at Cornell University. He earned his PhD at the University of North Carolina at Chapel Hill for his work on land, labor, and value among transnational soy farmers in Brazil. He holds degrees from Wageningen University (MS) for his ethnographic work with quinoa farmers and middlewomen in Bolivia, and from South Dakota State University (a BS in agronomy).

Katherine Strand is a PhD candidate in the Department of Anthropology at McGill University. Her ethnographic research within dryland farming communities began in the High Plains of the United States and now extends into the Prairie Provinces of Canada. Her work focuses on the historical development of concepts within agriculture that continue to shape farming practices including the NPK mentality and soil conservation. She currently lives and works with her partner on an organic grain and bison farm within the Palliser's Triangle of Saskatchewan.

Donald D. Stull is professor emeritus of anthropology at the University of Kansas, where he taught from 1975 to 2015. For the past thirty years his research and writing have focused on the meat and poultry industry in North America; rural industrialization and rapid growth communities; and industrial agriculture's impact on farmers, processing workers, and rural communities. Since 1998 he has studied the poultry industry in western Kentucky, where he is half-owner of a grain farm that has been in his family since the early nineteenth century. Stull coedited *Any Way You Cut*

It: Meat Processing and Small-town America (University Press of Kansas, 1995). He is the coauthor (with Michael Broadway) of *Slaughterhouse Blues: The Meat and Poultry Industry in North America* (Wadsworth, 2004, 2013).

Casey Walsh is professor and chair of anthropology at UC Santa Barbara. In *Building the Borderlands* (Texas A&M, 2008) and *Virtuous Waters* (UC Press, 2018) he employs a historical approach to political economy and culture to understand how humans engage with water and land over the long term. He is coeditor of the *Journal of Political Ecology*.

INDEX

Page numbers in italic indicate illustrations; page numbers with "t" indicate tables.

411

studies of, 336–40; transformation of, 352, 358; volunteers' shortage in, 348

rural credit, 301, 303

rural residents, 176, 183, 186–87, 189–92, 196, 199

safrinha, 304, 314, 315

Salinas River, 184, 189

Sanderson Farms, 35t, 64, 79

sanitation issues, 104, 115, 116, 119

San Luis Obispo county, 178, 196

Saskatchewan: branch stations in, 256; cash crops in, 252; farmers in, 258; illustration stations in, 256–57; lentil production in, 252

Saskatchewan Pulse Growers, 269, 271, 272

Sask Mustard, 269, 270, 271, 273

satellite farming. *See* precision agriculture

scientific community, 249, 257, 259, 265

scientific experiments, 254, 275

seasonal climate forecast, 238, 239

"See & Spray" machines, 150–51

seed(s): and Agbot Challenge, 149; and breeds, 22t, 30; companies, 25, 27t, 28–29, 91, 266, 267; cost issues, 143; herbicide tolerant, 17, 272; soybean, 295, 296, 303

semi-arid areas, 182, 253, 327

SENASAG organization, 102, 113–16, 119–20

Sierra Club, 80, 82

site-specific agriculture. *See* precision agriculture

slaughterhouses, 73, 92, 115, 116

small communities. *See* rural communities

small farmers, 128, 187, 189, 191, 194, 381

small farms, 2, 88, 189, 384, 386

smart farms, 135, 140, *141*, 147, 167, 169

Smithfield, 34, 35, 36, 91

snowball sampling procedure, 179, 215, 293

social class, 178, 179, 190, 380

social inequality, 7, 179

Socially Responsible Agriculture Project (SRAP), 94n1

social systems, 336, 338, 375

soil conditions, 142, *148*, 150, 168, 207, 231

soil erosion, 250, 257, 259, 283, 296

soil fertility, 3, 25, 30, 32, 40, 166

South Dakota State model, 313–14

soybeans: as animal feed, 118; demand for, 85; hybrid seeds, 295, 296, 303; prices for, 80, 82, 91, 118–19; regulation of, 118–19; traits space for, 29

soy production: in Bolivia, 117, 118; Brazil Model of, 290–320; conclusion about, 315–19; expansion of, 289–90; extractivist logic, 118; by municipality, *294*; and poultry production, 117–20

sprayers, 32, 139, 143, 252, 331

steam energy and engines, 137, 138

suppliers and vendors, 38, 39, 40, 125–27

surface water issues, 182, 193, 194, 198

sustainability: about, 8, 9, 10, 49, 50; achieving, 372; and balanced farming, 370–71; challenge of, 370; focus of, 373; and groundwater extraction, 183, 190, 196, 197; industrial agriculture, 92–93; and IPES, 371, 373; regenerative capacity for, 377; and right to food, 388, 389, 390; support for, 374

Sustainable Groundwater Management Act (SGMA), 176, 178, 194–200

Swift Current Research and Development Center (SCRDC): about, 250; conclusion about, 282–84; field days, 249, 251, 252, 261, 266–79; funding for, 271, 281, 282; research at, 250–53, 273–74; test plots at, 264–65, 269; wheat breeding at, 251

Taylor Farms, 145

technologies: about, 1, 3; agricultural, 144, 150, 162, 166, 297; and Brazilian farmers, 303; for crop production, 149–50; drones, 46, 142, 147, 275; GPS guidance systems, 25, 32, 143, 252; resistance to, 152–67, 339; RoboBees, 147; UAVs, 146. *See also* agricultural automation

technology transfer, 268, 274

test plots, 264, 267, 273, 275, 278, 279

Texas: climate change in, 211–12; farming practices in, 230–31; weather patterns in, 218; wheat cultivation and production in, 207–8, 211–12, 220–22

CPSIA information can be obtained
at www.ICGtesting.com
Printed in the USA
LVHW021617210422
716759LV00006B/39